JESUS' LACK OF EMOTION IN LUKE:

THE LUKAN REDACTIONS IN LIGHT

OF THE HELLENISTIC PHILOSOPHERS

A Dissertation

Submitted to the Graduate School

of the University of Notre Dame

in Partial Fulfillment of the Requirements

for the Degree of

Doctor of Philosophy

by

David G. George

_____

Gregory E. Sterling, Director

Graduate Program in Theology

Notre Dame, Indiana

April 2009

UMI Number: 3441729

Dissertation Publishing

ProQuest LLC
789 East Eisenhower Parkway
P.O. Box 1346
Ann Arbor, MI 48106-1346

JESUS' LACK OF EMOTION IN LUKE:

THE LUKAN REDACTIONS IN LIGHT

OF THE HELLENISTIC PHILOSOPHERS

Abstract

by

David G. George

This dissertation will argue that the author of Luke has redacted Mark in terms of

the characterization of Jesus. In the characterization of Jesus, the Lukan redactor has

removed strong emotion (and the actions which would result from these strong

emotions). Further, Luke has sometimes —transferred" these emotions to other characters

or groups. These redactions include the traditionally-viewed negative emotions grief,

neediness, stern speech, and especially anger. They also include some of the more

traditionally positive emotions including compassion, love, and general affection. It will

be shown that Luke consistently depicts (with two exceptions in the special —L" material)

the persona of Jesus (and only the character of Jesus) as bereft of strong emotion.

This dissertation will further attempt to explain *why* these redactions and

transferences have occurred by examining the Lukan redactions in light of the

philosophical traditions. Evidence will be presented from the Hellenistic, Jewish, and

Roman philosophical traditions on the subject of emotions in order to show that with notable exceptions (i.e., Aristotle), the primary philosophical view of the emotions was depreciatory and disapproving. This dissertation will conclude that it is primarily the Stoic tradition (and in particular the popular rendering of these in the Roman imperial authors) that leads the author of Luke to present his auditors with a Jesus character (quite to the contrary of Mark) without emotion, an exemplum of *apatheia*.

Dedicated to

Dr. James H. Charlesworth

My Mentor

who inspired me to pursue doctoral studies

and

Denise, Derek, Dominick and Dana

My Family

who offered tremendous support along a difficult journey

and

Lois J. George

My Mother

who taught me the value of education and a love of literature

CONTENTS

LIST OF GREEK TEXTS

ACKNOWLEDGMENTS

It is with great delectation that I acknowledge and thank the people whose friendship, support, and wisdom contributed to this dissertation. I wish to express my sincere thanks to my director, Greg Sterling, for directing me in the writing of this dissertation, for his knowledge of the field, for his attention to detail, and most importantly, for his encouragement and inspiration along the way. Without him, not only would the dissertation be of significantly lesser quality, it probably would have never come to fruition. I could not hope for a better *Doktorvater*.

I deeply appreciate the members of my dissertation committee – David Aune and Mary Rose D'Angelo, who along with Jerry Neyrey, challenged and encouraged me, and contributed much to my thinking about the biblical text in their Greco-Roman milieu. I am also thankful for Fabian Udoh, for his friendship and his willingness to share his wisdom of the ancient world. I am deeply indebted to Dan Brown, my former student, now at Georgetown University, for his constructive criticism on multiple drafts, for his encouragement, and mostly for his friendship.

During the years writing this dissertation, I received generous financial and logistical support from the Graduate School and the Theology Department at Notre Dame. In particular, I would like to thank Carolyn and Dorothy of the Theology

vi

Department, and Laura of the Dean's office. I also benefitted greatly from my involvement with the Kaneb Center. I would like to thank Alex, Kevin, Chris, Michelle, Terri, and Alisa, for their continuous support and friendship.

I would like to thank my first mentor, James Charlesworth, who whose friendship and counsel greatly influence my efforts as a teacher and scholar. For his inspiration, I dedicate this work to him.

I am blessed beyond belief for having the local support of my sister, Heather, and her family. I am thankful for the unwavering support from my in-laws, Geri and Dennis. I am grateful for my "noon-time" basketball buddies at RecSports, especially Mike, Tom, Lee, and Clark, who provided nourishment, both literal and figurative, along with a welcome respite from the daily rigors of Greek and Latin.

Most importantly, I am tremendously grateful for the love of my family, to whom this work is also dedicated. They have repeatedly demonstrated their love and encouraged me throughout my education. For my wife Denise, I am eternally thankful for her sacrifice and support. My sons Derek and Dominick, and my daughter Dana, have brought more joy to my life that I could ever have dreamed possible. Lastly, I cannot express the extent to which my mother, Lois, has influenced me, in her love of books, in her love of family, and in her love of life. Thank you.

CHAPTER 1

JESUS' EMOTION IN THE GARDEN AND THE EXTRAPOLATION

OF THE LUKAN REDACTIONAL PATTERN

Introduction

The New Testament documents were written in a milieu permeated with the ideas and slogans of Greek thinkers, whether Stoics, Cynics, or Epicureans. As the followers of Jesus moved steadily into the Greco-Roman world, they inevitably came in contact with these groups and their ideas in a variety of ways. Christians either found points of agreement with them, imitated them in terms of style and form, or engaged them in controversy.[1]

At its most basic level, this dissertation will argue that the author of Luke has

redacted Mark in terms of the characterization of Jesus.[2] In this characterization, the

Lukan redactor has consistently removed strong emotion (and the actions which would

result from these strong emotions). These redactions of the emotional persuasion include

the traditionally-viewed negative emotions grief, neediness, stern speech, and especially

---

[1] Jerome H. Neyrey, ―Acts, Epicureans, and Theodicy: A Study in Stereotypes‖ in *Greeks, Romans, and Christians* (eds. David L. Balch, Everett Ferguson, and Wayne A. Meeks; Minneapolis: Fortress Press, 1990), 118.

[2] I am assuming a modified ―two-source theory‖ to the ―synoptic problem.‖ The most important tenet of which (for the purposes of this dissertation), is that the author of Luke knew, used, and redacted the Markan source according to his purposes in undertaking his narrative task (see Luke 1:1-4). The present work proceeds on the general assumption that Luke had available the Gospel of Mark, and that he shared additional common source material with Matthew, but that the particular form of the shared material we cannot be too confident.

1

anger. They also include some of the more traditionally positive emotions including

compassion, love, and general affection.

Beyond the collection and categorization of the hard data to show that these

redactions have in fact occurred, this dissertation will attempt to explain *why* these

redactions have occurred.[3] In the attempt to locate the Lukan redactions, I will present

evidence from the Hellenistic, Jewish, and Roman philosophical traditions on the subject

of emotions. In chapter two, it will be shown that with notable exceptions (i.e. Aristotle),

the primary philosophical view of the emotions was depreciatory and disapproving. In

fact, one of the main distinctions among the schools was the *varying degrees* of

negativity in which they viewed them. The investigation of this motif of the emotions in

Hellenistic philosophy (including Latin representations) will be accomplished primarily

from the perspective of comparative religions. When examining each reference to the

emotions in a particular philosophical text, every effort will be made to interpret its

meaning and function within the context of that text itself.[4] When possible, the

dissertation will consider how philosophical notions of the emotions may have functioned

in their social milieu.[5]

---

[3] While this argument is more problematic and difficult, it is in a sense a ‑true scholarly question," an ‑issue truly open for debate." See Stuart Greene, ‑Argument as Conversation: The Role of Inquiry in Writing a Researched Argument," in *The Subject Is Research* (ed. W. Bishop & Pavel Zemliansky; Portsmouth, N.H.: Boynton/Cook Heinemann, 2001), 145-164.

[4] A case in point is Cicero. In order to deliberate and possibly reconcile Cicero's sometimes seemingly contradictory thoughts on the emotions, it will be necessary to distinguish his comments of a more proper philosophical nature and those on rhetoric.

[5] For example in an honor/shame society, rhetoricians trained polis elites in a type of judicial rhetoric called ‑forensic defense speech," which served as a pattern for Luke's portrayal of Paul in his various court speeches in Acts 22-26. See Bruce J. Malina and Jerome H. Neyrey, *Portraits of Paul: An Archaeology of Ancient Personality* (Louisville: Westminster John Knox Press, 1996), 64-91. Both Quintilian and Cicero emphasize a person's character (êthos) in describing this defense speech, whether the person in question be the speaker, plaintiff, or witness, and one important character depiction concerned emotion. Cicero spoke of emotion or feeling (*affectio*) as a temporary change of mind or body such as joy or fear (Inv. 1.24.35-

After delineating the major Hellenistic philosophical views of the emotions, especially the Stoics compared to the influential Platonic and Aristotelian streams, in chapter three, I will focus on texts from Greek-speaking Jewish authors. Using similar methodology, I will provide evidence from writers including Josephus and Philo, and works such as 4 Maccabees. In the attempt to expound upon and to differentiate among the different authors, I will give account as to *why* certain philosophical streams held these critical views of the emotions (for example, emotion was contrary to a highly held philosophical virtue such as reason or self-control).

While my presentation of the philosophical material is not meant to be exhaustive, the scholarly evidence will show a philosophical *pattern* of denunciation, even fulmination. The following two chapters will broadly and generally present evidence from the Hellenistic (with special attention to the four main schools), Roman (especially the popularization of Roman Stoic views in the imperial authors), and Hellenistic Jewish philosophical traditions (particularly those writers who are not philosophers in the technical sense, such as Josephus, for a research comparison to Luke) on the subject of emotions. I will argue that it is primarily the Stoic tradition (and in particular the popular rendering of these in the Roman imperial authors) that leads the author of Luke to present the reader with a Jesus character (quite to the contrary of Mark) as one bereft of strong emotion. I maintain that Luke was aware of and influenced by the general philosophical traditions (especially the Roman Stoics), not that Luke was a professional philosopher in

---

25.36). Quintilian described *commotio* as a temporary emotion such as anger or fear (Inst. Orat. 5.10.24-29). Ancients praised excellence (*aretê*) in living in accordance with a philosophical school's notion of virtue, thus conformity and constancy, not change, is valued. Malina and Neyrey further state (74) that emotion or feeling, "although celebrated in our modern individualistic culture, was by no means a valued or important thing in antiquity. If constancy counts and passions are suspect, then 'temporary change of mind or body' is noteworthy but hardly praiseworthy. Here an orator could indicate that persons are either subject to change and passion or masters of them." Therefore, one reason emotions were viewed pejoratively according to ancient social relations was due to their fleeting incongruous nature.

the technical sense. Thus the focus of the next two chapters will be on the philosophical traditions pertaining to emotional theory, primarily as it elucidates the philosophical ethos of the first century of the Common Era, in which the author of Luke redacts and constructs his Jesus.[6]

Research Methodology

Using essentially redaction critical methods, I propose three checks or research controls within my scholarly experiment, to buttress the contention that Luke has consistently removed Jesus' strong emotion from Mark. (1) As previously mentioned, I am not arguing that the author of Luke was a professional philosopher in the technical sense; only that he was aware of and influenced by the general philosophical traditions. Thus, Luke will be researched in light of other Hellenistic Jewish authors (chapter three), and perhaps most important for our analysis, those who are not philosophers in the technical sense (i.e. the author of 4 Maccabbees). (2) When appropriate, Matthew's use of the Markan source will be analyzed in comparison with Luke. To what degree and in which circumstance did Matthew also remove the emotion from the persona of Jesus? (3) In chapter five, I will examine the emotional portrayal of the characters in the Markan and Lukan narratives other than Jesus. Is Luke's consistent removal of Jesus' emotion representative of a larger Lukan pattern? In order to situate my claims within the larger

---

[6] An important assumption I share with many scholars is the partial break-down of borders among the various philosophical traditions in the first century and following. This concept dictates my use of language such as 'popular rendering' and 'popularization' when describing philosophical traditions during the time of Luke. This doesn't have to embrace fully the notion of philosophical 'eclecticism' that has sometimes been associated with the age; it is at the very least symptomatic of a constructive softening of school boundaries. See discussion in John Dillon and A. A. Long, eds., *The Question of „Eclecticism': Studies in Later Greek Philosophy* (Berkeley: University of California Press, 1988). See further chapter two.

scholarly community, I will also include an examination of the emotional characterization of the deity in Luke. To what degree does God show emotion in Luke?

Acts

Although I do not propose the most obvious fourth check, namely an analysis of Luke's second volume, Acts of the Apostles, it does fit with the general principles I lay out. My examination of Luke's gospel fits with what I argue is the larger agenda of Luke, namely, to make Christianity more compatible with Greco-Roman, especially imperial values, both in his gospel and in Acts.[7] My contention that Luke is making Jesus, and by extrapolation Christianity itself, more feasible to a Roman audience is similar to Crossan's and Reed's thesis in the recent volume *In Search of Paul*. I assert that Luke, through his redactional choices concerning characters' emotions, presents a Jesus in line with prevailing notions of Roman virtue. Crossan and Reed make an analogous asseveration in terms of Paul and Roman gender values. They argue that two absolutely divergent traditions claimed the name of Paul after his death.

> One moved him into an ultraconservative position of male-over-female superiority, the other into an ultraradical one of necessary male and female celibacy. The ultraconservative option is not just patriarchal misogyny. It demands male leadership, to be sure, but one that is noncelibate and nonascetic. Its leaders must be male, married, and fertile – in short, socially conventional.

---

[7] The case of Paul before the proconsul Gallio at Corinth in Acts 18:12-17, whether literal fact or metaphorical fiction, is a good example of Luke's defense of Christianity in general and of Paul in particular. John Dominic Crossan and Jonathan L. Reed implore their readers to, ―Look, therefore, at that judicial *bēma*, or tribunal, in Corinth and see it as the symbolic heart of Lukan rapprochement between Christ and Caesar, between the Christian church and the Roman Empire,‖ in *In Search of Paul: How Jesus's Apostle Opposed Rome's Empire with God's Kingdom, A New Vision of Paul's Words & World* (San Francisco: HarperCollins, 2004), 33. See also Joseph Fitzmyer, *The Acts of the Apostles* (AB 31; New York: Doubleday, 1998), 617-631. While I argue that Luke has constructed his narrative sympathetic to Stoic philosophy, the converse also seems to be true – that Luke argues against certain philosophic schools. See for example Abraham J. Malherbe, ―Hellenistic Moralists and the New Testament,‖ *ANRW* 26.1: 267-333.

Just like any decent Roman paterfamilias. The ultraradical option has both female and male leadership, but Thecla outdoes Paul in every way possible. The leadership there is female, unmarried, celibate, and virginal. And each claims to be Pauline and the only true Christianity. If, however, Roman authority thought that the ultraradical option was Christianity itself, it would probably have declared it an illicit religion. The ultraconservative option was one major step on the road from Christ to Constantine. It is sad, however, that the Christian tradition did not adopt a firm both/and rather than a strict either/or; that is, Christian life and leadership could be equally female or male, married or celibate, conventional or ascetic. That, certainly and regardless of his personal preferences for himself, was the authentic Pauline position for Christian converts and assemblies.[8]

It is of vast importance that Luke's Paul in Acts (like Luke's Jesus) is innocent according to Roman view.[9] In the theater in Ephesus, the town clerk declared that Paul's companions were ―neither temple robbers nor blasphemers of our goddess [Diana]" and then ―he dismissed the assembly" (19:37, 41). Claudius Lysias, the tribune at Jerusalem, wrote to the governor Felix, at Caesarea that Paul ―was accused concerning questions of their [Jewish' law, but was charged with nothing deserving death or imprisonment" (23:29). Two years later, the new governor, Festus, told Paul's case to the Jewish king Agrippa II and his sister Bernice and commented that ―they did not charge him with any of the crimes that I was expecting" and ―that he had done nothing deserving death" (25:18, 25). After Paul's speech, all three agree, ―This man is doing nothing to deserve death or imprisonment" (26:31). Importantly, Luke ends not with Paul's trial or execution, but this declaration: ―He lived there two whole years at his own expense and welcomed all who came to him, proclaiming the kingdom of God and teaching about the

---

[8] Crossan and Reed, *In Search of Paul*, 122-123. They use the Pauline corpus as one line of tradition and Luke in Acts of the Apostles, and in the later post-Pauline and pseudo-Pauline writings (important precisely because they were not written by Paul but were attributed to him by later writers) as the other.

[9] Crossan and Reed declare, ―... a final major theme in Luke's Acts is Roman reaction to Paul. Every Roman or Romanizing authority that Paul encounters declares him formally and explicitly to be innocent," in ibid., 32.

Lord Jesus Christ with all boldness and without hindrance" (28:30-31). Crossan and

Reed comment: ―To allow Christianity ‗without hindrance' should be Roman policy.

Jesus, Paul, and Christianity are encased by Luke in apologetic garments."[10] With a

Roman audience in mind, Luke's concluding emphasis is that Paul, his followers, and all

Christians are innocent.

While the purpose is not to examine all of Crossan and Reed's claims concerning

Paul and the Empire, our analysis is certainly part of this broader line of scholarship.

Luke, in his portrayal of Jesus (like his Paul) couched his brand of Christianity not only

as being *not antithetical to Roman values*, but as being *pro-imperial values*, with Paul to

a certain degree, and to an even greater degree, Jesus as the ideal embodiment of these

values.

An Extrapolation from an Examination

> [T]he third evangelist reshaped the traditions that he inherited by self-consciously
> situating them in the context of the larger Greco-Roman world."[11]

---

[10] Ibid., 33.

[11] Sterling, ―*Mors philosophi*," 394; see also idem, *Apologetic Historiography and Self-Definition: Josephos, Luke-Acts, and Historiography* (NovTSup 64; Leiden: Brill, 1992) 311-89.

330. Gethsemane[12]

Mark 14:32-38	Luke 22:39-46
[32]Καὶ ἔρχονται εἰς χωρίον οὗ τὸ ὄνομα Γεθσημανί,	[39]Καὶ ἐξελθὼν ἐπορεύθη κατὰ τὸ ἔθος εἰς τὸ Ὄρος τῶν Ἐλαιῶν· ἠκολούθησαν δὲ αὐτῷ καὶ οἱ μαθηταί. [40]γενόμενος δὲ ἐπὶ τοῦ τόπου
καὶ λέγει τοῖς μαθηταῖς αὐτοῦ, Καθίσατε ὧδε ἕως προσεύξωμαι.	εἶπεν αὐτοῖς, Προσεύχεσθε μὴ εἰσελθεῖν εἰς πειρασμόν.
[33]καὶ παραλαμβάνει τὸν Πέτρον καὶ τὸν Ἰάκωβον καὶ τὸν Ἰωάννην μετ᾽ αὐτοῦ, καὶ ἤρξατο **ἐκθαμβεῖσθαι** καὶ **ἀδημονεῖν**, [34]καὶ λέγει αὐτοῖς περίλυπός ἐστιν ἡ ψυχή μου ἕως θανάτου	
[35]καὶ προελθὼν μικρὸν	[41]καὶ αὐτὸς ἀπεσπάσθη ἀπ᾽ αὐτῶν ὡσεὶ λίθου βολήν,
ἔπιπτεν ἐπὶ τῆς γῆς, καὶ προσηύχετο ἵνα εἰ δυνατόν ἐστιν παρέλθῃ ἀπ᾽ αὐτοῦ ἡ ὥρα,	καὶ θεὶς τὰ γόνατα προσηύχετο
[36]καὶ ἔλεγεν, Αββα ὁ πατήρ, πάντα δυνατά σοι·	[42]λέγων, Πάτερ,
παρένεγκε τὸ ποτήριον τοῦτο ἀπ᾽ ἐμοῦ·	εἰ βούλει παρένεγκε τοῦτο τὸ ποτήριον ἀπ᾽ ἐμοῦ· πλὴν μὴ τὸ
ἀλλ᾽ οὐ τί ἐγὼ θέλω ἀλλὰ τί σύ.	θέλημά μου ἀλλὰ τὸ σὸν γινέσθω.
	[43][ὤφθη δὲ αὐτῷ ἄγγελος ἀπ᾽ οὐρανοῦ

---

[12] All Greek texts and parallel numbers/titles are taken from Kurt Aland, *Synopsis Quattuor Evangeliorum* (13th revidierte Auflage; Stuttgart: Deutsche Bibelgesellschaft, 1985), based on the Greek text of Nestle-Aland 26th edition. All English translations are mine (based on the NRSV), unless otherwise noted. The word(s) underlined in red indicate material omitted in Luke's version; dashed underlined in blue indicates emotion transferred from Jesus to another person or group; double-underlined in green indicates the omission or lessening of violence or emotion *to* Jesus; *italicized in orange* indicates a different word choice; waved underline in purple indicates emotional special ⌐L" material.

8

	ἐνισχύων αὐτόν.
	⁴⁴καὶ γενόμενος ἐν ἀγωνίᾳ
	ἐκτενέστερον προσηύχετο·
	καὶ ἐγένετο ὁ ἱδρὼς αὐτοῦ ὡσεὶ θρόμβοι
	αἵματος καταβαίνοντες ἐπὶ τὴν γῆν.]
	⁴⁵καὶ ἀναστὰς ἀπὸ τῆς προσευχῆς
³⁷καὶ ἔρχεται	ἐλθὼν πρὸς τοὺς μαθητὰς
καὶ εὑρίσκει αὐτοὺς καθεύδοντας,	
	εὗρεν κοιμωμένους αὐτοὺς
καὶ λέγει τῷ Πέτρῳ, Σίμων, καθεύδεις;	ἀπὸ τῆς λύπης
οὐκ ἴσχυσας μίαν ὥραν γρηγορῆσαι;	⁴⁶καὶ εἶπεν αὐτοῖς, τί καθεύδετε;
³⁸γρηγορεῖτε καὶ προσεύχεσθε,	
ἵνα μὴ ἔλθητε εἰς πειρασμόν·	ἀναστάντες προσεύχεσθε,
τὸ μὲν πνεῦμα πρόθυμον ἡ δὲ σὰρξ ἀσθενής.	ἵνα μὴ εἰσέλθητε εἰς πειρασμόν.

Like many scholarly undertakings, this dissertation began with a few simple questions derived from a few simple observations. The impetus for the inquiry was a discussion of the passion narrative in Luke, especially the scenes of Jesus praying at Gethsemane//Mount of Olives (Mark 14:32-42//Luke 22:39-46), during a Hellenistic Moral Philosophy Seminar at the University of Notre Dame. With Greg Sterling's thesis that "the third evangelist made selective use of Socratic traditions to transform an embarrassment [Mark's passion narrative] into an *exemplum* [Luke's account]" and a Greek synopsis, we proceeded to analyze the Lukan passion with respect to the Markan source and in light of the Socratic traditions.[13]

---

[13] Sterling's thesis as presented in "Mors philosophi: The Death of Jesus in Luke," was initially presented to the Luke-Acts Group of the Society of Biblical Literature at the annual meeting in November 1998, then as an unpublished paper distributed to members of the Hellenistic Moral Philosophy Seminar, University of Notre Dame, Fall 1999); it was then published in *HTR* 94:4 (2001): 383-402.

In support of his contention that the Socratic traditions influenced the Lukan passion narrative, Sterling offers as his primary evidence the "calmness" with which Jesus faced death in the third gospel, "The third evangelist consistently eliminated every hint of anxiety on the part of Jesus. This is most evident in the redaction of two major scenes: Gethsemane and the crucifixion."[14] In the pericope concerning the prayer at Gethsemane, Luke drops three Markan statements which indicated the struggles of Jesus: (1) Luke removes the Markan narrator's editorial, καὶ ἤρξατο ἐκθαμβεῖσθαι καὶ ἀδημονεῖν, (14:33).[15] (2) Luke omits the Markan narrator's introduction to Jesus' prayer, εἰ δυνατόν ἐστιν παρέλθῃ ἀπ' αὐτοῦ ἡ ὥρα, (14:35).[16] (3) Luke omits Jesus' impassioned declaration, περίλυπός ἐστιν ἡ ψυχή μου ἕως θανάτου (14:34).[17]

---

[14] Ibid., 395. Sterling argues (396-97) that the same rationale (analyzed below) underlies the replacement of the Markan cry of dereliction on the cross with the affirmation of dedication in Luke (Mark 15:34-37//Luke 23:44-46). Mark cites the Aramaic form, Ελωι ελωι λεμα σαβαχθανι; then the Greek translation of Ps 22:2, Ὁ θεός μου ὁ θεός μου, εἰς τί ἐγκατέλιπές με. Luke omits not only the citation but the entire episode it provoked. Luke substitutes Ps 31:6 for Mark's cry, Πάτερ, εἰς χεῖράς σου παρατίθεμαι τὸ πνεῦμά μου (23:46). Sterling contends (397): "[T]his change is best explained, I think, by the consistent elimination of any hint of an emotional struggle within Jesus." C.F. Evans makes a similar assertion, "It is thus possible to explain his briefer version as the result of a revision of Mark's which would depict a more serene Jesus and less faithless disciples," in *Saint Luke* (Philadelphia: Trinity, 1990), 809. It is also worth noting that Luke, as he does on occasion, compares the lack of emotion by Jesus with other characters' emotion. See, for example, the rich man (Mark 10:17-22//Luke 18:18-23), the disciples (here), and his enemies (the scribes and Pharisees, Mark 3:1-6//Luke 6:6-11). It is fitting, as will be seen in greater detail in chapter four, that Matthew (27:46-50) does not eliminate Jesus' cry, but maintains an almost exact linguistic copy.

[15] Many scholars recognize the martyrlogical elements of the story, but fewer recognize how the emotional omissions and transfers contribute to the martyrdom elements. Pace Green, who states, "Neither is it appropriate to attribute a martyrological interpretation to this Lukan scene," in *The Gospel of Luke* (Grand Rapids: Eerdmans, 1997), 777.

[16] Luke's concern over Jesus' anxiety is probably also the reason governing the shift in Jesus' posture in prayer. Mark states, καὶ προελθὼν μικρὸν ἔπιπτεν ἐπὶ τῆς γῆς, καὶ προσηύχετο ἵνα (14:35), which

It is of vital import that Luke not only omits the emotionally charged statement (Mark 14:34), but he "transfers" Jesus' grief (περίλυπος) to the disciples (λύπη). He expands the simple Markan description, καὶ ἔρχεται καὶ εὑρίσκει αὐτοὺς καθεύδοντας (14:37) into an explanation, ἐλθὼν πρὸς τοὺς μαθητὰς εὗρεν κοιμωμένους αὐτοὺς ἀπὸ τῆς λύπης (22:45b).[18] John Nolland comments on this redaction, "Luke explains and, in part, excuses their sleep, by adding that it was _from grief'; the sense of impending tragedy has brought them to emotional exhaustion."[19] While I view Luke's change as an explanation, it does not excuse their behavior, but is an indictment on it. Craig A. Evans states, "Luke may not intend this addition to excuse the disciples' failure to watch and pray. ... Their grief is a sign of spiritual weakness."[20] It is exactly because of their weak character, evidenced by them allowing their grief to cause them sleep, that

---

Luke rewrites, καὶ αὐτὸς ἀπεσπάσθη ἀπ' αὐτῶν ὡσεὶ λίθου βολήν, καὶ θεὶς τὰ γόνατα προσηύχετο (22:41). Sterling comments, "Luke replaced what he feared some might consider a sign of physical collapse with a posture of piety," in "Mors philosophi," 396. In agreement, I would further emphasize that the physical collapse in Mark is due to the extreme emotional turmoil of Jesus in Mark (ἐκθαμβεῖσθαι καὶ ἀδημονεῖν, v.33; περίλυπός ἐστιν ἡ ψυχή μου ἕως θανάτου, v.34), which is Luke's primary concern. In response to Luke's rewritten account of Jesus' prayer, Luke Timothy Johnson contends, "The description emphasizes Jesus' control and lack of emotional turmoil," in *Gospel of Luke* (SPS 3; ed. Daniel J. Harrington; Collegeville, Minn.: Liturgical Press, 1991), 351.

[17] Judith Lieu contends that the result of these redactions is the "softening of the sense of anguished inner conflict suggested by Mark," in *Luke* (London: Epworth Press, 1997), 185.

[18] This transfer is part of a larger shift in orientation throughout the passage. The testing of Jesus in Mark has become the testing of the disciples in Luke. For example, instead of Mark's, Καθίσατε ὧδε ἕως προσεύξωμαι, (14:.32), Luke's Jesus tells the disciples, Προσεύχεσθε μὴ εἰσελθεῖν εἰς πειρασμόν (22:40). See Sterling, "Mors philosophi," 395.

[19] Nolland, *Luke 18:35-24:53* (WBC 35C; Dallas: Word, 1982), 1084.

[20] Craig A. Evans, *Luke* (NIBCNT; Peabody, Mass.: Hendrickson, 1990), 329-330; see also Robert C. Tannehill, *The Narrative Unity of Luke-Acts* (2 Vol.; Minneapolis: Fortress Press, 1990), 1:263-64, 271.

Jesus' urgent, τί καθεύδετε, ἀναστάντες προσεύχεσθε, ἵνα μὴ εἰσέλθητε εἰς

πειρασμόν (Luke 22:46) resonates so powerfully.

Before we could extrapolate a larger pattern from these few scenes – Are these redactional changes concerning Jesus' emotion true for the entire gospel or only the specified Passion pericopae? – we came upon a possible exception in the famous textual *crux interpretum* of the angel giving strength to Jesus (Luke 22:43-44). This led to a debate, not only of the divided manuscript evidence,[21] but also how these verses fit or do not fit with Lukan themes.[22] Nolland states, ―After an earlier move in critical opinion toward accepting the verses, the more recent trend has been to question their presence in the original text of Luke."[23] He also states:

> The arguments for and against inclusion are finely balanced. Both addition and removal are explicable in terms of arguments over Christology. Much of the language is quite in line with Lukan use, but at the same time the material has an emotional tone that is otherwise quite absent from the Lukan account of the Gethsemane scene (contrast Mark).[24]

---

[21] In general, Alexandrian witnesses tend to exclude the verses (Luke 22:43-44), while Western witnesses tend to include them. Bruce Metzger states: ―The absence of these verses in such ancient and widely diversified witnesses as $\mathfrak{p}^{(69vid),75}$ $\aleph^a$ A B T W syr^s cop^{sa,bo} arm^{mss} geo Marcion Clement Origen *al*, as well as their being marked with asterisks or obeli (signifying spuriousness) in other witnesses (Δ^c Π^c 892$^{c\,mg}$ 1079 1195 1216 cop^{bomss}) and their transferral to Matthews' gospel (after 26.39) by family 13 and several lectionaries (the latter also transfer ver. 45a), strongly suggests that they are no part of the original text of Luke. Their presence in many manuscripts, some ancient, as well as their citiation by Justin, Irenaeus, Hippolytus, Eusebius and many other Fathers, is proof of the antiquity of the account. In *A Textual Commentary on the Greek New Testament* (New York: United Bible Societies, 1975), 128.

[22] See the excellent analysis in Bart D. Ehrman and Mark A. Plunkett, ―The Angel and the Agony: The Textual Problem of Luke 22:43-44," *CBQ* 45 (1983): 401-16. See also A. Feuillet, ―Le recit lucanien de l'agonie de Gethsemane (lc xxii. 39-46)," *NTS* 22 (1975-76): 397-417; W.J. Larkin, ―The Old Testament Background of Luke xxii, 43-44," *NTS* 25 (1978-79): 250-254; and T. Lescow, ―Jesus im Gethsemane bei Lukas und im Hebräerbrief," *ZNW* 58 (1967): 215-239.

[23] Nolland, *Luke 18:35-24:53*, 1080-81.

[24] Ibid., 1080. Judith Lieu acknowledges the evenly weighted evidence, ―Angels as divine messengers are part of Luke's narrative style (1.11, 26; Acts 5.19), but the verse do interrupt a natural flow from v.42 to

Pace Nolland, Michael Goulder not only argues for inclusion of the questionable verses but incredibly concludes: ―Without vv.43f, for which there is not obvious motive. The agony shows the cost of the cross, and is needed dramatically and theologically. Thus the case for including vv.43f seems overwhelming."[25] Thus, Nolland and Goulder similarly adjure to concerns of thematic harmony, though they come to completely opposite conclusions.[26]

While some scholars have appealed to text critical evidence and/or Lukan motifs, others have buttressed their arguments by accentuating the philosophical ethos of the first century. We have seen how Sterling advanced philosophical traditions associated with Socrates in arguing against inclusion of vv.43-44.[27] L.T. Johnson draws upon Epictetus

---

v.45; if they were originally part of Luke's text it is conceivable that scribes found them incompatible with their own more exalted view of Jesus and omitted them, yet it is equally possible that they were an independent tradition which became incorporated here at a later stage to add more drama to Luke's otherwise more emotionless scene." In *Luke*, 185.

[25] Goulder, *Luke: A New Paradigm* (JSNTSup 20; Sheffield: Sheffield Academic Press, 1989), 742.

[26] A number of scholars have argued for removal, not just in regard to the emotional elements, but also in terms of the fairly clear chiasmic structure of Luke's account without the verses (43-44) in question: v.39 is introductory; v.40 corresponds to vv.45c-46 (from εὗρεν κοιμωμένους…); v.41a (to … λίθου βολήν) corresponds to v.45b (ἐλθὼν πρὸς τοὺς μαθητὰς); v.41b (καὶ θεὶς τὰ γόνατα προσηύχετο) corresponds to 45a; with v.42 as the centerpiece emphasizing the divine will of God and Jesus' acceptance. See especially Ehrman and Plunkett, ―Angel and the Agony," 413. See also Mario Galizzi, *Gesù nel Getsemani* (Zurich: Pas, 1972), 137-38; D.M. Stanley, *Jesus in Gethsemane: The Early Church Reflects on the Suffering of Jesus* (Ramsey, N.J.: Paulist, 1980), 206-213.

[27] Sterling contends, ―There are, however, reasons for associating the elimination of emotions from the passion narrative with the Socratic tradition," in ―Mors philosophi," 397. After quoting Plato and Xenophon, it is important that he turns to the Stoic philosopher Seneca to bolster his review of the Socractic tradition, for the Stoics of the first century begin to incorporate Socrates and the Socratic tradition into their philosophic views; see preliminary Dillon and Long, *Question of 'Eclecticism'*; and David Sedley, ―The School, from Zeno to Arius Didymus," in *The Cambridge Companion to the Stoics* (ed. Brad Inwood; Cambridge: Cambridge University Press, 2003), 32. Other scholars who appeal to the Socratic tradition include John S. Kloppenborg, ―Exitus clari viri: The Death of Jesus in Luke," *TJT* 8 (1992): 106-20, who puts forth three arguments: the farewell discourse of Jesus, the presence of the disciples throughout the narrative, and the fearless demeanor of Jesus. See also Paul W. Gooch, *Reflections on Jesus and Socrates: Word and Silence* (New Haven: Yale University Press, 1996).

13

in defending Lukan composition. Johnson exposits on the verses in question: ―In just such fashion would Epictetus portray the philosopher's struggle for virtue in terms of an athletic contest (cf. Discourses 2, 18, 28; 3, 22, 59; 3, 25, 1-4). The angel strengthening Jesus is like a trainer, urging on his ‗eager prayer'."[28]

Jerome Neyrey employs general Stoic traditions, especially the cardinal virtues, along with an interpretation of ἀγωνία (based in part upon Philo) to reckon with the redactional changes, and ultimately concludes that Luke 22:43-44 was a part of the original Lukan text.[29] Neyrey agrees with Ehrman and Plunkett (and Sterling, and to a certain degree L.T. Johnson), that ―Luke's redaction of the Gethsemane scene is done with a view to the presentation of Jesus as ‗emotionally restrained'."[30] Neyrey further contends (pace Ehrman and Plunkett and Sterling): ―Lk 22:43-44 do not clash with this perspective at all, but indicate how Jesus strives as a virtuous person to maintain his virtue even when he is under attack. On the contrary, 22:43-44 *confirm* [his emphasis] Jesus as one not subject to passion."[31] At the crux of his interpretation is his definition of ἀγωνία (v.44), for he admits that ―it is improbable that Luke, who omits ‗grief' from

---

[28] Johnson, *Gospel of Luke*, 355. Johnson also seems to acknowledge (355) the humanity/divinity frame commonly applied by scholars to these and other texts concerning emotion, ―It would be a complete and insensitive misreading to think that Luke has diminished the humanity of Jesus by this portrayal, or engaged in a sort of docetism. Indeed, he portrays Jesus as engaging in the most fundamental sort of struggle for the human will." See conclusions in chapter six.

[29] Jerome H. Neyrey, ―The Absence of Jesus' Emotion: The Lucan Redaction of Lk. 22.39-46," *Bib* 61 (1980): 152-71; also idem, *The Passion According to Luke: A Redaction Study of Luke's Soteriology* (New York and Mahweh: Paulist, 1985).

[30] Neyrey, *Passion According to Luke*, 57; Ehrman and Plunkett, ―Angel and the Agony," 412.

[31] Neyrey, *Passion According to Luke*, 57.

14

Jesus, would attribute *agonia* (as ‗fear') to him."[32] While acknowledging ἀγωνία can

refer to a ―struggle for victory" as well as ―agony, anguish,"[33] he prefers the former

which he tweaks to ―victorious struggle" and then to ―soteriological combat" over

―evil."[34] Through an analysis based on the Adam-Christ typology of the πειρασμός in

Luke 4:1-13 (that he argues is continued in 22:3, 31), Neyrey contends that Jesus'

―struggle" *is* victorious, as Jesus is *not* ―in any way subject to passion, sin, or guilt."[35] He

concludes, ―Part of the reason for the description of the angel precisely as ‗strengthening'

Jesus may lie in Luke's desire to portray Jesus as not under the influence of ‗grief' by

showing him in strength, which grief characteristically destroys."[36] Therefore, Neyrey,

while ultimately disagreeing with Ehrman and Plunkett and Sterling *et al* as to the Lukan

composition of the text, basically agrees regarding the portrayal of an unemotional Jesus

---

[32] Ibid., 58.

[33] LSJ, 10. Neyrey (58) further acknowledges that in strands of Hellenistic philosophy, ―agonia is one of the subspecies of ‗fear', itself one of the cardinal passions. In this regard Philo cites it as the vanguard of ‗fear' (*Decal.* 145)." See also Ethelbert Stauffer, who also interprets these passages to refer not to fear but to concern for victory in the face of the approaching battle, in ―ἀγωνία," *TDNT* 1:140.

[34] Neyrey, *Passion According to Luke*, 58-62.

[35] Ibid., 62.

[36] Ibid., 63. My view is that the verses (43-44) in question were not originally part of the Lukan text. The external textual evidence, albeit fairly balanced, leans against inclusion. Neyrey's scholarly contribution is erudite and important, and if the verses were in fact original, he offers an intriguing option that maintains the view of Jesus as *exemplum* of *apatheia*. Though Neyrey re-inteprets ἀγωνία, Sterling's point that nearly all the early Christian authors seemed to accept the statement as a description of anxiety seems persuasive, and thus runs counter to the emotional composition of the narrative. Further, though Neyrey stresses victory over the struggle, Luke seems to de-emphasize even the emotional struggle of Jesus' testing. While I agree with Neyrey (against Ehrman and Plunkett) regarding the thematic continuity of 22:43-44 with 4:13, his appeal to Jesus' temptation in 4:1-13 is ultimately unconvincing as Jesus shows no emotion at all in the wilderness, similar to his serene portrayal in Luke 22 (without vv.43-44). I also find Ehrman and Plunkett's and Galizzi's chiastic structure (excluding vv.43-44) credible. In light of all the above, my view is very similar to John Nolland who concludes, ―I have excluded them [Luke 22:43-44] primarily on the basis of the emotional tone of the verses and secondarily on the basis of the chiasm," in *Luke 18:35-24:53*, 1080-81.

and also appeals to the philosophical traditions, albeit different ones which he uses in different ways.

Once the Lukan theme of omitting or at least significantly softening Jesus' emotion seemed fairly established, and in light of the above scholarly debate and mutual appeal to various Hellenistic traditions, I began to formulate the important "why" question. Luke Timothy Johnson, after commenting on the Lukan redactions,[37] makes a similar inquiry and offers a general response, "Why? Because these are understood by him (and his Hellenistic readers) to be signs of vice rather than virtue, and Luke is concerned to show that Jesus is not only prophet but true philosopher (*sophos*)."[38] He later states, "We notice, therefore, that the emotion of 'sorrow' (*lupē*) which is associated in Hellenistic moral literature with fear and cowardice as well as envy, is shifted from Jesus to the disciples."[39] *Summa summarum*, what is/are the primary tradition/s in which Luke self-consciously situates his gospel narrative as a whole, principally as it concerns his changes of Jesus' emotional characterization?

Although a character study into the lack of emotion shown by Jesus throughout Luke's gospel is strangely absent from many commentaries and monographs on Luke,[40]

---

[37] Johnson states, "He removes from him the need for companionship and the terrible fear and grief emphasized by Mark" in *Gospel of Luke*, 354.

[38] Ibid.

[39] Ibid.

[40] This is especially puzzling in scholars who pay particular attention to Greco-Roman parallels, and those commentaries focusing on redactional or narrative criticism. For some of the major commentaries who make no mention of this redactional pattern, see Hans Conzelmann, *The Theology of St. Luke* (London: Faber and Faber, 1960); I. Howard Marshall, *Gospel of Luke: A Commentary on the Greek Text* (NIGTC 3; Grand Rapids, Mich.: Eerdmans, 1978); Marshall, *Luke: Historian and Theologian* (Exeter: Paternoster Press, 1970); J. Jervell, *Luke and the People of God* (Minneapolis: Augsburg, 1972);

some important scholars have highlighted this redactional pattern.[41] Cadbury, Fitzmyer, and Powell give varying lists of the human emotions and expressions that have been omitted by the author of Luke, but their explanations of this phenomenon are unsatisfactory. Cadbury explains these omissions (apparently relying upon other scholars' work) by stating they are due to the reverence shown the person of Jesus in Luke. Powell, admittedly relying upon Fitzmyer, states that for the author of Luke, the attribution of any human emotion to Jesus detracted in some way from his nobility. What this means is not further explained by Powell or Fitzmyer. Further, Fitzmyer states emphatically, ―Certain redactional modifications of the Markan source material can be seen to stem from a delicate sensitivity which tends to make Luke eliminate anything that smacks of the violent, the passionate, or the emotional."[42] At the other end of the spectrum, François Bovon states, ―On a prétendu que Luc refoulait les émotions, surtout celles Jésus. Cela me paraît faux, car s'il ne spécule pas sur les sentiments, il dépeint les gestes qui les expriment."[43]

Schweizer, Eduard, *The Good News According to Luke* (Trans. David E. Green; Atlanta: John Knox Press, 1984); C. H. Talbert, *Reading Luke: A Literary and Theological Commentary on the Third Gospel* (New York: Crossroad, 1982); Tannehill, *Narrative Unity of Luke-Acts*; Loretta Dornisch, *A Woman Reads the Gospel of Luke* (Collegeville: The Liturgical Press, 1996); Lieu, *Gospel of Luke*; Barbara E. Reid, *Choosing the Better Part?* (Collegeville: The Liturgical Press, 1996); Jonathan Knight, *Luke's Gospel* (London and New York: Routledge, 1998).

[41] Henry J. Cadbury, *The Style and Literary Method of Luke* (Cambridge: Harvard University Press, 1920); Jospeh A. Fitzmyer, *The Gospel According to Luke: Introduction, Translation and Notes* (AB 28-28A; 2 vols.; New York: Doubleday, 1981-85); Mark Allan Powell, *What are They Saying about Luke?* (New York: Paulist Press, 1989).

[42] Fitzmyer, *Gospel According to Luke*, 94. See further conclusions in chapter six.

[43] Bovon, *L'Évangile selon Saint Luc 1-9* (Genève: Labor et Fides, 1991), 23. Bovon does not mention with whom he is disagreeing and his refutation is given by three examples with no explanation: John leaps in his mother's womb (1:41); the sinful woman pours forth tears (7:38); Jesus stoops down over Peter's mother-in-law (4:39). Only one of these has to do with Jesus, and in light of the plethora of examples where emotion is suppressed, he cites Jesus stooping down over Peter's ill mother-in-law as refutation?

This dissertation will attempt to enter this line of scholarship, and possibly further it, by arguing that the author of Luke, not just in specific scenes, but in the gospel narrative as a whole, has indeed redacted his Markan source by removing, or at least significantly softening the emotional characterization of Jesus. In conversation with those few scholars who have acknowledged this redactional pattern, I will offer explanation for this Lukan motif. Luke has constructed a Jesus sympathetic with the prevailing notions of virtue, primarily those of the Stoic traditions. I will further argue that Luke's vision of virtue is of the more popular variety, a Roman imperial version, a politicized version, which explains while Luke's portrayal is not merely Stoic, but includes popularized elements of philosophy such as the life and death of Socrates as philosophical model or archetype.

The Emotions in Contemporary Scholarship

> The current interest in the emotions is as widespread as it is interdisciplinary. From the cognitive and natural sciences to the humanities and social sciences, there is hardly a field of study that is not being invigorated or at least affected by ongoing research into the emotions.[44]

The increase of scholarly interest in the emotions has directly affected classics and most relevant to our inquiry, biblical studies, with important contributions to how emotion was viewed in antiquity from both fields. I stated that the impetus for the first

---

[44] John T. Fitzgerald, ‑The Passions and Moral Progress: An Introduction" in *Passions and Moral Progress in Greco-Roman Thought* (ed. John T. Fitzgerald; New York: Routledge, 2008), 1. A recent example of a thoroughly interdisciplinary analysis is D.M. Gross, *The Secret History of Emotion: From Aristotle's "Rhetoric" to Modern Brain Science* (Chicago: University of Chicago Press, 2006. Fitzgerald [p.16, n.3] puts forward the hypothesis that the reprinting in 1998 of Charles Darwin's pioneering *The Expression of the Emotions in Man and Animals*, first published in 1872, is a prime example of the contemporary interest in earlier investigations and theories.

proposed question, ‒Does this redactional pattern exist for the gospel as a whole?" was a discussion of the passion narrative in Luke. The search for an answer to the second (and more elusive) proposed query, ‒If Luke has redacted Mark in this way, why?" led to my foray into the scholarly field of ancient emotions via two influential (and recent at the time) collections of essays: *The Emotions in Hellenistic Philosophy* edited by Juha Sihvola and Troels Engberg-Pedersen[45] and *The Passions in Roman Thought and Literature* edited by Susanna Braund and Christopher Gill.[46] Three other recent collections of essays on ancient emotions are representative of the growing scholarly interest in the fields of classics: *Ancient Anger: Perspectives from Homer to Galen* edited by Susanna Braund and Glenn Most[47] and *Envy, Spite, and Jealousy: The Rivalrous Emotions in Ancient Greece* edited by David Konstan and N. Keith Rutter;[48] and in the field of biblical studies: *Paul and Pathos* edited by Thomas Olbricht and Jerry Sumney.[49]

It has been argued that the current interest in the emotions was ‒kick-started" by the 1994 publication of Martha Nussbaum's *The Therapy of Desire: Theory and Practice*

---

[45] *The Emotions in Hellenistic Philosophy* (ed. Juha Sihvola and Troels Engberg-Pedersen; Dordrecht: Kluwer Academic Publishers, 1998).

[46] *The Passions in Roman Thought and Literature* (ed. Susanna Braund and Christopher Gill; Cambridge: Cambridge University Press, 1997).

[47] *Ancient Anger: Perspectives from Homer to Galen* (ed. Susanna Braund and Glenn Most; YCS 32; Cambridge: Cambridge University Press, 2003).

[48] *Envy, Spite, and Jealousy: The Rivalrous Emotions in Ancient Greece* (ed. David Konstan and N. Keith Rutter; Edinburgh: Edinburgh University Press, 2003).

[49] *Paul and Pathos* (ed. Thomas Olbricht and Jerry Sumney; Atlanta: Society of Biblical Literature, 2001).

in Hellenistic Ethics.[50] Nussbaum's extremely influential work was not only a response

to the growing interest in the emotions but also a powerful catalyst for new research.[51]

Since Nussbaum's book was published, at least ten book-length scholarly investigations

on ancient emotions have appeared, as well as numerous book chapters, journal articles,

and other forms of publication.[52] These analyses have emphasized the importance (if not

individually, certainly collectively) and verified the veracity of the overarching premise

of Konstan's landmark volume on ancient Greek emotions, namely —that the emotions of

the ancient Greeks were in some significant respects different from our own, and that

---

[50] Martha Nussbaum, *The Therapy of Desire: Theory and Practice in Hellenistic Ethics* (Princeton: Princeton University Press, 1994).

[51] The pre-*Therapy* Nussbaum corpus in emotional research includes especially *The Fragility of Goodness: Luck and Ethics in Greek Tragedy and Philosophy* (Cambridge: Cambridge University Press, 1986); her edited collection *The Poetics of Therapy: Hellenistic Ethics in its Rhetorical and Literary Context* (Edmonton: Academic, 1990); and her edited (with Jacques Brunschwig) *Passions and Perceptions* (Cambridge: Cambridge University Press, 1993). Other significant contributions just prior to *Therapy* include Carlin Barton, *The Sorrows of the Ancient Romans: The Gladiator and the Monster* (Princeton: Princeton University Press, 1993); and Douglas Cairns, *AIDŌS: The Psychology and Ethics of Honour and Shame in Ancient Greek Literature* (Oxford: Clarendon, 1993). Julia Annas, who had already published on Epicurean emotions (—Epicurean Emotions," GRBS, 30 (1989): 145-64), examined both Stoic and Epicurean emotions in *Hellenistic Philosophy of the Mind* (Berkeley: University of California Press, 1992); see also Julia Annas, *The Morality of Happiness* (New York: Oxford University Press, 1993). Of course, scholarly interest on the emotions is not new to classicists. See especially William Anderson, *Anger in Juvenal and Seneca* (Berkeley: University of California Press, 1964); Ernst Milobenski, *Der Neid in der griechischen Philosophie* (Wiesbaden: Harrassowitz, 1964); W.W. Fortenbaugh, *Aristotle on Emotion* (London: Duckworth, 1975); Peter Walcot, *Envy and the Greeks: A Study of Human Behaviour* (Warminster: Aris & Phillips, 1978); Malcolm Schofield and Gisela Striker, eds., *The Norms of Nature: Studies in Hellenistic Ethics* (Cambridge: Cambridge University Press, 1986); and Susanna Braund, *Beyond Anger: A Study of Juvenal's Third Book of Satires* (Cambridge: Cambridge University Press, 1988).

[52] The most significant include: Richard Sorabji, *Emotion and Peace of Mind: From Stoic Agitation to Christian Temptation* (Oxford: Oxford University Press, 2000); William Harris, *Restraining Rage: The Ideology of Anger Control in Classical Antiquity* (Cambridge: Harvard University Press, 2001); Carlin Barton, *Roman Honor: The Fire in the Bones* (Berkeley: University of California Press, 2001); Margaret Graver's translation and commentary *Cicero on the Emotions: Tusculan Disputations 3 and 4* (tran. Margaret Graver; Chicago: University of Chicago Press, 2002); Teun Tieleman, *Chrysippus' On Affections: Reconstructions and Interpretations* (Leiden: Brill, 2003); Simo Knuuttila, *Emotions in Ancient and Medieval Philosophy* (Oxford: Clarendon Press, 2004); Peter Toohey, *Melancholy, Love, and Time: Boundaries of the Self in Ancient Literature* (Ann Arbor, Mich.: University of Michigan Press, 2004); Robert Kaster, *Emotion, Restraint, and Community in Ancient Rome* (New York: Oxford University Press, 2005). David Konstan, *The Emotions of the Ancient Greeks: Studies in Aristotle and Classical Literature* (Toronto: University of Toronto Press, 2006).

recognizing these differences is important to our understanding of Greek literature and Greek culture generally."[53]

Introduction to the *Pathē*: Towards a Translation and Definition

Georges Dryfus, in his famous essay, "Is Compassion an Emotion," said, "There is, or I should say there was, no Tibetan word for our word *emotion*. I said 'there was' because by now Tibetan teachers have been exposed to this question so many times that they have created a new word (*tshor myong*) to translate our *emotion*."[54] Contrary to the Tibetans, the ancient Greeks had a word that, at least in most contexts, is usually translated in English as *emotion*. That Greek word is *pathos* (plural *pathē*).

The differences between the ancient and modern understandings of the emotions are already signaled by the conceptual and linguistic difficulty of translating the standard terms that the Greeks used for "emotion" as a general concept and for the various "emotions" collectively, namely πάθος (*pathos*) and πάθη (*pathē*).[55] Both terms come from πάσχειν (*paschein*), which essentially indicates "to experience something,"

---

[53] Konstan, *Emotions of the Ancient Greeks,* ix. Kaster has convincingly shown the same is true of the Romans and their understanding of the emotions in *Emotion, Restraint, and Community*, iv-xxi.

[54] Georges Dreyfus, "Is compassion an Emotion? A Cross-Cultural Exploration of Mental Typologies," in *Visions of Compassion: Western Scientists and Tibetan Buddhists Examine Human Nature* (ed. Richard J. Davidson and Anne Harrington; Oxford: Oxford University Press, 2002), 31.

[55] The Greek word πάθη (at least in the authors and works analyzed here) is almost always the neuter plural (τὰ πάθη) of the singular noun τὸ πάθος. But πάθη in Greek is sometimes the feminine singular ἡ πάθη (plural αἱ πάθαι), a word that occurs as early as Herodotus and Plato, and for which LSJ gives "passive state," "what is done or happens to a person or thing," and "suffering, misfortune" as the basic meanings. See further Fitzgerald, "Passions and Moral Progress," 17, n.6.

21

whether positive or negative.[56] The latter was far more common than the former, so that

the meaning of the verb, over time, came to be understood as "to suffer."[57] The Greek

verb is thus distantly related to the Latin verb for suffering, *patior*, from which the

English words "passion" and "passive" derive.[58] Exactly how to render the Greek term

into English is difficult, for as Brad Inwood states: "no translation of the term is

adequate, for *pathos* is a technical term whose meaning is determined by the theory in

which it functions."[59] To further complicate precise definition, even restricting the

translation to how the term was used by one philosophical tradition (such as the Stoics)

does not settle the issue. Cicero already had (or feigned[60]) difficulty translating the Stoic

term into Latin when used of grief, fear, pleasure, and anger, and he was tempted to use

morbi, "diseases,"[61] arguing that it would be a word-for-word translation of *pathē* and

that the Greeks also used it not only of pity (*misereri*) and envy (*invidere*) but even of

exultation (*gestire*) and joy (*laetari*).[62] He finally settled for *perturbationes animi*,

"mental disturbances" (*Tusc.* 3.7; see also *Fin.* 3.35), though he does use *morbus* for

pathos in *Tusc.* 3.20.

　　　　There are three dominant English translations of *pathos* in current scholarship –

---

[56] BDAG, "πάσχω," 785; see also Graver, *Cicero on the Emotions*, 79.

[57] Fitzgerald, "Passions and Moral Progress," 2.

[58] Konstan, *Emotions of the Ancient Greeks*, 3.

[59] Brad Inwood, *Ethics and Human Action in Early Stoicism* (Oxford: Clarendon, 1985), 127.

[60] Graver correctly contends Cicero's discussion of how to translate *pathē* is an initial rhetorical ploy that he uses to gain an advantage at the outset of the discussion in *Cicero on the Emotions*, 79.

[61] This rendering of *pathos* is found in English in medical terminology, such as "pathogen" and "pathology," and by extension in certain phrases with negative connotations, such as "pathological liar."

[62] See Fitzgerald, "Passions and Moral Progress," 3.

emotion, passion, and affection. The most popular by an overwhelming margin is

"emotion," and is the preferable term here.[63] The next most popular translation of pathos

is "passion," which is the term used by Brad Inwood,[64] A.A. Long and D.N. Sedley,[65]

Susanna Braund and Christopher Gill in the title of *The Passions in Roman Thought and*

Literature, along with many others. "Passion" is derived from the Latin noun *passio*,

which also was a popular term used to render the Greek *pathos*. Augustine, for instance,

states that "the word *passio* for the Greek word *pathos* means a mental agitation (*motus*

animi) that is contrary to reason" (*Civ.* 8.17).[66]

The least popular English translation in current scholarship is "affection,"

preferred by Michael Frede and Teun Tielman, though for different reasons. Frede uses

the term "affection" primarily for the Platonic-Aristotelian tradition and speculates (and it

is presented as that without evidence):

> Perhaps the term *pathos* originally was restricted to … flagrantly irrational
> emotions, and only later came to refer to the emotions quite generally. … In this
> tradition the term *pathos* takes on the connotation of '*passio*', 'affect,' 'purely
> passive affection'.[67]

The Stoics, by contrast, "think that it is grossly misleading to think of the affection of the

soul as *pathē* in the sense of passive affection. They are rather *pathē* in the sense of

---

[63] Sorabji, for example, chose "emotion" in line with the Stoic theory of the *pathē* in *Emotion and Peace of Mind,* 7, 17.

[64] Brad Inwood, *Ethics and Human Action in Early Stoicism*, 127-28.

[65] A.A. Long and D. N. Sedley, *The Hellenistic Philosophers, I-II* (Cambridge: Cambridge University Press, 1987), I:410-23.

[66] See David Wiesen, trans., *Saint Augustine: The City of God against the Pagans* (3 vols.; Cambridge: Harvard University Press, 1968), 3:79.

[67] Michael Frede, "The Stoic Doctrine of the Affections of the Soul," in Schofield and Striker, *The Norms of Nature,* 96-97.

illnesses, diseases."[68] Tieleman, by contrast, chooses "affection" as the term "perhaps best suited to preserve the different shades of meaning of πάθος in its Stoic usage."[69]

There are, obviously, Latin precedents for translating the Greek words by terms belonging to the *affectio* (*adfecto*) / *affectus* (*adfectus*) word group. For example, Aulus Gellius reports a speech that he heard Herodes Atticus deliver in Greek at Athens about the important Stoic concept *apatheia*, which Herodes attacked: "no one, who felt and thought normally, could be wholly exempt and free from those *adfectionibus* of the mind, which he called πάθη, caused by sorrow, desire, fear, anger and pleasure" (*Noct. Att.* 19.12.3).[70] Cicero includes joy, desire, and fear as belonging to the category of *affectio* (*Inv.* 1.36) and he later calls annoyance, anger, and love "*affectionem animi*" (1.41).[71] Graver points out that most post-Ciceronian authors preferred to "render *pathos* by *adfecto* or *adfectus*."[72] Quintillian, for example, who presents *pathos* and *ēthos* as two emotional modes that can be used by the orator, says that "the Greeks call the one [mode] *pathos*, which we correctly and properly translate as *adfectus*" (*Inst.* 6.2.8). Further, he links *pathos* with tragedy and states that it is almost entirely concerned with anger,

---

[68] *Ibid.*, 99.

[69] Teun Tieleman, *Chrysippus' On Affections*, 16.

[70] Similarly, when speaking of anger, Gellius refers to "all the rest of the emotions, which the Latin philosophers call *affectus* or affections, and the Greeks *pathē*" (*Noct. Att.* 1.26.11).

[71] This usage is one of the factors that prompts Jakob Wisse to proclaim, "*Affectio* is roughly equivalent to Greek πάθος in its general sense" in *Ethos and Pathos from Aristotle to Cicero* (Amsterdam: Adolf M. Hakkert, 1989), 100, n.102.

[72] Graver, *Cicero on the Emotions*, 80.

hatred, fear, envy, and pity (6.2.20).[73]

In brief, there was no one word or word group used to render *pathos* and *pathē*. Augustine makes reference to this translation problem in *The City of God*:

> There are two opinions among the philosophers concerning the mental emotions [*animi motibus*], which the Greeks call *pathē*, while certain of our fellow countrymen, like Cicero, describe them as disturbances [*perturbationes*], others as affections [*affectiones*] or affects [*affectus*], and others again, like Apuleius, as passions [*passiones*], which renders the Greek more explicitly. (*Civ.* 9.4)[74]

Since there is no English word that fully corresponds to the exact meanings or nuances of πάθος, many modern scholars have avoided translating the same Greek word with a

single English term and use multiple English words. Representative of this approach is Martha Nussbaum, who uses ―emotions" and ―passions" ―more or less interchangeably" when speaking of the Stoics, and often augments with the term ―suffering," especially when describing the Epicureans and their desire to extricate themselves of the disturbing and frequently painful affects of certain *pathē*.[75] While my preferred rendering of *pathos* is ―emotion," an approach similar to Nussbaum will be employed in that ―passion" and ―emotion" will be used ―more or less interchangeably," and every attempt will be made

---

[73] Mario DiCicco claims that *adfectus* is ―coined" here by Quintillian as the Latin equivalent of the Greek *pathos*, but it would be more accurate to state that Quintillian is probably the first Latin author to equate the two terms explicitly with regard to rhetoric in *Paul's Use of Ethos, Pathos, and Logos in 2 Corinthians 10-13* (Lewiston: Mellen Biblical Press, 1995), 147 n.243. *Adfectus* in Latin was well established as a term for both ―emotion" and ―strong emotion" or ―passion" long before Quintillian and in equating the terms he is drawing on a common definition of *adfectus*. See David Konstan, ―Rhetoric and Emotion," in *A Companion to Greek Rhetoric* (ed. Ian Worthington; Oxford: Blackwell, 2007), 419-20.

[74] For Augustine's use and understanding of *affectus*, *passio*, and *perturbatio*, see Gerard O'Daly and Adolar Zumkeller, ―*Affectus* (*passio*, *pertubatio*)," in *Augustinus-Lexikon, vol.1: Aaron-Conuersio* (Basel: Schwabe, 1986), 166-180.

[75] Nussbaum, *Therapy of Desire*, 102 n.1, 319 n.4.

to augment this translation when appropriate in light of ancient context.

Πάθος had many connotations, but in its most general sense, meant ―something

that happens," referring to an ―event" or to a person affected by an outside agent, along

the lines of ―experience."[76] In classical Greek, *pathos* may refer more generally to what

befalls a person, often in the negative sense of misfortune or an accident, although it may

also bear the neutral significance of a condition or state of affairs.[77] In ancient

philosophy, *pathos* sometimes signified a secondary quality as opposed to the essence of

a thing.[78] Psychologically, it may connote a mental activity or phenomenon such as

remembering.[79] The specific sense of emotion is in large part conditioned by this

uncertainty of connotations. For example, in some connotations, *pathos* is a reaction to

an impinging event or circumstance, looking to the outside stimulus to which it responds.

Thus, every effort will be made to understand the context, both specific to the

philosopher, and generally to the broader culture, particularly where normally rendered

---

[76] Strong emotions were often seen as outside agents; both πάθος and its Latin equivalent *passio* connote something that ―happens to" a person who was usually regarded as a passive victim. Since these ―events" and ―experiences" could be either positive or negative, the term ―emotion," as previously mentioned above, is preferable in this survey to describe generally most of what the philosophers discussed under the heading of πάθη. See David E. Aune, ―The Problem of the Passions in Cynicism" in *Passions and Moral Progress*, 53-54. See further T. Gould, *The Ancient Quarrel between Poetry and Philosophy* (Princeton: Princeton University Press, 1990), 63.

[77] See further David Konstan, *The Emotions of the Ancient Greeks: Studies in Aristotle and Classical Literature* (Toronto: University of Toronto Press, 2006), 3-5.

[78] See Aristotle, *Metaph.* 1022b15-21; see also J.O. Urmson, *The Greek Philosophical Vocabulary* (London: Duckworth, 1990), 126-7.

[79] See Aristotle, *Mem. rem.* 449b4-7; see also 449b24-5 for *pathos* as memory of formerly perceived or contemplated things.

English linguistic equivalents may lead us to overlook significant differences.[80]

A Cursory Introduction to the Philosophers on the Emotions

‒Sing, goddess, the anger of Peleus' son Achilleus" – Homer, *Iliad*[81]

Ancient philosophers examined the emotions in a variety of contexts and genres, making them the general topic of analysis, as well as subjecting individual emotions to particular treatment. Given ancient philosophy's concern with concepts and expressions of virtue, inquiries into emotion were unavoidable. Emblematic is Galen who stated, ‒the doctrine of the virtues follows necessarily from the doctrine of the emotions (*PHP* 5.6.1). This is especially true of Stoics such as Posidonius, who ‒believes that the understanding of the nature of emotions is the basis of all ethical philosophy."[82] Ergo John Fitzgerald's summation: ‒From both a theoretical and a practical standpoint, to speak of virtue without giving due attention to the emotions was as impossible as it was inconceivable."[83]

It is not altogether clear who authored the first Περὶ παθῶν (*Peri pathōn*), *On*

---

[80] There is a large and multi-disciplined scholarly field on current understandings of the emotions that certainly references and debates classical formulations. Studies of the emotions, both philosophical and scientifically empirical, from Augustine to Aquinas and especially Darwin along with more recent landmark studies by Margaret Mead, Richard Rorty, and James Russell, have played a large role in the history of scholarship. Without impinging upon, but with due respect given to ongoing controversies over the emotions in such diverse areas such evolutionary psychology and sociobiology as well as philosophy and linguistics, my modest goal is to show broad general patterns in ancient philosophy.

[81] Interest in human emotion can be traced back to the very beginnings of Western literature – Homer's *Iliad*, whose opening line references Achilles' *mēnis*, rendered ‒anger" in Lattimore's translation, enjoys pride of place in the Greek text: μῆνιν ἄειδε, θεά, Πηληιάδεω Ἀχιλῆος. Homer's story shows the horrible consequences of the hero's angry passion. See Richmond Lattimore, trans., *The Iliad of Homer* (Chicago: University of Chicago Press, 1961), 59.

[82] Ludwig Edelstein, ‒The Philosophical System of Posidonius," *AJP* 57 (1936): 305.

[83] Fitzgerald, ‒Passions and Moral Progress," 5.

Emotions, but there is a scholarly consensus that the key impetus for these philosophical

analyses and debates came from Plato's Academy.[84] In describing the period that both

Xenocrates and Aristotle were students at the Academy, W.W. Fortenbaugh asserts:

> An investigation of emotion was undertaken which was to have profound effects
> upon the subsequent course of philosophical psychology, rhetoric, poetics, and
> political and ethical theory. Members of the Academy … focused upon emotions
> as distinct from bodily sensations and bodily drives and tried to explain the
> involvement of cognition in emotional response. *A satisfactory explanation was
> not immediately forthcoming* (emphasis added).[85]

Plato discussed emotion, especially in the *Philebus*, but did not devote any of his works

specifically to the *pathē*. Xenocrates wrote a one-volume tome *On Emotions* (D.L. 4.12),

perhaps when he was head of the Academy,[86] which may have been the first devoted

specifically to the passions.[87] It is probable that Aristotle wrote at least one book

specifically on the emotions, but no such work is extant.[88] Theophrastus, Aristotle's

successor at the Lyceum, wrote *On Emotions* (D.L. 5.45), which covered anger along

---

[84] See especially Simo Knuuttila and Juha Sihvola, ―How the Philosophical Analysis was Introduced,"
in *The Emotions in Hellenistic Philosophy*, 1-5.

[85] Fortenbaugh, *Aristotle on Emotion*, 9.

[86] See Fitzgerald, ―Passions and Moral Progress," 5-7.

[87] It is also possible that Xenocrates' *On Emotions* was a distillation of Plato's views on the emotions,
what Simon Hornblower calls an ―attempt to reproduce Plato's thought in a stereotyped and formalized
system," in ―Xenocrates," *The Oxford Classical Dictionary* (ed. Simon Hornblower and Antony Spawforth;
Oxford: Oxford University Press, 1996), 1628.

[88] There are two works mentioned in ancient lists of Aristotle's works with the term ―emotions" in the
title, though the lists vary (one appears in D.L. 5.22-7) and the exact nature of the works (if one or both
existed) is the subject of debate. See Paul Moraux, *Les listes anciennes des ouvrages d'Aristote* (Louvain:
Éditions universitaires de Louvain, 1951); and A.J.P. Kenny, *The Aristotelian Ethics: A Study of the
Relationship between the Eudemian and Nicomachean Ethics of Aristotle* (Oxford: Clarendon Press, 1978),
41-43.

with other emotions, as well as a work entitled Περὶ πένθους, *On Grief* (D.L. 5.44).[89]

The most famous early treatise, *On Grief* (D.L. 4.27) was written by Crantor, a member

of the Old Academy, and advocated moderation of the emotions instead of their

eradication.[90]

Epicurus himself began the Epicurean concern with the emotions by writing περὶ

παθῶν δόξαι πρὸς Τιμοκράτην, *Opinions on Emotions against Timocrates*.[91] After

Epicurus, much attention was given to the topic of the emotions throughout the history of

the school.[92] For instance, Philodemus wrote a number of treatises on various emotions

in the first century BCE.[93] Diogenes of Oenoanda (second century CE) inscribed the title

of his treatise, Περὶ παθῶν καὶ πράξεων, *On Emotions and Actions*, on the wall of a

stoa in Lycia.[94]

Among the Stoics, Zeno began the tradition with *On Emotions* (SVF 1.41, 211),

and was followed by Herillus (SVF 1.409), Sphaerus (SVF 1.620), and Chrysippus (SVF

---

[89] See further W.W. Fortenbaugh, P.M. Huby, R.W. Sharples, and D. Gutas, eds., *Theophrastus of Eresus: Sources for His Life, Writings, Thought, and Influence* (Leiden: Brill, 1992), 436.5 / 436.15.

[90] See David Sedley, ―Crantor,‖ *Oxford Classical Dictionary*, 405.

[91] The polemic is not extant (referenced in D.L. 10.28; Philodemus, *On the Stoics* col.III) but seems to have been aimed at Metrodorus‛ brother Timocrates, who belonged to the Epicurean school at one time, ―but later defected to become its leading detractor,‖ David Sedley, ―Metrodorus of Lampsacus,‖ in *Encyclopedia of Classical Philosophy* (ed. Donald J. Zeyl; Westport, Conn.: Greenwood Press, 1997), 342-43.

[92] See Annas, ―Epicurean Emotions,‖ 145-64.

[93] See Tiziano Dorandi, ―Filodemo: gil orientamenti della ricerca attuale,‖ *ANRW* 2.36.4 (1990): 2349-51.

[94] See Diskin Clay, ―The Philosophical Inscription of Diogenes of Oenoanda: New Discoveries 1969-1983,‖ *ANRW* 2.36.4 (1990): 2499.

3.456).[95] Dionysius of Heraclea on the Pontus wrote an extremely influential treatise

entitled Περὶ ἀπαθείας (usually translated *On Freedom from Passion* or *On the Absence*

of Emotion). It was probably the first work on the vital Stoic concept of *apatheia*, and

soon was the subject of a diatribe by Teles the Cynic (frg. 7).[96] During the Middle Stoa,

Panaetius discussed the emotions[97] and a Stoic version of a *consolatio* was written by

Posidonius and dealt with the alleviation of grief.[98] Comprehensive studies on the

emotions were composed by Hecaton of Rhodes (frg. 9; D.L. 7.110), who appears to have

been a voluminous (Περὶ παθῶν being among six works referenced by Diogenes

Laertius) and influential (frequently mentioned by Seneca, especially in his treatise *De*

Beneficiis) writer, though nothing is extant. As this brief survey indicates, the emotions

were a major concern of philosophers in Greco-Roman antiquity, but they were also

important for the historians, poets, novelists, etc. which the following examination will

consider when felicitous.

Posidonius' comprehensive treatments on the emotions were understood by

Plutarch, Galen, along with many modern scholars as attacking those of Chrysippus and

---

[95] Of all the Stoic writing on emotion, it was Chrysippus' that proved most important in subsequent periods, especially book 4 of *On Emotions*, which was know by its separate title *Therapeutics*. See Tieleman, *Chrysippus' On Affections*, 140-97.

[96] See David E. Aune, "The Problem of the Passions in Cynicism," 58-60.

[97] See Peter Steinmetz, "Die Stoa," in *Die Philosophie der Antike*, vol. 4 (ed. Hellmut Flashar; Basel: Schwabe, 1994), 694.

[98] See L. Edelstein and I.G. Kidd, eds., *Posidonius*, vol. 2: *The Commentary*, Part 1: *Testimonia and Fragments 1-149* (Cambridge: Cambridge University Press, 1988), 180.

rivaling if not surpassing them in importance.[99] Posidonius' work is sometimes considered the last great comprehensive treatment of the emotions by a Stoic philosopher; later Stoics preferring to summarize Stoic teachings – as Arius Didymus did in *Epitome of Stoic Ethics*[100] – or to write on particular emotions (especially anger) – as Seneca in *On Anger* and Epictetus in "That We Should Not Be Angry (χαλεπαίνειν) with People"

(*Diss.* 1.28) and "On Freedom from Fear" (*Diss.* 4.7).[101] The focus on anger among ancient philosophy was perhaps most identified with Stoicism, but hardly restricted to the Stoics or even to philosophy, it was a recurring theme in Greek and Roman literature as well.[102] Philosophical studies of anger were so numerous that Cicero could say to his brother Quintus, "I won't take it upon myself here to expound to you what philosophers are apt to say on the subject of irascibility, for I don't want to take too long, and you can find it in many books" (*Quint. fratr.* 1.1.37).[103]

From Luke's redaction of Jesus' emotions in the Passion pericopae (e.g., the transference of Jesus' *lupē* to the disciples), I propose a larger pattern of Luke consistently removing emotion from the character of Jesus throughout his gospel. With respect to the disagreement among biblical scholars concerning these redactions, I will

---

[99] See the discussion in Christopher Gill, *The Structured Self in Hellenistic and Roman Thought* (Oxford: Oxford University Press, 2006), 207-90.

[100] See especially 10-10e, a section introduced [9b] with the statement, "let us speak next about passions [περὶ παθῶν]" in *Arius Didymus: Epitome of Stoic Ethics* (ed. Arthur Pomeroy; Atlanta: Society of Biblical Literature, 1999).

[101] Fitzgerald, "Passions and Moral Progress," 10-11.

[102] See Braund and Most, *Ancient Anger*, 8-18.

[103] D.R. Shackleton Baily, ed. and trans., *Cicero: Letters to Quintus and Brutus, Letter Fragments, Letter to Octavian, Invectives, Handbook of Electioneering* (Cambridge: Harvard University Press, 2002), 39.

enter this line of scholarship and hopefully further it by offering explanation for them. It is in light of the ancient sources on the important philosophical topic of the πάθη, and with regard to the recent scholarly interest in the emotions, that I will explore Luke's redaction of Jesus' emotions in Luke.

CHAPTER 2

THE EMOTIONS IN HELLENISTIC PHILOSOPHY

Introduction

As stated in the general introduction, I maintain that the "true scholarly question"
is not that the author of Luke has redacted Mark in terms of his characterization of
Jesus,[104] but *why* Luke has chosen to redact the material in this particular manner. It is
the true scholarly question in the sense that why Luke has portrayed Jesus with little
emotion is a much more difficult argument to make; it is more speculative and open for
debate.[105] While my presentation of the philosophical material is not meant to be
exhaustive, the scholarly evidence will clearly show a philosophical *pattern*.

The following two chapters will broadly and generally present evidence from the
Hellenistic (with special attention to the four main schools), Roman (especially the
popularization of Roman Stoic views in the imperial authors), and Hellenistic Jewish
philosophical traditions (particularly those writers who are not philosophers in the
technical sense, such as Josephus, for a research comparison to Luke) on the subject of
emotions. This evidence will show a pattern, with notable exceptions (i.e., Aristotle),

---

[104] Chapters 4 and 5 systematically show that these redactions have in fact occurred.

[105] See Greene, "Argument as Conversation," 145-164.

that the primary philosophical view of the emotions was depreciatory and disapproving. I will argue that it is primarily the Stoic tradition (and in particular the popular rendering of these in Roman imperial authors) that leads the author of Luke to present the reader with a Jesus character (quite to the contrary of Mark) as one bereft of strong emotion.

I am arguing that Luke was aware of and influenced by the general philosophical traditions, not that Luke was a professional philosopher in the technical sense. Thus the focus of the next two chapters will be on the philosophical traditions pertaining to emotional theory, primarily as it elucidates the philosophical ethos of the first century of the Common Era, in which the author of Luke redacts and constructs his Jesus. Though seldom realized, a full philosophical education was understood ideally to involve training in all four of what were recognized as the principal sects -- Platonism, Aristotelianism, Stoicism, and Epicureanism.[106] Apollonius of Tyana, in the early to mid first century C.E., is said to have found for himself at nearby Aegae teachers of all four main philosophical systems, and for good measure a Pythagorean teacher too.[107] Galen, in the mid second century, was able to study with representatives of these same four schools at his native Pergamum.[108]

The focus of my presentation is on Platonism, Aristotelianism, Stoicism, and Epicureanism, though I include brief mention of others (e.g., Cynicism and

---

[106] An ideal philosophical education as a topos occurs as early as the first century before the common era, and there is some evidence for its actuality in subsequent centuries. Several emperors endowed chairs of rhetoric at Rome and elsewhere that embraced this multi-faceted philosophical study. Later for example, Marcus Aurelius set up four chairs of philosophy at Athens (for Platonism, Aristotelianism, Stoicism, Epicureanism). See Dio Cassius 71.31.3; see also J.P. Lynch, *Aristotle's School: A Study of a Greek Educational Institution* (Berkeley: University of California Press, 1972), 190; and J.M. André, ̶Les écoles philosophiques aux deux premiers siècles de l'Empire," *ANRW* II 36.1, 53.

[107] In Philostratus, *Vit. Apoll.* 1.7.

[108] *De cognoscendis curandisque animi morbis* 8 [*Scripta minora* 1.23-25].

Neopythagoreanism) primarily to compare and further elucidate the views of the emotions of the principal four and to show that over time sharp distinctions among them begin to erode. While I maintain it was the Stoics who most influenced Luke, an important assumption I share with many scholars is the partial break-down of borders among the various philosophical traditions in the first century and following.[109] Again, my contention is not that Luke was educated as an ideal philosopher in the four schools, but only that the traditions influenced Luke and during this period some traditional lines of distinction were softened. This concept dictates my use of language such as _popular rendering' and _popularization' when describing philosophical traditions during the time of Luke.

Part I: The Four Traditions

The Presocratics[110]

Blessed is he who has learned how to engage in inquiry,
with no impulse to harm his countrymen or to pursue wrongful actions,
but perceives the order of immortal and ageless nature,
how it is structured.[111]

---

[109] As stated in chapter one, this concept doesn't have to embrace fully the notion of philosophical _eclecticism' that has sometimes been associated with the age; but it is at the very least symptomatic of a constructive softening of school boundaries. See Dillon and Long, *The Question of ‚Eclecticism',* 5-15. It was in this philosophical milieu that narrow philosophical sectarianism was beginning to look obsolete. David Sedley describes this period as ‒one in which someone could be simultaneously a scholar of philosophical history, an author of ethical treatises, and a counselor to dynasts . . . that the _Roman' phase of Stoicism began life." In ‒The School, from Zeno to Arius Didymus," 32.

[110] In light of current debate over the term ‒Presocratic," I hesitate to use the term, which first appeared in Hermann Diels, *Die Fragmente der Vorsokratiker* (3 vols.; Berlin: Weidmann, 1903), 6, and despite the significant problems with ‒Presocratic," it is still the most widely used term in scholarship to describe those philosophers who (for the most part) are chronologically before Socrates. See A.A. Long, ed., *The Cambridge Companion to Early Greek Philosophy* (Cambridge: Cambridge University Press, 1999), 5-10.

[111] Euripides, fr. 910, from an unknown play, found in John Burnet, *Early Greek Philosophy* (New York: Meridian Books, 1957), 6. M.I. Finley argues, in an interesting and innovative manner, that

My analysis formally begins with Plato, and few scholars would question this decision or argue with Plato's great influence in philosophy or Western thought in general. This is not to ignore the important contributions of the "philosophers"[112] before Socrates (such as Pythagoras, Heraclitus, Xenophanes, Democritus, Parmenides, Protagoras, and Melissus to name just a few), it is just to acknowledge that Plato "was the first Greek thinker to theorise explicitly about the nature of philosophy."[113] Many of these philosophers attempted Aristotle's "inquiry into nature" without formally using the term or in Xenophanes' language to give "an account of all things" that differentiated them from other writers. Even in the Euripides quotation above, there is reference to query as a discipline, ethics, and the order of nature.

There are few direct references to the emotions as a type in the Presocratics, but especially in ethical treatments, we see mention of important concepts related to this examination of the emotions including reasonable action, rationality, good judgment, self-control, and moderation. Democritus is the earliest thinker reported as having explicitly posited a supreme good or goal, which he termed "cheerfulness" or "well-being."[114] A large part of this untroubled enjoyment of life was moderation, including

---

Euripides, especially in the *Bacchae*, pace Socrates, captures the actual psychology of the popular polis concerning the emotions and reason with respect to social class in *The Ancient Greeks: An Introduction to Their Life and Thought* (New York: Viking Press, 1969), 114-127.

[112] With the possible exception of Pythagoras, none of the Presocratics identified himself expressly as a "philosopher" or called his project "philosophy." Later in antiquity, Diogenes Laertius describes Pythagoras as "philosopher" (D.L. 1.12). See further Geoffrey Ernest Richard Lloyd, *Methods and Problems in Greek Science* (Cambridge: Cambridge University Press, 1991), 102-103.

[113] Long, *Early Greek Philosophy*, 3.

[114] See C.C.W. Taylor, "The Atomists" in *The Cambridge Companion to Early Greek Philosophy* (ed. A.A. Long; Cambridge: Cambridge University Press, 1999), 197-99.

moderation in the pursuit of pleasures, a type of enlightened hedonism, which is a forerunner of the Epicurean ideal.[115] Further, Julia Annas states that Democritus "came to be regarded, in the Hellenistic period, as something of an ethical pioneer, and was regarded as having adumbrated an ethical theory which Hellenistic thinkers took to be primitive, but recognizably like their own."[116] Democritus states:

> One should choose not every pleasure, but only that concerned with the beautiful (fr. 207).

> Moderation multiplies pleasures, and increases pleasure (fr. 211).

> The brave man is not only he who overcomes the enemy, but he who is stronger than pleasures. Some men are masters of cities, but are enslaved to women (fr. 214).

He describes the ethical goal as *athambia* (imperturbability), and later Stobaeus attributes to Democritus the term *ataraxia* (undisturbed) which would become important to both the Epicureans and the Pyrrhonists.[117] Protagoras calls for "good deliberation" (*euboulia*, *Prot.* 318e-319a), a concept which presupposes an ability to modify and control mental states, which some scholars have interpreted as including the emotions.[118]

Many Presocratics quarreled with the traditional poets on ethical topics, including Xenophanes, who asserts that "both Homer and Hesiod attributed to the gods all the

---

[115] See C.H. Kahn, "Democritus and the origins of moral psychology," *AJP106* (1985): 1-31, especially for a discussion of Democritus' views on reason and desire.

[116] Julia Annas, *The Morality of Happiness*, 18.

[117] See Everard Flintoff, "Pyrrho and India," *Phronesis* 25 (1980): 95-96.

[118] See Fernanda Decleva Caizzi, "Protagoras and Antiphon: Sophistic Debates on Justice," in *The Cambridge Companion to Early Greek Philosophy* (ed. A.A. Long; Cambridge: Cambridge University Press, 1999), 320-21.

things that are blameworthy and a reproach among men."[119] These include stealing, committing adultery, deceiving one another, and being quick to anger. Further, Heraclitus directly anticipates the Hellenistic schools in his proposition that the control of passion and desire (see especially frs. 85, 110) is the means to the almost godlike impartiality which he elsewhere seems to equate with his notion of ―wisdom" and living ―according to nature" (fr. 112). As Democritus' *athambia* paved the way for Epicurus' *ataraxia*, Heraclitus' declaration that the restraining of impulse is difficult but necessary to the soul's health (fr. 102) lays the foundation for the Stoic emphasis on intervening in the mental process that leads from sensation to action. Parmenides' *Way of Truth* endorses a distinction between lower and higher types of awareness, and to live by this higher awareness involves cultivation of a standpoint beyond the fluctuation of pleasure and pain.[120]

The above stated Presocratic motif of imperturbability (including *athambia* and *ataraxia*) was traditionally embodied by Socrates, whose life many philosophical traditions (even competing schools) would claim as a model of the philosopher-sage *par excellence*.[121] His students, especially Plato, would give account of the psychology of

---

[119] Hermann Diels, *Die Fragmente der Vorsokratiker,* 6, 337. See further Daniel Babut, ―Xénophane critique des poètes," *L'Antiquité Classique* 43 (1974): 83-117.

[120] See Thomas McEvilley, *The Shape of Ancient Thought: Comparative Studies in Greek and Indian Philosophies* (New York: Allworth Press, 2002), 597-598.

[121] In a related and fascinating discussion of the philosophically important notion of ―self-control" in Greece during the time of Socrates, see A.A. Long, *From Epicurus to Epictetus: Studies in Hellenistic and Roman Philosophy* (Oxford: Clarendon Press, 2006.), 7-10. Long argues that it was Socrates who first developed ―self-control," as a concept, which Long defines as ―a notion of self…over which their owners claim such complete authority that they find themselves in total charge of where their life is going and indulge their emotions and appetites only to the extent that they themselves determine" (7). See also Helen North, *Sophrosyne, Self-knowledge and Self-restraint in Greek Literature* (Ithaca, N.Y.: Cornell University Press, 1966). She detects mastery of the emotions in Euripides' interpretation of *sōphrosynē* and other Presocratics who develop *sōphrosynē* as the control of the emotions and appetites (69-70). Long argues

imperturbability, usually focusing on the process of pleasure and its habituation. He describes this process from sensation to action in the *Timaeus*:

> Now, when the souls be implanted in bodies by necessity and be always gaining or losing some part of their bodily substance, then, in the first place, it would be necessary that they should all have in them one and the same faculty of sensation, arising out of irresistible contacts; in the second place, they must have love, in which pleasure and pain mingle – also fear and anger and the emotions which are akin or opposite to them. If they conquered these they would live righteously, and if they were conquered by them, unrighteously (*Tim.* 42a).

Plato further elucidates how the emotions inundate around the recognition of the sensation and acts of avoidance or pursuit arise in a mechanical and automatic manner:

> When a man is carried away by enjoyment or distracted by pain, in his immoderate haste to grasp the one or to escape from the other he can neither see nor hear aright; he is in a frenzy and his capacity for reasoning is then at its lowest (*Tim.* 86c).

Plato argues that it is hypothetically possible to intervene in the emotional process and ―conquer‖ the emotional reactions.[122] This faculty to intervene is called *phronēsis*, which is often translated ―wisdom,‖ but in Greek ethical thought from Plato to Epicurus it is perhaps closer to ―mindfulness.‖[123] This emotional process, as we shall see, becomes an important subject of debate among the various Hellenistic philosophical schools, as they attempt to determine the exact point, and clarify techniques for intervention, where

---

that Sophist Antiphon was influenced by Socrates‘ oral discourse when he developed his notion of *sōphrosynē*.

[122] Though scholars disagree as to how Plato understands this intervention and some question if he is describing an intervention at all. See discussion in McEvilley, *The Shape of Ancient Thought*, 608-10.

[123] It is, in my opinion, rightly translated ―way of thinking‖ and especially ―frame of mind‖ in ―φρόνησις‖ *BAGD* 866. Epicurus states *phronēsis* ―patiently searches out the motives for every act of grasping and fleeing, and banishes those beliefs through which the greatest tumult enters the mind‖ (D.L. 10.129-132). Further, Epicurus asserts that ―all the other virtues have come by nature from *phronēsis*‖ in his *Letter to Menoeceus* (132).

these feelings of pleasure and pain (with or without cognitive identification) become

emotional reactions.

Plato and Platonism

In Plato's view the emotional reactions often entail misguided evaluations of contingent things. They bind the soul to earthly things in a way which disturbs the higher activities of the reasoning part. Emotions should be kept under strict control by continuously re-evaluating and often rejecting their behavioural suggestions. Aristotle did not share Plato's detached attitude to life. He thought that a considerable part of the good human life consists of participating in the various activities of civilized society and consequently in a complicated system of socially learned emotions which one should learn to feel in an appropriate manner.[124]

As mentioned above, it is well argued that philosophical inquiries pertaining to

the emotions were first formulated in the works of Plato and Aristotle, and that to a large

extent shaped Hellenistic and later ancient discussions.[125] In discussing the good state

and the good human life in his *Republic*, Plato divided the human soul into three parts,

the reasoning (λογιστικόν), the spirited (θυμοειδές), and the appetitive (ἐπιθυμητικός,

Resp. 4.435a-441c; 9.580d-583a.). The reasoning part is able to love wisdom and the

good. Ideally it should govern the entire soul. The appetitive part pursues immediate

sensual pleasure and avoids suffering, whereas the spirited part is the seat of emotions

connected with self-assurance and self affirmation. In the *Republic*, the reasoning part is

portrayed as immortal and purely rational. The lower parts are mortal and it is only

---

[124] Simo Knuuttila, *Emotions in Ancient and Medieval Philosophy* (Oxford: Clarendon Press, 2004), 5.

[125] See ibid., 1-5.

through the soul's union to the body that they belong to the composite (*Resp.* 10.608d-611a; see also *Tim.* 42c; 69c-d).

In his earlier dialogues, especially the *Phaedo*, Plato was inclined to see all appetites and emotions which are outside the reasoning part as changes in the body, thus stressing their irrational nature. The philosopher was understood to aim at complete detachment from all passions and desires of the mortal body.[126] In the *Phaedrus*, Plato gives a more positive role to the emotions, especially the erotic appetite through his simile of the two horses (246a-256d). The two horses represent the spirited and appetitive parts of the soul, and the charioteer represents reason which guides these two parts. The *Phaedrus* even seems to integrate the emotional responses with the immortal soul, but in *Timaeus*, a later dialogue, they are in the mortal soul again (69c-d).

Plato's ascetic ideal in the *Republic* and in earlier works was not very far removed from the Stoic ideal of *apatheia*, though Plato did not consider the complete elimination of the emotions possible, given the psychosomatic composition of humans. Plato tended to regard spontaneous desires and emotions as affective overvaluations of contingent and temporal matters.[127] They fill the soul with inappropriate interests and prevent it from focusing on higher values congenial to the all-important immortal part of the soul. Plato describes this ideal in the *Timaeus*:

> When a man is always occupied with his appetites and ambitions, and eagerly tries to satisfy them, all his thoughts must be mortal, and he must become entirely mortal as far as possible, because he has nourished this part. But he who has been serious in the love of knowledge and true wisdom and has exercised this part of himself more than any other part, must have immortal and divine thoughts, if he

---

[126] *Phaed.* 65e, 66b-c; For a more in-depth analysis of Plato's metaphysics in the *Phaedo*, see Martha Nussbaum, *The Fragility of Goodness*, 151-2.

[127] Knuuttila, *Emotions,* 24-25.

attains to truth, and he cannot fail to achieve immortality as fully as human nature is capable of sharing in it, and since he always looks after the divine part in himself and respects his inner divinity (*daimōn*), he will be happy (*eudaimōn*) above all others. (90b-d.)

In the *Laws* the emotions are taken to have more intrinsic value than in the *Republic*, but Plato is mainly interested in how to control them; moderated anger, feeling mildly, confidence, and shame (as fear of bad repute) appear useful in this respect.[128] He further states that young people should learn to love and to hate correctly, so that when their ability to reason is developed, there will be no disturbing conflicts between emotional inclinations and what reason suggests (*Leg.* 2.653b-c). Depending on one's scholarly view of Plato concerning the emotions, Plato either changes his mind (most scholars pinpoint this after the *Republic*) or is extremely careful to temper his positive and negative comments.[129] The idea of a positive epistemic role for the emotions suggested in the *Phaedrus* was qualified in the *Philebus*; since as mixtures of pleasure and distress the emotions were problematic and not reliable sources of information. While some of Plato's philosophical works give a slightly more positive role to the emotions than others, the consensus remains that Plato was skeptical of the value of emotions, and that one should strive to eliminate them as much as possible.

---

[128] *Leg.* 1.646e-649e; see also 5.731b-d.

[129] Nussbaum describes Plato's emotional theory as ―deepening" over time in *Fragility of Goodness*, 307-9. She posits that the deepened interest in the psychology of emotions visible in Plato's later works is reflected in Aristotle's approach to the emotions as the essential constituents of a person. Similarly, W.W. Fortenbaugh describes it as ―Plato's new bipartite psychology," in *Aristotle on Emotion: A Contribution to Philosophical Psychology, Rhetoric, Poetics, Politics and Ethics* (2nd ed.; London: Duckworth, 2002), 49.

Cicero

Just before Rome technically becomes the Empire, Cicero gives us a good indication of the standard Academic view[130] – walking a fine line between a notion which condemns the emotions (in line with Stoicism) and one more in line with the Aristotelian mean of feeling moderated emotion at the right in the right situation.[131] We see the standard Stoic position articulated by Cicero in his *Tusculan Disputations*. Cicero argued that virtue is the harmonious disposition of the soul, from which spring good inclinations, opinions, actions, and all that makes right reason, and its opposite is vice, from which comes the agitation of disorders. A disorder (πάθος) is an agitation of the soul alienated

from right reason and contrary to nature, thus, it amounts to an error in judgment (*Tusc*. 4.34ff). Therefore, for Cicero in *Tusculan Disputations*, emotion was an irrational disorder.

Like many philosophers (including Plato), Cicero was not totally consistent in his views (perhaps intentionally) throughout his works. This can particularly be seen in his writings on rhetoric and persuasive speaking, where he taught how to use effectively the very emotions he condemned.[132] In *De Oratore*, cast in the form of a conversation to the *ars rhetorica* of Aristotle and Isocrates, he argued that psychology is sometimes more important to persuasion than logical demonstration.

---

[130] Cicero is sometimes identified as a middle Platonist (middle Platonism developed in Cicero's lifetime), but he studied properly with the philosopher Antiochus of the Old Academy in Athens. See David E. Aune, ed., ―Marcus Tullius Cicero," in *The Westminster Dictionary of New Testament and Early Christian Literature and Rhetoric* (Louisville: Westminster John Knox Press, 2003), 97.

[131] Aristotelian virtue is ―having these feelings at the right time, on the right occasions, towards the right people, with the right aim and in the right way" (*Eth. nic.* 1109a26). See further below.

[132] See DiCicco, *Paul's Use of Ethos,* 121-132.

Now nothing in oratory, Catulus, is more important than to win for the orator the favor of his hearer, and to have the latter so affected as to be swayed by something resembling a mental impulse or emotion, rather than by judgments or deliberation. For men decide far more problems by hate, or love, or rage, or lust, or sorrow, or joy, or hope, or fear, or illusion, or some other inward emotion, than by reality, or authority, or any legal standard, or judicial precedent, or statute (*De or.* 2.42.178).

In a similar passage, he wrote about an expressive style of persuasive speech which:

excites and urges the feelings of the tribunal towards hatred and love, ill-will or well-wishing, fear or hope, desire or aversion, joy or sorrow, compassion or the wish to punish, or by it they are prompted to whatever emotions are nearly allied and similar to these passions of the soul, and to such as these. (*De or.* 2.44.185)

Given his aversion to the emotions in *Tusculan Disputations*, it is odd that he would not only advocate playing upon other peoples' emotions, but insisted that the orator genuinely feel the emotions one was trying to arouse in others in *De Oratore*. ―It is impossible for the listener to feel indignation, hatred or ill will, to be terrified of anything, or reduced to tears of compassion, unless all those emotions, which the advocate would inspire in the arbitrator, are visibly stamped or rather branded on the advocate himself‖ (*De or.* 2.44.187).[133] Antonius, the protagonist in *De Oratore*, lays particular emphasis upon those feelings eloquence has to excite in the minds of the audience: love, hate, wrath, jealousy, compassion, hope, joy, fear, and vexation.[134] In *De claris oratoribus*, Cicero

---

[133] On the requirement that the orator himself feel them in order to induce them the better, see also Quintilian, *Inst.* 6.2.26-36; and commentary by Jeroen Bons and R.T. Lane, ―Quintilian 6.2: On Emotion,‖ in *Quintilian and the Law: The Art of Persuasion in Law and Politics* (ed. Olga Tellegen-Couperus; Leuven: Leuven University Press, 2003), 141-44. On the importance of arousing emotions in the audience, see Ismene Lada, ―Empathic Understanding: Emotion and Cognition in Classical Dramatic Audience-Response,‖ *Proceedings of the Cambridge Philological Society* 39 (1993): 99-100.

[134] See *De or.* 2.47.194-53.214; and discussion in DiCicco, *Paul's Use of Ethos*, 124.

44

says that a crowd listening to a good speaker —feels joy and pain, laughs and cries, lauds and hates, scorns, envies, is moved to pity, shame, and disgust, grows angry, calms down, hopes, and fears."[135]

Cicero's use of Stoic practical ethics in the pre-imperial period is most predominant in *On Duties* (*De officiis*). This is substantially based on a book of Panaetius' on this topic, but it also draws on advice and casuistry (i.e., the analysis of key examples) going back at least to Diogenes and Antipater. A special feature of Panaetius' approach, reflected in Cicero, is the use of the theory of the four personae to differentiate our ethical and social roles, thereby providing the basis for specified advice about what is _appropriate' for us.[136]

Plutarch

—Reason makes use of the passions when they have been subdued and are tame and does not hamstring or altogether excise that part of the soul which should be its servant" (*Mor.* 451D-452A).[137]

Plutarch (c. 45-120), who regards himself as a Platonist (and who habitually

---

[135] *Brut.* 188: —gaudet, dolet, ridet, plorat, favet, odit, contemnit, invidet, ad misericordiam inducitur, ad pudendum, ad pigendum; irascitur, mitigatur, sperat, timet." See further John Marincola, —Beyond Pity and Fear: The Emotions of History," *Ancient Society* 33 (2003): 300-310.

[136] Another Ciceronian topic of practical ethics in which we see a Platonism laced with Stoicism concerns the πάθη and ontology. Πάθη are often understood in Stoicism as products of a specific kind of error; namely, that of treating merely _preferable' advantages as if they were absolutely good, which only virtue is. This type of mistake produces intense reactions (*pathē*), which constitute a disturbance of our natural psychophysical state. These disturbances are treated as _sicknesses' that need to be _cured' by analysis of their nature and origin and by advice. See further David Sedley, —The Stoic-Platonist Debate on *kathêkonta*," in *Topics in Stoic Philosophy* (ed. Katerina Ierodiakonou; Oxford: Oxford University Press, 1999), 130-3.

[137] Translations of *De Virtute morali* are from W.C. Hembold, trans., *Plutarch's Moralia*, vol. 6 (London: Heinemann, 1939).

attacked the Stoics), is representative of a Middle Platonic view. While remaining authentically Platonic,[138] he draws frequently upon the Peripatetic tradition and even incorporates Stoic traditions in his writing.[139] Operating from a Platonic-Aristotelian psychology, he divides the soul into three states: (1) capacity or potentiality (δύναμις); (2) passion (πάθος); and (3) acquired or settled disposition (ἕξις).[140] Plutarch describes capacity (or predisposition) as passion's starting point (ἀρχή) and matter (ὕλη), such as a proneness to anger (ὀργιλότης); passion proper as a stirring of the soul's capacity by anger (ὀργή) or shame, for instance; and the acquired disposition as the settled state of passion. This state can be either virtuous or vicious, depending on how the passion has been educated (*Mort.* 443D). This view is more in line with Aristotle's emphasis on training one's emotional state, having emotion at the correct time in the right situation, and the Aristotelian mean in general.[141]

For Plutarch, reason (λόγος) is the ―form" (εἶδος) that must be imposed on the matter" (ὕλη) of the passions if they are to be kept in check (*Mort.* 440D). In an intriguing (if slightly circular) argument, the emotions, when held in moderation, can

---

[138] Daniel Babut, *Plutarch: De la vertu éthique* (Paris: Les Belles Lettres, 1969), 66-75.

[139] For the Aristotelian aspects of *De Virtute morali*, see S.G. Etheridge, ―Plutarch's De virtute morali: A Study in Extra-Peripatetic Aristotelianism," (Ph.D. dissertation, Harvard University, 1961).

[140] See Richard A. Wright, ―Plutarch on Moral Progress," in *Passions and Moral Progress*, 140.

[141] Compare with *Eth. nic.* 2.5.2: ―we have a bad disposition in regard to anger if we are disposed to get angry too violently or not violently enough, a good disposition if we habitually feel a moderate amount of anger."

assist reason by intensifying virtue (*Vit. Mort.* 451D-452A). Plutarch even speaks propitiously about the passion that a person has for the dispositions of those whom he is trying to emulate (πάθος ὧν ζηλοῦμεν τὰ ἔργα τὴν διάθεσιν φιλεῖν καὶ ἀγαπᾶν, *Virt. prof.* 84E).[142]

The goal of the moral philosopher, according to Plutarch, is not the Stoic eradication of the passions (ἀπάθεια), which he argues is neither possible nor desirable.[143] The intent is rather their domestication, which consists in limiting their scope through the setting of a firm boundary (ὅρος) and in establishing order (τάξις) in regard to them.[144] Again, Plutarch is following the Academic-Peripatetic model of moderation (μετριοπάθεια) over against the Stoic position that the passions must be extirpated.[145] The moral virtues, generated by reason, do not eliminate the passions but are the ―due proportions of the passions" (συμμετρίας παθῶν) and a proper ―mean" (μεσότητας) between them (*Virt. Mor.* 443C-D). In describing Plutarch's view of emotional morality with respect to Hellenistic philosophy in general, J.P. Hershbell states Plutarch's ethical goal was ―to do away with defects and excesses of the passions, and to

---

[142] For Plutarch, one of the most important factors in living a moral life was finding virtuous exemplars in the lives of humans or even gods. See Wright, ―Plutarch on Moral Progress," 146.

[143] See John Dillon, *The Middle Platonists: A Study of Platonism 80 B.C. to A.D. 220* (Ithaca, N.Y.: Cornell University Press, 1977 [reprint 1996]), 193-95.

[144] Wright, ―Plutarch on Moral Progress," 140-41.

[145] For a discussion of Plutarch and *metriopatheia*, see George Depue Hadzsits, *Prolegomena to a Study of the Ethical Ideal of Plutarch and of the Greeks of the First Century A.D.* (Cincinnati: University of Cincinnati Press, 1906), 29-32.

find the proper mean, μεσότης, between the ἔλλειψις [deficiency] and ὑπερβολή

[excess] which, according to Aristotelian teaching, is the characteristic of ethical

virtue."[146]

Aristotle and the Peripatetics

Apart from Aristotle's acumen as an ethical thinker, he was the only one among the major Greek philosophers to accept the emotions as a natural and normal part of human life, attempting neither to abolish them utterly nor to reduce them to mere wraiths of living passion.[147]

Whereas Plato presented his views of the emotions primarily in his writings on

metaphysics, especially those concerning the nature of the soul, Aristotle's theories

regarding the emotions are predominantly found in his ethical and rhetorical writings,

principally *Nichomachean Ethics* and *Rhetoric*.[148] Aristotle's *Rhetoric*, book 1, sets forth

basic suppositions in emotional oratory such as the notion that listeners are more easily

persuaded ―when they are roused to emotion by his speech; for the judgments we deliver

are not the same when we are influenced by joy or sorrow, love or hate (*Rhet.* 1.2.5). But

---

[146] Jackson P.Hershbell, ―De virtute morali (Moralia 440D-452D)," in *Plutarch's Ethical Writings and Early Christian Literature* (ed. Hans Dieter Betz; Leiden: Brill, 1978), 138.

[147] Konstan, *Studies in Aristotle*, 41.

[148] This is not to say that we don't find discussions on the emotions in Aristotle's metaphysical works. For example, in *On the Soul,* Aristotle states that emotions do involve physical processes in the body, which will distinguish him from other philosophical schools of thought (*De An.* 403a16-27). Ever since Aristotle's famous definition of the soul as ―the primary actuality (ἐντελχεία) of a natural body with organs (σώματος φυσικοῦ ὀργανικοῦ" (*De An.* 412b5-6), there has been scholarly debate concerning the relationship of Plato's metaphysics to Aristotle's, especially the notion of the immortality of the soul. Hippolytus writes, ―In practically all matters Aristotle is in harmony with Plato, except for his teaching regarding the soul" (*Haer.* 1.20). Due to space constraints, I will focus on Aristotle's metaphysical theories only when they have direct bearing on my analysis of the emotions. For a useful scholarly history of the question with extensive bibliography, see Lloyd P. Gerson, *Aristotle and Other Platonists* (Ithica, N.Y.: Cornell University Press, 2005), esp. Ch. 5, ―Psychology: Souls and Intellects," 131-172.

it is Aristotle's *Rhetoric,* book 2, that we have the first extended analysis of singular emotions in Greek philosophy. In accordance with Platonic terminology, rational desire is βούλησις, and the two parts of non-rational desire are θυμός and ἐπιθυμία. (*Rhet.* 1369a2-7). An act has its origins in rational desire if reasoning concerning ends and means has taken place. Although Aristotle believed it was usually better to act on rational desire, there is a place for non-considered emotional responses (*Rhet.* 1369a17-24).

Aristotle thought that a good life consisted to a large extent of participation in various kinds of activities which constitute a civilized society. Such a life is based on a complicated system of socially learned emotions, and the quality of one's life depended greatly on whether one was habituated through education to feel them in an appropriate manner.[149] These thoughts are expounded in his *Nichomachean Ethics:*

> We can be frightened and bold and have desires and feel anger and pity and in general pleasure and pain both too much and too little, and both cases not well, but having these feelings at the right time, on the right occasions, towards the right people, with the right aim and in the right way, is the mean and the best thing, and this is characteristic of virtue. (*Eth. nic.*1106b18-23)

Aristotle thus sees emotions as part of the good life, and since emotions connect

---

[149] For general discussion of social emotional judgments of the ancient Greeks in light of modern Anglo-Saxon cultures, see Anthony S. R. Manstead and Agneta H. Fischer, "Social Appraisal: The Social World as Object of and Influence on Appraisal Processes" in *Appraisal Processes in Emotion: Theory, Methods, Research* (eds. Klaus R. Scherer, Angela Schorr, and Tom Johnstone; Oxford: Oxford University Press, 2001), 221-32. More specifically, Jon Elster, *Alchemies of the Mind: Rationality and the Emotions* (Cambridge: Cambridge University Press, 1999), characterizes the social world implied by Aristotle's account of the emotions in *Rhetoric* as "intensely confrontational, intensely competitive, and intensely public; in fact, much of it involves confrontations and competitions before a public. It is a world in which everybody knows that they are acting like judges, and nobody hides that they seek to be judged positively. It is a world with very little hypocrisy, or _emotional tact'." Elster concludes that "being ashamed of one's anger was not a typical Greek reaction" (75). I cannot agree with the totality of his statement, but it is entirely consistent with Aristotle's view of the emotions, since anger was not necessarily a vice or the sign of a malicious character (*Eth. nic.* 1108a4-6), whereas envy or spite, which are reprehensible (1107a8-11) would warrant such shame.

us to things that are not wholly under our control, the good life incorporates aspects not under our control. Plato on the other hand, understood the good life in such a way that links to changing reality should be limited at best (*Tim.* 421d). In fact, I postulate that the main reason for Plato's negative attitude to the emotions was his aim to achieve detachment from a changing reality.[150]

Aristotle's most extensive treatment of the emotions is found in his rhetorical treatment rather than in his treatise on psychology (*On the Soul*). Aristotle characterizes emotions as consisting of two basic elements: first, every *pathos* is accompanied by pain and pleasure; second, the *pathē* are, in Aristotle's words, those things –on account of which people change and differ in regard to their judgments" (*Rhet.* 1244c). Emotions, seen this way, are not static expressions resulting from impersonal stimuli, but rather elements in complex sets of interpersonal exchanges, in which individuals are conscious of the motives of others and ready to respond in kind. Aristotle's view of the emotions depends implicitly on a narrative context. The narrative context for an emotional display provides information on the stimulus, and thus shifts the emphasis back to the initial moment in the emotional process.[151]

Aristotle's approach to the *pathē* is in contrast to much of later Hellenistic philosophy, in which emotions were imagined as detached from external causes and reducible to eliminable disturbances of the soul.[152] One key consequence of these two

---

[150] For a different perspective, see Knuuttila and Sihvola, –How the Philosophical Analysis was Introduced," 16-17.

[151] Konstan, *Studies in Aristotle,* 27-28.

[152] Many scholars discuss this difference between Aristotle, who generally speaking views the emotions as responses to stimuli in the environment and later Hellenistic philosophers, who tend to view them as self-subsisting states that are recognized through their corporeal manifestations, as a change in cultural disposition between classical and Hellenistic Greece. For the changes in virtue with the decline of

orientations is that there is likely to be less interest in emotions or perhaps emotional states for which a stimulus is presumed to be obscure or even entirely absent, such as resentment or generalized anxiety, because Aristotle's attention is fixed on the stimulus of an emotion. Although primarily concerned with modern theories of emotion, Nancy Sherman critiques Aristotle's ―appraisal-based" view of the emotions in this light.[153] She asks of Aristotle's ―intellectualist" approach (which she describes as when ―emotional shifts are the result of cognitive shifts"), ―What Aristotle doesn't explore is why some emotions don't reform at the beck and call of reason?" and further ―why doesn't rational discourse undo irrational emotions?"[154]

Later, in the Hellenistic period, many philosophical schools did attempt to answer this question of why certain emotional responses seem to be incorrigible. The Epicureans in particular held that people may be mistaken about the cause of an emotion.[155] The Epicureans pointed to the repeated social reinforcement of false or vain beliefs (similarly

---

the classical city-state, see Arnaldo Momigliano, ―Freedom of Speech in Antiquity," in *Dictionary of the History of Ideas: Studies of Selected Pivotal Ideas* (ed. Philip P. Wiener; New York: Charles Scribner's Sons, 1973), 2: 252-63; on the rise of personal experience in rhetorical literature, especially his comparison of pity in Aristotle's *Rhetoric* and Cicero's *De oratore*, see Jakob Wisse, *Ethos and Pathos from Aristotle to Cicero* (Amsterdam: Hakkert, 1989), 292-294; on the varying depictions of the emotions in ancient Greek art, see Graham Zanker, *Modes of Viewing in Hellenistic Poetry and Art* (Madison: University of Wisconsin Press, 2004), 152-161; and especially see William V. Harris, *Restraining Rage* who describes, ―the change which occurred in the practice of Greek artists in the fourth century B.C." in which ―sculptors and painters began to represent emotional states for their own sake" (78). Harris cites Pliny, *Natural History* 35.98 on Aristeides: ―He, first of all, depicted the mind and attitudes [*animus et sensus*] of man – what the Greeks call ethos – and also emotions [*perturbationes*]."

[153] Nancy Sherman, ―Emotional Agents," in *The Analytic Freud: Philosophy and Psychoanalysis* (ed. Michael P. Levine; London: Routledge, 2000), 155.

[154] Ibid., 156-57.

[155] In discussing Lucretius' moral psychology, Kimberly R. Gladman and Phillip Mitsis maintain that the Epicurean notion of mistaken causes of emotions comes very close to describing a type of anxiety, in which the stimulus or object to fear is unknown or displaced, in ―Lucretius and the Unconscious" in *Lucretius and His Intellectual Background* (ed. K.A. Algra, M.H. Koenen, and P.H. Schrijvers; Amsterdam: Royal Netherlands Academy of Arts and Sciences, 1997), 217-218.

to Aristotle), which might be countered by living in Epicurean communities and constantly rehearsing Epicurus' doctrines. Of course the converse of unconstrained emotion is a lack of affect in the presence of an emotional stimulus. The Stoics regarded such passionlessness (*apatheia*) as the mark of the true sage.

Aristotle, like the Epicureans and many Hellenistic philosophers, placed great emphasis on the social factors which led to one's *hexis*, or formed disposition. In fact, concerning the emotions and *phronēsis*, the pre-eminence Aristotle gave to *hexis* greatly diminished the prominence of voluntary choice in the emotional process, which distinguishes his view from the Stoics in particular. Social repetition of actions imposed in childhood (by self, teachers, parents, etc.) does most of the *hexis*-formation. In Aristotle, it is unclear as to whether it is impossible or just extremely difficult to interfere with one's *hexis* after it has been developed to a certain point. In *Nichomachean Ethics* it seems that ―when a character has once been established it cannot be changed at will" (2.37a4-9), but then later: ―It is hard, if not impossible, to remove by argument the traits that have long since been incorporated in the character" (2.79b16-17).[156] At the very least, for Aristotle intervention in the emotional process does not seem likely to succeed, due to the dominance of one's early socially conditioned *hexis*.

> Moral virtue is a matter of pleasures and pains; it is for the sake of pleasure that we do what is bad, and because of pain we fail to do what is good. Hence we must be brought up from youth, as Plato says, to feel pleasure and pain about the right objects; that is right education. (*Eth. nic.*1104b8-13)

In some passages, Aristotle seems to believe there is some faculty for choice

---

156 See discussion and other Aristotle passages in Sarah Broadie, *Ethics with Aristotle* (New York: Oxford University Press, 1991), 64-67.

(*prohairesis*), which has some autonomy from the *hexis*, but not much.[157] The mind chooses responses according to its habituated disposition, and once *hexis* is firmly fixed, seems more or less unchangeable. Practically speaking emotion is not a choice in most cases, and in a sense determined by past events. The Stoics and Epicureans (though they often held opposing viewpoints) both attempted to mitigate this type of emotional determinism by insisting undeniably that *hexis* could be altered at any time in life using certain techniques.

In conclusion, Aristotle and the Peripatetic tradition stand in stark contrast to the general consensus in Hellenistic philosophy that the emotions were so harmful they should be abolished at all costs (or at least severely limited). To *not* feel sadness or fear or even anger at certain times was considered a vice not a virtue. In certain situations, one shows virtue (usually through moral training during youth) by becoming angry. For instance, a young man recognizes disrespectful treatment through the previously mentioned moral training,[158] and should this behavior be directed toward himself or those close to him, ―he exhibits his virtue by becoming angry and seeking appropriate *revenge*" [emphasis added].[159] As Theophrastus contends, ―Good men are angered on account of wrongs done to their own (close friends and relatives). ... It cannot happen that a good man is not angered by evil" (ap. Seneca, *Ira* 1.12.3, 14.1).[160]

---

[157] For discussion of Aristotle's view on *hexis* and moral virtue with respect to his well known (and previously mentioned) theory of the mean, see Friedo Ricken, *Philosophie der Antike* (Stuttgart: Kohlhammer, 1988), 177-92, esp. 188-89.

[158] For the importance of moral training, see preliminarily *Eth. nic.* 2.2, 3.7; *Pol.* 3.4.

[159] *Eth. nic.* 2.3; See W.W. Fortenbaugh, ―Aristotle and Theophrastus on the Emotions," in *Passions and Moral Progress*, 42-43.

[160] See also Fortenbaugh, Huby, Sharples, and Gutas, *Theophrastus of Eresus*, 446.1, 6-7.

Epicureanism

In Zeno's own day the Peripatetic school, founded by Aristotle and now maintained by his eminent successor Theophrastus, retained much of its prestige and influence, but for the remainder of the Hellenistic Age only the philosophically antithetical *Epicurean school* could compete with the Stoa as a doctrinal movement" [emphasis added].[161]

Whereas Stoicism came to prominence by claiming much of the Roman elite, Epicurus and Epicureanism generally shunned politics, and Epicureanism has been called ‑the only missionary philosophy produced by the Greeks."[162] Epicureanism was originally a challenge to Platonism, though later it became a rival to Peripateticism, but most importantly it became the main opponent of Stoicism. Epicurus and his early followers had strong views about the emotions, though these do not seem to have attracted much immediate attention outside their circle.[163] Though Epicurus was a prolific writer, only a small fraction of his work has survived. Our information about the details of Epicurus' doctrines are heavily dependent on secondary sources, especially the work of Roman poet Lucretius, a zealous proponent of Epicureanism who presents Epicurus' teaching as the only source of human salvation, who wrote more than 200

---

[161] Sedley, ‑The School," 11.

[162] Norman Wentworth DeWitt, *Epicurus and his Philosophy* (Minneapolis: University of Minneapolis Press, 1954), 329.

[163] This is most probably due to the nature of the movement. The community which Epicurus founded differed greatly from the Academy and Lyceum. The Garden of Epicurus and his followers offered little formal training, but its members were devoted to reading and copying Epicurus' books for both internal consumption and for dissemination to Epicureans outside Athens. See John Procopé, ‑Epicureans on Anger," in *The Emotions in Hellenistic Philosophy*, 186-7.

years after Epicurus' death.[164]

The Epicurean doctrine on the emotions is more in line with Aristotle and the Peripatetics, than the Stoics.[165] The influential Epicurean philosopher Philodemus[166] writes of a commendable anger which arises from insight into the nature of things and from avoiding false opinion (*Ir.* 37.33-39). He further adds –freedom from false opinion in correlating the losses inflicted and punishing those who do the damage."[167]

For Epicurus, the first of his *Key Doctrines* asserts that –the blessed and imperishable" Deity is susceptible neither to anger nor gratitude, –for all such is a mark

---

[164] See further A.A. Long, *Hellenistic Philosophy* (Berkeley: University of California Press, 1986), 14-19.

[165] As stated above, the subject of the emotions was a topic any philosopher of the age could be expected to discuss including the two main protagonists of the Epicureans – the Stoics and the Peripatetics. The Stoics maintained that human passions were intrinsically wrong, and the Peripatetics claimed that they were natural and beneficial so long as they remained –moderate," so long as reason maintains a certain control over them. The idea behind this –moderate emotion" (μετριοπάθεια) of the Peripatetics is the Aristotelian mean: –anyone can be angry – that is easy . . . but to be angry with the right person, to the right extent, at the right time, for the right moment and in the right manner is not something which anyone can do and it is not easy" (*Eth. nic.* 1109a26).

[166] Philodemus is especially important for our purposes due to his Greek educational roots, his later move to Rome, and overall influence in Roman culture and philosophy. He was a follower of Zeno of Sidon, head of the school in the Garden of Epicurus, outside Athens, before settling in Rome about 80 BCE. He was a friend of Lucius Calpurnius Piso Caesoninus, and was implicated in Piso's profligacy by Cicero (*Pis.* 68-72), who, however, praises Philodemus warmly for his philosophic views and for the *elegans lascivia* of his poems (see Horace, *Satires*, 1.2.120). Philodemus was the teacher of Virgil and an influence on Horace's *Ars Poetica*. There was an extensive library at Piso's Villa of the Papyri at Herculaneum, a significant part of which was formed by a library of Epicurean texts, some of which were present in more than one copy, suggesting the possibility that this section of Piso's library was Philodemus' own. See Marcello Gigante Dirk Obbink, *Philodemus in Italy: The Books from Herculaneum* (Ann Arbor: University of Michigan Press, 1995).

[167] *De ira* 37.33-39: . . .ἀπὸ τοῦ βλέπειν, ὡς ἡ φύσις ἔχει τῶν πραγμάτων, καί μηδὲν φευδοδοξεῖν ἐν ταῖς συμμετρήσεσι τῶν ἐλαττωμάτων καὶ ταῖς κολάσεσι τῶν βλαπτόντων. Compare Philodemus with Epicurus *Ep.* 3.130: τῇ μέντοι συμμετρήσει καὶ συμφερόντων καὶ ἀσυφόρων βλέψει ταῦτα πάντα κρίνειν καθήκει (–one must judge all such things by correlating one against another at what benefits and what does the opposite").

of weakness."[168] This seems to imply that although the Deity is unsusceptible to emotion, weaker humans may be liable to these emotions. In *De rerum natura*, Lucretius tells us that anger in human beings has a physiological basis, in the element of heat which, along with cold wind, peaceful air and an unnamed fourth element, makes up the soul (3.266-287.) Though a preponderance of such heat gives humans an irascible temperament which cannot be entirely eradicated, reason can expel the temperaments to such a degree that they will not prevent our leading a life worthy of the gods.

> And we must not suppose that faults can be torn up by the roots, so that one man will not too readily run into bitter anger, another be attacked somewhat too soon by fear, a third put up with an affront more meekly than he should. . . .One thing I see that I can affirm in this regard is this: so trivial are the traces of different natures that remain, beyond reason's power to expel, that nothing hinders our living a life worthy of gods. (3.289-90)

Diogenes Laertius admitted that the Epicurean wise man is indeed ―more susceptible than other men to some passions" but these ―will not impede his wisdom" (D.L. 10.117). There is the notion in Epicurean thought that the emotions, while not altogether good, are in one sense natural. They would affirm that pain is bad, but not to feel pain in certain instances is worse, a sign that something is seriously wrong.[169] When Philodemus was faced with the question of whether anger, for example, is good or evil, he replied:

> The passion itself [πάθος], taken separately, we declare to be an evil, since it is painful or analogous to painful; but taken in connection with the disposition, we consider that it could even be called good. For it arises from insight into the state of the nature of things and from avoiding false opinion in calculating the disadvantages and in punishing those who do harm. So in the same way that we described empty anger as an evil, since it springs from an altogether vile

---

[168] See also Philodemus, *Ir.* 43.14-41.

[169] See Epicurus, *Sent. Vat.* 5.73, see also *Ep.* 3.129.

disposition and brings innumerable vexations with it, we should describe natural anger as not an evil (its sting is minimal in extent); and . . . we shall say that not to be susceptible to natural anger is an evil, for anyone _ill spoken of' or ill treated _who is not roused to anger, carries the clearest mark of villainy', as Menander puts it. (*Ir.* 37.24-27)

Philodemus seems to be consciously trying to stake out middle ground – between an unduly favorable view of anger, which would be too similar to the Peripatetics, and the negative attitude of the Stoics. There are times when the Epicurean sage, detached, and not greatly affected by anything external, can look very much like a Stoic.[170] Seneca addressed this topic by making the simple declaration: —Epicurus says that the sage suffers only injuries which can be borne, we say that he suffers none at all" (*Ira* 16.1.) Further he asserts, —if . . . there is no room in his mind for great or frequent anger, why not free him of it altogether?" (*Ira* 2.6.3).

---

[170] There is currently a debate in scholarly circles as to where Epicurean views on the emotions in general, and Philodemus' views in particular, fits in Hellenistic Philosophy. At one end is Julia Annas, essentially arguing that the Epicurean view is equivalent to the Stoic view, albeit with different theoretical language. When commenting on Philodemus' *On Anger*, she states in *Hellenistic Philosophy of the Mind*:

> The affectively transformed Epicurean will, like the ideal Stoic, be free from the disturbances of emotion in our everyday sense, and motivated by emotions which have been transformed by a total restructuring of the beliefs that sustain them. Their behavior will not quite be the same – the Stoics have no room for approved forms of the hostile or negative emotions like anger, and the Epicureans do – but they will be equally far from our everyday state. [198-99]

David Armstrong strongly criticizes this view in particular in arguing for greater disparity between Philodemus (and the Epicureans) and the Stoics with regard to their teachings on the emotions in his essay —Be Angry and Sin Not: Philodemus Versus the Stoics on Natural Bites and Natural Emotions," in *Passions and Moral Progress*:

> It thus seems wrong to disparage Epicurus's and Philodemus's or even Lucretius's attitude toward the emotions as merely a milder version of the Stoics'. They do indeed allow that feelng at least some real emotions, and those important ones, is —natural" in the terms that they lay down; and they do not see that these —natural" emotions do any great damage. [109]

My view, as stated above, is closest to John Procopé who argues that Philodemus is consciously choosing a middle course, due to Philodemus' dispute with Nicasicrates, whom he accused of being a Stoic, though for Nicasicrates, anger is part of the human condition, affecting even the wisest (—Epicureans on Anger," 188-189). Though Armstrong mentions the intended audience of Philodemus and Lucretius in his analysis [120, n.40], more consideration is due to the innovations of Philodemus, away from conservative Epicureanism, especially after his move to Rome, which, in my opinion almost necessitated a slight move towards Stoicism, which resulted in his middle ground view. While Philodemus states that the pain of anger is —natural" to all humans, he also criticizes the Aristotelian notion of revenge, stating the pleasure of anger – revenge – is disturbingly obsessional and damages the person who feels it in the end more than the object of revenge (*Ir.* 40.20-21).

Stoicism

"The theory of the emotions in the Old Stoa is the subject of unusual agreement among scholars."[171]

There is little debate that Stoicism was the most important development in Hellenistic philosophy, and its influence was not confined to Classical antiquity. Further, Stoicism became the foremost popular philosophy among the educated elite in the Greco-Roman Empire, to the point where Gilbert Murray famously exclaimed, "nearly all the successors of Alexander . . . professed themselves Stoics."[172] Before an analysis proper of Stoic views on emotion with respect to their cosmology, ontology, psychology, and especially ethics, a brief excursus into rhetorical theory will indicate the stark differences between Aristotle and the Stoics on the emotions.

For Aristotle, pathos was one of the three basic types of artificial rhetorical proofs (πίστεις ἄτεvoι) making reasoned judgment (κρίσις) possible.[173] These three categories of proof were rhetorically named *inventio*, the "discovery [of arguments]," one of three parts of Aristotle's *officia oratoris*, i.e., duties of an orator, which for Aristotle were proofs, style, and arrangement (*Rhet.* 3.1.1). Aristotle's emphasis on the three types of

---

[171] Tad Brennan, "The Old Stoic Theory of Emotions," in *The Emotions in Hellenistic Philosophy*, 21.

[172] Gilbert Murray, *The Stoic Philosophy* (London: Watts & Co., 1915), 25. See also Bertrand Russell, *A History of Western Philosophy and Its Connection with Political and Social Circumstances from the Earliest Times to the Present Day* (Great Britain: Allen & Unwin, 1961).

[173] The other two were ethos and logos, *Rhet.* 1.2.3-6.

proofs (πάθος, "emotion," ἦθος, "character," and τὸ πρᾶγμα, the matter itself"),

however, is only rarely found in later rhetorical traditions.[174] Further, ethos and

especially pathos seemed to have dropped out of rhetorical handbooks after Aristotle, and

certainly after Hermagoras of Temnos (fl. 150 B.C.E.).[175] This is due mainly to the Stoic

tradition. The Stoics were very much interested in rhetoric, but, important for my

analysis, rejected emotional appeals and therefore obviously did not espouse Aristotle's

three-proof method. The absence of ethos and pathos from rhetorical handbooks is

reflected in a conversation attributed to the Academic philosopher Charmadas (ca. 102

B.C.E.):

> For he [Charmadas] was of the opinion that the main object of the orator was that
> he should both appear himself, and to those before whom he was pleading, to be
> such a man as he would desire to seem (an end to be attained by a reputable mode
> of life, as to which those teachers of rhetoric had left no hint among their
> instructions), and that the hearts of his hearers should be touched in such fashion
> as the orator would have them touched (another purpose only to be achieved by a
> speaker who had investigated all the ways wherein, and all the allurements and
> kind of diction whereby, and the judgment of men might be inclined to this side or
> that); but according to him such knowledge was thrust away and buried deep in
> the very heart of philosophy, and those rhetoricians had not so much as tasted it
> with the tip of the tongue.[176]

According to Diogenes Laertius, most of the Stoics – beginning with Zeno of

Citium – divided philosophical doctrine into three parts, one physical, one ethical, and

one logical (D.L. 7.40). For Stoics, the end of human life is the famous dictum "to live

conformably with nature" (*to homologoumenon têi phusei zên*, D.L. 7.87) or as some

---

[174] David E. Aune, ed., "Pathos," in *Westminster Dictionary of New Testament*, 340.

[175] See G.A. Kennedy, *Classical Rhetoric and Its Christian and Secular Tradition from Ancient to Modern Times* (Chapel Hill: University of North Carolina Press, 1980), 80; and especially Wisse, *Ethos and Pathos*, 80-83.

[176]Quoted in Cicero *De or.*1.87.

translators prefer, –living in harmony with nature."[177] Consequently, physics – that part

of philosophy that pertains to nature and that reveals the import of this Stoic mantra –

obviously has ethical significance. Most important for my examination are what might

be termed –large-scale Stoic philosophical themes" influencing physical doctrine. In

particular, the Stoic themes of the unity and cohesion of the cosmos and of an all-

encompassing divine reason controlling the cosmos are of fundamental importance to

Stoic physics, and by intimate correlation – ethics.[178]

Three Stoic doctrines have heavily influenced the course of later moral

philosophy:

1) Eudaemonism: the ultimate end of rational action is the agent's own happiness.
2) Naturalism: happiness and virtue consist in living in accord with nature.
3) Moralism: moral virtue is to be chosen for its own sake and is to be preferred above any combination of items with non-moral value.[179]

The Stoics take these three doctrines to be inseparable. The correct grasp of human

happiness shows that it consists in living in accord with nature, which requires living in

---

[177] Zeno's original formulation" living harmoniously" (*zên homologoumenon*) was appended by his successors as told in Stobaeus 2.75.11ff to include both the internal (harmony with oneself) and the external (harmony with the world at large). See discussion in A.A. Long, –Carneades and the Stoic *telos*" *Phronesis* 18 (1967): 59-90. Chrysippus (as found in D.L. 7.88, citing or paraphrasing book 1 of *Peri telon*) emphasizes both aspects in his use of the longer formula:

> It is living in accordance with the nature of oneself and that of the universe, engaging in no activity which the common law is wont to forbid, which is the right reason (*orthos logos*) pervading everything and identical to Zeus, who directs the organization of reality. The virtue of the happy man and his good flow of life consist in this: always doing everything on the basis of the concordance (*kata tēn symphōnian*) of each man's guardian spirit with the will of the director of the universe.

[178] See further Michael J. White, –Stoic Natural Philosophy (Physics and Cosmology)" in *The Cambridge Companion to the Stoics* (ed. Brad Inwood; Cambridge: Cambridge University Press, 2003), 124-25.

[179] For a discussion of Stoic Moral Philosophy with extensive bibliography, see T. H. Irwin, –Stoic and Aristotelian Conceptions of Happiness" in *The Norms of Nature: Studies in Hellenistic Ethics* (ed. Malcolm Schofield and Gisela Striker; Cambridge: Cambridge University Press, 1986), 205-244.

accordance with virtue in preference to any other aim.[180] As stated above, this

connection between happiness and virtue relies on Stoic claims about nature. Following

Aristotle, the Stoics take the human good to consist in the fulfillment of human nature,

understood as the nature of a rational agent.[181] The things that accord with this rational

nature include health, safety, wealth, and the other things that Aristotle calls _external

goods' and the Stoics call _preferred indifferents'; but they also include the exercise of

rational nature in rational efforts to achieve these objects. This exercise of rational nature

is virtue.[182]

Each virtue, according to the Stoics, includes some conviction about the value of

the actions it prescribes. The just person, for instance, not only does just actions, but also

does them for their own sake, in the conviction that they are worth doing simply because

they are just, and not because of some further causal result. Conceptions of the final good

that leave out rightness, including Epicurean and Cyrenaic views, demote the virtues to a

purely instrumental status that conflicts with the outlook of the virtuous person.[183] This

Stoic claim about the connection between moralism and eudaemonism asserts that we

have reason to value virtue and virtuous action as non-instrumentally good if and only if

we regard them as a part of happiness. Thus, the Stoics assert virtue to be identical to,

not simply the dominant element of, happiness.[184]

---

[180] See Cicero, *Off.* 3.2.1-8.

[181] D.L. 8.89; see also Stobaeus, *Ecl.* 2.76.16-23, 77.16-19.

[182] D.L 8.88; Stobaeus, *Ecl.* 2.75.11-76.15.

[183] Cicero, *Fin.* 2.35; see T.H. Irwin, ―Stoic Naturalism and Its Critics" in *The Cambridge Companion to the Stoics* (ed. Brad Inwood; Cambridge: Cambridge University Press, 2003), 345-47.

[184] See further T.H. Irwin ―Socratic Paradox and Stoic Theory" in *Ethics: Cambridge Companions to Ancient Thought 4* (ed. S. Everson; Cambridge: Cambridge University Press, 1998), 151-92; J. M. Cooper,

A summary of the Stoic position as described thus far is provided by A.A. Long in his analysis of the influence the Stoic traditions had on later philosophical traditions:

> Virtue, the Stoics will say, is necessary and sufficient for happiness because (1) it is the perfection of our rational nature; (2) our happiness is so conditioned by the cosmic Nature of which we are an integral part; and (3) nothing except happiness = moral virtue is a rational object of desire for beings whose nature is autonomous only in respect of their capacity to understand and assent to the causal sequence of events.[185]

Like Aristotle and Plato, the Stoic theory of the emotions can only be understood by reference to the broader theories (previously mentioned in brief) of psychology, ethics, epistemology and physics, and perhaps most importantly – the Stoic concept of the soul.[186] The Stoics claimed, in opposition to Platonists and Aristotelians, that humans are rational in the sense that they are *only* rational; the human soul is uniformly and monolithically rational, and does not contain irrational parts. Further, human beings pursue the good and whatever they conceive to be the good with their entire soul, unopposed by some other portion of the soul that might intrinsically pursue pleasure, honor, or something other than good. This Stoic soul has a resemblance to the reasoning portion of a Platonic or Aristotelian soul, but differs from a reasoning part, primarily by not being a part; the Stoic soul is unitary and undivided, without even the possibility of internal conflict.

Plato and Aristotle believed there to be irremovable emotional dispositions of the soul based on natural capacities which sensitize people to various objects of emotional

---

Eudaimonism, the Appeal to Nature, and Moral Duty' in Stoicism" in *Rethinking Duty and Happiness: Aristotle, the Stoics, and Kant* (ed. S. Engstrom and J. Whiting; Cambridge: Cambridge University Press, 1996), 261-84.

[185] Long, Stoicism in the Philosophical Tradition," 391.

[186] For the Stoic conception of the soul, see A.A. Long and D. N. Sedley, *The Hellenistic Philosophers*, 52A-Y.

response. When the emotional powers are actualized through judgments particular to them, people have specific feelings and are inclined to behave correspondingly.[187] Though scholars disagree as to the complexity and variety of Stoic therapeutic methods, it can be succinctly stated that the Stoics thought emotions are disturbances of the soul and that one should be disencumbered of them at all costs.[188]

The Stoics divided the emotions into four generic types: appetite or

desire (ἐπιθυμία), fear (φόβος), which relate to the future, and pleasure (ἡδονή), and

pain or distress (λύπη), which relate to the present. Various specific emotions were then

classified under these primary categories. The types are defined as follows:

> Desire is the opinion that some future thing is a good of such a sort that we should reach out for it.
> Fear is the opinion that some future thing is an evil of such a sort that we should avoid it.
> Pleasure is the opinion that some present thing is a good of such a sort that we should be elated about it.
> Pain is the opinion that some present thing is an evil of such a sort that we should be downcast about it.[189]

The author of the first-century treatise *The Passions*, putatively attributed to Andronicus

of Rhodes, describes the four generic emotions:

> Distress is an irrational contradiction, or a fresh opinion that something bad is present, at which people think it right to be contracted. Fear is an irrational leaning away, or escape from an expected danger. Appetite is an irrational reaching out, or pursuit of an expected good. Pleasure is an irrational elation, or a fresh opinion that something good is present, at which people think it is right to be

---

[187] See Knuuttila, *Emotions,* 47-51.

[188] Perhaps the most famous is Chrysippus' *On Emotions*, what Galen calls a "therapeutic" work (*PHP* 5.7.52).

[189] See further the classic discussion in Ioannes von Arnim, *Stoicorum veterum fragmenta* (4 vols.; Leipzig: B.G.Teubner, 1905-1924), 3.377-420. For similar lists, see Stobaeus 2.57.13-116.18; and Cicero *Tusc.* 4.11-22.

elated. (*SVF* 3.391)

Given these definitions of emotions, it is easy to see why the Stoics would have thought that the Sage never has them, and that it is always wrong to have them. They are mistaken opinions about what is truly valuable, and so they are also inconsistent with the Sage's or with God's (in some Stoic cosmologies) fully rational view of things. In the Stoic view, no action can proceed from anything but belief, or as one scholar describes the Stoic position, ―No number of shocks, bites, and frissons, no amount of internal thrilling and chilling, will have any affect on the movement of my limbs, unless I add to it the belief that I ought to take some action."[190]

According to Chrysippus, emotions are conjunctions of two false judgments. The first opinion that is wrongly assented to is that an external thing is either bad or good. It is accompanied by another belief, which is able to induce movement that a certain behavioral response is appropriate to the situation. The immediate responses (contraction in distress, elation in pleasure, deflation in fear, etc.) are psychosomatic changes which are followed by movements that end in external action.[191] Since the Stoics regarded the emotional movements as intentional, their analysis of the feeling component was different from that of Plato or Aristotle, who did not consider it as an act of choice in any ordinary sense.[192]

Since Chrysippus equated emotions with mistaken judgments, he thought of them

---

[190] Brennan, ―The Old Stoic Theory," 32.

[191] *SVF* 4.14-15; Stobaeus *Ecl.* 2.90.14-18; Pseudo-Andronicus, *Peri Pathon* 223.12-19; Galen *PHP* 4.2.1-4.

[192] It is my opinion that this Stoic description of the psychosomatic reaction as preparatory to hormetic motion was meant as an account of the feeling aspect of emotion. For a slightly different explanation of the technical variances, see Troels Engberg-Pederson, *The Stoic Theory of Oikeiosis: Moral Development and Social Interaction in Early Stoic Philosophy* (Aarhus: Aarhus University Press, 1990), 179-181.

as voluntary acts which one can basically ―learn away." This is different than most other ancient philosophical schools, especially those following Plato and Aristotle, who believed, that at least feelings, which belong to emotions, are externally caused reactions rather than chosen states of mind.[193] In his critical discussion of Chrysippus' approach, Posidonius attempted to examine what is voluntary and what is involuntary in emotional phenomena. Posidonius described affective motions (*pathētikai kinēseis*) as instinctive reactions to impressions, and their occurrences influence the formation of excessive emotional judgments.[194] These motions are not impulses but rather inclinations preceding emotional impulses, and therefore humans, like other animals, are subject to non-rational affective motions. Since Galen states the proper way is to follow one's reason, ―by nature similar to that which rules the whole world" (*PHP* 5.6.4), the goal of education is ―preparation of the emotional part of the soul in such a way that it may be most amenable to the rule of the rational part" (*PHP* 5.5.33-34).

Posidonius thought that he had improved upon Chrysippus' theory of the emotions by offering a plausible explanation for the simple fact that humans do show certain basic types of emotion.[195] Posidonius taught that emotions are impulses and normally depend on the assent of rational power, but the impulses can also be caused by appearances. Martha Nussbaum labels this view of the emotions ―non-cognitive" and describes Posidonius' vista as ―movements of a separate irrational part of the soul" that

---

[193] For example, see *Eth. nic.* 2.5, 1106a2-3.

[194] See Christopher Gill, ―Did Galen Understand Platonic and Stoic Thinking on Emotions?" in *The Emotions in Hellenistic Philosophy*, 124-28.

[195] Galen, *PHP* 5.5.21. See J.M. Cooper, *Reason and Emotion: Essays on Ancient Moral Psychology and Ethical Theory* (Princeton: Princeton University Press, 1999), 464-66.

are not affected by rational thought.[196] This is similar to Plato and Aristotle, who both

held the view that appearances are relevant to emotions.[197]

Stoic Disputations with Hellenistic Philosophy

A summation of the Stoic (especially in the Early and Middle periods, but in the

Later Roman as well, albeit in varying degrees) view of the emotions is simple – they are

bad. They are immoral because they are irrational, against reason. The emotions are

fleeting, in contrast with the rational consistency of Nature. They are against the

conditions of virtue, those things one should know if one is to know what is good:

orderliness, propriety, consistency, and harmony. A.A. Long sums up the Stoic position

bluntly:

> The Stoic sage is free from all passion. Anger, anxiety, cupidity, dread, elation,
> these…are all absent from his disposition. He does not regard pleasure as
> something good, nor pain as something evil….The Stoic sage is not insensitive to
> painful or pleasurable sensations, but they do ̵not move his soul excessively." [198]

As previously stated (in analyzing the Epicurean view), *ideal* manifestations of the main

philosophical schools' teachings on the emotions can look quite similar (especially the

Epicurean, and to a lesser extent the Platonic) to this Stoic Sage. In order to differentiate

these similarities, various technical philosophical variances (on the soul, for example)

between the Stoics and other traditions will be presented to expound further their views

of the emotions. Additionally, in light of the philosophic exigency to construe and

---

[196] Nussbaum, *Passions and Perceptions*, 100.

[197] See Richard Sorabji, *Emotion and Peace of Mind*, 109-115; for an in-depth technical discussion of Posidonius' physiognomy, see 258-59.

[198] Long, *Hellenistic Philosophy*, 206.

demarcate the Stoic (especially the important Later Roman renderings) position(s) of the emotions, significant Stoic disputations with philosophical traditions not represented above will be examined.

Psychology, Ontology and the Emotions

In their discussions of the self or soul compared to other schools of thought the Stoics maintained a materialistic and causal point of view while making concessions to the old Orphic supernaturalism as it was retained in a weakened form by Aristotle.[199]

Philosophical views of the soul and the nature of being greatly affected philosophers' positions of the emotions and sometimes even vice versa.[200] In Stoicism, the soul is, like everything real, corporeal; it exists only in conjunction with the body. But though it is material, its substance is not gross matter; rather, it is of the quintessence, or ether, the divine fire of the universe from which the soul in Plato's view also was formed (along with Aristotle's Prime Mover and active intellect).[201] This residual element of Orphic transcendentalism in the Stoic model of the soul is expressed with unusual frankness by Seneca, who calls the body the ―prison" of the soul (*Ep.* 65.16,

---

[199] McEvilley, *Shape of Ancient Thought*, 622.

[200] P.M. Blowers states in the introduction to his article on Maximus the Confessor: ―In classical philosophy as well as later patristic thought, the human passions presented a moral but inevitably also an ontological, or else physical, dilemma" in ―Gentiles of the Soul: Maximus the Confessor on the Substructure and Transformation of the Human Passions," *JECS* 4 (1996): 57. I follow Edgar Krentz, who responds to Blowers, ―I would argue he [Blowers] is certainly correct with respect to Stoic philosophy and its early Roman Empire representatives" in ―Πάθη and ἀπάθεια in Early Roman Empire Stoics" in *Passions and Moral Progress*, 6. Maximus, in fact, later advocates ἀπάθεια as the goal of the spiritual life and held that true Christians are those who ―pass beyond the disturbances brought about by the passions" (*Quaestiones ad Thalassium*, Ins.71-72), cited in Robert L. Wilken, *Remembering the Christian Past* (Grand Rapids, Mich.: Eerdmans, 1995), 146.

[201] See comprehensive discussion in ibid., 623-25.

25ff), declares that the soul longs to escape from it (*Ep.* 78.10 and 79.10-11), and says the soul escapes from the body as from "a foul and stinking womb" (*Ep.* 102.27-28).[202]

In light of their naturalistic psychology (and to a degree, their ontology), the Stoic account of the process which leads from sensation to action is directly related to their views on emotion. This process, like Epicurus', is based primarily on Aristotle's *Ethica nichomachea* and *De motu animalium* (with Plato in the more distant background), but – again like Epicurus' version – with avenues opened up toward revision of the *hexis*.[203] At the first stage, sensation occurs (*aisthesis*), resulting from contact of an object with a sense organ. In the second stage, still similar to Aristotle and Epicurus, a *phantasia*, or image, arises in the mind, already bearing a tonality of pain or pleasure; this pain or pleasure aspect gives initial directionality to an emerging impulse (*hormē*) of either grasping or shunning (either *orexis*, a stretching out toward, or *ekklisis*, a leaning away from). In the third stage, the *orexis* or *ekklisis* will be decided in its overall directionality and also articulated in its nuances of texture, urgency, and ambiguity by the *hexis* or formed disposition, which in the Stoic view contains a stock of general conceptions, or *prolēpseis*.[204] These are formed by generalizing from the data of experience, and are

---

[202] A trace of this view of the soul may also remain in Epicurus' nearly mystical "nameless" atoms which make up the most sensitive part of the soul and are the smallest and finest atoms in the universe. The "nameless kind of atom is the only purely theoretical entity in Epicureanism" says Annas, *Hellenistic Philosophy of the Mind*, 139. See also p. 55, n.46.

[203] As stated above, I prefer to translate *hexis* as "disposition," but it has also been translated as "state" or more recently "active state." *Hexis* is contrasted with *energeia* (in the sense of activity or operation) in *Nichomachean Ethics* 1.8.1098b33 and *Eudemian Ethics* 2.1.1218b. See Joe Sach's discussion and translation of *Nichomachean Ethics* (Newbury, Mass.: Focus Pub./R. Pullins, 2002), 3-30.

[204] Pace Zeno, who felt that judgments are without emotion. Chrysippus, in an interesting but somewhat circular argument maintained that "judgments must have some kind of emotional coloring." See J.M. Rist, *Stoic Philosophy* (Cambridge: Cambridge University Press, 1969), 30, 34-35.

immediately activated when a sense-impression is received."[205]

At this point, the model is not all that different from Aristotle's, but with an important addition: the Stoics posit a factor of free will or choice (*hairesis*) which has the power to either assent to or dissent from the impulse.[206] In this worldview, the *prohaeretic* faculty has more autonomy than in Aristotle's. It can intervene in the sensation-to-action sequence at the point of the *hormē* or impulse. For the Stoics then, emotions arise from a psychological process which may appear to be automatic – the arising of impulsive actions from the collaboration of pleasure/pain with early conditioning (the *hexis* or disposition) – but which in fact contains a somewhat concealed element of free will. This obscured force, the *prohairesis*, can be uncovered by self-study and brought into a controlling position over one's activities. That is the achievement of the sage.

The primary tool which can avail against the *pathē* is reason (*logos*). According to Chrysippus, at some point in one's development, ―Reason supervenes as the craftsman, or technician, of impulse" (D.L. 7.86). McEvilley emphasizes that the Stoic view of reason includes, ―the ability to cut through habitual confusions and delusions and forestall the unhealthy impulses that arise from them."[207] Until reason ―supervenes," the *hormetic* process is more or less mechanical, but reason has the unique power to

---

[205] Long and Sedley, *The Hellenistic Philosophers*, 1.240.

[206] Rist states for the Stoic, ―All human activities without any exceptions whatever involve some degree of assent. A totally non-voluntary act is an impossibility," *Stoic Philosophy*, 42. Seneca, for example, says, ―impulse never exists without the mind's assent" *Ira* 2.4. Although this seems extreme (what about one's breathing or heartbeats?), Zeno seems to have thought even those bodily functions usually regarded as involuntary involve a voluntary assent, however hidden, which can be rescinded by exercise of free will. According to tradition (D.L. 7.28), he died by voluntarily stopping his breath.

[207] McEvilley, *Shape of Ancient Thought*, 628.

reprogram one's *hexis*.

In *De finibus* 3.20-21, Cicero reports a five-stage model of the process which is based on an increasing accumulation of ―selection" impulses: (1) first are infantile pre-rational impulses where selection is only based on pleasure and pain; (2) then, early exercise of socially oriented selection occurs under parental and other influences, without much involvement of reason yet; this may be the stage with which selection-development ceases for many; but (3) for one exposed to philosophy, there may supervene some conscious application to the task of selecting impulses that will be in harmony with reason and nature; (4) in a lifetime devoted to this task, the continuous performance of this process of selection will be conducive to the development of virtue; (5) virtue is understood as approaching natural selection at all times. Theoretically, stages three to five – which comprise a self-willed (re)programming of oneself – can affect a transition from one *hexis* to another which contradicts it.

This ―self-willed programming" becomes increasingly important as ―self-control" as a philosophical tool on par with reason becomes more and more important in the first centuries BCE-CE for both the Roman Stoics (especially in political thought, usually *temperantia*) and the Hellenistic Jewish writers (usually σωφροσύνη). Thus the true

Sage, often portrayed in an idealized form (e.g., an ideal Roman statesman), can and does control (and even eliminate) one's emotions through sheer power of will. This is a sign of true power and authority.

A related (and representative of the time) area of debate in this period concerns the passions and ethical psychology.[208] Three questions tend to be linked in this debate: (1) whether the motions should be moderated *or* extirpated; (2) whether human psychology is to be understood as a combination of rational and non-rational aspects *or* as fundamentally unified and shaped by rationality; and (3) whether ethical development is brought about by a combination of habituation and teaching *or* only by rational means. On these issues, thinkers with a Platonic or Peripatetic affiliation tend to adopt the first of these two positions and Stoics the second.[209]

Plutarch's essay, *On Moral Virtue*, encapsulates this debate. Plutarch articulates the first (Platonic-Aristotelian) position and criticizes the Stoic one. This position is, as previously argued, characteristic of Plutarch, who regards himself as a Platonist and frequently attacks the Stoics with vigor, although he adopts a view of the passions somewhat more sympathetic with the Stoic view (at least with a popularized Roman notion of Stoicism) elsewhere, which is testament to the partial breakdown of hard borders among various philosophical traditions.[210]

Galen takes a broadly similar line to Plutarch in Books 4-5 of *On the Doctrines of Hippocrates and Plato*. Galen was a philosophically minded doctor who aimed to reconcile Hellenistic philosophy with the findings of medical science, including the

---

[208] See comprehensive discussion in Sihvola and Engberg Pedersen, *The Emotions in Hellenistic Philosophy*, 32-37.

[209] For a similar contrast between positions, but here expressing the Stoic side and criticizing the Peripatetic, see Cicero, *Tusc.* 3.22, 4.39-46; Seneca, *Ira* 1.7-14. However, Platonic and Stoic positions were sometimes linked, for instance, by Eudorus and Philo.

[210] For example, in less doctrinaire essays, such as *On Peace of Mind* and *On Freedom from Anger*, Plutarch sometimes praises the (Stoic ideal) of *apatheia* (freedom from passions) rather than moderation of the passions. See John Dillon, *The Middle Platonists*, 189, 193-8; also Daniel Babut, *Plutarque et le Stoicisme* (Paris: Presses Universitaires de France, 1979), 298-301, 316-7, 321-33.

71

Alexandrian discovery of the anatomic and psychological role of the brain and nerves.[211] In Books 1-3, Galen takes up the related question of the contrast between a tripartite psychological model, in which the brain, heart, and liver are regarded as distinct motivational sources, with different locations; the Stoic unified model, centered on the heart, is treated as the locus of rationality as well as emotions.[212]

For Galen, the passions are, in principle, correctable faults or, as he would prefer, diseases of the soul that can be cured. Galen describes those men who are ―caught in the violent grip of these diseases, for in such men the disgrace is clearly seen" (*Passions* 1.7). According to Galen these diseases of the soul are ―anger and wrath [*thymos* and *orgē*] and fear and grief and envy and excessive desire"; he further states that ―loving or hating anything too much" should also be regarded as pathos (*Passions* 1.3). Only the best or wisest can escape these morbid conditions.[213] It is of vital importance that a non-philosopher of the second century CE engaging the philosophical traditions, drawing upon Platonic psychology, criticizing Old Stoic ideas in some respects, sympathetic in other ways (―an eclectic compendium of popular mainly Stoic philosophical teaching")

---

[211] Galen, writing in the second century, provides vital evidence of what I have termed popular Stoic philosophy. He was foremost a prominent Greek physician and not a philosopher, but his treatises, including the above *On the Doctrines of Hippocrates and Plato*, and perhaps even more importantly, his short *On the Passions of the Soul*, provide ―the main primary source for the Stoic theory of the passions," Brennan, ―Stoic Epistemology," 115-120. Loveday Alexander rightly recognizes that *On the Passions of the Soul*, ―presents an eclectic compendium of popular (mainly Stoic) philosophical teaching on the passions" in ―The Passions in Galen and the Novels of Chariton and Xenophon," in *Passions and Moral Progress*, 175.

[212] See James Hankinson, ―Action and Passion: Affection, Emotion, and Moral Self-management in Galen's Philosophical Psychology," in *Passions and Perceptions* (ed. Jacques Brunschwig and Martha Nussbaum; Cambridge: Cambridge University Press, 1993), 160-63. On Galen's disagreements with traditional Stocism, especially his criticisms of Chrysippus, see Jaap Mansfield, ―The Idea of the Will in Chrysippus, Posidonius, and Galen," *Boston Area Colloquium in Ancient Philosophy* 7 (1991): 107-45; also Teun Tieleman, *Galen and Chrysippus on the Soul: Argument and Refutation in the de Placitis Books II-III* (Leiden: Brill, 1996); Gill, ―Did Galen Understand," 119-124.

[213] See Alexander, ―The Passions in Galen," 176-78. See also Susanne Bobzien, *Determinism and Freedom in Stoic Philosophy* (Oxford: Oxford University Press, 1998), 359.

calls ‑loving" too much a disease of the soul that only the best of humanity can escape.[214]

The ultimate aim of philosophical training is to induce self-discipline, a system of ‑training" (*askēsis*) comparable to a ‑prolonged course of training in rhetoric or medicine" (*Passions* 1.4). Alexander states this *askēsis* in self-control ‑ultimately will enable the addressee to live a life in which the passions are firmly under the control of the rational mind."[215] Galen, along with many of the Roman Stoics, places dual emphasis on rationality and self-control. He further describes this training in rational self-control:

> If you do this, some day you will be able to tame and calm that power of passion within you which is as irrational as some wild beast. Untamed horses are useless, but horsemen can in a short time make them submissive and manageable. Can you not take and tame this thing which is not some beast from outside yourself but an irrational power within your soul, a dwelling it shares at every moment with your power of reason? Even if you cannot tame it quickly, can you not do so over a longer period of time? It would be a terrible thing if you could not. (*Passions* 1.5)[216]

The emotions in Galen were viewed as irrational ‑pathological diseases" which must be ‑cured" through ‑training in self-control" in order to bring the passions under the auspices of the rational mind.

Neopythagoreanism, Skepticism, and Cynicism

---

[214] See also *Passions* 1.7, love, along with grief and fear are forms of ‑pain" that any sensible person will seek to avoid.

[215] Alexander, ‑The Passions in Galen," 177.

[216] It is noteworthy that Galen's prescription places the passion within oneself, which is contrary to many traditional lines of philosophy. It is a type of modified Stoicism, which traditionally placed emphasis on assent and the ability to make rational judgments. I contend it is indicative of the type of popular Stoicism I have been advocating.

Neopythagoreanism, Skepticism, and Cynicism

While the term ―Neopythagorean" itself is imprecise,[217] the pseudepigraphic

Pythagorean treatises,[218] mostly written in Doric, show a remarkable homogeneity in

their views of the passions.[219] The psychological framework for the ethics of the

Pseudopythagorica is a Platonic tripartite division of the soul into rational and irrational

(including spirited and appetitive) parts, with virtue resulting when there is harmony

(συναρμογά) between the parts.[220] Following the Peripatetic tradition, the

Pseudopythagorica contend that all ethical action is accompanied and influenced by

emotions such as pleasure and pain (called ultimate (ὑπέρτατα) emotion, Theages, *De*

virt. 192.6; Metopus *De virt.* 119.8-10). Further, the passions are considered the very

---

[217] Our evidence for the existence of such a movement primarily comes from Cicero, who referred to the revival of the Pythagorean *disciplina* by his friend Nigidius Figulus (Tim. 1.1), though the authenticity of Cicero's comments has come under scholarly scrutiny. See Christoph Riedweg. *Pythagoras: Leben, Lehre, Nachwirkung; eine Einführung* (München: Beck, 2002), 138-39, 161-62; for a more positive view of the sources see Bruno Centrone, *Introduzione a i Pitagorici* (Rome: Laterza, 1996), 164-70. Johan Thom states, ―Neopythagoreanism does not constitute a conceptually homogeneous philosophical tradition, nor does it have very definite chronological boundaries" in ―The Passions in Neopythagorean Writings," in *Passions and Moral Progress*, 67.

[218] The date and place of origin of these pseudo-Pythagorean treatises is difficult to determine, but most seem to have been composed between 150 BCE and 100 CE. Rome and Alexandria are the most likely places of origin. For a summary of positions see Centrone, *Pseudopythagorica Ethica*, 14-16.

[219] The treatises are included in my survey largely because of (1) the numerous references to the passions in a considerable number of texts, including Archytas' Περὶ νόμου καὶ δικαιοσύνης (*De leg.*) and Περὶ παιδεύσεως ἠθικῆς (*De educ.*), Metopus' Περὶ ἀρετῆς (*De virt.*), and Theages' Περὶ ἀρετῆς (*De virt.*), and the scholarly debated *Tabula of Cebes* (see Sorabji, *Emotion and Peace of Mind*, 294-95); and (2) the consistency of the positions regarding the emotions. There is one apparent contradiction: in *De leg.* 33.17-18, attributed to Archytas, he favors the emotional theory of *apatheia*, while in *De educ.* 41.16-18 he argues for *metriopatheia*. See Paul Moraux, *Der Aristotelismus bei den Griechen: von Andronikos bis Alexander von Aphrodisias* (Berlin: De Gruyter, 1984), 661-66.

[220] For example, Metopus, *De virt.* 119.28-20.1: καθόλω μὲν ὦν ἀρετὰ συναρμογά τις ἐντὶ τῶ ἀλόγω μέρεος τᾶς ψυχᾶς ποτὶ τὸ λόγον ἔχον (―In general, therefore, virtue is a harmony of the irrational part of the soul with the rational element").

matter" (ὕλα) of virtue.[221]

From their Peripatetic ethics underscored by a Platonic psychological system, it obviously follows that the Pseudopythagorean authors not only favored the Aristotelian ideal of *metriopatheia* (μετριοπάθεια), moderation of the emotions, but also vehemently opposed the Stoic *apatheia* (ἀπάθεια), which called for the elimination of the emotions. Virtue was seen as the "mean" (μεσότας), or as the "due proportion" (συμμετρία) of the passions (Theages, *De virt.* 191.28-29; 192.11; Metopus *De virt.* 120.4-5, 23-25).[222] Theages explicitly states, "Virtue does not consist … in eliminating the passions from the soul, but in bringing them into harmony" (οὐκ ἐν τῷ ὑπεξελέσθαι τὰ πάθεα τᾶς

ψυχᾶς … ἁ ἀρετὰ πέπτωκεν, ἀλλ' ἐν τῷ ταῦτα συναρμόζ εσθαι, *De virt.* 192.7-8).

Metopus similarly argues that "the passions should not be removed from the soul…, but joined in harmony with the rational part" (*De virt.* 121.10-12).

Like other Stoic opponents, the Pseudopythagorean authors were critical of *apatheia* because they thought it unattainable; it was beyond human ability (i.e., Archytas, *De educ.* 41.9-18). Further, they considered *apatheia* inhumane. According to Becchi, the Pseudopythagorica's strong stance against *apatheia* was a "deliberate attempt" to provide a more humane theory of moral action. Instead of the perfect and

---

[221] The Peripatetics of the imperial period also considered passions the very matter of virtue. See Moraux, *Der Aristotelismus bei den Griechen*, 661.

[222] See Thom, "Passions in Neopythagorean Writings," 69.

Stoic *sophos* (σοφός), a "professional of rationality" without any emotion, they proposed

the concept of *agathos* (ἀγαθός).[223] Becchi describes this as, "the ideal of moral

excellence that does not exist in purifying the soul of passions, but in moderation and

self-control, in a just equilibrium vis-à-vis pleasure and pain … thus tempering pleasure

with moral rectitude."[224]

Carneades, an influential Academic Skeptic, took up debate with the Stoics as

well as the Epicureans on the topic of the passions (πάθη). He did not publish any

written version of his arguments, leaving it to his successors (e.g., Clitomachus) and

adversaries to quarrel over their actual philosophical intentions. Plutarch tells us that, "In

matters of importance, Carneades remarked that unexpectedness is the whole and entire

cause of grief and dejection" (*Tranq. an.* 47e-f). Cicero tells us that Carneades argued

with Chrysippus against his approval of a passage of Euripides emphasizing the

inevitability of suffering.[225] Somewhat surprisingly, Cicero tells us that Carneades agrees

with the Stoics that the sage would feel no distress at the fall of his country to enemy

forces (*Tusc.* 3.54).

The Stoic sense of ethical values was derived closely from the Cynics (and vice

versa) and featured the Cynic ideals of *apatheia* (passionlessness or non-reactiveness)

---

[223] F. Becchi, "L'ideale della metriopatheia nei testi pseudopitagorici: A proposito di una contraddizione nella Ps.-Archita," *Prometheus* 18 (1992): 102-20.

[224] Ibid., 116.

[225] For example, see *Tusc.* 3.59-60.

and *autarkeia* (self-rule).[226] According to the Stoic concept of cosmic harmony, the goal was to ―live in agreement with nature" as Zeno avowed or similarly Chrysippus, ―for our own natures are parts of the nature of the whole" (D.L. 8.87-88). An inclination to position oneself in conflict with nature amounts to a *pathos*, which ―could be properly located as a subdivision of ‗impulses'…"[227] As Stobaeus stated, ―They say emotion (*pathos*) is impulse which is excessive and disobedient to the dictates of reason, or a movement of soul which is irrational and contrary to nature."[228]

The goal of ethical philosophy for both the Stoic and Cynic was to bring personal preferences and aversions into harmony with those of the ruling principle of the universe, variously called ―Zeus," ―Reason" (*logos*), and ―Nature," depending on the author and especially the time period. For example, Cleanthes (usually classified as a Stoic, but who studied in Athens under Crates the Cynic, as well as Zeno) wrote in his *Hymn to Zeus* as

---

[226] In my survey of the positions of the philosophical traditions with respect to the emotions, I have omitted a separate discussion of the Cynics, choosing instead to discuss them only in light of other traditions for a number of reasons. Since Cynic views of the πάθη, as with most other topics of Hellenistic philosophy, were never given a systematic treatment in dialogue with other philosophical traditions, has opined, ―There is nothing particular to say of the Cynics, for they possess but little philosophy, and they did not bring what they had into a scientific system" in G.W.F. Hegel, *Lectures on the History of Philosophy* (trans. E.S. Haldane, 3 vols; Lincoln: University of Nebraska, 1995), 1.479. The Cynics were omitted from Long and Sedley's important *Hellenistic Philosophers* as ―non-standard" (1.xii). In the influential *Therapy of Desire*, Nussbaum (8) states: ―There is, I believe, far too little known about them and their influence, and even about whether they offered arguments at all, for a focus on them to be anything but a scholarly quagmire in a book of this type. With some regret, then, I leave them at the periphery." Whether one ultimately agrees with the notions of ―they posses little philosophy," ―non-standard," or whether they deserve peripheral treatment, there the fact remains that the literature produced by the Cynics, especially the early Cynics, has mainly perished, and our knowledge is largely confined to anecdotes of dubious historicity. Further, Cynicsm was not a philosophical school in any way comparable to Stoicism, Epicureanism, or even Scepticism, for it lacked both an organizational structure and a central body of teaching. Cynicism never produced a system of philosophic doctrines, whether in esoteric oral form or in exotic written form, that could be subject to discussion, criticism, and elaboration in a school setting (Julian, Or. 6.186B). For a comprehensive treatment of difficulties associated with the Cynics and the emotions, see David E. Aune, ―The Problems of the Passions in Cynicism," 48-53.

[227] Long and Sedley, *The Hellenistic Philosophers*, 1.346.

[228] D.L. 2.88.8; see also ibid., 410.

preserved in Stobaeus, ―Zeus leads the willing person, the unwilling he drags." One must develop the ability to block personal impulses when Reason or Nature says otherwise. During these moments, one needs the qualities of imperturbability and mental detachment from the *hormē*. For this detachment the Cynics (and the Stoics) used the previously mentioned term *apatheia*, or nonemotional response.[229]

Zeno wanted to preserve this essential Cynic virtue – its relentless and uncompromising cultivation of imperturbability – while refining other aspects of the doctrine to make it socially useful.[230] Not everyone could be expected to attain the same level of freedom and imperturbability as the infamous Diogenes of Sinope.[231] According to Diogenes Laertius, Zeno himself did attain a comparable freedom, but did not expect it of everyone. Society, in his view, should be guided by a few individuals who have

---

[229] Rist argues that the Cynic and Stoic uses of this word were different. He argues that the Cynic *apatheia* meant actual emotionless, while the Stoic *apatheia* meant a certain kind of rational guidance or control. I agree to a considerable extent with his assessment of the Stoic *apatheia*, but remain skeptical of his claim that the Cynics held absolute ―unfeelingness" to be the ideal (e.g., Crates was a strong advocate of compassion, *philanthropia*). See J.M. Rist, ed., ―The Stoic Concept of Detachment," in *The Stoics* (Berkeley: University of California Press, 1978).

[230] A controversy arose between Zeno and his disciple Ariston of Chios, who disliked Zeno's compromises for the sake of social stability (a concern the Cynics did not share) on a number of issues, including the Cynic categorization of indifference (*adiaphora*), along with virtue and vicious, whereas Zeno introduced other categories to make a total of seven: virtuous, preferred, appropriate, indifferent, inappropriate, avoided, vicious. See C.O. Brink, ―Oikeiosis and Oikeiotes: Theophrastus and Zeno on Nature and Moral Theory," *Phronesis* I (1955): 12-145, for the suggestion that Zeno was influenced in this compromise of Cynic principles by the Academician Polemon. Both Cynics and Epicureans attacked the Academy as the stronghold of reactionary thought.

[231] Along with Antisthenes, Crates of Thebes, and Xeno, Diogenes is considered one of the founders of Cynicism. He taught by living example that wisdom and happiness belong to the man who is independent of society. Diogenes scorned not only family and political social organization, but property rights and reputation. He rejected normal ideas about human decency, and is said to have eaten (and masturbated) in the marketplace, urinated on a man who insulted him, defecated in the amphitheatre, and pointed at people with his middle finger. See D.L. 6.20 and Luis Navia, *Diogenes of Sinope: The Man in the Tub* (Westport, Conn.: Greenwood Press, 1989).

attained real *apatheia* and *autarkeia*,[232] while the general population of course should be encouraged to develop these qualities as much as they were able. The purpose of this development of *apatheia* is essentially eudemonistic as happiness is related to tranquility and equanimity, not the fleeting nature of emotion. ―What is a happy life? Peacefulness and constant tranquility."[233]

Related to the philosophical notion of imperturbability with regard to the emotions, ―self-control" was a key term for the Cynics as well as the Later Stoics.[234] Moore and Anderson state, ―And it was the Stoics who, following the Cynics, fully unfurled the philosophical motif of the moral struggle of the sage."[235] In the Cynics, we encounter the emotions primarily through vice and virtue lists. In Dio Chrysostom (usually labeled a Cynic, sometimes a Stoic), we find anger listed several times in his extensive vice lists in his *Discourses*.[236] We also find lists that include emotions such as fear, grief, and joy, but these lists usually (not always) contain qualifying adjectives, such as vain glory or senseless joy.[237] In 4.126, he concludes his vice list, ―...contentious, foolish, conceited, vain glory, jealousy, and all such difficult emotions." While certainly we do not find the elimination of all emotion as in the Stoic outlook, in the virtue lists we find many references to temperance, self-control, moderation, true sobriety, and

---

[232] McEvilley argues that Zeno's societal notions were related to Plato's notion of philosopher-kings and may show the influence of Polemon, Plato's third successor as head of the Academy, in *Shape of Ancient Thought*, 625.

[233] Seneca, *Ep.* 92.3, as translated by Long and Sedley, *The Hellenistic Philosophers*, 1.396.

[234] The Greek word is usually ἐγκράτεια but other words, such as σώφρονα, connote similar ideas.

[235] Stephen D. Moore and Janice Capel Anderson, ―Taking It Like a Man: Masculinity in 4 Maccabees," *JBL* 117 (1998): 259.

[236] 1.13; 2.75; 3.33; 49.9; 62.2; 75.2.

[237] 1.13; 3.33; 23.7; 32.5.

mildness.[238] We also find negative references to the emotions in the *Cynic Epistles*, particularly anger, fear, and grief.[239]

Part II: The Roman Stoics [240]

> [Socrates] is the first to have called philosophy down from the heavens, planted it in the cities, and even introduced it into houses, and forced them to ask about life, ethics, good evil" (Cicero, *Tusc.* 5.10).

Since I argue it is the Roman rendering of the Stoics in particular that serves as the primary influence to Luke, I will summarize and accentuate certain features of Roman Stoicism germane to my analysis of the Lukan redactions. The previously mentioned Cicero serves as an influential and hinge figure between Republic and Empire in Rome and the above quote leads to a few preliminary observations. Though he wouldn't have described himself as a Stoic (hence my analysis in the Platonism section), he has some clear sympathies with them, and his influence (not just in his philosophical positions, but in his wording and the manner in which he framed the issues) is unquestioned.[241] The

---

[238] 1.4-6; 3.58; 23.7; 29.14; 32.27; 35.3; 38.35, 44.10; 51.6; 62.3-4; 77/78.39.

[239] See Abraham J. Malherbe, *The Cynic Epistles* (SBLSBS 12, Missoula: Scholars Press, 1977).

[240] I use the term "Roman Stoics" synonymously to the more conventional designations "Late Stoics" or "Later Stoics." I prefer "Roman Stoics" primarily in order to emphasize the sociopolitical challenges of imperial Rome facing such Stoics as Seneca, Musonius Rufus, and Marcus Aurelius, as well as Greek thinkers Arius Didymus and Epictetus. For a classical overview of Stoicism during this time, see Edward Arnold, Roman Stoicism: Being Lectures on the History of the Stoic Philosophy (Cambridge: The University Press, 1911). More recently, Annas has described Roman Stoicism as favoring discussion that was "edifying and moralizing" that "gave little indication of the philosophical structure of their positions" in "Stoicism," *Oxford Classical Dictionary*, 1446. While I would not go so far as to affirm "little indication," the Stoics of the time did emphasize ethics and due to the breakdown of hard lines delineating traditions, the philosophical structures were certainly both de-emphasized and harder to determine.

[241] See further Andrew Erskine, "Cicero and the Expression of Grief" in *The Passions in Roman Thought and Literature*, 185.

Roman Stoics tend to emphasize social responsibility more than their Greek forbears, along with a general prioritization of ethics over logic and physics, particularly in societal function.[242] They rely heavily on *their version* of Socrates' behavior as a moral exemplum.[243] They have appropriated Socrates to accentuate their philosophical claims about the good life.[244]

According to the stereotypical view, in the period of the Roman Empire, Stoicism was philosophically uncreative. The dominant theme was ethics, and the main surviving works are largely exercises in practical morality based on philosophical ideas constructed centuries before. There was no institutional school as in the Hellenistic Age, and Stoicism was eventually replaced as the dominant philosophy by a revived Platonism along with a form of Christianity that was increasingly more sophisticated.[245]

While recognizing an element of truth to this stereotype, Stoicism remained the dominant philosophical movement in the Roman imperial period, and perhaps most important for my analysis of Luke's redactions was the fact that it was strongly

---

[242] Cicero, for example, argues that a politician should follow the Stoic ideal of *apatheia* or detachment, because only one who is indifferent to personal advantages, or to the advantages of a single group of people, can truly serve the common good (*Tusc.* 1.85). See also Gretchen Reydams-Schils, *The Roman Stoics: Self, Responsibility, and Affection* (Chicago: University of Chicago Press, 2005), 2-4.

[243] For example, in the *Discourses* of Epictetus, Socrates is the philosopher extraordinaire, a person idolized more often and with more detail than any other Stoic sage – more than Diogenes, Antisthenes, or Zeno. ―The honorable and good man neither fights with anyone himself, nor, as far as he can, does he let anyone else do so. Of this as of everything else the life of Socrates is available to us as a model (*paradeigma*), who not only himself avoided fighting everywhere, but did not let others fight" (4.5.1-4). See further A.A. Long, *Stoic Studies* (Cambridge: Cambridge University Press, 1996), 1-34.

[244] This is especially true in relation to their main antagonist and rival with regard to the ―Socratic paradigm" during this time – Platonism. See further Pierre Hadot, *Exercices spirituels et philosophie antique* (Paris: Institut d'études augustiniennes, 1993), 75-116; Ilsetraut Hadot, *Seneca und die griechisch-römische Tradition der Seelenleitung* (Berlin, de Gruyter, 1969), 179-90; and A.A. Long, *Epictetus: A Stoic and Socratic Guide to Life* (Oxford: Clarendon Press, 2002), 67-96.

[245] See discussion in Christopher Gill, ―The School in the Roman Imperial Period," *The Cambridge Companion to the Stoics* (ed. Brad Inwood; Cambridge: Cambridge University Press, 2003), 33-34.

embedded in Greco-Roman culture and in political life. In the Julian-Claudian era (from Augustus to Nero), numerous Stoic philosophers held high positions in the Empire, often in the inner-circle of the Emperor. Augustus maintained two Stoic philosophers who combined the roles of moral advisor and philosophical scholar – Athenodorus of Tarsus and Arius Didymus. Under Nero, Seneca also combined these roles, but was even more important politically and philosophically. The ideal of living a properly Stoic life remained powerful well into the third and fourth centuries; Stoicism was assimilated, not replaced. Neoplatonic and Christian writers built upon these ideas and ideals and absorbed them into their systems.[246]

Though the different nuances within Stoicism during the imperial Period are not to be devalued, the Roman Stoic view of the emotions is clearly seen to be pejorative. Most Stoics regarded the emotions as intentional movements, entirely within the control of the person experiencing some ―pre-emotion." This view was somewhat different from that of Plato or Aristotle, who did not consider emotion wholly within the realm of choice. For example, after the immediate psychosomatic response to pleasure being that of elation, the emotional movement from elation to joy would be considered nothing less than a disorder of the soul. Emotions were disorders of the soul because they were irrational and subject to change. The ideal of the sage would be to *control* the immediate response to avoid the irrational emotions.

Arius Didymus, writing during the time of Augustus, serves as a great example of the preceding contentions. He is never accused of being overly creative, but provides a great summary of traditional Stoic thought with an emphasis on imperial values. His

---

[246] See further Sorabji, *Emotion and Peace of Mind*, 15-22.

approach to the emotions follows an orderly and systematic approach to ethics in general,[247] and clearly shows how important the discussion of the passions was in Roman Stoicism.[248] He argues that reason can control the emotions, which are contrary to that which should control human beings, their nature as rational beings.[249] And perhaps most importantly, since we can control our judgments, we are responsible for our passions and so are to blame for them. In this, he picks up the important "cognitive" element in the Stoic interpretation of the emotions as represented by Chrysippus.[250] Arius Didymus describes the πάθη as follows:

> They say a passion is an impulse [ὁρμή] which is excessive, disobedient to the choosing reason [τῷ αἱροῦντι λόγῳ] or an irrational motion of the soul contrary to nature [φύσις]. All passions belong to the controlling part [τὸ ἡγεμονικόν] of the soul. Hence also every agitation [πτοία] is a passion, and again every passion is an agitation.
>
> First in genus are these four: appetite [ἐπιθυμία], fear [φόβος], pain [λύπη], and pleasure [ἡδονή]. Appetite and fear lead the way, the former toward the apparently good, the other toward the apparently evil. Pleasure and pain come after them: pleasure whenever we obtain that for which we had an appetite or escape from that which we feared; pain whenever we fail to get that for which we

---

[247] See his extended discussion on virtue preceding this treatment of the *pathē* in 8-9b = Stobaeus *Ecl.* 2.85-88. Arius Didymus is usually identified with the Arius whose works are quoted at length by Stobaeus, who was summarizing Stoic, Peripatetic and Platonist philosophy. See Sedley, "The School, from Zeno to Arius Didymus," 32.

[248] Long and Sedley, *The Hellenistic Philosophers*, 1.419-21.

[249] Krentz, "Πάθη and ἀπάθεια in Early Roman Empire Stoics," 124-126.

[250] Nussbaum argues that there were two Stoic interpretations of the emotions in *Passions and Perceptions*, 100-01. Posidonius (following Diogenes of Babylon) presents the "non-cognitive view" as discussed above. The "cognitive view" of Chrysippus (following Zeno) holds that emotions are rational judgments that assent to appearance and hence are subject to intellectual education. Nussbaum contends that Arius Didymus, Seneca, and Epictetus follow Chrysippus. It is obvious that Arius Didymus and Epictetus follow this approach. Seneca's view, in my opinion, is more nuanced and complicated. See discussion below. Nevertheless, the "cognitive" view dominates Roman Stoicism.

had an appetite or encounter that which we feared.

The terms "irrational" and "contrary to nature" are not used in the usual sense, but irrational as equivalent of "disobedient to reason" [ἀπειθὲς τῷ λόγῳ]. For every passion is overpowering, just as when those in the grips of passion often see that it would be useful not to do this, but carried away by its violence, as if by some disobedient horse, are led to doing this.

Contrary to nature" [παρὰ φύσιν] in the description of passion is taken as something which occurs contrary to correct and natural reasoning [παρὰ τὸν ὀρθὸν καὶ κατὰ φύσιν λόγον].

But those in the grips of passion, even if they know or have been taught that they need not feel pain or be afraid or be involved at all in the passions of the soul, nevertheless do not abandon them, but are led by their passions to being governed by their tyranny.[251]

Arius then lists the emotions subsumed under each of the four primary passions. Under appetite, he lists anger, violent cases of erotic love, cravings, yearnings, and cases of fondness for pleasure or wealth or esteem. Under pleasure, he lists joy at others' misfortune, self-gratification, charlatanry (γοητεῖαι). Fear includes hesitancy, anguish, astonishment, shame, commotions, superstitions.[252]

As stated in the introduction to this chapter, sharp distinctions among the main philosophical schools began to erode, especially during this imperial period. An apt illustration is the classic rivalry between the Stoics and the Epicureans. Chrysippus is said to have devoted his life to a demolition of Epicurus' doctrines, yet the later Stoics including Seneca, Epictetus, and Marcus Aurelius, sought common ground between the two points of view and actively syncretized them. Case in point, the Stoic philosopher emperor Marcus Aurelius gave state salaries to the heads of all Epicurean

---

251 Arius Didymus 10-10a = Stobaeus *Ecl.* 2.88.8-90.6; translation from Pomeroy, *Arius Didymus*, 57, 59.

252 See Krentz, "Πάθη and ἀπάθεια in Early Roman Empire Stoics," 125.

schools.[253]

Seneca and Epictetus

In the influential Seneca, we have a bridge between earlier Stoic philosophy and Roman imperial values. Like earlier Stoic philosophers, Seneca focused on the emotion of anger, but the emphases and reasons for his pejorative attitudes went in a slightly different direction. In *De ira*, Seneca describes anger as ―the most hideous and frenzied of all the emotions (*affectum*). For the other emotions have in them some element of peace and calm . . . this one is wholly violent" (1.1). He immediately tells his readership why anger is so bad. ―Anger is temporary madness, for it is equally devoid of self-control (*aeque enim impotens sui est*) . . . closed to reason and counsel (*rationi consiliisque praeclusa,* 1.2)." He then states that anger is an ―ugly and horrible" vice (*Ira* 1.5). Seneca is articulating the ever-growing concern with self-control in the Empire. Whereas previous philosophers (especially in the Stoic and Cynic traditions) alluded to self-control, the main reason as to the pejorative view towards the emotions was rationality. Now, both reason and self-control are enunciated jointly as being contrary to the *affectum*.

An important Senecan concept, for both ancient and even modern understandings of the emotions, is his notion of ―propassion."[254] Seneca's doctrine of the first motions or

---

[253] See further DeWitt, *Epicurus and His Philosophy*, 326-329.

[254] Seneca's discussion of key terms such as ‗feeling, ‗assent‗, and ‗judgment‗ are surprisingly relevant to modern formulations of emotion, especially in terms of cognition. Recent investigators in several disciplines have increasingly recognized that emotions typically, and perhaps necessarily, involve a substantial cognitive component. Some theorists, in fact have interpreted emotions as nothing more than judgments. Richard Lazarus writes that ―cognition is both a necessary and sufficient condition of

propassions was, at least to some extent, an attempt to revise the theory of feeling. In *De ira* 2, Seneca described the origins of anger as first being a mental agitation induced by an appearance of injustice which is accompanied by bodily changes. This first motion of the mind is involuntary (*Ira* 2.3). Seneca calls it a preparation for emotion, because it suggests an emotional interpretation of the situation. For example, something hurts me, therefore I should exact revenge. The presence of this proposition in the mind, even if it is voluntarily cogitated, is not an emotion, since the assent of the mind is needed in addition. Unlike the first movement, the assent is voluntary. Emotional assent implies that people are ready to act in accordance with it, whereas those having a preliminary

---

emotion," in ―Cognition and Motivation," *American Psychologist* 46 (1991): 353. Robert Solomon states simply and boldly, ―emotions are judgments," in *The Passions: Emotions and the Meaning of Life* (Indianapolis: Hackett, 1993), viii.

Many modern debates have led to an increased study and new interpretations of ancient texts. Perhaps most important for our analysis of ancient emotional theories, Martha Nussbaum defends an extreme cognitivist interpretation in *Upheavals of Thought: The Intelligence of Emotions* (Cambridge: Cambridge University Press, 2001). Nussbaum describes her view as neo-Stoic when she stipulates that emotions ―involve judgments about important things" (19). She asserts, ―The neo-Stoic claims that grief is identical with the acceptance of a proposition that is both evaluative and eudaimonistic, that is, concerned with one or more of the person's important goals and ends" (41). She describes mourning as:

just the awareness that a person whom I love and who has been central to my well-being [her rendering of *eudaimonia*; she also uses ‗flourishing'] is dead. The loss of such an individual is not a neutral event, but bears directly on my sense of what is valuable to me. Thus, the proposition that expresses such a loss carries an intensity that distinguishes the emotion from more narrowly intellectual beliefs, without, however, altering its character as a judgment. The real, *full recognition of that terrible event*...is the upheaval (emphasis added, 45).

David Konstan questions Nussbaum's neo-Stoic outlook in light of his interpretation of Aristotle:

One may question whether the intensity characteristic of certain kinds of judgments – namely, those concerning matters that are important for our life goals – can be simply folded into judgment itself, as opposed to constituting an additional element carrying precisely the affective charge that we associate with the category of emotion. Aristotle specified that emotions are necessarily accompanied by pain and pleasure, which are not, on his view, judgments but rather sensations (*Studies in Aristotle*, 21).

Pace Nussbaum, many modern investigators, like Aristotle, stipulate that emotions are positively or negatively inflicted, and identify additional components in emotions such as physiological changes, characteristic facial expressions and other surface manifestations, accompanying desires or motives, and so forth. Aristotle himself recognized that emotions involve physical processes in the body (e.g., *De an.* 403a16-27). See Andrew Ortony, Gerald Clore, and Allen Collins, eds., *The Cognitive Structure of Emotions* (Cambridge: Cambridge University Press, 1988), 13ff; Brian Parkinson, *Ideas and Realities of Emotion* (London: Routledge, 1995), 230-36; Angela Schorr, ―Appraisal: The Evolution of an Idea," in *Appraisal Processes in Emotion: Theory, Methods, Research* (ed. Klaus R. Scherer, Angela Schorr, and Tom Johnstone; Oxford: Oxford University Press, 2001), 31; and William Reddy, *The Navigation of Feeling: A Framework for the History of the Emotions* (Cambridge: Cambridge University Press, 2001), 21-25.

acceptance think that it can be qualified by further thoughts.[255]

In light of my contention of the blurring of philosophical traditions during the imperial period, Seneca's views of the emotions (along with other convictions) cannot always be categorized as strictly Stoic. In his writings on practical ethics, he does not present himself as a Stoic teacher. He often states his doctrinal independence, as he bluntly asserts in *Natural Questions* 7.22.1: ―I do not agree with the views of our school." Also, in his *Letters*, he frequently refers with a level of interest and tolerance bordering on favor to the ideas of other schools, notably those of Epicureans.[256] Even with these examples, Seneca's practical writings are, on the whole, strongly shaped by Stoic principles, particularly his views of the emotions. In *De ira*, Seneca emphasizes emphatically the Stoic need to extirpate rather than simply moderate passions such as anger.[257] At one point (2.4), Seneca offers an account of the process by which passions occur that is in some respects familiar and others perhaps innovative. He introduces the notion of ―pre-passion" and includes the idea that an emotion, once formed, makes one determined to act in a given way ―at all costs" (whether right or wrong). Seneca's notion of a _pre-passion' (i.e., an instinctive or impulsive reaction not yet rationally adopted) may go back to Posidonius, and has some parallels elsewhere in Stoic sources.[258] I suggest that Seneca seems to be taking the essence of the orthodox Stoic view of

---

[255]Knuuttila and Sihvola, ―How the Philosophical Analysis was Introduced,"13-14.

[256] Pace Cooper and others who argue Seneca is only intent to show that Epicurean insights support Stoic views. See J.M. Cooper, ―Posidonius on Emotions" in *The Emotions in Hellenistic Philosophy*, 83-84.

[257] See, for example, 1.9-10, 17; 3.3.

[258] See Cooper, ―Posidonius on Emotions," 85.

emotions – that they depend on the rational assent of the person involved but that, once formed, they can outrun rational control – and recasting them using his own vivid, nontechnical terms.[259]

In line with Seneca, Epictetus views the emotions as a vice primarily because they go against reason, show a lack of self-control, and are fleeting.[260] In describing this internal moral struggle between reason and self-control on the one hand and the passions on the other in terms of athletic imagery, Victor C. Pfitzner writes:

> The true Agon of the sage is one of the most frequently recurring pictures in the moral discourses of Epictetus, Seneca, Marcus Aurelius, and Plutarch. The contest into which a man struggles against the desires and passions, and the whims of fortune which threaten to disrupt his peace of mind, is the Olympic contest of life itself."[261]

At the outset of his *Diatribai* (*Dissertationes*), Epictetus asserts the primacy of reason (ἡ λογικὴ δύναμις, *Diatr.* 1.1). It is the only faculty that stands in judgment over itself (αὐτῆς θεωρητικῆς, *Diatr.* 1.1.4) and thus over all other faculties as well. One's

---

[259] Questions of orthodoxy and eclecticism lead naturally to that of relations with other schools. The fact that there was controversy about Stoic ideas is evidence of their continued significance in the intellectual life of the period; it also shows that traditionally, the Stoics had clearly defined boundaries on certain issues. The use of Stoic ideas by thinkers of different allegiances as well as philosophers in the Stoic tradition referencing and incorporating other traditions indicate a more fluid side of intellectual life at this time, but this should not be taken to mean that allegiance is meaningless or that boundaries have vanished entirely. On the question of Seneca's orthodoxy or innovation, see Max Pohlenz, *Die Stoa: Die Geschichte einer geistigen Bewegung* (2 vols.; Göttingen: Vandenhoeck und Ruprecht, 1948), 305-9; Pierre Grimal, ‑Seneque et le Stoicisme Romain," *ANRW* II 36.3 (1989): 1962-92; J.M. Rist, ‑Seneca and Stoic Orthodoxy," *ANRW* II 36.3 (1989): 1993-2012; Sorabji , *Emotion and Peace of Mind*, Chs. 3-4.

[260] We also find similar themes in the earlier Dionysius of Halicarnassus' *Roman Antiquities*, particularly this theme of Roman self-control compared to the lax manners of the Greeks; see especially 2.27.1. For the specific relationship between self-control of anger and control of the household, see Plutarch's *De Cohibenda Ira*.

[261] Victor C. Pfitzner, *Paul and the Agon Motif: Traditional Athletic Imagery in the Pauline Literature* (NovTSup 16; Leiden: Brill, 1967), 29.

decisions (προαίρεσις) are all that is in one's power (τὰ ἐφ' ἡμῖν); therefore, an ethical action lies in moral decision (2.5.4-5).[262] Nature (φύσις) becomes the criterion of the rational, since humans are to live according to nature (κατὰ φύσιν ζῆν), in logical consistency with nature (ὁμολογουμένως τῇ φύσει), and in harmony with nature (συμφώνως τῇ φύσει) (1.2.6; 3.1.25). Education (παιδεία), for Epictetus, is necessary ~~to~~ learn to correlate our concept of rational and irrational to particular cases in a manner consonant with nature."[263]

For Epictetus (and for the Stoic tradition in general), there is a rational harmony among virtue (and progress toward virtue through education) and key Stoic terms, such as εὐδαιμονία, ἀπάθεια and εὔροια: ~~V~~irtue [ἡ ἀρετή] promises to produce happiness, freedom from passions, and serenity; certainly the progress in relation to each of these is progress" (*Diatr.* 1.4.3).

Throughout *Diatribai*, he advocates ἀταραξία[264] along with ἀπάθεια.[265]

---

[262] Gisela Striker, ed., *Essays on Hellenistic Epistemology and Ethics* (Cambridge: Cambridge University Press, 1996), 279.

[263] μαθεῖν τοῦ εὐλόγου καὶ ἀλόγου πρόληψιν ταῖς ἐπὶ μέρους οὐσίαις ἐφαρμόζειν συνφώνως τῇ φύσει (*Diatr.* 1.2.6).

[264] For ἀταραξία, see 1.4.27; 2.1; 2.5.2; 2.18.29; 4.6.9; and Jason Xenakis, *Epictetus: Philosopher–Therapist* (The Hague: Martinus Nijhoff, 1969), 81-82.

[265] Krentz (127) interprets Epictetus use of ἀταραξία and ἀπαθεια: ~~B~~y these, however, he does not mean noninvolvement or disinterestedness; rather they describe imperturbability, *the triumph of mind over disturbance arising from without*, the mastery of circumstances, against which anger, fear, *love*, hatred, despair, *friendship*, desire, and the like work. One should not be apathetic like a statue; no one must keep

Like Arius Didymus and traditional Stoicism, the emotions from which one is to be freed

include: fear [φόβος], desire [ἐπιθυμία], grief [λύπη], and pleasure [ἡδονή]. Emotions

(πάθη) arise when that which makes human beings what they are, their logical and

rational nature, the governing faculty (τὸ ἡγεμονικόν), no longer governs their life.

Emotions are internal motions of the mind that react to external stimuli (φαινόμενα).[266]

> Epictetus further defines the πάθη:

> For a strong emotion [πάθος] does not arise except a desire fails to attain its
> object, or an aversion falls into what it would avoid. This is the field of study
> which introduces to us confusions; and sorrows, lamentations, envies; and makes
> us envious and jealous – passions which make it impossible for us even to listen
> to reason [λόγος]. (*Diatr.* 1.2.3)

Epictetus later describes the freedom associated with a person who is able to control

his/her emotions, ―However, the necessary principles, those which enable a man, if he

sets forth from them, to get rid of grief, fear, passion, hindrance, and become free . . .‖

(4.6.16). In a quotation attributed to Epictetus by Aulus Gellius, it is similarly said that a

wise man may be disturbed by terrible appearances, but he neither consents to them nor

sees anything in them that ought to excite fear.[267]

---

the natural and acquired states, *as a pious person*, a son, a brother, a father, *a citizen* (3.2.4)" [emphasis
added]. In ―Πάθη and ἀπάθεια in Early Roman Empire Stoics." Krentz' interpretation of Epictetus
emphasizes the cognitive element of Roman Stoicism, the inclusion of positive emotions in
imperturbability, and the relation of *apatheia* to piety and citizenship, all of which are of vital importance
to our analysis of Luke.

[266] Epictetus actually denounces Greek tragedies for they stress the emotions arise from externals
(1.4.26). See Krentz, ―Πάθη and ἀπάθεια in Early Roman Empire Stoics," 128-29.

[267] Aulus Gellius, *Noct. Att.*, 19.1.17-18.

Epictetus, associating an ideal Cynic with a Stoic sage, provides a perfect

summary of Roman Stoicism, emphasizing public citizenship and asserting the necessity

of an *apatheia* which includes ―positive‖ emotions. In a lecture subtitled ―On the Cynic,‖

he recapitulates:

> It is necessary for you to remove desire absolutely, to turn your avoidance to the
> things that within the province of your choice [ὄρεξιν ἆραί σε δεῖ παντελῶς,
> ἔκκλισιν ἐπὶ μόνα μεταθεῖναι τὰ προαιρετικά]; you should have no anger, no
> wrath, no envy, *no mercy* [σοὶ ὀργὴν μὴ εἶναι, μὴ μῆνιν, μὴ φθόνον, *μὴ*
> *ἔλεον*]; no little girl should appear fair to you, *no little public reputation*, no
> young boy, no little darling [μὴ κοράσιόν σοὶ φαίνεσθαι καλόν, *μὴ δοξάριον*,
> μὴ παιδάριον, μὴ πλακουντάριον]. In short, *say no to all emotions, positive or*
> *negative*, in all areas of life. (Emphasis added, *Diatr.* 3.22.13)

Seneca and Epictetus give us emotional theory in the Stoic tradition with an

emphasis on practical ethics, with perhaps some slight innovations (such as ―propassion‖

or ―preparation for emotion‖ as a fully realized concept, and a more prominent pejorative

emphasis on ―positive‖ emotion), and incorporations from other philosophical

traditions;[268] all of which I maintain are indicative of first century Greco-Roman

philosophical culture on which Luke models his portrait of Jesus.

---

[268] Another illustration of the softening of philosophical lines in this period is found in Gretchen
Reydams-Schils, *The Roman Stoics*, 38-45. Similarities between a passage on ethics attributed to the Cynic
Demetrius in Seneca‘s *De Beneficiis* 7.1 and an ethical fragment (fr. 175) by Epictetus showing certain
Cynic sympathies leads Reydams-Schils to remark, ―it is very hard to draw a sharp line between Stoics and
Cynics in the imperial period‖ (39).

Roman Poetry

Aeneas stopped his right hand; and now, now Turnus' speech had begun to affect him and make him pause, when he was struck by the unhappy baldric of Pallas . . . when he drank in the spoils that reminded him of his savage grief (*saeui monimenta doloris*), then, inflamed by fury and terrible in his anger (*furiis accensus et ira terribilis*) . . . boiling (*feruidus*), he buried the sword full in Turnus' breast.[269]

As previously stated, by the late Republican period, philosophy had come to play a significant part in the education of upper class Greeks and Romans.[270] One of the corollary features of this occurrence is the influence that philosophy had on Roman literature, including poetry.[271] In Roman literature, the presence of philosophy, especially Stoicism, is marked in poetry, as well as prose, from the end of the first century C.E. and throughout the first century C.E.[272] The question of Stoicism's influence in particular on Roman epic poetry is more complex. Though the extent of the influence is a matter of scholarly debate, there is little question that for Virgil, Lucan, Silius Italicus, and probably Statius, Stoicism helps to shape the conceptual structure of

---

[269] Virgil, *Aeneid* 12, lines 938-952.

[270] For starters see Gill, ―The School in the Roman Imperial Period, 56ff.

[271] For a general introduction to the acculturation of Hellenistic civilization, especially art and philosophy, by Rome see Paul Zanker's discussion in light of Horace's famous dictum ―*Graecia capta ferum victorem cepit et artis intulit agresi Latio* (Captive Greece captured the victor and brought the arts to rustic Latium)" Epode 2.1.156 in *The Power of Images in the Age of Augustus* (trans. Alan Shapiro; Ann Arbor: University of Michigan Press, 1990), 1-4.

[272] My main assertion is that certain poetic passages demonstrate the extension of Stoic thought into more popular literature. For an analysis on the influence of Stoicism on Roman prose and poetry with extensive bibliography, see M.C. Colish, *The Stoic Tradition form Antiquity to the Early Middle Ages* (2 vols.; Leiden: Brill, 1985), esp. vol.1 ch. 6; For the influence of Stoicism on Roman law, see David Johnston, ―The Jurists," in *The Cambridge History of Greek and Roman Political Thought* (ed. Christopher Rowe and Malcolm Schofield; Cambridge: Cambridge University Press, 2000), esp. 622-3, 630-3.

the poems.[273] Arguing for a *primarily* Stoic ethical framework in the *Aeneid,* for example, is beyond the scope of this examination, but a brief excursion into select Roman epic poetic passages can further elucidate *popular* depictions of ethics, the emotions, and the characterizations of such, during the time in which Luke composes *Luke-Acts*.

Before undertaking Virgil and the above-quoted provocative end to the *Aeneid* in light of Stoicism, we begin with poetry that certainly shows Stoic influence – Seneca's tragedies.[274] Seneca's tragedies offer repeated and complex descriptions of the passions in action and of the effects of passions on both agents and victims, including for example, Atreus' thirst for revenge, Thyestes' quivering determination to resist passion, and especially Medea's and Phaedra's destructive love.[275] The specific Stoic notion of *propatheiai* (pre-emotions) or *principia proludentia adfectibus* (preliminary stimuli to emotions) provides the conceptual framework for reading the passions in Senecan tragedy, and in particular, for apprehending the dissent into madness of Media and Phaedra.[276]

---

[273] See Andrew Wallace-Hadrill, *Augustan Rome* (London: Bristol Classical Press, 1993), 98-100, on Ovid, Virgil, and Horace in Rome.

[274] Some scholars caution against assuming that Seneca's presentation of the emotions in his tragedies can be straightforwardly or uniformly identified as Stoic. See especially Alessandro Schiesaro, ‑Passion, Reason, and knowledge in Seneca's tragedies," in *The Passions in Roman Thought and Literature*, who argues that the emotional characterization in Seneca's tragedies (e.g., in Seneca's *Medea*) does not fully align with Stoic psychological theory (90-8). While I, following most scholars, disagree ultimately with his assessment, I accept the notion that other influences, from the poetic and philosophical traditions, are palpable, and further evidence my notion of the popular presentation of Stoicism in the imperial period. Pace Schiesaro, see Denis and Elisabeth Henry, *The Mask of Power: Seneca's Tragedies and Imperial Rome* (Warminster: Aris & Phillips, 1985); and Charles Segal, *Language and Desire in Seneca's ‚Phaedra'* (Princeton: Princeton University Press, 1986).

[275] For a useful introduction to Seneca's tragedies, see Thomas G. Rosenmeyer, *Seneca Drama and Stoic Cosmology* (Berkeley: University of California Press, 1989), esp. 3-31.

[276] For the Stoic *propatheiai* (that I suggest serves as Seneca's framework) as an argument directed specifically against the Epicureans, see D.P. Fowler, ‑Epicurean Anger," in *The Passions in Roman Thought and Literature*, 185.

In the Stoic theory of the passions (including the Senecan pattern), the emotions are categorized as, in different senses, both rational and irrational. They are rational in that they involve beliefs and reasoning. In terms of Stoic psychology, it is only when one _assents' to a rational _impression' that one has the impulse to action (*hormē*) that constitutes an emotion. More precisely, the assent is to certain kinds of impressions, those involving the thought that something is good or bad and that it is right to react accordingly. However, the *pathē* are irrational in two related senses. The beliefs involved are false and reflect a misguided understanding of what is genuinely good and bad. Emotions are also irrational in the different (though related) sense that they often involve intense, even violent, psychological reactions which disrupt normal functioning. The person concerned can feel _taken over' by their own passions, even unto _madness'.[277]

Seneca stresses the existence of these *propatheiai*, involuntary or instinctive reactions of fright or impatience that anyone can feel. These only become full-scale emotions (and thereby become overwhelming and irrational states) when one _assents' to the _impression' (e.g., it is right for one to react in this way).[278] In *De ira* 2, Seneca offers strategies for countering these pre-emotions such as childhood training (similar to Aristotle's emphasis on early socially conditioned *hexis)* and self-management (contrary to Aristotle and his diminished, if any, faculty for choice, *prohairesis*). These two Stoic notions of assent to *propatheiai* and the ability to overcome them through socially

---

[277] See Galen, *PHP* 4.1.14-2.44.

[278] See *De ira* 2.2.1-4.2, esp. 2.2.5 and 2.4.1-2. Janine Fillion-Lahille argues that Seneca's _pre-emotions' are based on Posidonius' _affective motions' in *Le De ira de Sénèque et la philosophie stoïcienne des passions* (Paris: Klincksieck, 1984), 164-7; Further, Gill suggests that Seneca's strategy for dealing with anger in *De ira* 2 is based on Posidonian ideas about how to build up character-structures that can resist affective motions in –Passion as Madness in Roman Poetry," in *The Passions in Roman Thought and Literature*, 226.

training offer insights into the Senecan characterization of Phaedra and Medea, especially with respect to Euripides' ancient Greek plays, which originally portrayed them.

Euripides' *Hippolytus*, especially Phaedra's great speech, recounting her attempts to cope with the passionate love for her stepson (391-402) and his *Medea*, especially the great monologue (1021-80), both show the central figure distancing herself from one or another aspect of herself. In Medea's monologue for example, she adopts the _voice' of one of her other possible selves, sometimes addressing the other self directly.[279] Phaedra's great speech identifies what she sees as the only effective way of not acting on her love, namely suicide.[280] Euripides' illustrations are indicative of Greek tragic _madness' in general, which is conceived as an occurrent state, not deriving from deep-rooted features of the personality. It arises, typically from outside (as opposed to the Stoic/Senecan model of internal psychologicalization), either from divine intervention or from a special set of pressures, such as those operating on Orestes when he sees the Furies after murdering his mother.[281]

In light of his Stoic framework in comparison to his ancient parallels, Seneca presents Phaedra and Medea as cautionary examples of the consequences of assenting to, rather than counteracting, pre-emotions; and their own acknowledgement of their internally formed (due to their misguided, and in a sense irrational, assent to false beliefs

---

[279] *Med.* 1021-48, 1056-64, 1067-80; on disowning the other self, see esp. 1028, 1079-80.

[280] *Hipp.* 400-2, defended further in 403-30; there is no indication that she assents to the nurse's initiative (507-24), especially in the Stoic sense of ἀκρασία, acting against one's better judgment.

[281] See Ruth Padel, *Whom Gods Destroy: Elements of Greek and Tragic Madness* (Princeton: Princeton University Press, 1994). In a full-scale study of Greek tragic madness, she takes as central to the genre the type of raving, god-induced madness, marked by distortions in perception and identification, and violent behavior that she finds in Aeschylus' Io, Sophocles' Ajax, and Euripides' Heracles.

of what is genuinely good and bad) madness. In the prologue of the *Phaedra*, we are

shown Phaedra thinking her way into her passionate love for her stepson, Hippolytus,

through a type of reasoned justification. When the nurse urges self-control, citing the

unnaturalness of Phaedra's lust (165-77), Phaedra replies:

> I know what you say is true, nurse; but frenzy (*furor*) compels me to follow the
> worse course of action. . . . What could reason (*ratio*) do? Frenzy (*furor*) has won
> and rules, and a powerful god (*Amor*) dominates my whole personality (*tota
> mente dominatur*) (177-9, 184-5).

The nurse counters that such talk of the divine power of love (an external deific force) is

simply a rationalization of her internal lust (*libido*). There is no external source for her

soon-to-be madness, only her own _assented to' passion. There is also no countering her

passion (i.e., through self-management) as it turns into intense violent madness as she

kills Hippolytus, then takes her own life (1176-1193).

A parallel to the interpretation above in the *Phaedra* takes place in Medea's

monologue near the end of *Medea* (893-977). In Seneca's description of Medea's inner

conflict, she vacillates between herself as mother and her motherly duty (*pietas*), on the

one hand, and, on the other, the mad frenzy (*demens furor*), bitter grief (*dolor*) and anger

(*ira*) of the outraged wife (937-44). She finds resolution to this conflict, by re-conceiving

the surrender to passion as a way of appeasing her guilt at her former crimes, especially

her killing and dismemberment of her brother (945-53). She justifies her resurging anger

as the act of _the ancient Fury' (*antique Erinys*) and then, in her dissent into madness,

declares, ‒anger, I follow where you lead" (952-7). Through his tragedies, Seneca seems

to be repudiating the notion that the gods are the cause of passion. The madness

depicted, being the combination of passion (in Medea's case, bitter anger) and guilt, in

this final stage resembles that in the final scene of the *Phaedra*.

We have another depiction of the emotions most probable in the Stoic tradition, in the *Thebaid* of Statius, a work written a generation after Seneca and Lucan.[282] The passions are presented as harmful to one's rational forces that eventually lead (as in the Senecan tragedies) to a kind of madness and self-destruction.

> Immediately passions are stirred beneath the brothers' breasts, and their inherited madness takes over their hearts, and envy distressed by good fortune and fear, the begetter of hate. From this source come the savage love of ruling, and the violation of their turns, and ambition intolerant of the second claim, and the sweeter charm of one man standing at the peak of power, and strife, the companion of divided rule.[283]

Statius provides the psychological motivation for hatred in the emotions of fear and envy, which Seneca and Plutarch also present as the source of human hatred.[284] Along with the jealousy (*inuidia*) of Polynices, and the fear (*metus*) felt by the tyrannical Eteocles, Statius adds the passion of desire as sources of hatred.

In Virgil's *Aeneid*, the extent of Stoic influence is a matter of great debate,[285] but most scholars agree to at least some Stoic propensities, especially the unequivocal presentation of uncontrolled passion as generating madness, destruction and in particular

---

[282] Statius' classification is debated; see discussion in Elaine Fantham, —Envy and Fear the Begetter of Hatred': Statius' *Thebaid* and the Genesis of Hatred," in *The Passions in Roman Thought and Literature*, 185-88.

[283] *Thebaid* 1.123-30. The raw emotions are realized in terms of the obsession with undivided rule, similar to Seneca's portrayal of Euripides in *Phoenissae*. See David Vessey, *Statius and the „Thebaid'* (Cambridge: Cambridge University Press, 1973), 570-575.

[284] Seneca, *Ep.* 14.14-16, 105.10-14; Plutarch, *Mor.* 86b-92a.

[285] The Punic Wars of Silius Italicus seem to be much more shaped by Stoicism, for example, notably in the contrasted and strongly ethical characterization of the main Carthaginian and Roman generals. See debate and bibliography in Margarethe Billerbeck, —Stoizismus in der römischen Epik neronischer und flavischer Zeit," *ANRW* II 32.5 (1986): 3116-51.

self-destruction.[286] For example, as soon as Dido surrenders herself (described as *akratic* by the narrator, 4.15-19), her behavior is characterized as ‗mad', being intensely emotional and uncontrolled.[287] Her ―madness" is intensified by the news of Aeneas' departure: ―She goes wild, and loses control of her mind (*saeuit inops animi*), and runs inflamed (*incensa*), like a Bacchant (*bacchatur*) throughout the city" (300-1). Her speeches thereafter are marked by a combination of intense emotions: continuing passionate love, violent anger, and extreme guilt at breaking her vow to her former husband. The comparison at one point (465-73) of Dido's state of mind to the madness of tragic figures such as mad (*demens*) Pentheus and Orestes accentuates that the (internally-generated ‗assented to' Senecan) ‗madness' involved is not the raving (ancient Greek Euripidean) insanity of Pentheus and Orestes. There is also the description of her final moments of rationality before her suicide, when she reviews her life with a type of cosmic detachment (651-8), reminiscent of the Stoic *apatheia*. This Stoic ideal of ―passionlessness" or ―non-reactiveness" is embodied in Roman political rhetoric of the imperial period. The state of mind is that of the person whose commitment to public service is so great that ordinary emotions and desires, and attachments other than those to the state, count as nothing.[288]

---

[286] There is great scholarly interest particularly in the above quoted end to the *Aeneid*. Karl Galinsky uses the Aristotelian tradition to justify Aeneas' enraged killing of Turnus as wholly appropriate in *The Interpretation of Roman Poetry: Empiricism or Hermeneutics?* (New York: P. Lang, 1992), 215-20; M.R. Wright also sees it justifiable in light of Aristotelian ethics in ―*Ferox uirtus*': Anger in Virgil's ‗*Aeneid*'," in *The Passions in Roman Thought and Literature*, 169-184. Conversely, Michael Putnam argues that Aeneas' final action is reprehensible, to be condemned in Stoic terms as incompatible with wisdom, revealing lack of moderation, moral blindness, and ultimate failure as either a hero or a symbol of Roman *exemplum* in *Virgil's ‗Aeneid': Interpretation and Influence* (Chapel Hill: University of North Carolina Press, 1995), 293-302. While I see the *Aeneid* as a whole being more Stoic that any other tradition, the ending is problematic, as an Aristotelian reading makes the most sense to me. Perhaps this is indicative of the popularization of Stoicism that I argue is characteristic of the time period, or just bluntly in the words of Christopher Gill a ―paradox" that the poem ends with the ―figure who is the principal bearer of world-historical rationality, as well as the one on whom the claims of passionless virtue are most strongly impressed, gives way to an ethical misjudgment that constitutes a kind of madness" in ―Passion as Madness," 241.

[287] See esp. 68-9 (―in a frenzy," *furens*); 78-9 (―madly," *demens*); 91, 101 (―frenzy," *furentem*).

[288] Regulus, in one of Horace's *Odes*, is a striking *exemplar* of this state of mind. See *Carm.* 3.5, esp. 41-56.

Our short examination into the poetry of Seneca, Statius, and Virgil, has provided us with depictions of ethics in general, of the emotions in particular, and of the literary characterizations (even redactions of the emotions in acknowledgment of Euripides' original portrayals) of these in Roman popular literature during the time of Luke. The primary point of relevance is that the psychological and ethical portrait (especially concerning the contrast between reason and passion, and madness as internal assent) found in the *Aeneid*, for example, is in the Stoic tradition at the broadest level. I am not arguing that the poetic vision of the poem is only Stoic as many scholars see the ethics and psychology as having Aristotelian and Homeric elements.[289] In a sense, I am using Virgil as a parallel to Luke in my contention that the visions of the passions found in their epics are not just or even definitively Stoic, but their depictions of the passions can certainly be located in the broad general Stoic traditions. Further, both the *Aeneid* and *Luke-Acts* are indicative of the type of Stoicism (which I have, for lack of a better term, designated 'Popular Stoicism') found in this (Roman imperial) period.

Conclusion

I have presented evidence from Hellenistic philosophy that shows the subject of the πάθη was of primary concern for the philosophers. The overall philosophical view towards the emotions was clearly pejorative, but certain patterns emerge along a philosophical spectrum. The Stoics were unmistakably at the negative end of the continuum. They advocated eradication of all emotion at all costs (ἀπάθεια), and expended a great deal of effort in defining, classifying and debating them. At the other

---

[289] See discussion in Gill, The School in the Roman Imperial Period, 57; also Colish, *The Stoic Tradition*, 194-203, 225-52.

99

end of the spectrum was the Aristotelian tradition, calling for moderation

(μετριοπάθεια), even espousing a view that it would be unethical and unjust to *not* show

emotion in certain contexts.[290]

In between these extremes, we have the Platonic tradition, exhorting the immortal

reasonable part of the soul to control the mortal part which holds the dreadful but

unavoidable παθήματα, closer to the Stoic end. With respect to the current scholarly

debate (as discussed above) of where exactly the Epicurean view of the emotions fits

along this continuum, I maintain the Epicurean position was closer to the Peripatetic end

of the spectrum, especially the earlier Epicureans, with Philodemus taking a more middle

position along the continuum. While they held a generally disapproving view of the

emotions, Philodemus, for example, writes of a commendable and natural anger.

Some of the differences among schools or philosophers were more theoretical or

psychological, with the final ethical view of the emotions similar. Julia Annas argued

that the Epicurean view is equivalent to the Stoic view in practical matters. When

commenting on Philodemus' *On Anger*, she contends, The affectively transformed

Epicurean will, like the ideal Stoic, be free from the disturbances of emotion in our

everyday sense. …Their behavior will not quite be the same – the Stoics have no room

for approved forms of the hostile or negative emotions like anger, and the Epicureans do

– but they will be equally far from our everyday state.[291]

---

[290] Of course, at the actual end of the positive spectrum were the Cyrenaics, who were one of the minor Socratic schools. The school was founded by Aristippus, a follower of Socrates. The Cyrenaics are notable mainly for their empiricist and skeptical epistemology and their sensualist hedonism. The Cyrenaics had the most positive stance toward the πάθη, which functioned for them as a basic epistemological category, since they maintained that one could have no knowledge of things except through the medium of the πάθη. See David E. Aune, ―The Problem of the Passions in Cynicism," 54. See also Voula Tsouna, *The Epistemology of the Cyrenaic School* (Cambridge: Cambridge University Press, 1998).

[291] Annas, *Hellenistic Philosophy of the Mind*, 198-99.

While some philosophers consciously chose a stance between two competing schools, others sought to syncretize rival traditions, especially during the Roman period. Cicero was a self-described Platonist (hence my analysis under Middle Platonism), yet had sympathies with Stoicism, especially on practical ethical matters, like the emotions. Galen sought to reconcile his medical learning with philosophy, including a preference for Platonic psychology. The resulting general ethic and specifically his labeling of the emotions as ―diseases of the soul" was more in line with the Stoicism of the time.

This syncretization is emblematic of the breakdown of traditional philosophical boundaries during the Roman period, in which Luke constructs his Jesus. There is also more emphasis on ―self-control" as a philosophical notion and a symbol of authority and commitment to ―proper" citizenship during this period. Whereas the disparaging view of the emotions in Plato was primarily due to their irrationality, in the Roman writers, especially the Stoics and Cynics, emotions are immoral because they show a lack of self-control as well as being irrational. I have presented evidence that has shown the traditionally ―negative" emotions, especially anger, were seen as particularly egregious (save for Aristotle who still thought it dangerous) in Hellenistic philosophy. In the Roman period, the ―positive" emotions, including love, were often also regarded as disorders of the soul, especially within Roman Stoicism. The emphasis on self-control, particularly in public figures, along with increased disparagement of the ―positive" emotions during the Roman period are key concepts that influence Luke's construction of a Jesus much more in the tradition of ἀπάθεια than μετριοπάθεια.

CHAPTER 3

THE EMOTIONS IN HELLENISTIC JUDAISM

Introduction

Early Christian and Jewish texts responded to Roman imperial moral propaganda with varying combinations of accommodation and resistance.[292]

The general contention of this dissertation is that Luke has re-formulated his Markan source material, particularly in his view of the emotions concerning the characterization of Jesus, in order to make it more accessible to the dominant Greco-Roman culture. In chapter two I presented evidence from Hellenistic philosophy, especially from the four main traditions, that showed a philosophical disposition toward the emotions (with notable exceptions including Aristotle) that was primarily depreciatory and disapproving. This presentation culminated with the asseveration that the author of Luke, in his depiction of an emotionless Jesus, drew upon the Stoic tradition

---

[292] Mary R. D'Angelo, ―*Eusebeia*: Roman Imperial Family Values and the Sexual Politics of 4 Maccabees and the Pastorals,‖ *Biblical Interpretation* 11 (2003): 139.

in general, principally in its popular Roman rending of the first century C.E., in which the author of Luke creates and acclimates his Jesus.

In order to situate further and compare the Lukan redactional agenda, we turn to the presentation of the emotions in the Hellenistic Jewish traditions. Though I will use the Philonic material (and the Josephan corpus to a lesser extent) generally with the purpose of completing the philosophical presentation of the emotions in antiquity, I will also employ the Hellenistic Jewish authors for means of comparison. The Jewish writers share with Luke issues of accommodation with and resistance to the prevailing notions of virtue in the Greco-Roman cultural milieu. Further, Luke is comparable to a majority the Hellenistic Jewish writers analyzed below in that they are *re-writing* a body of literature to make it more acquiescent to the regnant *mise en scène*. Accordingly, I will briefly analyze how the Jewish authors (e.g., Josephus and Philo) have rewritten or allegorically (re-)interpreted select biblical passages concerning virtue and the πάθη. Of particular importance will be the portrayal of major heroes and figures of authority with regard to their emotions, including Abraham and Eleazar, and especially Moses.

Philio

The history of Christian philosophy begins not with a Christian but with a Jew, Philo of Alexandria.[293]

Though his work was not widely accepted at the time, it is hard to overestimate Philo Judaeus' importance for Judaism or early Christianity, or even for philosophy and religion in late antiquity *en masse*. Philo represents the philosophical epitome of Hellenistic Judaism.[294] Philo sheds light on a number of issues important to the philosophical ethos in the first century of the Common Era, including the highly-debated

---

[293] Henry Chadwick, "Philo," in *The Cambridge History of Later Greek and Early Medieval Philosophy* (ed. A.H. Armstrong; Cambridge: Cambridge University Press, 1976), 137.

[294] Though not the main topic of this examination, the concept of Hellenization is important and always in the background, especially through the influential formulation of Adolf von Harnack more than a hundred years ago; *History of Dogma* (trans. Neil Buchanan; 7 vols.; Boston: Little, Brown & Co., 1896-1905), 1:48. For the historian of early Christianity, "Hellenization" usually refers to Greek culture from the time of Alexander the Great (356-323 B.C.E.) as it made its way throughout the Greco-Roman Empire. It manifested itself in popular philosophies such as Platonism, Stoicism, and Cynicism, and its ethos is somewhat distinct from that of the PreSocratics, Plato, and Aristotle, despite the short chronological distance from the latter. Symbolically, it is best represented by the city of Alexandria, the center of learning and culture founded by Alexander the Great in 331 B.C.E. See discussion in Barry W. Henaut, "Alexandria or Athens as the Essence of Hellenization" in *Hellenization Revisited: Shaping a Christian Response within the Greco-Roman World* (ed. Wendy E. Helleman; Lanham, Md.: University Press of America, 1994), 99-106. The general acceptance of this broad definition of "Hellenization" for the historian may be recognized in New Testament textbooks which begin with Alexander the Great rather than with Athens and Plato. See for instance Normin Perrin and D.C. Duling, *The New Testament: An Introduction* (New York: Harcourt Brace Jovanovich, 1982), 1-22. To a lesser extent, see Bart Ehrman, *The New Testament: A Historical Introduction to the Early Christian Writings* (Oxford: Oxford University Press, 2004), 17-34.
   A brief discussion of Hellenization is necessary especially as it relates to von Harnack's unfortunate contrast between an increasingly Hellenistic Christianity and a non-Hellenistic Judaism (which he termed "exclusive Judaism" which is "as yet unaffected by any foreign influence," 1:47 n.1) If Hellenization, as it is scholarly accepted, refers to the spread of Greek culture throughout most of the Mediterranean world, it makes no sense to regard Judaism "exclusive" or even an increasingly Hellenistic Christianity, implying a Christianity "unaffected by foreign influence," for Christianity was truly Hellenistic from the very beginning, including its development from a thoroughly Hellenistic Judaism. As Martin Hengel (along with a plethora of others) has shown, "From about the middle of the third century B.C.E. all Judaism must really be designated "Hellenistic Judaism" in the strict sense, and a better differentiation could be made between the Greek-speaking Judaism of the Western Diaspora and the Aramaic/Hebrew-speaking Judaism of Palestine and Babylonia." In *Judaism and Hellenism: Studies in their Encounter in Palestine during the Early Hellenistic Period* (trans. John Bowden; 2 vols.: London: SCM, 1974), 1:104.

topic of the emotions. Though their differences certainly outnumber their similarities,[295] Philo, like Luke, uses Hellenistic forms, arguments, and traditions to further his religious agenda, albeit with much more erudition and overall *savoir vivre*. Thus Henry Chadwick could declare the philosophically sophisticated works of Philo the inauguration of Christian philosophy.

There are few biographical details concerning Philo in his own works, and the only event in his life that can be determined chronologically is his participation in the embassy which the Alexandrian Jews sent to the emperor Caligula at Rome as the result of civil strife between the Alexandrian Jewish and Hellenized communities in 40 C.E. (*Legat*. 28-31). We find a brief reference to Philo by the first century Jewish historian Josephus. In *Antiquitates judaicae*, Josephus tells of Philo's selection by the Alexandrian Jewish community as their principal representative before the Roman emperor Gaius Caligula. According to Josephus, Philo and the larger Jewish community refused to treat the emperor as a god, to erect statues in honor of the emperor, and to build altars and temples to the emperor. The importance of Philo's social situation of being a philosopher as well as a Jew in the Greco-Roman empire, especially in its similarity to the social milieu of Luke, allows for the full citation of Josephus' brief comments:

> There was now a tumult arisen at Alexandria, between the Jewish inhabitants and the Greeks; and three ambassadors were chosen out of each party that were at variance, who came to Gaius. Now one of these ambassadors from the people of Alexandria was Apion, who uttered many blasphemies against the Jews; and, among other things that he said, he charged them with neglecting the honors that belonged to Caesar; for that while all who were subject to the Roman empire built altars and temples to Gaius, and in other regards universally received him as they

---

[295] Most importantly, as previous emphasized, I am not claiming that Luke was anything close to a professional philosopher, only that he knew enough philosophy to employ certain patterns, allusions, and typologies, familiar to semi-educated people (see discussion of audience in chapter three), in order to recast Mark's Jesus more in line with prevailing notions of emotional virtue.

received the gods, these Jews alone thought it a dishonorable thing for them to erect statues in honor of him, as well as to swear by his name. Many of these severe things were said by Apion, by which he hoped to provoke Gaius to anger at the Jews, as he was likely to be. But Philo, the principal of the Jewish embassage, a man eminent on all accounts, brother to Alexander the alabarch, and one not unskillful in philosophy, was ready to betake himself to make his defense against those accusations; but Gaius prohibited him, and bid him begone; he was also in such a rage, that it openly appeared he was about to do them some very great mischief. So Philo being thus affronted, went out, and said to those Jews who were about him, that they should be of good courage, since Gaius's words indeed showed anger at them, but in reality had already set God against himself. (*A.J.* 18.257)

In *In Flaccum*, Philo tells indirectly of his own life in Alexandria by describing how the situation of Jews in Alexandria changed after Caligula became the emperor of Rome. Philo says Flaccus, the Roman governor over Alexandria, permitted a mob to erect statues of Caligula in Jewish synagogues, an unprecedented provocation (43). This invasion of the synagogues was perhaps resisted by force, since Philo then says that Flaccus —was destroying the synagogues, and not leaving even their name" (53). In response, Philo says that Flaccus next —issued a notice in which he called us all foreigners and aliens... allowing any one who was inclined to proceed to exterminate the Jews as prisoners of war" (54).[296] Philo even states, —the most merciless of all their persecutors in some instances burnt whole families, husbands with their wives, and infant children with their parents, in the middle of the city, sparing neither age nor youth, nor the innocent

---

[296] Philo states that in rejoinder, the mobs —drove the Jews entirely out of four quarters, and crammed them all into a very small portion of one ... while the populace, overrunning their desolate houses, turned to plunder, and divided the booty among themselves as if they had obtained it in war" (62). In addition, Philo says their enemies, —slew them and thousands of others with all kinds of agony and tortures, and newly invented cruelties, for wherever they met with or caught sight of a Jew, they stoned him, or beat him with sticks" (66). See especially Pieter Willem van der Horst, *Philo's Flaccus: The First Pogrom : Introduction, Translation, and Commentary* (Philo of Alexandria commentary series, vol. 2; Leiden: Brill, 2003).

helplessness of infants" (68).[297] Flaccus was eventually removed from office and exiled, ultimately suffering the punishment of death.[298]

In light of his *Sitz im Leben*, much of Philo's philosophy served to defend and justify Jewish religious truths, even those treatises not explicitly apologetic. With this end in view Philo adapted as well as traversed from his great knowledge of Greek philosophy.[299] Philo regards the Bible as the source not only of religious revelation, but also of philosophic truth; for the Greek philosophers also have borrowed from the Bible.[300] Perhaps most famous for his allegorical method, Philo used allegory to fuse and

---

[297] Some men, he says, were dragged to death, while ‑those who did these things, mimicked the sufferers, like people employed in the representation of theatrical farces." Other Jews were crucified (71-72).

[298] All English translations, unless otherwise noted, are from Loeb Classical Library, *Philo* (trans. F.H. Colson and G.H. Whitaker, 10 vols.; Ralph Marcus, 2 sup. vols.; Harvard: Harvard University Press, 1929-1962).

[299] The breadth of his profundity is especially impressive. His model of creation comes from Plato's *Timaeus*, though the direct agent of creation is not God himself (described in Plato as Demiurge, Maker, Artificer), but the Logos (*Conf.* 41; *Leg.* 1.319, 3.10, 3.96; *Opif.* 8-9, 22, 81; *Somn.* 1.76; *Spec.* 1.328). See David T. Runia, *On the Creation of the Cosmos According to Moses* (Philo of Alexandria commentary series, vol. 1; Leiden: Brill, 2001). His dualistic contrast between God and the world, between the finite and the infinite, appears in both Neo-Platonism and in Neo-Pythagorism. The soul as a divine emanation is similar to Plato's νοῦς. He even quotes the epic poets with frequency. The influence of Pythagorism also appears in number-symbolism, to which Philo frequently refers; see the seminal Carl Gustav Adolf Siegfried, *Philo von Alexandria als Ausleger des Alten Testament: an sich selbst und nach seinem geschichtlichen Einfluss betrachtet* (Jen: Verlag von Hermann Dufft, 1875), 139-151, 245-7. The influence of Stoicism is unmistakable in the doctrine of God as the only efficient cause, in that of divine reason immanent in the world, and in that of the powers emanating from God and suffusing the world. In the doctrine of the Logos, various elements of Greek philosophy are united. As Max Heinze argues in *Die Lehre vom Logos in der griechischen Philosophie* (Oldenburg: Neudruck, 1872; repr. Aalen: Scientia, 1984), 204-209, this doctrine touches upon the Platonic doctrine of ideas as well as the Stoic doctrine of the γενικώτατον and the Neo-Pythagorean doctrine of the type that served at the creation of the world; and in the shaping of the λόγος τομεύς it touches upon the Heraclitean doctrine of strife as the moving principle. See also the introduction by David Winston in *Philo of Alexandria: The Contemplative Life, The Giants, and Selections* (tran. David Winston; Preface by John Dillon; New York: Paulist Press, 1981), 7-20.

[300] Heraclitus, according to *Quis rerum divinarum heres sit* 1.503; Zeno, according to *Quod omnis probus liber sit* 2.454.

harmonize Greek philosophy and Judaism.[301]

Philo's treatment of the emotions, like other facets of his philosophy, can generally be described as a blending of Platonic psychology with Stoic moral theory.[302] Philo most commonly adopts the Platonic tripartite division of the soul into parts which are rational (*logikos*), high-spirited (*thumikos*), and lustful (*epithumētikos*), which he links, with the head, chest, and stomach, respectfully (*Leg.* 2.99, 3.115-18; *Agr.* 30; *Her.* 167, 185, 232).[303] In a limited sense (usually determined by his biblical exegesis), he also accepts the Stoic division of the soul into eight faculties (*Leg.* 1.69-70; *Agr.* 30; *Mut.* 111; *Abr.* 29). Philo also offers the standard Stoic definition of passion as both an

—inordinate and excessive impulse" (ἄμετρος καὶ πλεονάζουσα ὁρμὴ) and an

—irrational and unnatural movement of the soul" (τῆς ψυχῆς ἡ ἄλογος καὶ παρὰ ψύσιν

---

[301] His method followed the practices of both Jewish exegesis and Stoic philosophy. Greek allegory had preceded Philo in this field. As the Stoic allegorists sought in Homer the basis for their philosophic teachings, so the Jewish allegorists, and especially Philo, went to the Bible. Following the methods of Stoic and Pythagorean allegory, Philo found much material for his complex symbolism in the Hebrew Bible. See Siegfried, *Philo von Alexandria,* 16-37. See also Jaap Mansfeld, —Sources" in *The Cambridge History of Hellenistic Philosophy* (ed. Keimpe Algra et al; Cambridge: Cambridge University Press, 1999), 9-19. Philo could follow in many points the tradition handed down by his allegorizing predecessors; see *Contempl.* 2.481.

[302] Philo apparently devoted a separate treatise to this topic, which is no longer extant, though it may represent a project that was never carried out; see discussion in Clara Kraus Reggiani and Roberto Radice, *La filosofia mosaic: La creazione del mondo secondo Mosè* (Milano: Rusconi, 1987), 493. Max Pohlenz makes the interesting observation that no part of Greek philosophy appears so frequently in Philo as the Stoic doctrine of the emotions in *Kleine Schriften* (ed. H. Dörrie; 2 vols.: Hildesheim: Olms, 1965), 1.353.

[303] Described in detail at *Leg.* 1.69-70. For this background in Plato, see especially *Phaedrus* 246ff.; *Timaeus* 69C; and *Republic* 439D. Sometimes the division of the soul is presented as bipartite, with a simple distinction made between rational and irrational elements. See further the helpful discussion in Brad Inwood, *Ethics and Human Action in Early Stoicism* (Oxford: Clarendon Press, 1985), 139-43.

κίνησις).[304] He accepts the Stoic tetrachord (*Opif.* 79; *Leg.* 2.8, 3.113; *Contempl.* 2) and

from his extensive use of medical terminology it is clear that Philo also accepts the Stoic

notion of passions as diseases of the soul.[305] In discussing this Platonic-Stoic conflation

David Winston contends:

> The fusion of Platonic and Stoic terminology and conceptuality in Middle
> Platonism enabled Philo to superimpose the monistic Stoic analysis of the
> passions, which he found so appealing, on his dualistic Platonic understanding of
> the human psyche.[306]

Since Philo's doctrine of virtue is primarily Stoic, his preferred emotional state is

complete dispassionateness (ἀπάθεια, e.g., *Leg.* 3:45), but there is also the acceptance of

moderation (μετριοπάθεια, *Abr.* 2.137) as the true virtuous condition in certain

circumstances for some people. Philo typically identifies virtue with divine wisdom, and

he frequently identifies the Logos with divine wisdom. The Garden of Eden is ―the

wisdom of God‖ and also ―the Logos of God‖ and ―virtue.‖ The fundamental virtue is

---

[304] *Spec.* 4.79; see also *Leg.* 3.185, where passion is likewise described as an ―irrational impulse‖
(*alogos hormē*). For the Stoic background, see *SVF* vol.3, especially fragments 391, 459, 462, 463, 480;
Colson, *Philo*, 4.57.

[305] *Deus* 67: *tas tēs dianoias nosous*; *Prob.*12: *noson psuchēs*, and the description of the Therapeutae
in *De vita contemplativa* 2: ―Their [therapy] treats also souls oppressed with grievous and well-nigh
incurable diseases, inflicted by pleasures and desires and griefs and fears, by acts of covetousness, folly and
injustice and the countless host of the other passions and vices.‖

[306] Winston, ―Philo of Alexandria on the Emotions,‖ in *Passions and Moral Progress in Greco-Roman
Thought* (ed. John T. Fitzgerald; New York: Routledge, 2008), 202. His contention speaks also to the
eclectic nature and breakdown of strict philosophical barriers during this period, which I have elsewhere
argued is emblematic of popular Stoicism. It seems to be representative of Middle Platonism as well, thus
whether Philo is ultimately categorized as a Middle Platonist, as is most common, or a Middle Stoic, it
ultimately is not that useful, as even individual philosophical topics (e.g., the emotions) are difficult to
classify. See especially Greg E. Sterling, ―Platonizing Moses: Philo and Middle Platonism,‖ *SPhilo* 5
(1993): 96-111; and David T. Runia, ―Was Philo a Middle Platonist? A Difficult Question Revisited,‖
SPhilo 5 (1993): 112 -140. Philo's philosophical fusion was already found in Cicero's *Tusculanae
disputationes* (e.g., 4.10-11); see Inwood, *Early Stoicism*, 141.

goodness; and from it proceed four cardinal virtues—prudence, courage, self-control, and justice (φρόνησις, ἀνδρία, σωφροσύνη, δικαιοσύνη) — as the four rivers proceeding from the river of Eden.[307]

Imitating God, who is completely ἀπαθής,[308] the sage must achieve a state of ἀπάθεια. The wise man must convert all of his irrational diseased emotions (πάθη) into rational emotions (εὐπαθείη). David Winston, in his analysis of *apatheia/eupatheia*, concludes:

> Thus, for example, the wise man would never experience the morbid emotion of fear, but only the completely rational feeling of caution or wariness, which requires no further moderation or modification. Grief, on the other hand, he would not be subject to in any form, experiencing at most a mental sting or minor soul contractions, which are morally neutral and betray not the slightest trace of irrationality.[309]

The product of Philo's Platonic-Stoic synthesis is the notion that the ―high-spirited" and ―lustful" divisions of the soul (as well as the corresponding parts of the body – the chest, stomach and what lies below the stomach) are by nature irrational and diseased. The philosophical goal of moral perfection is to rid oneself of these irrational portions of the soul. The majority, those who are unable to attain perfection, must remain

---

[307] See discussion of Philo's ethical modifications made in *QG* 2.57 in John Dillon and Abraham Terian, ―Philo and the Stoic doctrine of *Eupatheiai*," *SPhilo* 4 (1976-77): 18-22.

[308] See *Op.* 8; *Leg.* 3.2, 81, 203; *Cher.* 44, 46, 86; *Sacr.* 101; *Det.* 54-56; *Deus* 7, 22, 52, 56.

[309] Winston, *Philo of Alexandria*, 30. See discussion below of Abraham, who is allowed a moderate amount of grief at Sarah's death, and Isaac, who is the symbol of σοφός, no longer has to struggle in his state of *apatheia/eupatheia*; see for example *Abr.* 201-204, *Fug.* 166-67; *Sobr.* 8; *Det.* 46.

content with allowing the rational portion of the soul to rule over the irrational elements.

Like a charioteer (taken from Plato's similar analogy), reason has been placed over these

"high-spirited" and "lustful" elements to control (*epistomizein*) or at least contain

them.[310] In his interpretation of Deuteronomy he compares the emotions with excrement.

Like the stake which the Israelites used for digging latrines outside the camp, reason is

used to dig out the passions from the soul and to prevent them from spreading out beyond

their proper bounds.[311] Since the Torah contains the actual utterances of God, which are

the "royal road" of true and genuine philosophy (*Post.* 101-12), to obey the Torah means

to be guided by "divine reason"[312] and to live "according to nature."[313]

In his philosophical hierarchy, Philo considers some emotions to be more

troublesome than others. Philo's discussion of ethical matters usually develops out of an

allegorical interpretation of specific biblical texts. In his treatment of Genesis 3, for

example, Philo associates pleasure (*hēdonē*) with the serpent in the Garden of Eden and

declares it to be the source of the other three:

> Because it [pleasure] is, we may say, at the bottom of them [the passions] all, like
> a kind of starting-point and foundation. Desire comes into play through love of
> pleasure; pain arises as pleasure is withdrawn; fear again is engendered owing to a
> dread of being without pleasure. It is clear, then, that all the passions depend on

---

[310] The analogy of the charioteer is a favorite of Philo's: see especially *Leg.* 3.118, 127-28, 138. In an enlightening analogy, Philo interprets God leading his people out of Egypt as God leading them out of their bodily passions (*Leg.* 3.160).

[311] *Leg* 3. 153, on Deut 23:13 (LXX). Philo also adds to his discussion Exod 12:11, "Your loins should be girded up," and states, "For God would have us gird up our passions and not wear them flowing and loose."

[312] This concept is variously described in *Leg.* 3.118 as "sacred reason" (*hieros logos*), in *Cher.* 36 as "divine reason" (*logos theios*), and in *Sacr.* 51 as "right reason" (*orthos logos*).

[313] See Helmut Koester, "Nomos Phuseōs: The Concept of Natural Law in Greek Thought," in *Religions in Antiquity: Essays in Memory of Erwin Ramsdell Goodenough* (ed. Jacob Neusner; Leiden: Brill, 1968), 521-41.

pleasure. (*Leg.* 3.113)

Building upon the idea that the serpent was cursed to slither on his breast (*stēthos*) and on

his belly (*koilia*), Philo argues that passion comes to reside in the lower regions of the

body, which correspond to the lustful (*epithumetikōs*) part of the soul.[314] Further, in his

exposition of the tenth commandment, Philo claims that desire is the most problematic

because it originates ―with ourselves and is voluntary (*hekousios*)" (*Decal.*142-53).

Elsewhere, Philo argues that desire is the source of evil: ―But of all the passions there is

not one so grievous as a covetous desire.... So great and so excessive an evil is covetous

desire; or rather, if I am to speak the plain truth concerning it, it is the source of all

evils.[315]

   As previously stated, Philo accepts the fact that most people will not achieve

complete mastery over pleasure, desire and the other passions, even by obeying the

Torah. Philo's treatment for the passions is often described as a two-stage ethical

program in which few ever attain *apatheia* but many can attain *metriopatheia*, a limited

control over, or moderation of, the passions.[316] According to Philo, the highest goal for

---

[314] See further A. Peter Booth, ―The Voice of the Serpent: Philo's Epicureanism" in *Hellenization Revisited*, 159-72.

[315] *Spec.* 4.80, 84. On this point, Philo is in agreement with many other Jewish writers of the Roman period. See, for example, *Apoc. Mos.* 19.3: ―desire (*epithumia*) is the origin (*kephale*) of every sin," and *Apoc. Ab.* 24.9: ―I saw there desire and in her hand (was) the head of every kind of lawlessness." All quotations from the Old Testament Pseudepigrapha are taken from James H. Charlesworth, ed., *The Old Testament Pseudepigrapha* (2 vols.; Garden City, N.Y.: Doubleday, 1985), unless otherwise noted.

[316] While primarily espousing *apatheia*, and explicitly attacking the milder Peripatetic view (*Det.* 6-9), Philo also proposes a milder view in line with the Aristotelian mean (*Her.* 285-86). In *Deus* 162-65, the middle path leads to God (cf. *Spec.* 4.102; *Post.* 101). See David Winston, ―Philo's Ethical Theory," *ANRW* II.21.1 (Berlin: Walter de Gruyter, 1984), 401 n.4. See further Salvatore Lilla, ―Middle Platonism, Neoplatonism and Jewish-Alexandrine Philosophy in the Terminology of Clement of Alexandria's Ethics," *Archivio Italianoperia StoriaDelia Pieta* 3 (1962): 30-36. For the position that Philo's program for self-mastery is more adaptable see Émile Bréhier, *Les idées philosophiques et religieuses de Philon d'Alexandrie* (Paris: J. Vrin, 1925), 250-310.

humankind is to become like God,[317] who, as mentioned above, is without emotion.[318] Thus Philo describes *apatheia* as an *ideal* ethical state.[319] Failure to attain this ideal state is not always an indictment upon those in process. Philo accepts there are different stages in moral development and acknowledges that advancement toward the ideal can be a good in itself.[320] In *De Agricultura* 159, Philo divides humanity into three categories: the beginners (ἀρχομένοις), those making moral progress (προκόπτουσι) and those who have reached perfection (τετελειωμένοις).[321]

Philo is particularly important among the philosophers for my ultimate goal (of ascertaining the *raison d'être* of the proposed Lukan redactions concerning Jesus'

---

[317] For example, *Virt.* 168: "A man should imitate God as much as may be and leave nothing undone that my promote such assimilation as is possible." See also *Spec.* 4.188; *Fug.* 63; *QG* 4.188. Eudorus of Alexandria also uses this formulation, which became common among Middle Platonists. See preliminarily John M. Dillon, *The Middle Platonists, 80 B.C. to A.D. 220* (Ithaca, N.Y.: Cornell University Press, 1977), 120-25. See also Wendy Helleman, "Philo of Alexandria on Deification and Assimilation to God," *SPhilo* 2 (1990): 51-71. See further T. Rüther, *Die sittliche Forderung der Apatheia in den beiden ersten christlichen Jahrhunderten und bei Klemens von Alexandrien* (Freiburg: Herder, 1949), 17-18.

[318] *Abr.* 202: "But the nature of God is without grief or fear and wholly exempt from passion of any kind, and alone partakes of perfect happiness and bliss."

[319] Philo states definitively and unequivocally in *Leg.* 3.131: "God assigned to the wise man a share of surpassing excellence, even to the power to cut out the passions. You observe how the perfect man always makes perfect freedom from passion (ἀπάθειαν) his study." See further *Leg.* 2.99-102, where *apatheia* is described as *soteria* (salvation) and *Virt.* 31, where the ideal soldier is described as one for whom passion has found no entry.

[320] For adaptability as a pedagogical strategy in antiquity, see Stanley K. Stowers, "Paul and Self-Mastery" in *Paul in the Greco-Roman World: A Handbook* (ed. J. Paul Sampley; Harrisburg, Penn.: Trinity Press International, 2003), 353-7.

[321] See extended discussion of Philo's three-stage development in Bréhier, *Les idées philosophiques,* 267-71, esp. n.16. Elsewhere, Philo maintains that, like physicians who are willing to treat hopeless cases, those making moral progress should try to rescue persons being overcome by evil, "and if some seed of recovery should appear in him, however little, it should be cherished as we fan an ember with every care" (*Sacr.* 123). Therapy for the passions should also take into consideration a person's willingness to be healed: "All the above are lessons and instructions, which stand recorded in many places of the law, urging the tractable in gentle, the intractable in sterner terms to despise the bodily and external goods, holding the life of virtue to be the one sole end and pursuing after everything else that is conducive to it" (*Virt.*15).

emotional depiction) in that he not only discusses the emotions as a philosophical *topos*, but actually provides illustrations of his philosophical theories in his representations of biblical figures. Especially concerning his adaptable ascetic program, an important trio for Philo is that of Abraham, Isaac and Jacob, three distinct types which represent the movement toward perfection in varying ways. Abraham's moral journey is illuminating in that his self-mastery is described as a conquest of certain emotions and the moderation of others, especially grief. Abraham's personal pilgrimage is representative of all humanity leaving pagan practices for a knowledge of the one true God, as well as a symbol of the soul's journey leaving sensuality and turning to reason (*Abr.* 66-71). Philo praises Abraham as a ―sage"[322] who passes ―the chief part of his life in glad-hearted contemplation of what the world has to show" (*Abr.* 207). In describing Abraham's willingness to sacrifice Isaac, Philo uses language which suggests complete mastery over his passions: ―[Abraham] showed no change of colour nor weakening of soul, but remained steadfast.... Mastered by his love for God, he mightily overcame (*ana kratos*) all the fascination expressed in the fond terms of family affection" (*Abr.* 170). Later, Abraham proves himself to be victorious over the four passions and the five senses, again ―fully strengthened" (*ana kratos*) for the task (*Abr.* 244).

Philo portrays Abraham as one who has successfully conquered his emotions throughout his life, with one important exception – grief. Philo's informative depiction of Abraham after Sarah's death allows for the moderation of his grief. After recognizing the importance of reason as the antagonist of passion, Philo clarifies Abraham's moral situation:

---

[322] One of the most common appellations for Abraham is σοφός: *Abr.* 77, 80, 83,132,142,199, 202, 207, 213, 255, etc.

He gave strength and high courage to the natural antagonist of passion, reason [*logismon*], which he had taken as his counselor throughout his life… The advice was that he should not grieve over-bitterly as at an utterly new and unheard-of misfortune, not yet assume an indifference as though nothing painful had occurred, but choose the mean rather than the extremes and aim at moderation of feeling [*metriopathein*], not resent that nature should be paid the debt which is its due, but quietly and gently lighten the blow. (*Abr.* 256-7)

Though strongly resembling an Aristotelian position, Philo's carefully nuanced stance on grief is not unheard of in antiquity among philosophers who similarly advocate a position on the emotions normally along the lines of the Stoic ideal *apatheia*. Plutarch and Cicero both quote Crantor's *Peri Penthous*, which advocates *metriopatheia* in dealing with grief.[323]

Isaac is perhaps the best example of Philo's typology of virtue and perfection. Isaac is perfect from the beginning: perfection is a part of his nature (φύσις); and he can never lose it (αὐτήκοος καὶ αὐτομαθής). Philo depicts Isaac as a self-taught sage, who represents moral perfection in the form of joy (*chara*), one of the allowable, even good passions (*eupatheiai*).[324] Isaac's perfection is a divine gift; endowed with a simple and pure nature, he has no need of training (*askēsis*) or education (*Congr.* 36). Isaac is thus described as being the only example of *apatheia* among his kind (*en genesei*).[325]

The third member of Philo's holy triad, Jacob, acquires virtue by training

---

[323] Plutarch, *Cons. Apoll.* 102D and Cicero, *Tusc.* 3.12. See further F. H. Colson, *Philo*, 6.598-99.

[324] See especially *Sacr.* 7: ―[Isaac has] dispensed with the instruction of men and has become an apt pupil of God...‖ See also *Fug.* 78 and *Abr.* 168.

[325] Colson translates *Det.* 46, saying that Isaac is ―the only example of freedom from passion beneath the sun.‖ The fuller context suggests a comparison between Isaac and his extended family members, especially Abraham and Jacob.

(*askēsis*).[326] Jacob represents those who, through discipline and ascetic practice, receive the victorious prize of ―seeing God.‖[327] Trained by his grandfather Abraham, Jacob achieves a healthy state through his studies (*Sacr.* 44) and passes on this moral strength to his descendants (49). Sometimes, those ―trained in wisdom‖ emerge victorious in both the practical and contemplative aspects of life.[328] At other times, the *asketai* are less successful in finishing the ethical journey, ―For many, after beginning to practise virtue, have changed at the last‖ (*Leg.* 1.89).

It is of the utmost importance for Philo that Moses, the giver of the law, did in fact achieve a state of *apatheia*. In fact, while Philo depicts Isaac as an exemplar of the Stoic apathic ideal, Moses‗ depiction transcends even this virtually unattainable moral standard. Moses enjoys the unique privilege of having entirely eliminated his irrational soul-components, a privilege commensurate with his unique status as a heavenly soul that was sent down on loan to mere earthlings to whom he was appointed as a god (*Sacr.* 9; *Det.* 161-62; *Leg.* 1.40; *Migr.* 84; *Mut.* 19).[329] In *De sacrificiis Abelis et Caini* 9, Moses is described as being sent by God ―as a loan to the earthly sphere,‖ gifted with ―no ordinary excellence ... wherewith to hold sway (*ana kratos*) and sovereignty over the

---

[326] Jacob is often described as ―supplanter‖ of the passions (*Leg.* 3.89) and ―the wrestler‖ or the one in training (*Leg.* 3.18, 190-91).

[327] Philo interprets taking the name of ―Israel‖ to mean ―one who sees God‖ (*Mut.* 81); see also *Som.* 171. See Ellen Birnbaum, *The Place of Judaism in Philo's Thought: Israel, Jews, and Proselytes* (Atlanta: Scholars Press, 1996).

[328] Philo describes those ―schooled to hold things indifferent as indeed indifferent, armed against the pleasures and lusts, always eager to take their stand in a position above the passions. . .‖ (*Spec.* 2.44-46).

[329] Philo‗s more realistic portrayal of Moses as well as his (re-)interpretation of life events surrounding Moses in *De vita Mosis* is sometimes at odds with his idyllic description elsewhere as the perfect embodiment of *apatheia*. For example, Philo is compelled to justify Moses‗ occasional fearful and indignant disposition (ἄθυμος and δυσχερής, *Mos.* 1.40) in Midian as youthful indiscretion (*Mos.* 1.50). See analysis of specific Josephan redactions in comparison with Philo‗s portrait of Moses in *Mosis* below.

passions of the soul." Moses is the highest example of the virtuous life by combining the qualities of king, philosopher, law-giver, priest and prophet in his personhood (*Mos.* 2.3-7).[330] Using typical medical imagery, Moses is the master surgeon, who considers it necessary to excise and cut out all of the *thumos* from the soul, not being content with *metriopatheia* but only complete *apatheia*.[331] The outcome of this ethical surgery is that the "remainder [after the emotions have been excised], the better portion of the soul, the rational part, that is left, may exercise its truly free and noble impulses towards all things beautiful, with nothing pulling against it any longer and dragging it in another direction" (*Migr.* 67).[332]

Philo's portrayal of Moses as an exemplum of *apatheia*, as having eradicated all passion, is in direct contrast to Aaron, who can only control his emotions. Further, not only does Moses exscind the spirited element entirely, but in a corresponding manner he

---

[330] In *De vita Mosis* 1.154, Philo gives us a veritable catalogue of the virtues that Moses constantly exhibited: self-control (ἐγκράτειαι), perseverance (καρετερίαι), temperance (σωφροσύναι), shrewdness (ἀγχίνοιαι), sagacity (συνέσεις), knowledge (ἐπιστῆμαι), laboriousness (πόνοι), endurance of suffering (κακοπάθειαι), contempt for pleasure (ἡδονῶν ὑπεροψίαι), justice (δικαιοσύναι), exhortation to excellence (προτροπαὶ πρὸς τὰ βέλτιστα), lawful censure and punishment of wrongdoers (ψόγοι καὶ κολάσεις ἁμαρτανόντων νόμιμοι), and praise and honor of those doing rightly, again according to the law (ἔπαινοι καὶ τιμαὶ κατορθούντων πάλιν σὺν νόμῳ). As we will see below in discussing specific Philonic redactions of the biblical text in *de vita Mosis*, Moses' capacity as a "king" is generally de-emphasized in *Mosis*, probably due to audience concerns. *Mosis* was intended for non-Jew auditors primarily in response to the misunderstandings, disparagement, and maligning of Moses; thus Philo's portrayal of Moses often varies in his other treatises. Romans, particularly the Roman emperors themselves, avoided the word "king." See Louis H. Feldman, *Philo's Portrayal of Moses in the Context of Ancient Judaism* (Notre Dame, Ind.: University of Notre Dame Press, 2007), 11-16; also Erwin R. Goodenough, "Philo's Exposition of the Law and His *De Vita Mosis*," *HTR* 26 (1933): 109-125. Pace Feldman, see Victor Tcherikover, "Jewish Apocalyptic Literature Reconsidered," *Eos* 48 (1956): 169-93.

[331] *Leg.* 3.129: Μωυσῆς δὲ ὅλον τὸν θυμὸν ἐκτέμνειν καὶ ἀποκόπτειν οἴεται δεῖν τῆς ψυχῆς, οὐ μετριοπάθειαν ἀλλὰ συνόλως ἀπάθειαν ἀγαπῶν.

[332] Moses is further described as "being a most admirable physician of the passions and diseases of the soul, has proposed to himself one task and one end, namely, to eradicate the diseases of the mind by the roots" (*Deus* 67).

also scours away all pleasure. Conversely, Aaron, unable to act in so radical a fashion, admits simple and necessary pleasures, declining only what is superfluous and excessive in the way of delicacies (ἐπεντρώσεις).[333] In Philo's interpretation of Lev 9:14 ("He washed the entrails and the legs and, with the burnt offering turned them into smoke on the altar"), Moses washes out the entire belly and the pleasures that it and the parts adjoining it yield, rejecting even necessary food and drink, being fed instead by the contemplation of things divine (*Leg.* 3.140-41).[334] In refusing pleasure, Moses renounces the other emotions too, for the filling of the belly is the dwelling place of the emotions (*Leg.* 3.113).[335]

It is important that in his attainment of *apatheia*, Moses experiences no pain or toil (*ponos*):

> Without pain is the one on whom God bestows with great abundance the good things of perfection. The one who acquires virtue by means of pain is found to fall short of perfection, as compared with Moses, who received [virtue] easily and without pain from God. (*Leg.* 3.135)[336]

For Philo, since God created and sustains the world without toil (*aneu ponou*, *Sacr.* 40), "lack of weariness" (*akamatos*) is an almost divine condition. To the extent that Moses

---

333 Perhaps tellingly, ἐπεντρώσεις is an Epicurean term; see Hermann Usener, ed., *Epicurea* (Lipsiae: in aedibus B.G. Teubneri, 1887), frag. 413; see further Leopold Cohn, Yizhak Heinemann, and Maximilian Adler, eds., *Die Werke Philos von Alexandria in deutscher Übersetzung* (6 vols.; Breslau: M. & H. Marcus, 1909), 3.130 n.2.

334 So we read in Exod 24:18 that Moses was on the mountain for forty days and nights and ate no food and drank no water when listening to God (*Somm.* 1.36).

335 Importantly, Moses does all this without God's bidding, while Aaron acts under orders. See Epictetus, *Ench.* 48; and Plutarch, *Virt. mor.* 446e.

336 In contrast, see Philo's prolonged analysis about the benefits of *ponos* for those still making moral progress, *Sacr.* 35-42.

represents God in a state of near divinity,[337] he too achieves this perfection without

ponos.[338] David Winston concludes his analysis of Philo's characterization of Moses:

> It would seem, then, that Philo has provided us with the extraordinary phenomenon of a *supersage*, whose perfected reason requires no epithymetic impulse to motivate it to compute the body's needs and satisfy them in the best possible way. …Thus Moses' mind lives in lower, impulse-free conjunction with his body, and with the sole exception of joy (*chara*), it is unaccompanied by the ordinary sage's rational emotions. The *Mosaic mind is accordingly the closest possible approximation to the Divine Mind*, as neither of them is characterized by the usual rational emotions. [emphasis added][339]

To elucidate further Philo's moral prescriptions concerning the emotions consider

the antipodean paragon of Aaron, whose prescription is *metriopatheia*. Aaron is

representative of one who is "making moral progress" (*prokoptōn*).

> But he who eradicates them being next to him, that is Aaron, labours to arrive at a state in which the passions have only a moderate power, as I have said before; for he is unable to eradicate the breast and the angry passions. But he bears the oracle, on which is distinctiveness and truth even beyond the guide himself, together with the appropriate and kindred virtues of language (*Leg.* 3.131-2).[340]

Unable to expunge the passions entirely, Aaron controls them and bridles them through

reason and virtuous conduct. Again relying extensively on medical imagery, Philo's

Aaron does not perform surgery on the passions but cures them with the saving medicines

---

[337] For an in-depth discussion of the (near) divinity of Moses in Philo compared with other Graeco-Jewish literature, including Josephus, the Dead Seas Scrolls, the Pseudepigrapha, and even Rabbinic literature, see Feldman, *Philo's Portrayal of Moses*, 331-357.

[338] Winston, "Ethical Theory," 401 n.4, states that since Philo's sages achieve the state of *apatheia* without toil, they differ from the Cynic sages for whom toil was an important part of the process of perfection.

[339] Winston, "Philo of Alexandria," 211.

[340] As emphasized in chapter two, the moderation of the emotions, *metriopatheia*, was the position advocated by the Peripatetics, many Epicureans, and even a few Platonists. It is possible that Philo is here engaged in a polemic against those philosophical positions which were unwilling to accept the Stoic notion of moral perfection in *apatheia*.

(*sōtēriois pharmakois*) of reason and virtue (*Leg.* 3.128-29). The containment and management of the emotions is a process for the *prokoptōn*, who needs to be constantly fixated on the ―thought of God" in order to experience the healing of this sicknesses of the soul (*Leg.* 3.215-16).[341]

For Philo, the ascetic communities of the Essenes and the Therapeutae (and the Therapeutrides) represent existent examples of successful self-mastery.[342] Although he admits that those who attain great goodness are rare (*Prob.* 63), Philo emphasizes that they can be found: ―[B]ut that the number of those who are prudent, and just, and virtuous, is very small; but that of which the numbers are small, though it may be rare, is nevertheless not non-existent" (*Prob.* 72). The Essenes are presented as examples of virtuous behavior who, through close study of the Mosaic law and commitment to strict communal principles, attain a high degree of piety and self-mastery.[343] Likewise, the Therapeutae remain celibate and practice a simple lifestyle of contemplation, study and prayer. Although Philo does not use the term *apatheia* to describe their ascetic achievements, members of this community (especially the women, the Therapeutrides)

---

[341] Philo holds that good moral endowment takes precedence over teaching and practice. Virtue is not necessarily the result of hard labor, but fruit maturing on its own. The biblical character Noah represents the preliminary stage. Noah is praised, though good deeds are rarely attributed to him, due to his good disposition. Noah is praised only in comparison with his contemporaries, and his characterization is from perfect.

[342] Descriptions of the Essenes can be found in *Prob.* 75-91 and *Hyp.* 11.1-18. Philo devoted *De vita contemplativa* to a description of the Therapeutae. For an analysis in light of other writers in antiquity, who devoted entire works (or portions of larger narrative) to specific religious or philosophical groups, see Gregory E. Sterling, ―Athletes of Virtue': An Analysis of the Summaries in Acts (2:41-47; 4:32-35; 5:12-16)," *JBL* 113/4 (1994): 679-696. Philo's idealized presentation of these communities has received much scholarly consideration; see especially, G. Vermes, ―Essenes and Therapeutae," *Revue de Qumran* 3 (1961): 495-504; D. Mendels, ―Hellenistic Utopia and the Essenes," *HTR* 72 (1979): 207-22, and V. Nikiprowetzky, ―Le 'De Vita Contemplativa' revisite," in *Sagesse et Religion: Colloque de Strasbourg Octobre 1976* (ed. E. Jacob; Paris: Presses Universitaires de France, 1979), 105-25.

[343] These ―athletes of virtue" achieve their exemplary state of near moral perfection by ―intently working at the ethical part [of philosophy], taking the laws of their fathers as their trainers" (*Prob.*80).

have found a successful ―cure" for the passions through their life of devotion (*Contempl.* 68).[344]

In Philo's ethical system, while very few individuals attain the (Stoic) ideal of *apatheia*, many are able to achieve a certain moderateness of passion (*metriopatheia*). Philo's moral program takes into account a variety of factors such as one's natural ability and one's place along the path of moral development. Not only can we examine Philo's ethical philosophy, we can see how this translates in his depiction of biblical heroes (and members of certain ascetic communities). Abraham, Isaac and Jacob, represent three distinct types which represent the movement toward perfection in varying ways, with Isaac exemplifying *apatheia* as ―the only example of freedom from passion beneath the sun." Moses is portrayed as a kind of supersage, able to transcend even this virtually unattainable moral standard; incredibly, Moses achieves this *ne plus ultra* without toil (*aponia*). Moses' emotional portrayal as beyond *apatheia* is distinguished from Aaron's *metriopatheia*. Aaron, who is unable to expunge his emotions entirely, represents one who is ―making moral progress" (*prokoptōn*). Aaron labors to arrive at a state in which he is able to control his passion through reason and virtuous conduct.

---

[344] It is important to note that although Philo idealizes these highly ascetic communities, control of one's passions does not come about automatically by withdrawal from the world. In a rare glimpse into his own attempts at self-mastery, Philo reflects:

> Many a time have I myself forsaken friends and family members and country and come into a wilderness, to give my attention to some subject worthy of contemplation, and derived no advantage from doing so, but my mind scattered or bitten by passion has wandered off to matters of the contrary kind. Sometimes, on the other hand, while in the midst of a great throng I have a clear mind. God has dispersed the crowd around my soul and taught me that a favorable and unfavorable condition are not brought about by differences of place, but by God who moves and leads the carriage of the soul in whatever way He pleases. (*Leg.* 2.85)

4 Maccabees

> 4 Maccabees represents the attempt by a pious Jew to make a continued commitment to the traditions of the ancestors, particularly the Torah, reasonable and even advantageous in the eyes of fellow Jews. It is a remarkable synthesis of Hellenistic philosophy and Jewish piety, which stands as a milestone in the ongoing task of reinterpreting tradition in the light of changing world-views and cultural environments. Rather than heaping up pious phrases from Jewish tradition that may have rung hollow in the ears of his audience, the author uses Greek rhetorical forms and philosophical ideas in order to make being Jewish in a thoroughly Hellenized world both tenable and sensible.[345]

Any thorough analysis of Hellenistic Judaism must necessarily include Philo of Alexandria and it is hard to overestimate his importance. However, when considering the theme of regulating or even subjugating human passions (often termed ‑self-mastery"), 4 Maccabees is of vital import. Further, despite significant differences, there are important foci of correspondence between the author of 4 Maccabees and Philo. Most important for this analysis, both state that human emotions should be controlled (and even conquered) and both argue repeatedly that the Jewish religion offers a superior method for achieving self-mastery.

It is generally accepted that Stoicism, with a few important modifications and admitting a certain eclecticism, provides the primary philosophical background for the ethical theory of both Philo (as discussed above) and the author of 4 Maccabees.[346] In chapter two, we showed that Stoics viewed the πάθη as diseased irrational impulses of

---

[345] David A. deSilva, *4 Maccabees* (Sheffield: Sheffield Academic Press, 1998), 11.

[346] See discussion above, especially Winston, ‑Philo's Ethical Theory," 400-14. Philo's eclecticism is stressed in D. Hay, ‑Psychology of Faith," *ANRW* 20.2 (1984): 898-902. Robert Renehan shows connections between 4 Maccabees and the ‑Middle Stoicism" of Posidonius in ‑The Greek Philosophical Background of Fourth Maccabees," *Rheinisches Museum für Philologie* 115 (1972): 223-38.

the soul, often categorized under the previously analyzed —Stoic tetrachord": pleasure (*hēdonē*), desire (*epithumia*), grief (*lupē*) and fear (*phobos*). The highest ethical ideal for the Stoics was the attainment of *apatheia*, which signified the elimination (in varying degrees depending on the Stoic philosopher) of the *pathē*. Those who attain *apatheia* are guided by right reason and are therefore free from anything that is contrary to nature (which in some cases was equivalent to the will of God).[347]

The book of 4 Maccabees is a homily or philosophic —tractate" praising the supremacy of pious reason (εὐσεβὴς λογισμός) over the emotions.[348] The work consists of a prologue and two main sections; the first advances the philosophical thesis while the second illustrates this supposition using examples drawn from 2 Maccabees (principally, the martyrdom of Eleazer and the Maccabean youths under Antiochus IV Epiphanes). Probably an Alexandrian Jew writing to other Jews around the mid-first century C.E.,[349] the author combines Stoic ideas with his own particular understanding of Judaism.[350] His rhetorically sophisticated thesis, that —pious reasoning" can master the passions, and

[347] See chapter two and further Martha Nussbaum, —The Stoics on the Extirpation of the Passions," *Apeiron* 20 (1987): 129-77. See further Dillon and Terian, —Philo and the Stoic doctrine of *Eupatheiai*," 20-24.

[348] While basically agreeing with my contention, de Silva's analysis of the form leads him to classify further the genre as —epideictic oratory" with —deliberative rhetorical elements" in —The Noble Contest: Honor, Shame, and the Rhetorical Strategy of *4 Maccabees*," *JSP* 13 (1995): 31-57.

[349] See Thomas Tobin,"4 Maccabees," in *The HarperCollins Study Bible* (New York: HarperCollins, 1993), 1814-15. See also the arguments advanced by E. Bickerman, —The Date of Fourth Maccabees," in *Louis Ginzberg Jubilee Volume* (ed. S. Lieberman et al.; New York: The American Academy for Jewish Research, 1945), 105-12. For a more recent and somewhat contrary view, see David A. deSilva, *4 Maccabees: Introduction and Commentary on the Greek Text in Codex Sinaiticus* (Boston: Brill, 2006), xvii-xxv.

[350] Preliminarily see John Collins, *Between Athens and Jerusalem* (New York: Crossroad, 1983), 187-94; H. Anderson, —4 Maccabees: A New Translation and Introduction," *OTP* 2.531-64; and especially Stanley K. Stowers, —4 Maccabees," *Harper's Biblical Commentary* (San Francisco: Harper and Row, 1988), 923-34. See also André Dupont-Sommer, *Le Quatrieme Livre des Machabees* (Paris: Champion, 1939); and Moses Hadas, *The Third and Fourth Book of Maccabees* (New York: Harper and Bros., 1953).

his method for developing that thesis, a series of logical arguments and encomiums on heroic figures in the past, could easily have been presented in the Greek philosophical schools of his time.[351] Furthermore, a comparison of this document with its most important primary source, 2 Maccabees, shows that the elaborations and additions are often directly informed by moral philosophy.[352] In effect, the author uses a *Greek* literary form to argue that the standard virtues celebrated by *Greek* culture can best be attained by meeting the obligations of the *Jewish* law.[353]

The Hellenistic Jewish 4 Maccabees advocates a position similar to the previously discussed philosophical traditions, namely the subjugation of the emotions or passions to reason. Further, like Philo's emphasis on self-control (σωφροσύνη) as one of the four cardinal virtues in his rivers in Eden allegory, the author of 4 Maccabees likewise accentuates the primacy of self-control (ἐπικρατεία) in his moral philosophy. The first sentence provides the thesis of the author: ―As I am going to demonstrate a most philosophical proposition, namely, that religious reasoning (εὐσεβὴς λογισμός) is absolute master of the passions (παθῶν), I would willingly advise you to give the utmost

---

[351] See Clara Kraus Reggiani, *4 Maccabei: a cura di Clara Kraus Reggiani* (Genova: Marietti, 1992), 7-19.

[352] See especially Dupont-Sommer, *Quatrieme Machabees*, 30-34, on the relationship between the two books. Dupont-Sommer shows that the discussion of Greek virtues, the description of the martyrs as ―philosophers," and even the notion that reason masters the passions are all absent from 2 Maccabees.

[353] On the ―Law" in 4 Maccabees with respect to the larger Greco-Roman cultural milieu, see Paul L. Redditt, ―The Concept of *Nomos* in Fourth Maccabees," *CBQ*: 45 (1983), who states: ―The term *nomos* refers to the Pentateuch in the Hebrew Bible, which the author of 4 Maccabees considers divinely promulgated. Further, *nomos* functions to inspire not simply pious behavior, but *rational living* [emphasis added]" (249-50).

heed to philosophy" (1:1).[354] The author then goes on to discuss the relationship between reason, self-control, and the emotions:

> For the subject is essential to everyone who is seeking knowledge, and in addition it includes the praise of the highest virtue – I mean of course, rational judgment. If then, it is evident that reason rules over those emotions that hinder self-control (ἐπικρατεῖν), namely, gluttony and lust, it is also clear that it masters the emotions that hinder one from justice such as malice, and those that stand in the way of manliness, namely anger, fear, and pain (1:2-4).

The author methodically answers the questions (using the same Greek root words as indicated above) of primary importance to him: "The question, therefore, is, whether reasoning be absolute master of the passions? Let us determine, then, what is reasoning? And what is passion? And how many forms of the passions? And whether reasoning bears sway over all these?" (1:13-14).

The author of 4 Maccabees classifies the passions under two main headings: pleasure (*hēdonē*) and pain (*ponos*, 1:20-27). The analogy provided is that of two branches, pleasure and pain, growing respectively out of the body and the soul, each with multiple offshoots. Associated with pleasure are desire (*epithumia*), joy (*chara*) and other passions related to a malicious disposition (*kakoēthēs*). Fear (*phobos*) and grief (*lupē*) are associated with pain. Anger (*thumos*) is common to both pleasure and pain.

While this categorization of the passions is inquisiturient and rather unconventional, its uniqueness can most likely be explained by the author's literary desiderata.[355] Pleasure and pain are accentuated as passions in order to emphasize that

---

[354] All 4 Maccabees quotes taken from the NRSV unless otherwise noted.

[355] As seen in chapter two, particularly with the Cynics, lists of the passions were very common among the Hellenistic philosophers, but those who categorized the passions under the rubric of "pleasure and pain" typically used *lupē* (often translated "grief"), not *ponos*. For example, see Plato, *Phileb.* 31c, Aristotle, *Eth. nic.* 1105 b 21, and Albinus' *Epitome doctrinae platonicae* (*Didaskalikos*), esp. 32.3. Furthermore, the author of 4 Maccabees lists joy (*chara*), an emotion sometimes considered to be a good

the Maccabean martyrs are not led astray by the pleasures of this world, and are able to endure terrible amounts of pain without succumbing to their torturer's demands. Other variations can be explained by the primacy of obedience to the law over every other aspect of life. Due to the gruesome descriptions of torture in the second half of the treatise, it is important to note that the author construes *pathos* to include both excessive impulses and human suffering.[356]

Considering that I will show that the author of Luke has consistently removed strong emotion in his characterization of Jesus, including not only the more obvious ―negative" emotions (e.g., anger and grief), but also the so-called ―positive" emotions (mercy, love and affection), 4 Maccabees is indispensible to my study. In 4 Maccabees 15 the author argues that even the seemingly positive emotions of joy and parental love can be regarded as destructive passions if they prevent one from following the law.

> Two courses were open to this mother, that of religion, and that of preserving her seven sons for a time, as the tyrant had promised. She loved religion more, the religion that preserves them for eternal life according to God's promise (2-3). Nevertheless, though so many factors influenced the mother to suffer with them out of love for her children, in the case of none of them were the various tortures strong enough to pervert her reasoning (11).[357]

---

emotion (*eupatheia*, see Philo above), even in the Stoic tradition, as a *pathos* associated with pleasure. For the ways in which 4 Maccabees compares with other ―passion lists," see the excellent Urs Breitenstein, *Beobachtungen zu Sprache, Stil und Gedankengut des Vierten Makkabäerbuchs* (Basel/Stuttgart: Schwabe, 1978), esp. 134-43.

[356] For the connection between the passions and human suffering, see David Seeley, *The Noble Death: Graeco-Roman Martyrology and Paul's Concept of Salvation* (Sheffield: JSOT Press, 1990), 96-97. See also the introductions in J. W. van Henten and Friedrich Avemarie, eds., *Martyrdom and Noble Death: Selected Texts from Graeco-Roman, Jewish, and Christian Antiquity* (London: Routledge, 2002); and Arthur Droge and James D. Tabor, *A Noble Death: Suicide and Martyrdom Among Jews and Christians in the Ancient World* (San Francisco: HarperSanFrancisco, 1991).

[357] See also, for example, 4 Macc 2:10-14:
> For the law prevails even over affection for parents, so that virtue is not abandoned for their sakes. It is superior to love for one's wife, so that one rebukes her when she breaks the law. It takes precedence over love for children, so that one punishes them for misdeeds. It is sovereign over the relationship of friends, so that one rebukes friends when they act wickedly. Do not consider it

While I argued that the author's categorization of the passions is peculiar, his phrase "devout reasoning"[358] is arresting both in its similarity to Philo and its ultimate uniqueness. According to the *Thesaurus Linguae Graecae*, 4 Maccabees is the only occurrence of *ho eusebēs logismos* in Greek literature prior to the second century C.E.[359] It is similar, however, to certain of Philo's formulations, especially "holy reasonings" (*hosious logismos*) which are separated from unholy reasonings by those who love God (*Her.* 201). The author of 4 Maccabees uses *ho eusebēs logismos* to signify "reasoning in accordance with the ways of God," or in other words, ratiocination in conformance with a strict interpretation and application of Torah.[360] A specific method for mastering the passions by "pious reasoning" is advanced throughout his discourse, a method which is almost identical to that which Philo prescribed above for the *prokoptōn*.

While the author of 4 Maccabees maintains that the passions can be mastered, he asserts they cannot be completely eradicated in a number of important passages. One of the most prominent in this regard is 4 Maccabees 3:2-5:

> paradoxical when reason, through the law, can prevail even over enmity. The fruit trees of the enemy are not cut down, but one preserves the property of enemies from marauders and helps raise up what has fallen.

---

[358] The NRSV translates as "devout reason," while Thomas Tobin, in his notes to the NRSV text in "4 Maccabees," 1814, uses the more common and traditional "religious reason" after the influential translation in Moses Hadas, ed. and trans., *The Third and Fourth Books of Maccabees* (New York: Ktav, 1953). R.B. Townshend uses "inspired" in "The Fourth Book of Maccabees," in *The Apocrypha and Pseudepigrapha of the Old Testament* (ed. R.H. Charles; Oxford: Oxford UniversityPress, 1913), 2.653-54. C.W. Emmet translates as "God-directed" in *The Fourth Book of Maccabees* (London: Society for Promoting Christian Knowledge, 1918), 19-21.

[359] The *TLG* is an ongoing project based at the University of California at Irvine; an exhaustive listing of the texts in this databank can be found in Luci Berkowitz, et al, *Thesaurus Linguae Graecae: Canon of Greek Authors and Works* (New York: Oxford University Press, 1986). For a similar view see S. Lauer, "Eusebes Logismos in 4
Maccabees," *JJS* 6 (1955): 170-71.

[360] See further Collins, *Between Athens and Jerusalem*, 187-92, who argues that one of the most distinctive features of 4 Maccabees is the defense of "the Jewish law in all its particularity" (187 n.37).

No one of us can eradicate [*ekkopsai*] that kind of desire, but reason can provide a way for us not to be enslaved by desire. No one of us can eradicate anger from the mind, but reason can help with anger. No one of us can eradicate malice, but reason can fight at our side so that we are not overcome by malice. For reason does not uproot the emotions but is their antagonist.[361]

This text in particular has led some scholars to suggest that the author of 4 Maccabees rejects Stoicism in favor of a type of Middle Platonism or at the very least a more eclectic philosophical position. While certainly not in the lines of early Stoicism, the views expressed here have much in common with the Middle Stoicism of, for example, Posidonius, who likewise argued for mastery and control but not complete extirpation of the passions.[362] Contrary to Philo, the author of 4 Maccabees seems to reject the Platonic tripartite division of the soul: ―Now when God fashioned human beings, he planted in them emotions (pathē) and inclinations (ēthē), but at the same time he enthroned the mind among the senses (*noun . .. dia tōn aisthēstēriōn*) as a sacred governor over them all" (2:21-3). Since passions are not part of a lower, ―lustful" portion of the human soul, he does not conceive of them as being completely removed from the soul.

However, while the author of 4 Maccabees consistently emphasizes mastery rather than extirpation, the examples of Eleazar and the seven brothers approximate the previously discussed notion of *apatheia*. If we take as our definition for *apatheia* the elimination of *pathē*, the freedom from external forces contrary to nature, and the

---

[361] Similarly, the use of agricultural imagery suggests control rather than extirpation: reason is the ―niversal gardener [who] purges, prunes, binds up, waters and thoroughly irrigates and thus tames the wild growth of inclinations and passions" (1:29).

[362] See Renehan, ―Philosophical Background," 223-38, esp. n.4. I further contend that one facet of Middle Stoicism, especially during the time of 4 Maccabees (middle to late first century C.E.) is a more eclectic type of Stoicism, with softer edges, incorporating aspects of other philosophic traditions. For a contrary view, see Anderson, ―4 Maccabees," 538: ―As the Jewish philosopher par excellence (5:4), Eleazar, far from endorsing Stoic principles, indeed opposes them, as when, for example, he insists against Stoicism that reason does not eradicate but only controls or directs the passions."

accompanying experience of *aponia* ("toil-lessness" or lack of pain),[363] we see that the author of 4 Maccabees believes the attainment of *apatheia* to be possible by strict adherence to the law. Essentially, for the author of 4 Maccabees, complete mastery of the passions is equivalent to the attainment of *apatheia*.

Like the sage in Stoic philosophy, there is an ideal person in control of her/his emotions, but not all people fall into this category. At the conclusion of his encomium to the martyred Eleazar, the author of 4 Maccabees notes that "some men seem to be ruled by their passions (παθοκρατεῖσθαι) because of the weakness of their reason . . . Only the wise and manly individual (ἀνδρεῖος) is ruler of the passions" (7:20-23). This sets the scene for all that ensues. The torture of the "heroes" is occasioned by the inability of Antiochus to control his own passions, especially his rage. Moore and Anderson, in discussing the virtues on display in 4 Maccabees, state, "the physical torture of the youths and the psychological torture of their mother will prove their remarkable self-control, and hence their _manliness'."[364]

The author of 4 Maccabees portrays Eleazar as an example par excellence of one who overcomes passion through his extraordinary powers of reason. When Eleazar is tortured, he is "in no way moved" (*oudena tropon metetrepeto*),[365] and although his body

---

[363] In Philo, we noted the supersage characterization of Moses' *aponia*, which is in direct contrast to Aaron as one who is "making moral progress" (prokoptōn). Aaron labors to arrive at a state in which the passions have only a moderate power, for he is unable to expunge the passions entirely (*Leg.* 3.131-2).

[364] Stephen D. Moore and Janice Capel Anderson, "Taking It Like a Man: Masculinity in 4 Maccabees," *JBL* 117 (1998): 254. See further Mary R. D'Angelo, "*Eusebeia*: Roman Imperial Family Values and the Sexual Politics of 4 Maccabees and the Pastorals," *BibInt* 11 (2003): 139-165.

[365] The verb μετατρέπω and its cognates are used throughout the Fourth Maccabean text to describe a turning or swerving from pious reason; BADG, 513. See especially 7:12: "Eleazar … remained unmoved

129

collapses, his reasoning remains "upright and unswerving" (6:7). Eleazar is extolled as one who "broke the maddening waves of emotion," a model priest, philosopher and king (7:5ff).[366] Although he is compared with the biblical figures of Isaac and Aaron, there are also close parallels between the description of Eleazar and those of the Cynic wise men (especially Antisthenes and Diogenes) idealized by Stoic writers of the Roman period.[367]

The characterization of the mother is perhaps the most nuanced and complex, as well as the most debated.[368] In many ways she is depicted as being completely free from the passions which tormented Eleazar and the brothers. The mother is presented as enduring mental anguish and exhibiting heroic amounts of courage and perseverance (15:29-31). In her steadfastness and endurance she is portrayed as having super-human strength and heroism: she is both a "champion of the Law" who carried away the prize "in the contest of the inner parts" (15:29) and a "soldier of God" who "vanquished even the tyrant" (16:14). Even her ultimate death through a type of suicide is offered as the epitome of virtue. By flinging herself into the fire rather than allowing herself to be

---

in his reason," and 15:11: "the manifold tortures [of the mother] could not influence a swerving of her reason."

[366] See further translation notes in Hadas, *Third and Fourth Maccabees*, n.37.

[367] See Diog. Laert. 6.3,5,13. On the relationship between Eleazar and the Stoic sage see Stowers, "4 Maccabees," 51 n.37.

[368] The exact emotional portrayal of Eleazar, the seven brothers, and the mother in particular is a matter of scholarly debate. David C. Aune argues that the Maccabean depiction of "Eleazar, the seven brothers *and* the mother *clearly* suggest the *apatheia* which was attained by the Cynic and Stoic sages" (emphasis added) in "Mastery of the Passions: Philo, 4 Maccabees and Earliest Christianity" in *Hellenization Revisited*, 136. Against this position, A. O'Hagan, contends, "[the author of 4 Maccabees] does not slip into the Stoic philosophic extreme of insensitivity and complete indifference, the technical terms ἀπαθεία and ἀναισθηρία never occur in 4 Maccabees" in "The Martyr in the Fourth Book of Maccabees," *SBFLA* 24 (1974): 101. Though the technical terms are not present, the mother's idyllic portrayal, especially in her lack of grief, does seem to "slip" into the "Stoic philosophic extreme."

defiled by the hands of her assailants, she exemplifies extraordinary moral fortitude (17:1).[369]

On the other hand, David deSilva warns of the author's hyperbole and calls for caution in assessing the author's claim that the mother did not weep (15:19), nor shed tears (15:20), nor wail, lament, and "grieve as they were dying" (16:12).[370] He cites the author's description of the mother in the last verse of chapter 15: "[S]o you, O guardian of the law, overwhelmed from every side by the flood of your emotions and the violent winds, the torture of your sons, endured nobly and withstood the wintry storms that assail religion" (v.32), and concludes:

> In these statements, we hear nothing of 'toil-lessness' and everything of brave endurance in the face of the experience of horrific pains. Indeed, the whole point of the *ekphrasis* of 15.14-15, 18-22 is to amplify the audience's sense of the magnitude of the mother's sufferings (15.13, 16-17) and thus her achievement (15.11-12, 14, 23). It is not that she remains untouched by these sufferings, but that she remains unmoved in her moral purpose by them (15.11, 14).[371]

While acknowledging the hyperbolic rhetorical strategy by the author of 4 Maccabees as well as a degree of complexity in the martyrs' portrayal (especially the mother), I still maintain that the presentation of the emotions has much in common with the popular rendering of first-century Stoic *apatheia*.

In line with Eleazar and the mother, the brothers likewise step forward, one by one, and willingly endure the horrible tortures, fearlessly proclaiming their faith until

---

[369] On the mother, see further R. D. Young, "The 'Woman with the Soul of Abraham': Traditions about the Mother of the Maccabean Martyrs," in *Women like This: New Perspectives on Jewish Women in the Greco-Roman World* (ed. A.J. Levine; Atlanta: Scholars Press 1991), 67-81.

[370] David A. deSilva, "The Perfection of 'Love for Offspring': Greek Representations of Maternal Affection and the Achievement of the Heroine of 4 Maccabees," *NTS* 52 (2006): 264-67.

[371] Ibid., 264-65.

finally they are silenced by death. For example, the first brother boldly states: ―Cut my limbs, burn my flesh and twist my joints; through all these tortures I will convince you that children of the Hebrews alone are invincible where virtue is concerned" (9:17-18). By repeatedly emphasizing that these virtuous martyrs experience no human suffering, the author remonstrates his main thesis that ―pious reason" overcomes the passions.

An important question for the author of 4 Maccabees, as it was for Philo, is whether or not moral perfection is attainable. The author of 4 Maccabees argues that mastery of the passions (which I have argued is essentially equivalent to the attainment of *apatheia*) *is* possible for those who are fully devoted to God.

> Some may say that not all are able to master their emotions, because not all possess sound judgment in their reasoning (*phronimon ton logismon*). But, as many as attend to piety with their whole heart will be able to master the passions of their human nature, believing that they, like the patriarchs Abraham, Isaac and Jacob, do not die to God but live to God. Therefore, no contradiction arises when certain ones are not able to master their passions because of weak reason (*asthene logismon*). Who, then, living as a philosopher by the whole rule of philosophy, trusting in God and knowing that it is blessed to endure all pain for the sake of virtue would not be able to master their passions because of their devotion to God? For only the wise and courageous person is master of the passions. (7:17-23)

Contrary to Philo and his two-stage ethical program in which few ever attain *apatheia* but many can attain *metriopatheia*, the author of 4 Maccabees does not advocate any adaptable program of ascetic practice: all persons, whatever their stage of moral development, and whatever their natural abilities, should expect to master their passions completely if they obey the law. The author depicts the martyrs disencumbered by the obstacles of old age, youth and gender. The philosophical argument builds from Eleazar, ―an aged man" (7:16) through the seven ―young men" (8:1) to the mother, who represents the climax of the story because ―the mind of woman [sic] despised even more diverse agonies" (14:11). When he reaches the exhortation to ─obey this Law" (18:1), the author has in effect stated that it is possible for all persons to do so, whatever their inherent disabilities. Failure to attain mastery of the passions is due to the weakness (or, sickness)[372] of one's reason (7:20), which is strengthened (or healed) by obedience to the Torah.

Further, the author of 4 Maccabees asserts that even an *aponos apatheia* is achievable by those who live according to pious reason. For Philo, one test of true *apatheia* is whether it can be accomplished without *ponos*, i.e. the previously mentioned depiction of exemplar Moses over and against Aaron, who has to labor in making moral progress. Similarly in 4 Maccabees (pace deSilva), even those most vulnerable to pain are characterized as being able to overcome it and, veritably, be free from it. In their speeches, for instance, the second brother declares: ─I relieve the burden of pain by the pleasures which come from virtue" (9:31) and the sixth reaffirms: ─Your fire is cold to us, and the catapults painless (*aponos*), and your violence powerless ...; therefore, unconquered, we hold fast to reason" (11:26-27). To borrow Philo's language of ethical maturation, the author of 4 Maccabees maintains that even the *prokoptōn* can attain *apatheia* through strict obedience to the law.

Other Hellenistic Jewish Literature

Pseudo-Phocylides is an apocryphal work claiming to have been written by Phocylides, a Greek philosopher of the 6th century, though it is usually dated between the first century B.C.E. and the first century C.E., since it is evident that the writer knows the

---

[372] The word *asthenēs* is often used by philosophical writers to describe moral weakness in the sense of sickness, oftentimes synonymous with *nosos,* see *SVF* 3.421 and 473.

Septuagint.[373] Pseudo-Phocylides consists of about 250 aphorisms seriatim, perhaps

reminiscent of the Noachian Laws, to propagate some universal principles of religion and

ethics without the intention of making proselytes.[374] While there have been many

attempts to systemize Pseudo-Phocylides, most scholars have agreed to the eclectic

nature of his ethical dictions. Though van der Horst observes "contradictory statements"

which are "uttered so unsystematically" and he recognizes "there is no unifying

conception behind the poem and no coherence exists," he argues generally for a Jewish

ethic shaped by Stoicism.[375] Though the language used in the formulation of his moral

philosophy could be seen as Stoic at times, the poet's emphasis on moderation is more

compatible with a Jewish ethic shaped by the Aristotelian tradition.[376]

---

[373] See Pieter Willem van der Horst, "Pseudo-Phocylides: A New Translation and Introduction" in *OTP*, 565-573. See also his full-length commentary with Greek text *The Sentences of Pseudo-Phocylides* (SVTP 4; Leiden: Brill, 1978).

[374] The exact purpose (e.g., apologetic, propagandistic) and audience (e.g., Jews, "sympathizers") of Pseudo-Phocylides is debated. See Walter T. Wilson, *The Sentences of Pseudo-Phocylides* (New York: Walter de Gruyter, 2005); John Collins, "Jewish Ethics in Hellenistic Dress: The Sentences of Pseudo-Phocylides," in *Jewish Wisdom in the Hellenistic Age* (Louisville: Westminister John Knox, 1997), 158-177; Johannes Thomas, *Der jüdische Phokylides: formgeschichtliche Zugänge zu Pseudo-Phokylides und Vergleich mit der neutestamentlichen Paränese* (Göttingen: Vandenhoeck & Ruprecht, 1992). A number of verses in Pseudo-Phocylides run parallel to passages in Philo's *Hypothetica* and Josephus' *Contra Apionem* which figure in an apologetic and propagandistic context. James Crouch has even suggested that all three of them had a common source which had its origin in a "wide-spread Jewish missionary activity which promoted ethical monotheism" in *The Origen and Intention of the Colossian Haustafel* (Göttingen, Vandenhoeck & Ruprecht, 1972), 89. He further states, "The original impulse and intention of the Jewish mission lay . . . not in an extension of Judaism as a national religious cult but in the proclamation of the one God and his universal, ethical standards" (94). For a general overview on this issue, see Gregory E. Sterling, review of Hans Conzelmann, *Gentiles, Jews, Christians: Polemics and Apologetics in the Greco-Roman Era*, SPhilo 5 (1993): 238-242.

[375] van der Horst, "Pseudo-Phocylides," 565, 570-1.

[376] van der Horst sees a piece of Stoic casuistry behind "but if rage is excessive, it is wrath" (line 64) that distinguishes three kinds of anger. Although such a distinction does exist in some Stoic traditions, they saw all anger as a disease of the soul to be extirpated, in contrast to the moderation found in Pseudo-Phocylides, which I argue is more in line with Aristotle.

Pseudo-Phocylides stresses the concept of self-control similarly to contemporaneous texts 4 Maccabees and *Joseph and Aseneth*.[377]

Practice self-restraint (σωφροσύνη), and abstain from shameful deeds (line 76).

This is particularly true in terms of anger:

Do not be rash with your hands, but bridle your wild anger (57)
but if rage is excessive, it is wrath (64)

Anger, like other emotions, should be tempered, not eradicated, for even God has (justifiable) anger.

Do not dig up the grave of the deceased, nor expose to the sun (100)
what may not be seen, lest you stir up the divine anger (101)

Excessive anger leads to a loss of control, irrationality, and mental instability, affecting one's ability to make sound rational judgments, an important virtue in Pseudo-Phocylides.

Anger that steals over one causes destructive madness (63)

Insanity can be caused by emotions other than anger.

Do not become mad in your mind by reveling in boastfulness (122)

The above lines from Pseudo-Phocylides could fit into most of the philosophic traditions, a broad pejorative view of the emotions, but the emphasis on moderation instead of complete abolishment is resonant with the Aristotelian legacy. Moderation (μέτρον, literally "measure") is a virtue in general:

Moderation is the best of all, and excesses are grievous (36)
Eat in moderation, and drink and tell stories in moderation (69)

---

[377] See for example 4 Macc 1:31 and *Jos. Asen.* 4:7. Later see also *T. Jos.* 4:2, 9:2, 10:2-3, and Josephus, *Ag. Ap.* 2.195.

> Moderation is the best of all, excesses are grievous (69b)
> It is better to entertain guests with a simple meal quickly (81)
> than extensive festivity drawn out beyond the right time (82)

μέτρον is a specifically important virtue concerning one's emotional disposition:

> Let your emotions be moderate, neither great nor overwhelming (59)
> Excess, even of good, is never a boon to mortals (60)
> And a great luxuriousness draws one to immoderate desires (61)
> Love of virtue is worthy, but love of passion increases shame (67)

Even more specific in his categorization, Pseudo-Phocylides advocates moderation in the grieving process:

> Be moderate in your grief; for moderation is best (98)

At their most basic classification, the emotions in Hellenistic philosophy fall under either the Stoic summons for eradication or the Aristotelian mean; it is clear that Pseudo-Phocylides' enjoinment for μέτρον is the latter.

Although not always categorized as a ―Hellenistic Jewish" text, *Joseph and Aseneth* was almost certainly written in Greek during the Second Temple period (probably between 100 B.C.E. and 100 C.E.), and at the very least enhances our understanding of Greek-speaking Judaism around the time of the present era.[378] From a literary point of view it represents, like Pseudo-Phocyclides and the *Sibylline Oracles*, an

---

[378] Marc Philonenko suggests a rural milieu outside Alexandria because he argues *Joseph and Aseneth* is less intransigent toward paganism than an Alexandrian like Philo in *Joseph et Aséneth: Introduction, texte critique, traduction et notes* (Leiden: Brill, 1974), 106ff.

attempt to adapt forms of Greek belletristic literature.[379] Though the subjugation of the emotions is not the main theme of this Greco-Jewish work as it is in 4 Maccabees,[380] the "good" characters, especially Joseph, are depicted as having (to varying degrees) overcome their emotions, particularly anger, primarily through the practice of self-control. Aseneth's father, Pentephres, describes Joseph:

> Joseph the Powerful One of God is coming to us today. And he is chief of the whole land of Egypt, and the king Pharaoh appointed him king of the whole land, and he is giving grain to the whole land, and saving it from the ongoing famine. And Joseph is a man who worships God (θεοσεβής), and self-controlled (σώφρων), and a virgin (παρθένος) like you today, and Joseph is also a man powerful in wisdom and experience, and the spirit of God is upon him, and the grace of the Lord is with him (4:7).

Joseph and Aseneth does not use εὐσέβεια (the key term in overcoming the emotions in 4 Maccabees), but instead uses θεοσεβής to describe Jews who worship God and also observe high ethical standards. Self-controlled (σώφρων) here is not associated with sexual practice but with the control of one's behavior, demeanor, and emotion.[381]

---

[379] See Christoph Burchard, "Joseph and Aseneth: A New Translation and Introduction," in *OTP*, 194-195.

[380] Most scholars see mixed-marriage and/or conversion as the major issue(s) in *Joseph and Aseneth*. See especially Randall D. Chesnutt, *From Death to Life: Conversion in Joseph and Aseneth* (JSPSup 16; Sheffield : Sheffield Academic Press, 1995). See also Howard Clark Kee, "The Socio-Religious Setting and Aims of *Joseph and Aseneth*" (ed. George MacRae, *SBLSP* 10; Missoula, Mont.: Scholars Press, 1976), 187.

[381] The reasons for my rendering of self-control as self-mastery in a general sense and not a sexual one are two-fold. Textually, I read "a man who worships God (θεοσεβής) and self-controlled (σώφρων), and a virgin (παρθένος)" as three separate, albeit related, character traits, not three synonyms for the same ethical ideal. Lexically, σώφρων can denote chasity (very rarely), though even when describing womanly virtue, it usually means decent or modest. Aristotle uses σώφρων to refer to self-control in *Eth. nic.* 3.15.

In Genesis 34, Levi and Simeon destroy the city of Shechem in revenge for the rape of Dinah, seizing the wealth of the city, and killing the men. When Jacob hears about the destruction of Shechem by Simeon and Levi, he castigates them for it (30-31). *Joseph and Aseneth* also portrays Simeon as having violent anger, but Levi is now contrasted with Simeon as a man of self-control: ―. . and there was not the least bit of anger in him" (23:10). Levi even curbs Simeon's violent anger against Pharaoh's son:

> And Simeon was a daring and bold man, and he intended to lay his hand on the handle of his sword and draw it from its sheath and strike Pharaoh's son, because he had spoken defiant things to them. And Levi saw the intention of his heart, because Levi was a prophet, and he was sharp-sighted with both his mind and his eyes, and he used to read what is written in the heart of men. And Levi trod with his foot on Simeon's right foot and pressed it and thus signaled him to cease from his wrath. And Levi said to Simeon quietly, ―Why are you furious with anger (ὀργῇ θυμοῦσαι) with this man? And we are men who worship God, and it does not befit us to repay evil for evil" (23:8-9).

In the penultimate chapter it is Aseneth who calms Simeon's vengeful anger:

> And Aseneth stretched out her right hand and touched Simeon's beard and kissed him and said, ―By no means, brother, will you do evil for evil to your neighbor. To the Lord will you give the right to punish the insult done by them. And they are your brothers and your fathers, Israel's line, and they fled far from your presence. Anyway, grant them pardon." And Levi went up to her and kissed her right hand and perceived that she wanted to save the men from their brother's anger so that they would not kill them. (28:14-15)

Josephus

> Josephus was a first-century Jew whose life as a diplomat, general, and historian was crammed with contradictions. He studied in the desert but wrote in the city. He was a pacifist who went to war, a military commander who (to our

---

In Titus' virtue list, the NRSV translates σώφρων as prudent (2:2); in the qualifications of Bishops in 1 Timothy, it is translated as sensible (3:2).

knowledge) had no training in the martial arts but fought as if he had. He battled the Romans, yet was befriended by them. He joined a suicide pact but survived, while thirty-nine lay dead around him. He was the mortal foe of a future emperor – who later brought him into the family! Schooled in Aramaic, he wrote a massive history in Greek for a Roman audience, writings which have either been disdained or called ―next to the Bible in importance.‖ Many of the historical works that he used have perished but his own have survived. He was scorned by his fellow Jews but honored by Christians. He has been labeled a traitor, quisling, lackey, or banal opportunist on the one hand, as well as a survivor, prodigy, sage, and indispensable source on the other. His exploits and achievements – pulsing with paradox – are discussed as much today as they were nineteen centuries ago.[382]

Beyond all debate over Josephus as bane or blessing is his position as a first-century Jewish historian.[383] Perhaps aside from references to the biblical texts themselves, the phrase ―according to Josephus‖ is the single most familiar refrain in

---

[382] Paul L. Maier, *The New Complete Works of Josephus* (Grand Rapids, Mich.: Kregel, 1999), 7.

[383] Josephus, often designated Flavius Josephus due to his clientage with the Flavian dynasty, was of Hasmonean royal descent on his mother‘s side, and of priestly descent on his father‘s, introducing himself in Greek as ―Iosepos (Ἰώσηπος), son of Matthias, an ethnic Hebrew, a priest from Jerusalem‖ (*Vita* 1.1-2; *B.J.* 1.3). He studied the principal Jewish sects – the Pharisees, Sadducees, and Essenes – favoring the last when he lived for three years in the wilderness with a hermit named Banus. He eventually joined the Pharisees, for whom he would later offer criticism (*Vita* 9-12). Some Recent commentators have sought to move scholarly perceptions forward by demonstrating that Josephus was not a Pharisee but an orthodox Aristocrat-Priest who became part of the Temple establishment as a matter of deference and not willing association; see Steve Mason, *Flavius Josephus on the Pharisees: A Composition-critical Study* (Leiden: Brill, 1990); and Todd S. Beall, *Josephus' Description of the Essenes Illustrated by the Dead Sea Scrolls* (Cambridge: Cambridge University Press, 1988), 9-11.
     The particulars of the debate are beyond the scope of my examination, though it is important to note (and there is general scholarly agreement) that Josephus *did receive a Jewish education* (*A.J.* 20.264; *C. Ap.* 1.54) and at least acquired a rudimentary level of Greek proficiency (the degree of which is a matter of dispute). Sterling (in *Historiography*, 229-240) argues that since Josephus was an ambassador to Rome at age 26, this ―presupposes some ability to communicate in the *lingua franca* of the Roman world‖ (230 n.19), and therefore concludes Jospehus ―stands in the same social tradition as Berossos, Manethon, and Eupolemos and should be considered *unus ex nobilibus* as Suetonius says‖ (230).
     Due to a series of extraordinary events, he ended up in Rome as a client of the three Flavian emperors (Vespasian, Titus, and Domitian). He was granted Roman citizenship, an apartment in Vespasian‘s former mansion, and an annual pension for his literary endeavors (*Vita* 422-30). Under imperial patronage, Josephus composed *Bellum Judaicum* (The Jewish War), *Antiquitates judaicae* (Jewish Antiquities), *Vita* (Life), and *Contra Apionem* (Against Apion). See further Denis Lamour, *Flavius Josèphe* (Paris: Les Belles Lettres, 2000), 37-72.

biblical and Second Temple scholarship.[384] The writings of Josephus provide a vital

political, topographical, economic, social, intellectual, and religious supplement to

biblical information – crucial for comparing, interpreting, and extending our knowledge

of the times. Due to the sheer size of the Josephan oeuvre,[385] my focus will be on the

general content, form, and function of the texts (primarily *Antiquitates judaicae*) in

ascertaining Josephus' broad view of virtue and the emotions.[386] More specifically and

importantly, I will focus on how this view contributes to his rewritten portrayal of

biblical heroes, particularly Moses, which I can then compare with Philo (and perhaps

Luke) in content, form, and/or function.

Among those authors I have chosen in my examination of the emotions in

antiquity, Josephus is most similar to Luke in many ways. Josephus and Luke share the

---

[384] Robert A. Spivey, D. Moody Smith, and C. Clifton Black claim that Josephus' *Jewish Antiquities* ―is at once our best single historical source for the so-called intertestamental period and a monumental effort to make Jewish history intelligible to the wider world" in *Anatomy of the New Testament* (6th ed.; Upper Saddle River, N.J.: Pearson Prentice Hall, 2007), 45.

[385] Equally as impressive as the size of the Josephus corpus is its survival. The massive Josephan texts are preserved virtually in tact (with only a small string of verses missing in the *Antiquitates*). See especially Heinz Schreckenberg, *Die Flavius-Josephus-Tradition in Antike und Mittelalter* (Leiden: Brill, 1972). See also Folker Siegert, Heinz Schreckenberg, and Manuel Vogel, eds., *Flavius Josephus Aus meinem Leben (Vita): Kritische Ausgabe, Übersetzung und Kommentar* (Tübingen: Mohr Siebeck, 2001), 3-9.

[386] *Contra Apionem* and *Vita* will be used only as they elucidate elements of other texts or certain aspects of Josephus' life. Though beyond the scope, I side with those scholars who read *Contra Apionem* straightforwardly as a sequel to *Antiquitates judaicae* (*C. Ap.* 1.1-5), with common themes and similar language; see Heinz Schreckenberg, ―Text, Überlieferung und Textkritik von Contra Apionem," in *Josephus' Contra Apoinem: Studies in its Character and Context* (eds. Louis H. Feldman and John R. Levison; Leiden: Brill, 1996), 49-51; and Per Bilde, ―Contra Apionem 1.28-56: Josephus' View of His Own Work in the Context of the Jewish Canon" in *Josephus' Contra Apoinem*, 94-114. Pace S. J. D. Cohen, ―Respect for Judaism by Gentiles according to Josephus," *HTR* 80 (1987): 420-25; and Seth Schwartz, *Josephus and Judean Politics* (CSCT 18; Leiden: Brill, 1990), 54-6, esp. n.127. His complex and even contradictory personal life is of scholarly interest for many reasons, in particular his unique social status of being Jewish and a Roman citizen (even an imperial client).

same broad genre – apologetic historiography.[387] They were both heavily influenced by and quote Jewish scripture extensively. Josephus and Luke use similar conventions in their histories, including the use of prefaces (a common and important feature in ancient historical accounts) and extensive speeches for the leading characters.[388] They both have sequels which reference themselves (with additional prefaces). Luke and Josephus both have literary patrons who are dignitaries of some kind (Theophilus, Epephroditus) which they describe with similar language (Lk 1:3; *Vita* 430, *C. Ap.* 1.1). In fact, Josephus is unique in that all hermeneutical components (content, form, and function) correspond in some way to Luke. We can compare the content (how Josephus and Luke portray characters), the form (they both alter a previous text for their purposes – Luke redacts Mark, Josephus in *Antiquitates* rewrites or paraphrases the Jewish Bible), and the function (redactions to portray their Jewish heroes in a positive Greco-Roman light).[389]

---

[387] Gregory E. Sterling defines apologetic historiography as ‒the story of a subgroup of people in an extended prose narrative written by a member of the group who follows the group's own traditions but Hellenizes them in an effort to establish identity of the group within the setting of the larger world" in *Historiography and Self-Definition: Josephos, Luke-Acts and Apologetic Historiography* (Leiden: Brill, 1992), 17. Important also in this survey of certain Josephan (as well as Lukan) characterizations is the assertion of Arnaldo Momigliano that the distinction during the Hellenistic period between history and biography has been less than generally accepted in *The Development of Greek Biography* (Cambridge, Mass.: Harvard University Press, 1971), 1-7.

[388] Due to rhetorical training, these speeches often become the primary vehicle for conveying the authors' themes. The agenda of the authors is revealed through the voice of their characters. On speeches in Greco-Roman historiography see David E. Aune, *The New Testament in its Literary Environment* (Philadephia: Westminster, 1987), 91-93 and bibliography on 113-14. For Josephus' speeches in particular, see David E. Aune, ‒Josephus," 253-55, and for rhetorical speeches in Luke-Acts see ‒Luke-Acts," 281-88, both in *The Westminster Dictionary of New Testament and Early Christian Literature and Rhetoric* (Louisville: Westminster John Knox Press, 2003). See also the important work, Eduard Schweizer, ‒Concerning the Speeches in Acts," in *Studies in Luke-Acts* (eds. Leander E. Keck and J. Louis Martyn; Philadelphia: Fortress, 1980), 208-216.

[389] Though not as specifically related to my analysis of Josephus' view and depiction of the emotions as *Antiquitates*, the first of his literary efforts, *Bellum Judaicum*, is important in its parallel with what I have stated is Luke's broad agenda – to make his message, his gospel story, his non-emotional Jesus more amenable to a Greco-Roman audience. Josephus' Greek version of *Bellum* (the only extant version) was directed to a Greco-Roman readership, as an attempt to influence them positively in their perception of the Jews. In fact, the standard scholarly view for much of the twentieth century was that Josephus wrote *Bellum* as a lackey of the Romans, on retainer to quell any further revolutionary hopes. H. St. John

The *Antiquitates judaicae* (*Archaiologia* or ‑Ancient History") appeared some fifteen years after *Bellum Judaicum* was published. Josephus' longest and most complicated work, it provides a voluminous ‑introduction" to the Jewish War by presenting the whole panorama of Jewish history from creation and the patriarchs up to 62 C.E. and the ‑gathering war clouds of the Jewish revolt."[390]

While stating that historical accuracy was his central aim (similar to Luke's stated purpose in his preface, Lk 1:4), Jospehus also attempted to make his account acquiescent and entertaining:[391]

Thackeray, distinguished Josephus scholar and Loeb translator, concludes dismissively, ‑Josephus was commissioned by the conquerors to write the official history of the war for propagandistic purposes" in *Josephus: The Man and the Historian* (New York: Jewish Institute of Religion, 1929), 27.

While an in-depth discussion of this topic is beyond the scope, the cause of the war (which he attributed primarily to the Jewish revolutionaries and their demagogic leaders, whose subsequent internal strife also doomed Jerusalem, *B.J.* 1.9-10) was an important facet of his agenda in writing *Bellum*. Like Josephus, Luke must also show that his religion is not opposed to Roman order, although from a different perspective. Josephus had to account for the Revolt. Luke must explain why their leader was executed by the Roman Empire. *Indicium ne multa*: Luke presents the Roman authorities positively and friendly to the Jesus movement. Pilate emphasizes the innocence of Jesus (Lk 23:4, 14-15, 22), and puts the blame squarely on the Jewish authorities (Acts 2:23; 3:15; 4:10; 5:10). Whereas, for example, John's gospel blames the Jews for Jesus' death as a polemic after the Christian/Jewish divergence, I contend that Luke is primarily motivated (like Josephus) in making his religion congenial to his Greco-Roman audience. Further, *Bellum* is filled with philosophical themes (e.g., fate, free will, and providence) that were familiar to Hellenistic culture, and he often paused to reflect on current issues in historiography or Hellenistic philosophy; see Hadas-Lebel, *Flavius Josèphe*, 251. In the conclusion to his brief analysis of the Greek content, form, and function of *Bellum*, Steve Mason writes, ‑In short, the Greek War fits perfectly within the Greco-Roman literary context," in *Josephus and the New Testament*, 59.

[390] Maier, *Works of Josephus,* 11. Patterned after the twenty books of *Antiquitates Romanae* by Dionysius of Halicarnassus, *Antiquitates judaicae* was also written in twenty books, the first ten of which cover the period up to the Babylonian captivity, while the last ten encompass the return under Cyrus through the Second Temple and New Testament eras to the outbreak of the war. Scholars have termed the first ten of its twenty books ‑a complex example of rewritten Bible" (Aune, ‑Josephus," 253) or ‑expanded and embellished paraphrase" (Ben Zion Wacholder, ‑Josephus" in *The Oxford Companion to the Bible* (eds. Bruce M. Metzger and Michael D. Coogan; New York: Oxford University Press, 1993), 384).

[391] Especially through his importation of Hellenistic novelistic features, see discussion of Louis H. Feldman's analysis of the Josephan Hellenizations below. Luke-Acts has also been described by scholars as a Greco-Roman novel, see for example Richard I. Pervo, *Profit with Delight: The Literary Genre of the Acts of the Apostles* (Philadelphia: Fortress, 1987); and Susan M. Praeder, ‑Luke-Acts and the Ancient Novel," (SBLSP 20; Chico, Cal.: Scholars Press, 1981), 269-92. For a comparison of Acts to Greek romance novels see the interesting article Loveday Alexander, ‑In Journeying Often': Voyaging in Acts of the Apostles and in Greek Romance," in *Luke's Literary Achievement* (ed. C.M. Tuckett; *JSNTSup* 116;

For while the relation and the recording of events that are unknown to most people because of their antiquity require charm of exposition, such as is imparted by the choice of words and their proper arrangement and by whatever else contributes elegance to the narrative, in order that readers may receive such information with a certain degree of gratification and pleasure, nevertheless what historians should make their chief aim is to be accurate and hold everything else of less importance than speaking the truth to those who must rely upon them in matters of which they themselves have no knowledge. (*A.J.* 14.2-3)

In communicating to his Greco-Roman audience, *Antiquitates* draws heavily from the Septuagint, along with extrabiblical traditions and the writings of the Greek and Roman historians (such as Dionysius mentioned above).[392] Josephus also formulates his message, even within his Jewish apologetic (i.e., the antiquity and attractiveness of Judaism), in philosophical terms.[393] The thesis of *Antiquitates* contends:

But, speaking generally, the main lesson to be learned from history by any who care to peruse it is that men who conform to the will of God, and do not venture to transgress laws that have been excellently laid down, prosper in all things beyond belief, and for their reward are offered by God's happiness (εὐδαιμονία) whereas, in proportion as they depart from the strict observance of these laws, things

---

Sheffield: Sheffield Academic Press, 1995), 17-49. For a general introduction to the ancient novel see the excellent treatment by Thomas Hägg, *The Novel in Antiquity* (Berkeley: University of California Press, 1983). J.R. Morgan and R. Stoneman, eds., *Greek Fiction: The Greek Novel in Context* (London: Routledge, 1994) is a wide-ranging and stimulating collection of essays. Reinhold Merkelbach makes the still interesting thesis that all the ancient novels, Greek and Roman, were fundamentally religious narratives culminating in the achievement of salvation in *Roman und Mysterium in der Antike* (München: Beck, 1962).

[392] Some scholars downplay the significance of the LXX in Josephus' work, most notably Shaye J. D. Cohen, who argues Josephus often works from a Hebrew or Aramaic text observing that Josephus' paraphrase of the Bible bears little linguistic resemblance to the LXX in *Josephus in Galilee and Rome* (Leiden: Brill, 20002), 36. See further the introduction to *The Works of Josephus* (trans. William Whiston; Peabody, Mass.: Hendrickson, 1987), ix-x.

[393] Though *Antiquitates* is rightly recognized as having an apologetic purpose, Josephus' intentions are numerous and often complex. He was not a critical historian of the caliber of a Thucydides, and he shared with many ancient historians a propensity to exaggerate. *Antiquitates* is dedicated to Epaphroditus (as is *Vita* and *Contra Apionem*), who must have been a friend or patron. Unlike *Bellum*, it was not directly commissioned by the emperor, who is named only once – and thus it serves a less Rome-glorifying purpose.

practicable become impracticable, and whatever imaginary good thing they strive to do ends in irretrievable disasters (1.14).

Josephus argues that obedience to the Jewish law will result in happiness (*eudaimonia*), the recognized goal of philosophical schools in his day.[394]

In the preface to *Antiquitates* Josephus continues to present Judaism much more as a philosophy than as an ethnic cult.[395] He provides philosophical reflections on nature, reason, and law, which Josephus argues is entirely in keeping with the ―nature of the universe" (*A.J.* 1.25). He portrays key Judaic heroes including Abraham, Solomon, and Daniel, as philosopher exemplars, with Moses as the founding philosopher who drafted a constitution in accordance with natural law (*A.J.* 1-19-20). He describes the Pharisees, Sadducees, and Essenes as philosophic schools (*A.J.* 13.171-173; 18.12-18), even using the technical term for philosophical schools – *hairesis*. He compares the Essenes to Pythagoreans (*A.J.* 13.171) and the Pharisees to Stoics (*Vita* 12). The issues dividing the Jewish philosophical schools were the same as those dividing the Hellenistic ones – differences over their understanding of fate, free will, human nature, and the soul (*A.J.*

---

[394] For example, Epictetus, *Diatr*. 1.4.32, and especially Aristotle, who names *eudaimonia* as the main goal of philosophy. *Eth. nic.* 10.6.1. Later, Lucian brilliantly satirizes the philosophers' competing and contradictory recipes for *eudaimonia* (i.e. *Philosophies for Sale, Hermotimus*). See further H.F. Weiss, ―Pharisäismus und Hellenismus: zum Darstellung des Judentums im Geschichtswerk des jüdischen Historikers Flavius Josephus," *Orientalistische Literarzeitung* 74 (1979): 427-28. Though *eudaimonia* is missing from the Greek Bible, Josephus uses the word forty-seven times in his rewritten Bible to present Judaism not only as a philosophical option, but as the preferred option.

[395] Steve Mason asserts that Josephus construes Moses' laws within a Stoic framework. Mason's assertion is made primarily according to his understanding of the Stoic emphasis on a single unifying principle (usually Nature or Reason) in all of life in *Josephus and the New Testament*, 67. My contention is that while certainly *parts* of Josephus' massive corpus could be labeled Stoic, his work does not show a reliance on one tradition over another. For instance, Joseph Sievers argues that Josephus draws primarily on the Platonic tradition for his ontological views of the soul, immortality, and the afterlife in ―Josephus and the Afterlife" in *Understanding Josephus: Seven Perspectives* (ed. Steve Mason; JSPSup 32; Sheffield: Sheffield Academic Press, 1998), 20-34. I argue that Luke (being similar to Josephus in that he is not primarily a philosopher), however, *does* show a reliance on Stoicism over other philosophical traditions.

13.171-73).   He includes in his preface a series of rhetorical appeals directly to the

reader (*A.J.* 1.15):

> At the outset, then, I entreat (παρακαλῶ) those who will read these volumes to
> fix their thoughts on God and to test (δοκιμάξειν, ‒prove") whether our lawgiver
> has had a worthy conception of His nature (τὴν φύσιν ἀξίως αὐτοῦ
> καταενόησε) and has always assigned to Him such actions as befit his power,
> keeping his words concerning Him pure of that unseemly mythology current of
> others.

Josephus concludes his preface: ‒Should any further desire to consider the reasons for

every article in our creed, he would find the inquiry profound and highly philosophical"

(*A.J.* 1.25).[396]

Many scholars have systematically shown that Josephus has rewritten his source

material to convey the previously mentioned themes as Josephus sets forth in his

preface.[397] In his telling of Balaam for example, Josephus emphasizes the happiness of

the Judean nation; Balaam states that Judea is happier than all the other nations under the

sun (πάντων εὐδαιμονέστεροι τῶν ὑπὸ τὸν ἥλιον) because it alone has been granted

---

[396] Josephus employs his polemical contrast (σύγκρισις) over and against other traditions, not as a
member of a beleaguered community trying desperately to fend off slander, but as a fellow Roman making
a philosophical argument. Steve Mason summarizes, ‒This forthright challenge to discover for oneself the
superiority of the Judean constitution fits precisely with what we know of the implied reader via
Epaphroditus, with the paradigm of the LXX translation, and with Josephus' repeated claim that the Judean
laws bring happiness to anyone who follows them," in ‒The *Contra Apionem* in Social and Literary
Context: An Invitation to Judean Philosophy" in *Josephus' Contra Apoinem*, 200.

[397] The Josephan oeuvre is immense as is the secondary literature on Josephus' rewritten or
paraphrased Bible. See preliminarily Harold W. Attridge, *The Interpretation of Biblical History in the
Antiquities Judaicae of Flavius Josephus* (Missoula: Scholars Press, 1976); Thomas W. Franxman, *Genesis
and the "Jewish Antiquities" of Flavius Josephus* (Rome: Biblical Institute Press, 1979); Christopher T.
Begg, *Josephus' Account of the Early Divided Monarchy (Ant. 8, 212-420): Rewriting the Bible* (Leuven:
Leuven University Press, 1993); and especially Louis H. Feldman, *Studies in Josephus' Rewritten Bible*
(Leiden: Brill, 1998). Thus, my focus is necessarily on the previously mentioned *general* agenda and how
it corresponds to Luke's, but I will also analyze specific passages where Josephus rewrites a passage to
make it more compatible to his Greco-Roman audience, i.e. his retelling of the Korah pericope.

God's providence (πρόνοια) as an eternal guide (4.114). Louis H. Feldman espouses

that Josephus has hellenized the biblical narrative in three basic ways, which we could

also loosely apply (in varying degrees) to the Lukan texts.[398] Firstly, he imports

appropriate novelistic features including heroism, suspense, and romance.[399] Secondly,

Josephus cast the biblical characters in terms clearly redolent of classical models from

Euripides or Sophocles.[400] Thirdly, he ascribes to his heroes the four cardinal virtues of

wisdom, courage, temperance and justice, plus the additional (Jewish) virtue of piety.[401]

Since a full discussion of Josephan Hellenizations would be impossible, my brief

sojourn into *Antiquitates* will focus on Josephus' portrayal of key religious heroes

(especially Moses), and how his recast characterizations might compare with the Lukan

redactional agenda. Josephus paints portraits of religious leaders as typical national God-

---

[398] See any number of Feldman's works on Josephus and the major biblical characters over the past forty years, many of which are recast in the previously noted *Studies in Josephus' Rewritten Bible*. See specifically on the above over-arching methodological concerns ―Use, authority, and Exegesis of Mikra in the Writings of Josephus," in *Mikra: Text, Translation, Reading, and Interpretation of the Hebrew Bible in Ancient Judaism and Early Christianity* (ed. J. Mulder; Philadelphia: Fortress, 1988), 485-494. See also P. Villalba i Varneda, *The Historical Method of Flavius Josephus* (*ALGJ* 19; Leiden: Brill, 1986), 64-241; and Sterling, *Historiography*, 290-95.

[399] See ―Luke-Acts as novel" bibliography above. My view is that Acts in particular follows these conventions especially in its epic scale.

[400] As discussed in chapter one, Greg Sterling and John Kloppenborg examine the death of Jesus in Luke in light of Hellenistic noble death traditions, particularly in Luke's usage of Socrates as a model. Previously, I argued that the use of Socrates as an exemplar was as much a part of Middle Stoicism as it was Middle Platonism.

[401] Paul Spilsbury finds Feldman's argument that Josephus has invoked the four cardinal virtues ―unassailable in and of itself" and that Feldman ―is prone to over-play his hand in this regard" in *The Image of the Jew in Flavius Josephus' Paraphrase of the Bible* (Tübingen: Mohr Siebeck, 1998), 33. I maintain that Josephus is drawing on philosophical traditions in general (as noted above in response to Mason's Stoic contention, and contrary to my thesis that Luke is drawing upon specific Romanized Stoic traditions). I would therefore argue against a notion that Josephus is drawing upon specific Stoic traditions (which were the most popular) of the four cardinal virtues. The cardinal virtues were certainly a part of numerous traditions, and especially with the breakdown of traditional philosophical schools in Josephus time, I would contend, at least on the most general level, that Josephus does invoke the four cardinal virtues.

like heroes, such as were popular in antiquity, with emphasis (and often the previously mentioned theme of exaggeration)[402] on them as statesmen, philosophers, logicians, rhetoricians, scientists and romantic heroes.[403] Channeling Plato, Philo depicts Solomon, for example, as a philosopher as well as a king, ultimately becoming the wisest philosopher-king in history (8.42-50).

Using the model of Thucydides' Pericles,[404] Josephus depicts Abraham as an ideal statesman,[405] accentuating those attributes which would appeal to a Roman audience, such as persuasive speaking.[406] Thus, Josephus describes Abraham (1.154), not just as one possessing intelligence (δεινὸς ὢν συνιέναι) in all matters, but persuasive with his hearers (πιθανός τοῖς ἀκρωμένοις),[407] and not mistaken in his inferences, thus leading

---

[402] Exaggeration shows in Josephus' ebullient summary of David's career (8.390-91): ―He was a most excellent man and possessed of every virtue (ἀρετή) which should be found in a king entrusted with the safety of so many nations; there was no one like him for bravery (ἀνδρεῖος), and in the contests fought on behalf of his subjects, he was the first to rush into danger, encouraging his soldiers against the opposing lines by his labours in the fight, and not by commanding them like a master. He was also most apt in perceiving and understanding the course of future events and in dealing with the immediate situation, prudent (σώφρων), mild (ἐπιεικής), kind (χρηστὸς) to those in trouble, just (δίκαιος) and humane (φιλάνθρωπος), -- qualities which only the greatest kings are expected to have; and, with so great a measure of authority, never once did he do wrong, except in the matter of Uriah's wife. Moreover he left behind such wealth as no other king, whether of the Hebrews or other nations, ever did.

[403] Louis H. Feldman, *Judaism and Hellenism Reconsidered* (Leiden: Brill, 2006), 323.

[404] Thucydides, *History of the Peloponnesian War*, 2.60.

[405] For Thucydides' portrayal of Pericles as a statesman, see Arnaldo Momigliano, *The Classical Foundations of Modern Historiography* (Sather Classical Lectures 54; Berkeley: University of California Press, 1990), 39-52.

[406] Aristotle (*Rhet.* 1355a21) professes that those speaking the truth have an obligation to be persuasive. Cicero further asserts that oratory was a ―virtue" of the good person in *De oratore* 1.83; 3.65.

[407] ἀκροάομαι was a technical term associated with students who listen to lectures given in the philosophical schools, *BAGD* 31-33.

147

him to more lofty conceptions of virtue (φρονεῖν μεῖζον ἐπ' ἀρετῇ).[408] Through his

superior reasoning, Abraham was the first to conceive of God as one (1.156) and the first

to teach science to the Egyptians (1.167).[409] Beyond linguistic parallels, Abraham's

sophisticated teleological proof for the existence of God (1.156) from the irregularities of

the heavenly bodies is in the *form* of the proofs for the existence of God promulgated by

the Greek philosophical schools.[410] Josephus communicates through philosophical terms

and language (content) as well as philosophical forms reminiscent of important

philosophical discussions in order to communicate more effectively to his Greco-Roman

audience (function).[411]

---

[408] Though not a concept original with Josephus, he places great importance on Abraham as a philosophic innovator in astronomy and especially logic. See Pseudo-Eupolemus, *inter alios*, and most importantly, Philo, who depicts Abraham as a philosophical innovator in *De Abrahamo* 71-74.

[409] According to Josephus, Abraham's God (using language familiar to his Greco-Roman audience: Plato, *Leg.* 10.886a; and Aristotle in Sextus Empiricus, *Math.* 1.22) is the creator of the universe and is one. *Apocalypse of Abraham* (ch. 7), *Jubilees* (12.17), and the rabbinic sources (*Genesis Rabbah* 39) all emphasize the concept that Abraham arrived at the idea of monotheism through his own reasoning. In the rabbinic sources Abraham observed how the elements subdued each other in arriving at his proof. Josephus is distinct in that his Abraham inferred monotheism from the irregularities of heavenly bodies. See Louis Ginzberg, *The Legends of the Jews* (trans. Henrietta Szold; Philadelphia: JPS, 1952), 5.210 n.16; 217-18 n.49.

[410] Scholars debate the particular philosophical form of the passage. Feldman argues convincingly that Josephus is specifically combating a Stoic teleology though importantly shows the widespread philosophical concern for the topic in ―Abraham the Greek Philosopher in Josephus,‖ *TAPA* 99 (1968): 146-49. While the general philosophical content is important, I am using Josephus particularly to show a *form* and *function* similar to Luke, namely the redaction of previous source material to portray their Jewish heroes in a positive Greco-Roman light.

[411] At the conclusion to *Antiquitates,* Josephus proudly declares no one else, Jew or Gentile, could so accurately deliver these accounts to the Greek world (20.262).

The Josephan and Philonic redactions[412]

Since Josephus sought to present Moses in the highest possible light, we can extrapolate those qualities of virtue that were most important to Josephus. Moses is a wise philosopher,[413] a great orator (contrary to the biblical account), a superior general (e.g., an extended extrabiblical account of Moses' commanding of the Egyptian army against the Ethiopians, *A.J.* 2.238-53), the greatest prophet, the greatest lawgiver,[414] the most pious,[415] and most important in this perusal, had complete control of his passions. Josephus summarizes Moses' career in eulogy (4.328-331):

> He departed ... having surpassed (ὑπερβαλών) in understanding (συνέσει) all men that ever lived and put to noblest use the fruit of his reflections. In speech and in addresses to a crowd he found favour in every way, *but chiefly through his thorough command of his passions (τῶν παθῶν αὐτοκράτωρ), which was such*

---

[412] The Josephan redactions analyzed are found in *Antiquitates judaicae*; the Philonic redactions are found in *De vita Mosis*. Moses, though of course depicted as the epitome of virtue by Philo, is not described in the same idyllic totally perfect supersage manner in *Mosis* as he is in other texts (as noted above). *Mosis'* Moses is more realistic, and Philo keeps closer to the biblical text, probably due to the fact that *Mosis*, in a sense, serves as a type of official biography intended for a non-Jewish Greco-Roman audience. See discussion of audience above and further Samuel Sandmel, *Philo of Alexandria: An Introduction* (New York: Oxford University Press, 1979), 45-49.

[413] *A.J.* 3.66-74. Michael Hardwick argues convincingly that Eusebius drew heavily from Josephus' portrayal of Moses in his introduction of a thoroughly Hellenized portrait of Moses as preeminent philosopher and lawgiver into *Christian* literature in "Contra Apionem and Christian Apologetics" in *Josephus' Contra Apoinem*, 399.

[414] In his first reference to Moses in *Antiquitates* (1.6), without even naming him, Josephus refers to Moses as a lawgiver (νομοθέτης). Revealing of Josephus' agenda, Aaron's role is downgraded in the lawgiving process, not to denigrate Aaron but to elevate Moses. Josephus omits Aaron's presence at Sinai (Exod 24:1//*A.J.* 3.84). Compare further the following eulogy of Moses to the fact that Aaron is given no word of encomium in Josephus (Num 20:22-29; Deut 34).

[415] Εὐσέβεια is the fifth and most important cardinal virtue for Josephus. Moses is described as pious numerous times. In his very first mention of "the great lawgiver," Josephus states that it was in piety (εὐσέβεια) and in the exercise of the other virtues that the Israelites were trained under him (A.J. 1.6). Josephus asserts that once Moses had won their submission to the principles of piety (εὐσέβεια), he was able to persuade the Israelites of all the rest (1.21).

that he seemed to have no place for them at all in his soul (ψυχῇ), and only know their names through seeing them in others rather than in himself. As a general he had few to equal him, and as prophet none, insomuch that in all his utterances one seemed to hear the speech of God Himself. ...and never were Hebrews oppressed by grief so profound as that which filled them then on the death of Moses. Nor was he regretted only by those who had known him by experience, but the very readers of his laws have sadly felt his loss, deducing from these the superlative quality of his virtue (ἀρετῆς). He had few equals as a general and none as a prophet, to the extent that in all his pronouncements, one seemed to hear the voice of God himself. [emphasis added][416]

In Josephus' final tribute to Moses, Moses is eulogized as having had complete control of his emotions, as having irradiated them from his soul, which is certainly in line with the Stoic view of *apatheia*. However, Josephus' depiction of Moses throughout *Antiquitates* stresses the moderation (σωφροσύνη) of Moses (and even the moderation of the laws, *A.J.* 4.184), especially compared to other immoderate characters (e.g., Korah). Moderation of the emotions is more in line with Aristotle and the Peripatetics, which evidences my contention that Josephus did not rely on a single philosophical tradition, but used varying traditions generally in support of his overall agenda in writing his apologetic historiography. Similar to the Lukan redactional program concerning Jesus' emotions, the Josephan redactional paradigm consists of Josephus' *omitting* those narratives most troubling or most inconsistent with his perspective of virtue (e.g., the golden calf incident, Exod 32), and *rewriting* other biblical pericopae in light of his convictions regarding the emotions (e.g., Moses and the revolt of Korah, Num 16).

---

[416] Josephus, like Philo, depicts Moses as a Stoic-like sage in this, his final eulogy for Moses, but does not depict Moses as going to the extreme of sexual abstention, except for begetting children, that we find in Philo; see Feldman, *Philo's Portrayal of Moses*, 331-357.

While scholars have shown that Josephus is not fully consistent, Josephus has omitted many biblical texts of potential embarrassment, either to his Greco-Roman audience and/or the Jewish people.[417] This general principle of omission is similar to Luke's (albeit more consistent) redactional pattern of omitting emotions concerning the character of Jesus (which would have been embarrassing according to popular first-century Stoicism, upon which I argue Luke relies). Gone are the stories of Isaac's lie about Rebekah (Gen 26:6-11), Jacob's selective breeding of Laban's herd (Gen 30:35-43), Judah and Tamar (Gen 38), the circumcision of Zipporah's son (Exod 4:24-26), the slanders of Miriam (and her subsequent leprosy) and Aaron against Moses (Num 12),[418] Moses at Meribah (Num 20:2-13), the bronze serpent (Num 21:4-9), David's eating of the bread of presence (1 Sam 21:1-9; vv. 3-6 are omitted in *A.J.* 6.242-44).

Of particular interest to this analysis of the emotional portrayal of Moses is the Josephan omission of the narrative concerning Moses' slaying of the Egyptian (Exod 2:11-15). In the biblical version, not only does Moses kill an Egyptian who was beating a Hebrew, but he is described as ―afraid" (וַיִּרָא; ἐφοβήθη, v.14). Philo includes the incident,[419] but justifies Moses' slaying by stressing that the Egyptian was the most

---

[417] Shaye Cohen compares the Josephan omissions with the *Letter of Aristeas'* exclusions. He asserts Josephus *usually* omits long lists of Semitic names, incidents embarrassing (see above) or difficult (the mention of Goliath in 2 Sam 21:19), a few miracles which he thought a bit too much (the pillars of cloud and fire of Exod 13; Elijah's translation to heaven), though inconsistently does include Semitic lists (A.J. 1.79, 83-88; 2.4-6; 8.35-37), embarrassing incidents (kidnapping of Joseph, revolt of Korah), and fantastic miracles (Balaam's ass; Jonah and the fish) in *Josephus in Galilee*, 37.

[418] This narrative was perhaps omitted due to the troubling portrayal of Yahweh's anger against Aaron and Miriam (וַיִּחַר אַף יְהֹוָה בָּם; Καὶ ὀργῇ θυμοῦ Κυρίου ἐπ' αὐτοῖς, Num 12:9).

[419] Philo, somewhat surprisingly, describes Moses as ―grieved and indignant" (ἀθυμῶν καὶ δυσχεραίνων) in not being able to assist those oppressed before he slays the oppressor (*Mos.* 1.40).

violent of the oppressors and had persecuted many Hebrews to the point of death (*Mos.* 1.44).[420] Philo does omit the following episode of the story, that of the two Israelites fighting; hence he omits Moses' fear.[421]

Further, Philo not only lessens the actual biblical description of Moses' violent action and then justifies the action as being pious (εὐαγὲς, *Mos.* 1.44), but also emphasizes the contrast in virtue between Moses and the king (Pharaoh in the biblical text) through their differences in emotional disposition. The Hebrew Bible states pithily that the Pharaoh ―sought to kill Moses‖ (v.15); the account in Philo is expanded, primarily to compare the emotional temperaments of Moses and the king. The Philonic narrator first construes the king as ―very indignant‖ (ἠγανάκτει δεινὸν ἡγούμενος, 1.45),[422] then describes in detail his jealousy of Moses (1.45-48). While the king was deliberating,

> Moses was carrying out the exercises of virtue with an admirable trainer, the reason (λογισμὸν) within him… He was ever opening the scroll of philosophical doctrines, digested them inwardly with quick understanding… for he desired truth rather than seeming, because the one mark he set before him was nature's right reason (φύσεως λόγον), the sole source and fountain of virtues. (1.48)

---

[420] Feldman argues that a major reason for Philo's *inclusion* of this text is the tendency for Philo, wherever possible, to adhere to the biblical text, though doesn't account for Philo's omission of the following episode of the story, that of the two Israelites fighting (2:13-14).

[421] An interesting example of the difference between Philo's treatment of the same episode is provided by his interpretations of this passage (Exod 2:11-25) in *De vita Mosis* and *Legum allegoriae*. In *Leg.* 3.14 Philo explains allegorically that Moses' conflict with the Pharaoh was not with Pharaoh, but with his passions (τῶν παθῶν αὐτοῦ), and that he did not flee, but withdrew temporarily to renew the attack later with greater force. In *Mos.* 1.45 Philo rather presents two extra-biblical factors that led Moses to leave Egypt, namely the suggestions that Moses intended to seize power from the Pharaoh and the Pharaoh's anger that his own daughter's son utterly disagreed with him.

[422] The Lukan narrator (18:16) also omits Jesus' ἀγανακτέω (Mk 10:14), a common term for ―anger‖ or ―indignation.‖

152

Philo provides his auditors with an inclusio, concluding his comparison of Moses' and

the king's emotions with a description of the king as having "relentless wrath" (ὀργὴν

ἀμείλικτον, 1.49), while Moses is the epitome of calm.

Josephus and Philo both omit Moses' anger during the monitory to Pharaoh

concerning the final plague (Exod 11//*Mos.* 134). While warning Pharaoh of the

upcoming slaying of the firstborn, the Bible describes Moses' emotional state when

leaving as burning hot anger (בחרי-אף, Exod 11:8; LXX: μετὰ θυμοῦ, Exod 11:9).

Feldman contends that Philo removes Moses' anger "because a leader must exercise

greater self-control."[423] Feldman's contention is typical of what I have termed popular

Stoicism of the time period, especially in its Roman renderings, when "self-control"

receives greater emphasis in the philosophers and rhetoricians, particularly when they

write of the virtuous characteristics necessary in their civic leaders. Whereas

traditionally the emotions were viewed pejoratively primarily due to their irrationality, in

the Middle Stoicism of the first century expressly, the emotions were a sign of the lack of

self-control which was *de rigueur* for public figures of authority.[424]

The most famous incident of Moses' anger[425] (and perhaps Yahweh's as well) is

---

[423] Feldman, *Philo's Portrayal of Moses*, 365.

[424] Philo and Josephus both augment Moses' portrayal as an authority figure and leader, not just in terms of emotional disposition, but generally, in areas such as physical virility and organizational skills. Philo's Moses has more physical stamina compared to the biblical description of a decrepit leader who is barely able to hold up his hands (Exod 17:12//*Mos.* 1.218). Philo omits Jethro's organizational advice to Moses (Exod 18//*Mos.* 1.19). Philo's Moses has greater organizational responsibility with regard to the military, though, of course, he places less stress than Josephus on Moses' military ability; see above.

[425] See the numerous depictions of Moses' anger in the golden calf incident in a variety of popular art works throughout history, especially during the Italian Renaissance.

found in the biblical account of the golden calf (Exod 32). Moses is upon Sinai as the Israelites, led by Aaron, make and then offer sacrifices to a golden calf. Yahweh commands Moses to go down at once, ―Now let me alone, so that my wrath may burn hot against them (ויחר - אפי בהם; θυμωθεὶς ὀργῇ) and I may consume them; and of you I will make a great nation (v.10). Instead of immediately returning to camp, Moses coolly and rationally convinces Yahweh to change his mind:

> But Moses implored the Lord his God, and said, ―O Lord, why does your wrath burn hot [יתרה אפך; θυμοῖ ὀργῇ] against your people, whom you brought out of the land of Egypt with great power and with a mighty hand? Why should the Egyptians say, ‗It was with evil intent that he brought them out to kill them in the mountains, and to consume them from the face of the earth'? Turn from your fierce wrath [מחרון אפך; ὀργῆς τοῦ θυμοῦ]; change your mind and do not bring disaster on your people. Remember Abraham, Isaac, and Israel, your servants, how you swore to them by your own self, saying to them, ‗I will multiply your descendents like the stars of heaven, and all this land that I have promised I will give to your descendents, and they shall inherit it forever'." And the Lord changed his mind about the disaster that he planned to bring on his people. (11-14)

Ironically, after Moses soothes Yahweh's anger, he returns to the Israelite base, hears chanting, and speaks briefly with Joshua. As soon as he came near camp and saw the calf and the dancing, *Moses'* anger burned hot (ויחר אף משה; ὀργισθεὶς θυμῷ), and he threw the tablets from his hands and broke them at the foot of the mountain. He took the calf that they had made, burned it with fire, ground it to powder, scattered it on the water, and made the Israelites drink it (19-20). Now Moses is on the receiving end as Aaron pleads with Moses, ―Do not let the anger of my lord burn hot (אל-יחר אף אדני; μὴ ὀργίζου κύριε); you know the people, that they are bent on evil" (v.22). Unlike Yahweh

154

upon hearing Moses implorations, Moses does not change his mind upon hearing

Aaron's. Moses calls and then commands the clan of Levi:

> —Thus says the Lord, the God of Israel, _Put your sword on your side, each of you! Go back and forth from gate to gate throughout the camp, and each of you kill your brother, your friend, and your neighbor'." The sons of Levi did as Moses commanded, and about three thousand of the people fell on that day. (27-28)

The anger and violence (both from Moses the national hero and Yahweh the universal

God) would have been embarrassing to the Jewish people and troubling to the Romans,

so instead of radically rewriting the incident (as in the following Korah pericope),

Josephus omits the golden calf narrative altogether.

Philo, who, as previously noted, generally remains close to the biblical narrative,

includes a version of the golden calf episode that remains quite faithful to the text (Mos.

2.161-73). Philo omits some of the embarrassing details, both the problematic

theological issues (e.g., convincing Yahweh not to smite them all)[426] and the troubling

ethical depictions. He softens Moses' violent actions and his anger somewhat, but

certainly does not remove all of Moses' strong emotions or commands. In contrast with

his characterization of Moses as the paragon of *apatheia* in his other writings, Moses, in

de vita Mosis, is hardly an unperturbed supersage. Philo removes Yahweh's —burning

wrath" from his command to Moses (32:10)[427] and Moses' violent actions of breaking the

tablets, grinding the calf, and making the Israelites drink it (19-20). Philo omits Moses'

---

[426] Moses' success in changing Yahweh's mind is reminiscent of Abraham's argument with Yahweh concerning the wickedness of the Sodomites (Gen 18:22-33). In *Quis rerum divinarum heres sit* 16-29, Philo describes Moses as being on such close terms with Yahweh that he could be frank with Yahweh as no one else, yet in this episode, he omits this detail, rather than attempting a theologically complicated explanation.

[427] Philo does not have Yahweh explicitly threaten the Israelites through direct discourse as in the biblical text, though the narrator does make a later reference to Moses softening the —wrath of the Ruler" (2.166).

burning anger (v.19), but describes Moses' emotional disposition (2.166) as "dejection" (κατηφῶν) and then "ready to burst with dejection and heaviness" (κατηφείας, συννοίας), implying sorrow, shame, and anxiety.[428] Though Philo omits Aaron's plea to Moses, he does include perhaps the most troubling aspects – Moses commanding the Levites to slay 3000 Israelites, the Levites obeying, and Moses rewarding their "virtuous" deeds (2.171-73).

Along with eliminating numerous biblical stories seen by Josephus to be disconcerting and/or embarrassing according to his ethical viewpoint, especially concerning troubling biblical portrayals of emotion, Josephus has recast certain biblical stories according to his moral agenda. A prime example is the revolt and ultimate divine killing of Korah, Dathan, and Abiram (Num 16) – troubling for a Greco-Roman audience in a number of ways. Particularly disconcerting is the biblical presentation of Moses' (and Yahweh's) extreme anger which leads to Yahweh's definitive actions. Korah and his company complain about the central priestly authority located in Moses and Moses' nepotistic choosing of Aaron (16:1-3). Moses demands they make sacrifice to atone for their uprising and further summons Dathan and Abiram, who refuse his request. Moses becomes very angry (ויחר למשה מאד; καὶ ἐβαρυθύμησεν Μωυσῆς σφόδρα; v.15) and demands that Yahweh not accept their sacrifice. Yahweh refuses the sacrifice of the group and commands Moses and Aaron to separate themselves from the group so he can consume the congregation (20-21). Moses and Aaron petition Yahweh (v.22), "Shall one

---

[428] Κατηφέω / κατήφεια connotes depression (even to the point of muteness in some contexts) from horror or grief; σύννοια connotes anxiety, often with remorse, LSJ, 422; 777.

person sin and you become angry (תִּקְצֹף; ὀργή) with the whole congregation?" Their

petition is successful in the sense that Yahweh ultimately kills only the rebels and their

families (250 people) by fire and/or by being swallowed alive by the earth (23-35) as a

warning to the others. Yahweh's warning is not successful and on the next day the

congregation assembles against Moses and Aaron (41-42). There is no petition this time

around, and Yahweh kills fourteen thousand seven hundred, besides those who died in

the affair of Korah through a plague begat by divine wrath (הַקֶּצֶף, 16:46; ὀργή, 17:11).

Josephus rewrites this story in a number of ways to make it more congenial to his

audience. Josephus softens the tragedy and violence by adding the editorial comment

that one might commiserate with the victims (the 250) of the exhibition of God's mighty

power (thus also softening God's wrath), even stating that the victims were obliterated so

fast they felt no pain (*A.J.* 4.51-53). Further, the most important facet of Josephus'

editorial comments is that the lesson to be learned is moderation (σωφροσύνης, 4.49).[429]

Josephus omits entirely the second half of the pericope, the smiting through plague, in

which Yahweh kills over fourteen thousand.

Josephus heavily alters the depiction of the main characters' emotions. Korah in

particular is contrasted with Moses as one who is controlled by his emotions while Moses

is in control of his. Though not altogether free of anger (ἐζυβρισάντων, 4.14), Moses is

---

[429] Moderation (σωφροσύνης) is an important theme for Josephus, probably due to the fact that the Bible (Num 12:3) cites it as Moses' prime virtue; see Feldman, *Philo's Portrayal of Moses*, 249-50. σωφροσύνης is also used by Josephus to connote sexual chastity (*A.J.* 2.48; 18.180). Context provides clear distinction.

noticeably less angry. Moses' actions are less rash; and even when harsh, they are the result of deep rational thought. Moses' two long speeches (a typical Josephus *topos*) defend himself against false accusations and the coming violence in general, and appeal to justice and even providence (4.25-34; 40-50).[430] Josephus also stresses that Moses was not afraid despite all the circumstances (4.24). Like Moses', God's wrath is still seen, but it is justified (4.60).

Contrary to the moderated emotional presentation of Moses and Yahweh, Korah is portrayed as one who revolts with more intensity (his assemblies are presented with more potential violence, 4.22) and defiance to the laws, not on behalf of the people, but for his own gain (4.14-16). Korah has outrage (βιάζεσθαι, 4.16), is prone to violence (4.17), is full of malice (4.21), behaves disorderly with uproar (4.22), is impious (ἀσεβές, piety being a fifth cardinal virtue for Josephus, 4.31), and is especially seditious, unparalleled among the Greek or barbarians (4.12, 32). Josephus asserts that the basis of Korah's impious hostility was envy (4.14). Likewise, Dathan and Abiram are also portrayed as more violent and disobedient to the law (37-39). Even the congregating masses, which are ultimately spared in Josephus' version, assemble in disorderly fashion with clamor and uproar, and are hell bent on stoning Moses (4.22).

Philo gives less attention to the revolt of Korah than does Josephus because the contest was primarily between Korah and Aaron, with whom Josephus as a priest especially identified. Whereas Josephus compared the moderateness of Moses' disposition with the extreme passion of Korah, Philo says nothing about Korah at all,

---

[430] Moses is allowed to weep in order to persuade his audience during his second oration (*A.J.* 4.51).

158

nothing about his wealth, genealogy, or emotions; in fact, Philo doesn't even mention his name (in either major account, *Mos.* 2.174-79; 2.275-87). Philo is more concerned with refuting the charges and Korah's (the mob's) impiety, than with Moses' portrayal. While Philo, like Josephus, emphasizes Moses' mildness (πραότατος) and gentleness (ἡμερώτατος, *Mos.* 2.279), his overall portrayal of Moses is even more emotional than the original biblical source. Philo states that Moses was ―distressed" (ἀνιαθείς, 2.177) and ―greatly pained" (περιαλγήσας, 2.279). Moses' anger, though exonerated as legal and justifiable, is described in fervent terms; Moses' anger is certainly not eradicated or even controlled. Moses anger is described as justified (δικαίαν ὀργήν, 2.279) and his intense (ζέων, ―boiling" and πεπυρωμένος, ―inflamed") indignation lawful (νομίμου διαγανακτήσεως, 2.280). His emotions are the inspiration for his prophetic oracle explaining the coming destruction, which is even more violently limned than the biblical version.[431]

Similarly, in other narratives, Josephus either portrays Moses as moderate or emphasizes the importance of moderation through Moses' deeds and words. Though clearly upset by Zimri's brazen action in marrying a foreign wife, Josephus' Moses refuses to provoke him further (4.262). In an extrabiblical addition, Josephus, through Moses, emphasizes that the goal of the treatment of the rebellious son is that he should

---

[431] The account of the seditious leaders being swallowed up by the earth and burned alive by heavenly fire (Num 16:31//*Mos.* 282-87) is given a longer and more detailed treatment by Philo. It is important to note however, that Philo, like Josephus, omits the second judgment, in which Yahweh kills 14,700 people via a plague.

return to more moderate (σωφρονέστερον) ways (4.262). In his farewell address to the Israelites (4.184), he obliges them to follow the moderation (σωφροσύνη) of the laws and orderliness of the constitution.

Though Philo usually follows the biblical text closely in *de vita Mosis*, and therefore does not omit Moses' strong emotions and actions as often as Josephus, Philo often chooses simply to recast Moses as a model of Stoic-like patience, especially in pericopae where the biblical description of Moses *does not* include a passionate temperment. As noted above, Philo contrasts Moses' insouciant state with the strong emotions of his pursuer (the king after Moses justifiably slays the Egyptian oppressor, Exod 2//*Mos.* 1.44). In addition to this antithetical comparison, Moses' calm disposition is consistently contrasted with the querulousness of the Israelites. Beginning with his rewriting of the Red Sea crossing (Exod 14), Philo stresses Moses' halcyon constitution by expanding on the bitterness with which the Israelites complained on their sojourn. As the Egyptians pursued them, the Israelites complained to Moses:

> Was it because there were no graves in Egypt that you have taken us away to die in the wilderness? What have you done to us, bringing us out of Egypt? Is this not the very thing we told you in Egypt, ‑Let us alone, and let us serve the Egyptians?" For it would have been better for us to serve the Egyptians than to die in the wilderness. (14:11-12)

Philo includes these biblical verses, and simply expands the level of the Israelites' vociferousness, both in narrator description (‑panic-stricken;" ‑bitterness of their hearts;" ‑broken down;" ‑troubled," *Mos.* 1.170) and direct discourse:

> Was it because there were no tombs in Egypt where our dead bodies could be laid that you brought us out to kill and bury us here? Is not any slavery a light ill than death? You enticed this multitude with the hope of liberty, and then have saddled

160

it with the greater danger which threatens its life. Did you not know our unarmedness, and the bitterness and savage temper of the Egyptians? Do you not see how great are our troubles, how impossible to escape? What must we do? Can we fight unarmed against the armed? Can we fly, surrounded as in a net by merciless enemies, pathless deserts, seas impassable to ships, or, if indeed they are passable, what supply of boats have we to enable us to cross? (*Mos.* 1.171-72)

Despite their panic-stricken complaints, Moses –discoursed, still calm and composed" (*Mos.* 1.175).

Similarly, in the wilderness the Israelites complained to Moses concerning their hunger, –If only we had died by the hand of the Lord in the land of Egypt, when we sat by the fleshpots and ate our fill of bread; for you have brought us out into this wilderness to kill this whole assembly with anger" (16:3).[432] Philo again expands the carping of the Hebrews, while accentuating the serene demeanor of Moses. The Israelites were in –despair" and –despondency" (*Mos.* 1.192) and eventually –they were roused to anger" (1.193) clamoring:

We left the country in the hope of freedom, and yet we have no security even of life. Our leader promised us happiness; in actual fact, we are the most miserable of men. What will be the end of this long, interminable journey? Every traveler by sea or land has before him some goal to come to, market or harbour for the one, city or country for the other; we alone have before us a pathless wilderness, painful journeying, desperate straits. For, as we proceed, there opens out before us, as it were, an ocean, vast, deep, impassable, ever wider day by day. He exhorted and puffed us up with his words, and filled our ears with empty hopes, and then tortures our bellies with hunger, not providing even the barest nourishment. With the name of colonization he has deceived this great multitude, and first carried us from an inhabited to an uninhabited world, then led us on to the grave along the road which brings life to its end. (1.193-95)

---

[432] See also the previous incident when, –the people complained against Moses, saying, –What shall we drink?" (Exod 15:22). Philo, according to the proposed pattern, augments the biblical text with increased grumbling from the people. Philo uses narration to represent the emotional disposition in light of their physical thirst. The Israelites were –thoughtless," –of feeble piety," –engaged in lamentations," –weak," and –despondent" (*Mos.* 1.184-85). Philo concludes by stating that as soon as the people drank the formerly bitter water, the bitterness in their hearts also went away (1.186).

Moses responds with annoyance,[433] but Philo emphasizes that Moses was annoyed

(ἐδυσχέραινεν), not from the insulting slander against him as a personal emotional

response, but his δυσχέρεια was a type of vicarious emotional suffering on behalf of the

Israelites (1.196). While Josephus and especially Philo often describe Moses as

achieving the Stoic state of *apatheia*, in their specific revisions of the biblical text

(*Antiquitates judaicae*; *de vita Mosis*), they portray Moses in less idyllic terms,

emphasizing a Moses more in line with *metriopatheia*.

Conclusion

Philo, Josephus, and the author of 4 Macabees are perhaps the three most

important authors for my analysis of Luke, both for their chronological proximity as well

as their (re-)interpretations of the philosophic tradition in light of Judaism. They serve as

salient agnates to Luke in the sense that they also have rewritten their religious traditions

with the purpose of making them more acquiescent to a Roman milieu. Other Hellenistic

Jewish texts such as *Joseph and Aseneth* and Pseudo-Phocylides also offer valuable

insight into the period, especially with their emphasis on self-control, and their varying

takes on moderation.

Philo is particularly important among the philosophers for my goal of attempting

to answer why Luke has removed Jesus' emotion. Philo not only discusses the emotions

---

[433] Colson translates ‑indignation" and Yonge renders ‑grieved." I prefer annoyed, as δυσχεραίνω
seems to connote a certain frustration or displeasure; see LSJ, 217.

as a philosophical *topos*, but we actually see his philosophical emotional theories in practice through his portraits of key biblical characters. Philo's treatment of the emotions can generally be described as a Stoic ethic within a Platonic psychological framework. Abraham, Isaac and Jacob, represent three distinct types toward the ideal of *apatheia*, with Isaac a symbol of virtue and perfection. Philo consistently portrays Moses as having eradicated all passion, with no pain or toil (*aneu ponou, apatheia*), as compared to Aaron, whose prescription is *metriopatheia*, representing one who is "making moral progress" (*prokoptōn*).

The book of 4 Maccabees is a philosophic treatise lauding the preeminence of religious or pious reason in overcoming the emotions, as exemplified by the martyrs' apathic-like ability to over their emotions even under traumatic circumstances. For the author of 4 Maccabees, the emotions are irrational and provisional, common objections found throughout the philosophical traditions. As in most of the material analyzed, reason (in this case, that of the religious variety) should be the master of the passions. Qualities associated with reason as the highest good include manliness, justice, and particularly self-control, which was stressed as virtuous most notably for public figures of authority in first century Stoicism.[434]

Philo and 4 Maccabees, despite their similarities, represent different perspectives on self-mastery. Philo, who (usually) has a Platonic tripartite understanding of the human soul, suggests that moral perfection consists in a complete elimination of the diseased *pathē*. But since *apatheia* is very rare, the vast majority of humans will spend their lives struggling to control their passions by right reason. Adducing moral exemplars

---

[434] 4 Maccabees also gives us further evidence of the negativity towards both the "positive" and "negative" emotions, which was characteristic of Middle Stoicism; see chapter two.

from Hellenistic philosophy and the Jewish scriptures (and even the ascetic communities of his day), Philo offers an adaptable ascetic program which acknowledges that some persons go further in moral advancement than others. The author of 4 Maccabees, on the other hand, while not presenting the passions as being entirely rooted out or even using the term *apatheia*, suggests that complete mastery over the passions is possible for anyone who is willing to obey the law. As a rhetorical tractate with many encomiastic features, there is no program of asceticism prescribed in 4 Maccabees. Alternatively, we have a highly idealized account of Jewish heroes who experience complete freedom from their passions, especially pleasure and pain, through their resolute obedience to the commandments of God.

Through additions, omissions, and rewrites, Josephus presents major biblical heroes and important biblical narratives in a more congenial manner to a Roman world. He relies on Hellenistic conventions within the genres of history and philosophy, appealing to various traditions in general ways (contra Luke). He is often not consistent in his omissions and additions, which would support the view that he is not beholden to a specific philosophical tradition. In his encomium, Josephus argues that Moses had eradicated the emotions from his soul in line with the Stoic *apatheia*. However, in his portrayal of Moses in *Antiquitates judaicae*, Josephus emphasizes the moderation (σωφροσύνη) of Moses more in line with Aristotle and the Peripatetics. Josephus does omit material that Romans might find generally embarrassing, and though he does not *consistently* remove emotion from his heroes' accounts, he often softens it.[435]

---

[435] In fact some scholars have pointed out that Josephus himself shows less emotion that many of his characters, even when describing horrendous acts of war. When commenting on Josephus' language in *Bellum* 8.148 concerning the destruction of the Temple by the Romans, Hadas-Lebel observes, ―Quels

There is universal agreement among scholarship that the most lauded biblical hero for Philo is Moses. There is further agreement that the portrayal of Moses in the Philonic oeuvre is of a sage who has completely conquered his emotions without toil (*aponia*), seen further in his comparison with Aaron's *metriopatheia*. Somewhat contrarily,[436] Philo's Moses in *de vita Mosis*, retains many of his strong emotions as found in the biblical text, and is sometimes shown as having even stronger emotion in *Mosis*. While omitting some troubling and/or embarrassing pericopae or parts of pericopae, Philo more often recast his Moses as one of moderation, especially as compared with his kingly pursuer's strong emotion and the Israelites' complaining.

---

furent ses sentiments quand il vit apparaître ensuite les dépouilles prises aux Juifs et notamment le mobilier du Temple? Aucune emotion ne perce dans son récit quand il énumère celui-ci." in *Flavius Josèphe*, 215.

[436] It seems to me the best explanation is that Philo is greatly concerned with remaining true to the biblical text.

CHAPTER 4

LUKE'S REDACTIONS OF MARK:

THE CHARACTER OF JESUS

The Lukan Portrait of Jesus

> [Portraits] give life to historical persons, freed from the bonds of mortality.
> Portraits stock the picture galleries of my memory with the vivid images of
> people, once known or previously unknown, now registered, preserved, and
> accessible though works of art that have become momentarily transparent. It is as
> if the art works do not exist in their own material substance but, in their place, real
> persons face me from the other side or deliberately avoid my glance.[437]

Donald Capps incorporates this famous Richard Brilliant quote to also include

biographical portraits, specifically in the context of recent attempts by biblical scholars to

shed new light on biblical personages.[438] Capps replicates the social scientific language

of Bruce J. Malina and Jerome H. Neyrey, and more relevant to his psychological

biographical reconstruction of Jesus, he echoes the many historical Jesus scholars who

use the word ―portrait."[439] After assimilating Brilliant's (and Wendorf's[440]) scholarship

---

[437] Richard Brilliant, *Portraiture* (Cambridge: Harvard University Press, 1991), 7.

[438] Donald Capps, *Jesus: A Psychological Biography* (St. Louis, Miss.: Chalice Press, 2000), 3.

[439] Capps, *Jesus,* 3. See Malina and Neyrey, *Portraits of Paul*; Marcus J. Borg, ―Portraits of Jesus" in
Jesus in Contemporary Scholarship (Valley Forge, Penn.: Trinity, 1994); and Mark Allan Powell, *Jesus as
a Figure in History: How Modern Historians View the Man from Galilee* (Louisville: Westminster John
Knox, 1998).

on portraiture, Capps reviews and assesses critically the "renaissance" in historical Jesus studies en route to offering his own "portrait" of Jesus. Capps states, "Each portrait or Gestalt is interesting in its own right as a construal of the traditions about Jesus."[441] He further asserts:

> A portraitist's decision *whether or not to incorporate a given image* is an important statement about who the portraitist understands Jesus to have been. A related, underlying assumption is that Jesus' identity was complex, that it is unlikely that he was a unidimensional figure. The more of such images an author incorporates into his "overall portrait," the more complex the portrait becomes, especially if one or more of these images appears not only to complement another image, *but stands in some sense or degree in conflict with it.* [emphasis added][442]

While Capps puts forward his theories in reference to current historical Jesus reconstructions as "portraits" with the Jesus scholars as portraitists, I propose that we see the third evangelist in the same way: as one of many portraitists whose gospel was his ancient canvas. I thus turn to the Lukan Gestalt of Jesus, especially in his decisions of what to incorporate of the Markan one.[443]

---

[440] Richard Wendorf, *The Elements of Life: Biography and Portrait-Painting in Stuart and Georgian England* (Oxford: Clarendon, 1990), 6-11.

[441] Capps, *Jesus*, 5.

[442] Ibid.,7.

[443] Determining the thought or theology of an evangelist is "notoriously difficult," as stated by Stephen Moore, *Literary Criticism and the Gospels: The Theoretical Challenge* (New Haven: Yale University Press, 1989), 61-62. My analysis of the characterization of Jesus in Luke is greatly advantaged by the availability of a source with which to compare Luke. Hence my methodology is primarily that of redaction criticism with the admitted problems and limitations as stated briefly in the introduction. See further Paul Borgman, *The Way according to Luke: Hearing the Whole Story of Luke-Acts* (Grand Rapids, Mich.: Eerdmans, 2006), 5-7. My analysis follows the redactional critical methodology as developed by scholars such as Joel B. Green, "Preparation for Passover (Luke 22:7-13): A Question of Redactional Technique," in *The Composition of Luke's Gospel: Selected Studies from "Novum Testamentum"* (ed. David E. Orton; Leiden: Brill, 1999); Fitzmyer, *Luke*; Jan Lambrecht, *The Sermon on the Mount: Proclamation and Exhortation* (GNS 14; Wilmington, Del.: Michael Glazier, 1985); Helmuth L. Egelkraut, *Jesus' Mission to Jerusalem: A Redaction Critical Study of the Travel Narrative in the Gospel of Luke, Luke 9:51-19:48* (Frankfurt: Peter Lang, 1976); Tim Schramm, *Der Markus Stoff bei Lukas: Eine literarkritische und redaktionsgeschichtliche Untersuchung* (NTSMS 14; Cambridge, University Press,

Luke's Redactional Program

A great many scholars begin their study of Luke by comparing his Gospel to that of Mark, noting what has been changed, and asking ―why?"[444]

As stated in the general introduction, and examined in detail in the *status quaestionis,* scholars such as Sterling, Neyrey, and Kloppenborg have shown important redactional changes concerning Jesus' emotions with respect to *specific* Lukan scenes including the Garden of Gethsemane, the trial of Jesus, and the death of Jesus. I argue that these specific scenes are part of a larger redactional pattern. In the characterization of Jesus, I will show that Luke has *consistently* removed strong emotion (and the actions which would result from these strong emotions) from Mark. These redactions of the emotional persuasion include the traditionally-viewed negative emotions grief, neediness, stern speech, and especially anger. They also include some of the more positively viewed emotions including compassion, love, and general affection.[445]

"Negative" Emotions

Anger/Indignation

Mark 3:5	Luke 6:10	Luke removes anger from Jesus
Mark 10:14a	Luke 18:16	Luke removes anger/indignation from Jesus
Mark 11:15-16	Luke 19:45	Luke removes Jesus' angry and violent actions

Anger / Stern Speech

Mark 1:43-44	Luke 5:14a	Luke softens tone of Jesus' speech
Mark 3:12	Luke 6:19/4:41	Luke removes Jesus' harsh speech

1971); and Henry J. Cadbury, ―Four Features of Lucan Style," *Studies in Luke-Acts: Essays Presented in Honor of Paul Schubert* (ed. Leander E. Keck and J. Louis Martyn; Nashville: Abingdon Press, 1966).

[444] Mark Allan Powell, *What Are They Saying about Luke*, 20.

[445] The Lukan redactions concerning these so-called ―positive" emotions are vital because they speak to Luke's overall philosophical presentation of Jesus, which I argue is more in line with the Stoic ideal *apatheia,* as opposed to a less stringent alternative such as *metriopatheia.*

Mark 5:19a	Luke 8:38b	Luke softens tone of Jesus' speech
Mark 5:40,43	Luke 8:53,56	Luke removes Jesus' harsh speech, Luke softens tone of Jesus' speech
Mark 6:8a	Luke 9:3a	Luke removes harsh tone of Jesus' speech
Mark 9:9	Luke 9:36	Luke removes Jesus' admonition to the disciples
Mark 8:30	Luke 9:21	Luke softens tone of Jesus' command
Mark 8:32-33	Luke 9:22	Luke removes Jesus' stern speech and harsh rebuke
Mark 11:14	Luke 13:6-9	Luke removes Jesus' cursing of the fig tree

Grief / Sadness

Mark 2:25a	Luke 6:3a	Luke removes Jesus' "emotional" neediness
Mark 3:5a	Luke 6:10a	Luke removes Jesus' state of grief
Mark 8:12a	Luke 11:16/12:54	Luke removes sadness or anger from Jesus[446]

"Positive" Emotions

Compassion / Mercy

Mark 1:41	Luke 5:13	Luke removes Jesus' compassion
Mark 6:34	Luke 9:11a	Luke removes Jesus' compassion and sentimentality
Mark 5:19-20	Luke 8:39	Luke removes Jesus' self-described mercy

Love / Affection

Mark 10:21	Luke 18:22	Luke removes Jesus' love
Mark 9:36	Luke 9:47-48	Luke removes Jesus' signs of affection
Mark 10:15-16	Luke 18:17	Luke removes Jesus' signs of affection

---

[446] I do not include this pericope of the Pharisees seeking a sign (Mark 8:11-13//Luke 11:16, 12:54-56) as primary evidence for the proposed pattern. Along with most scholars, I do not view it as a true parallel (though it is listed in *Synopsis Quattuor Evangeliorum* as no. 154, pp. 225-26), as it is part of the block of texts termed "the great omission" or "big omission." At the very least it demonstrates Mark's Jesus as showing strong emotion. Mark characterizes Jesus (8:12) as "καὶ ἀναστενάξας τῷ πνεύματι," ("sighed deeply in his spirit"), implying being disturbed, troubled, and upset; see "ἀναστενάζω," *BAGD*, 61. See also Mark 7:34, "Then looking up to heaven, he sighed (ἐστέναξεν) and said to him" (7:34a). See further Cadbury, *Style and Literary Method*, 96.

The above list constitutes a summary of my textual analysis of the Lukan redactions (not including the previously discussed passion pericopae) to be examined in detail with respect to two redactional lists put forward by two prominent scholars – Henry Cadbury and Joseph Fitzmyer. Henry Cadbury includes almost all of these in his indispensable tabulation.[447] Cadbury does not include the narrative of Jesus plucking grain on the Sabbath (Mark 2:25a//Luke 6:3a). Many scholars also reject this pericope as evidence of an *emotional* redaction and see it instead as a story of physical neediness (see analysis below). Cadbury does not include four of the above listed parallels of Luke's linguistic choices concerning Jesus' speech: Jesus' harsh command to the unclean spirits (Mark 3:12//Luke 6:19), Jesus' harsh command to the Gerasene Demoniac (Mark 5:19a//Luke 8:38b), Jesus' harsh command in the commissioning of the twelve (Mark 6:8a//Luke 9:3a), and Jesus' admonition to the disciples (Mark 9:9//Luke 9:36).[448]

Joseph Fitzmyer also includes a similar list of emotional redactions, which are discussed in light of six general Lukan redactional principles he has proposed.[449] (1) Luke frequently improves the Greek style and language of the Markan stories.[450] (2) Luke often abbreviates Markan narratives, especially parables. (3) Certain episodes considered duplicates by Luke are omitted from his Markan material. Fitzmyer continues:

Fourth, Luke deliberately omits from his source-material what does not contribute

---

[447] Cadbury, *Style and Literary Method*, 90-96.

[448] He does include Jesus' stern speech and harsh rebuke of/by Peter (Mark 8:32b-33//Luke 9:22) in his list of redactions, though oddly, he later includes a section of Lukan changes in Markan speech patterns, though these are not included, Cadbury, *Style and Literary Method*, 100-101.

[449] Fitzmyer, *Luke I-IX*, 92-97.

[450] See further ibid., 107-8.

to the over-all literary plan that he imposes on the story of Jesus. His depiction of Jesus as preoccupied with Jerusalem as a city of destiny and his concern to move Jesus resolutely toward it result in the omission of geographical designations and certain episodes that are explicitly located in Mark.[451]

Fitzmyer explains the ―Big Omission" (Mark 6:45-8:26) by this Lukan redactional principle.[452] (5) Likewise, he also explains the transposition of some Markan material by Luke's literary concerns.[453]

Most important for this study, Fitzmyer concludes his examination of Luke's redactional principles with a discussion of the violent and emotional alterations to the Markan source, ―Sixth, certain redactional modifications of the Marcan source material can be seen to stem from a delicate sensitivity which tends to make Luke eliminate anything that smacks of the violent, the passionate, or the emotional."[454] Fitzmyer gives six examples of Luke softening or eliminating violence from his source:

1.) Mark 6:17-29//Luke 3:19-20   The imprisonment of John the Baptist
(recounted as the summation of Herod's evil;
we learn of John's death subsequently in 9:9)

2.) Mark 3:21//Luke omits   Jesus' relatives (*hoi par' autou*) want to take hold of him, thinking him to be beside himself

3.) Mark 11:15b-16//Luke 19:45   The violent details of Jesus' purging of the Temple

4.) Mark 14:62-65//Luke 22:70   The striking of Jesus at the interrogation of the Sanhedrin (but cf. Luke 22:63-64)

---

[451] Ibid., 94.

[452] This is relevant as an important emotional redaction is found in the pericope of the Pharisees seeking a sign (Mark 8:11-13//Luke 11:16, 12:54-56); see further above.

[453] See further ibid., 71-72.

[454] Ibid., 94.

| 5.) Mark 15:15//Luke 23:16,22,25 | The scourging of Jesus becomes a mere suggestion |
| 6.) Mark 15:16-20//Luke omits | The crowning with thorns and mockery of Jesus[455] |

Fitzmyer's third example is the only one that actually refers to *Jesus'* actions and is included in my list. Four of the examples (2, 4, 5, 6) are evidence of a type of corollary to my proposed redactional theorem that Luke has consistently removed strong emotion from the character of Jesus. These four examples point to a redactional maxim that violence and strong emotion *to* Jesus are often omitted or softened by Luke.[456] The example of John the Baptist is the only one given to support his broad thesis that Luke has eliminated ―*anything* that smacks of the violent, the passionate, or the emotional" [emphasis added].[457] I will present evidence that repudiates this broad generalization in chapter five, as I maintain Fitzmyer's contention is true only for the character of Jesus.[458] Fitzmyer's thesis is only true concerning the emotions and the emotional violence

---

[455] Ibid., 94-95.

[456] Though space does not permit an in-depth analysis, I do accept this redactional principle. In addition to the above pericopae, the disciples' accusation of Jesus' lack of concern (Mark 4:38//Luke 8:24) fits this principle. See also the following discussion of Luke's omission of Peter's rebuke of Jesus followed by Jesus' rebuke of Peter, who is ultimately called Satan (Mark 8:32b-33).

[457] There is a further broad principle (though not to the degree of Jesus' actions and actions to Jesus) that Jesus' harsh *teaching* in Mark is mitigated by Luke, and exacerbated in Matthew. Characteristic of the latter two writers is Luke's complete omission of Mark's stern passage (9:43-47) about cutting off the offending hand (v.43) or foot (v.45) and casting out the offending eye (v.47), while Matthew actually uses it twice (18:8-9; 5:29-30). This principle is generally true for ―Q" material as well. See the foundational essay H.G. Wood, ―Some Characteristics of the Synoptic Writers" in *The Parting of the Roads: Studies in the Development of Judaism and Early Christianity* (ed. F.J. Foakes-Jackson; London: Edward Arnold, 1912), 134-171, esp. 160-170.

[458] Luke often keeps the emotions (and violence) of the characters other than Jesus, including those seen as favorable (e.g. the women at the tomb), unfavorable (Jewish authorities), and mixed/neutral (e.g. disciples, crowd/people). A secondary, but important, related Lukan theme is the portrayal of the disciples, especially the oft-noted ―rehabilitation" of Peter many commentators propose. Therefore, in relevant pericopae, the disciples' depiction will be given serious consideration.

exhibited by Jesus (the main thesis of this dissertation) as well as the emotion showed and violence done *to* Jesus (a corollary to the main thesis).

With regard to the emotional portrayal of Jesus, Fitzmyer makes a contention similar to my overall thesis, ―Similarly [to the list of redactions concerning violence], the description of Jesus moved by human emotions in the Marcan Gospel is normally eliminated in the Lucan story, even if they are expressions of *love, compassion, or tenderness.* [emphasis added]"[459] Fitzmyer's list of Luke's redactions is quite similar to Cadbury's list.[460] Like Cadbury, he does not include the speech redactions of Jesus' harsh command to the unclean spirits (Mark 3:12//Luke 6:19), Jesus' harsh command to the Gerasene Demoniac (Mark 5:19a//Luke 8:38b), Jesus' harsh command in the commissioning of the twelve (Mark 6:8a//Luke 9:3a), or Jesus' admonition to the disciples (Mark 9:9//Luke 9:36), but (like Cadbury) does emphasize the Lukan omission of Jesus' stern speech and harsh rebuke of Simon Peter (Mark 8:32b-33//Luke 9:22). Fitzmyer rejects Cadbury's inclusion of the cursing of the fig tree (Mark 11:12-14//Luke 13:6-9).[461]

The Lukan redactions concerning Jesus' emotion are sometimes meager and often

---

[459] Fitzmyer's important recognition of Luke's removal of these ―positive" emotions is vital to my broad thesis that Luke's redactions are typical of first century Stoicism (*Luke I-IX*, 95). See further chapter two.

[460] Fitzmyer seems to have relied heavily on Cadbury in his analysis of the Lukan redactions in general. Though not cited directly (as he does, for example, Talbert's *Literary Patterns, Theological Themes, and the Genre of Luke-Acts* one paragraph later), he does state (96), ―For further details in this sort of study of Luke's use of his sources, see H. J. Cadbury, *Style and Literary Method*, 73-205," near the end of his ten-plus page analysis, though it is difficult to determine if Fitzmyer cites Cadbury generally on the Lukan redactions or specifically for the questionable (from a text-critical viewpoint) verses about the so-called bloody sweat (Luke 22:43-44); see *status quaestionis*.

[461] In his introduction to Luke via a survey of scholarship, Mark Allan Powell (along with my analysis) broadly accepts Fitzmyer's redactions, though questions the particulars of his explanations (i.e., detracting from Jesus' nobility and Luke's aversion to describing violence) in *What Are They Saying about Luke*, 19-20.

subtle. Further, there are often multiple factors contributing to these Lukan changes, not just emotional considerations. Thus it is important to show the consistency and pervasiveness of the pattern, because individually, all of the pericopae listed above have numerous possible interpretations and show evidence of divers Lukan themes and conventions. The –cleansing" of the Temple (Luke 19:45-46//Mark 11:15-17) is a great example of Luke removing problematic angry actions on the part of Jesus, and thus provides strong evidence for the proposed pattern. But since this pericope is important to Luke for a wide variety of reasons,[462] I will rely on the ubiquitous weight of the textual evidence.

Anger[463]

47. The Man with the Withered Hand

Mark 3:4-5[464]	Luke 6:9-10
καὶ λέγει αὐτοῖς	εἶπεν δὲ ὁ Ἰησοῦς πρὸς αὐτούς
ἔξεστιν τοῖς σάββασιν	ἐπερωτῶ ὑμᾶς εἰ ἔξεστιν τῷ σαββάτῳ
ἀγαθὸν ποιῆσαι ἢ κακοποιῆσαι,	ἀγαθοποιῆσαι ἢ κακοποιῆσαι,

---

[462] Many commentators correctly point out themes of eschatology, soteriology, and history, to name but a few, which are mostly beyond the scope of this examination. See analysis below and preliminarily Hans Conzelmann, *Die Mitte Der Zeit* (Tübingen: Mohr Siebeck, 1953); Marshall, *Gospel of Luke*; Donald Juel, *Luke-Acts: The Promise of History* (Atlanta: John Know, 1983).

[463] In my examination into the Lukan emotional redactions, I proceed in rough chronological order and by category beginning with the most commonly redacted emotion – anger. The word(s) underlined in red indicate material omitted in Luke's version; dashed underlined in blue indicates emotion transferred from Jesus to another person or group; double-underlined in green indicates the omission or lessening of violence or emotion *to* Jesus; *italicized in orange* indicates a different word choice; waved underline in purple indicates emotional special –L" material.

[464] All Greek texts and parallel numbers/titles are taken from Kurt Aland, *Synopsis Quattuor Evangeliorum* (13th revidierte Auflage; Stuttgart: Deutsche Bibelgesellschaft, 1985), based on the Greek text of Nestle-Aland 26th edition. All English translations are mine (based on the NRSV), unless otherwise noted.

ψυχὴν σῶσαι ἢ ἀποκτεῖναι;	ψυχὴν σῶσαι ἢ ἀπολέσαι;
οἱ δὲ ἐσιώπων.	
καὶ περιβλεψάμενος αὐτοὺς	καὶ περιβλεψάμενος πάντας αὐτοὺς
μετ᾽ ὀργῆς,	
συλλυπούμενος ἐπὶ τῇ πωρώσει	
τῆς καρδίας αὐτῶν,	
λέγει τῷ ἀνθρώπῳ	εἶπεν αὐτῷ
ἔκτεινον τὴν χεῖρα.	ἔκτεινον τὴν χεῖρα σου.
καὶ ἐξέτεινεν,	ὁ δὲ ἐποίησεν,
καὶ ἀπεκατεστάθη ἡ χεὶρ αὐτοῦ.	καὶ ἀπεκατεστάθη ἡ χεὶρ αὐτοῦ.
καὶ ἐξεθόντες οἱ φαρισαῖοι	αὐτοὶ δὲ
εὐθὺς μετὰ τῶν Ἡρῳδιανῶν	**ἐπλήσθησαν ἀνοίας,**
συμβούλιον ἐδίδουν κατ᾽ αὐτοῦ,	καὶ διελάλουν πρὸς ἀλλήλους
ὅπως αὐτὸν ἀπολέσωσιν.	**τί ἂν ποιήσαιεν τῷ Ἰησοῦ.**

The most common emotion the Lukan redactor has omitted from Jesus' character is anger.[465] In a scene at the synagogue (Mark 3:1-6//Luke 6:6-11), the scribes and Pharisees were watching Jesus to see if he would heal on the Sabbath. In a close linguistic parallel, Jesus asks them if it is lawful to heal on the Sabbath, to do good or harm, save life or kill (Mark 3:4//Luke 6:9). Then the Markan account (3:5) states, καὶ περιβλεψάμενος αὐτοὺς *μετ᾽ ὀργῆς, συλλυπούμενος ἐπὶ τῇ πωρώσει τῆς καρδίας αὐτῶν,* λέγει τῷ ἀνθρώπῳ ἔκτεινον τὴν χεῖρα. καὶ ἐξέτεινεν, καὶ ἀπεκατεστάθη ἡ χεὶρ αὐτοῦ. The Lukan redaction (6:10) simply reads, καὶ περιβλεψάμενος πάντας

---

[465] Luke never uses ὀργή/ ὀργίζεσθαι of Jesus, whose calmness in this pericope in particular, contrasts sharply with his opponents' ἄνοια; see further Goulder, *Luke: A New Paradigm* I, 339.

αὐτοὺς εἶπεν αὐτῷ ἔκτεινον τὴν χεῖρα σου. ὁ δὲ ἐποίησεν, καὶ ἀπεκατεστάθη ἡ χεὶρ αὐτοῦ. Luke omits the narrator's "with anger" (μετ᾽ ὀργῆς, as well as "grieved at their hardness of heart," συλλυπούμενος ἐπὶ τῇ πωρώσει τῆς καρδίας αὐτῶν, see analysis of grief below) in referring to how Jesus looked at the Pharisees.[466]

Despite I. Howard Marshall's assertion of this passage that the "alterations made by Luke to his source are insignificant, and contribute, as often, simply to the clarification and better styling of the narrative,"[467] this pericope is essential for my analysis in showing a number of relevant Lukan redactional principles. **(1)** As stated above, Jesus' anger is omitted from Luke. Obviously, this scant example of Luke removing anger from Jesus' characterization is tenuous in and of itself; but it is a vital piece of evidence indicative of a larger pattern. Despite his claims to the contrary (see the general introduction), even François Bovon admits, "A vrai dire, il affaiblit et les sentiments de Jésus (μετ᾽ ὀργῆς, συλλυπούμενος, <<avec colère, attristé>>, Mc 3,

---

[466] Some groups of manuscripts "correct" this omission by adding "μετ᾽ ὀργῆς" or "ἐν ὀργῇ" following the Markan parallel, a phrase about which Bruce Metzger states (similarly to Cadbury both in language and further elaboration), "Luke is not likely to have used (from a sense of reverence)" in *A Textual Commentary*, 140. See further Albert Huck and Heinrich Greeven, *Synopse der drei ersten Evangelien* (13th ed.; Tübingen: Mohr-Siebeck, 1981), 67. The "corrected" textual traditions seem to favor gospel agreement over Lukan thematic consistency.

[467] Marshall, *Gospel of Luke*, 233. Other commentators that recognize the Lukan redactions though deny, ignore, or understate their importance: R. Alan Culpepper, *The Gospel of Luke: Introduction, Commentary, and Reflections* (NIB 9; Nashville: Abingdon Press, 1995), 134-35; Walter Radl, *Das Evangelium nach Lukas: Kommentar, Erster Teil: 1,1-9,50* (Freiburg: Herder, 2003), 344-48; L.T. Johnson, *Gospel of Luke*, 102; C.F. Evans, *Saint Luke* (Philadelphia: Trinity, 1990); John Nolland puzzlingly asserts without further explanation: "it [reference to Jesus' emotion omitted by Luke] presupposes a fixed attitude on the part of the Pharisees for which Luke is not yet ready" in *Luke 1-9:20*, 262.

5)."[468] This narrative also shows that Luke redacts emotions other than anger concerning his portrayal of Jesus. Jesus' grief at the hardness of their hearts (συλλυπούμενος ἐπὶ τῇ πωρώσει τῆς καρδίας αὐτῶν) is also omitted from the Lukan narration.[469] (2) This passage is also evidence for Luke's transference principle as I contend Jesus' anger in Mark is transferred (and even intensified) to the scribes and Pharisees in Luke (see further chapter five). Mark states that the scribes and Pharisees went out and immediately discussed with the Herodians how to destroy Jesus. Luke (6:11) adds that when the scribes and Pharisees discussed what they might do they were filled with a type of maddening rage (ἐπλήσθησαν ἀνοίας). (3) Further, this pericope points to the Lukan principle of omitting or lessening the violence (or the threat of violence) and strong emotion *to* Jesus as discussed above. The threat of violence to Jesus is softened in Luke where the scribes and Pharisees only discuss what they might do (τί ἂν ποιήσαιεν) to Jesus (6:11), whereas Mark states they counseled with the Herodians how they might destroy (ἀπολέσωσιν) Jesus (3:6).[470] In conclusion, Luke redacts Jesus' emotion, removing Jesus' grief (see further below) and transferring Jesus' anger to the disciples, while lessening the threat of violence to Jesus.

---

[468] Bovon, *Saint Luc 1-9*, 266.

[469] See complete analysis of other emotions and the proposed transference principle below and in chapter five.

[470] Robert C. Tannehill, who understates the importance of Luke's omission of anger and grief, but (in accordance with my third Lukan principle), emphasizes, ―Luke considerable softens the end of the scene, for in Mark the Pharisees begin to plot Jesus' death" in *Luke* (Nashville: Abingdon, 1996), 112. See also Judith Lieu, who argues that the Lukan version ―is not as dark as that which climaxes Mark's telling of the story," in *Gospel of Luke*, 47-49.

As stated in the general introduction as the proposed second scholarly check, *Matthew's* use of the Markan source (especially in comparison with the Lukan redactions) will further elucidate the Lukan redactional agenda.[471] Though the Lukan version of the passage is much closer to Mark linguistically than Matthew is to Luke,[472] Matthew, like Luke, removes the references to anger and grief (Matt 12:12-13//Mark 3:4-5//Luke 6:9-10).[473] Leon Morris uses the omission of Jesus' anger and grief in Matthew and Luke as his primary evidence in asserting that ―Mark is franker than [Matthew and Luke] in depicting Jesus' humanity,‖[474] though no further analysis or citation is provided, either to show further the equivalency of the Matthean and Lukan portrayals or to provide a definition of humanity/divinity as applied to emotion.[475]

---

[471] See preliminarily Eric Franklin, ―Comparing Luke and Matthew‖ in *Luke: Interpreter of Paul, Critic of Matthew* (JSNTSup 92; Sheffield: Sheffield Academic Press, 1994), 164-173.

[472] Michael Goulder uses this passage as evidence that Luke had access to Matthew's gospel as well, due to Luke and Matthew both removing the emotions and later the Herodians. Thus Luke's agenda is seen in the differences in light of both Matthew and Mark. Although I disagree with his ultimate assessment, Goulder does emphasize (1) the removal of emotion (the argument is actually more forceful because Luke chooses to follow the Markan text but keeps the Matthaean redactions in Goulder's paradigm) as well as (3) the softening (more so than in Matthew) of potential violence against Jesus. Despite a parallel linguistic analysis of Luke 6:11, Goulder fails to acknowledge (2) the transference of emotion from Jesus to the Pharisees. See Goulder, *Luke: A New Paradigm I*, 339-40.

[473] Interestingly, Matthew's version, while omitting the Markan narrator's description of Jesus' gaze altogether (and thus removing Jesus' anger and grief), does not follow the other two Lukan redactional principles. Matthew does not transfer Jesus' anger to the disciples, and though he removes Mark's reference to the Herodians, he keeps the Markan phase exactly ―ὅπως αὐτὸν ἀπολέσωσιν‖ (Mark 3:6//Mt 12:14).

[474] Leon Morris, *Luke: An Introduction and Commentary* (Grand Rapids, Mich.: Eerdmans, 1988), 53.

[475] Pace Morris, C.F. Evans argues that Luke ―can be seen rewriting a Markan story so as to make it humanly more intelligible‖ in *Saint Luke*, 66. Though not the space for an extended discussion, there are two reasons why the emotional redactions by Luke (and to an extent Matthew) should not be seen in terms of humanity/divinity. There is ample evidence that divine beings in antiquity were portrayed as emotional beings, both in Greek mythology and in the Hebrew Bible. For example, see the extended analysis of the Josephan omissions of embarrassing biblical narratives with regard to emotion, especially the omission of Yahweh's and Moses' emotional anger in the golden calf incident, in chapter three. With respect to the gospel texts, John's Jesus is characterized both as more divine and more emotional than Luke's.

As we will see, Matthew has many of the same redactions as Luke (though the Matthean pattern is not nearly as broad or consistent), and often for the same reason.[476] Anger, as previously shown, was troubling in almost every philosophical presentation (albeit in varying degrees and circumstances), including many of the Hellenistic Jewish sources. Obviously, the loaded emotional phrase "μετ' ὀργῆς, συλλυπούμενος ἐπὶ τῇ πωρώσει τῆς καρδίας αὐτῶν" would have been troubling to Matthew's Jewish worldview as well.[477]

253. Jesus Blesses the Children

Mark 10:13-14	Luke 18:15-16
Καὶ προσέφερον αὐτῷ παιδία	Προσέφερον δὲ αὐτῷ καὶ τὰ βρέφη
ἵνα αὐτῶν ἅψηται	ἵνα αὐτῶν ἅπτηται ἰδόντες
οἱ δὲ μαθηταὶ ἐπετίμησαν αὐτοῖς	δὲ οἱ μαθηταὶ ἐπετίμων αὐτοῖς
ἰδὼν δὲ ὁ Ἰησοῦς **ἠγανάκτησεν**	ὁ δὲ Ἰησοῦς
καὶ εἶπεν αὐτοῖς	προσεκαλέσατο αὐτὰ λέγων

---

[476] While it is beyond the scope of my inquest, the in/consistency Matthew/Luke comparison concerning emotional redactional patterns is indicative of the respective gospels and their overall agendas in many ways. Graham Stanton argues that "we may simply have to accept that the evangelist [Matthew] was . . . less consistent than some of his modern students have supposed" in *The Interpretation of Matthew* (Philadelphia: Fortress Press, 1983), 16. Whereas many scholars argue that Luke is an author working out a consistent point of view. See Gerhard Schneider, *Das Evangelium nach Lukas* (2 vols.; Würzburg: Echter-Verlag, 1984), 23-28; R.J. Dillon, "Previewing Luke's Project from his Prologue," *CBQ* 43 (1981): 205-208.

[477] Traditionally, scholarship has designated Matthew (and Mark) as Jewish and Luke as the Greek gospel. Adolf von Harnack, for example, has famously stated the whole synoptic tradition is Palestinian and has had nothing to with Gentile Christian circles except in the redaction of Luke in *New Testament Studies I. Luke the Physician: The Author of the Third Gospel* (Williams & Norgate; G.P. Putnam's Sons, 1907), 166. Even if one rejects the too-simplistic distinction of Matthew as the Jewish gospel and Luke as the Greek gospel (as I do along with most scholars) and recognizes there is considerable similarity (as well as Jewish elements in Luke and Greek ones in Matthew), there is scholarly consensus that Matthew emphasizes Jesus upholding the Law and the Hebrew Bible for example *more than* Luke. See the important commentary W. F. Albright and C.S. Mann, *Matthew: Introduction, Translation, and Notes* (AB 26; Garden City, N.Y.: Doubleday, 1971), xix-cxci. And considering Jerome's dictum that Luke "was the most learned in the Greek language among all the evangelists" (*Epist.* 20.4), I begin with this broad distinction.

ἄφετε τὰ παιδία ἔρχεσθαι πρός με,	ἄφετε τὰ παιδία ἔρχεσθαι πρός με
μὴ κωλύετε αὐτά	καὶ μὴ κωλύετε αὐτά
τῶν γὰρ τοιούτων	τῶν γὰρ τοιούτων
ἐστὶν ἡ βασιλεία τοῦ θεοῦ	ἐστὶν ἡ βασιλεία τοῦ θεοῦ

In a narrative concerning Jesus' teaching on the kingdom of God and children (Mark 10:13-16//Luke 18:15-17), the Markan narrator makes a similar observation to the scene at the synagogue (Mark 3:1-6//Luke 6:6-11). When the disciples of Jesus rebuke the people for attempting to bring children to Jesus (10:14), Mark describes Jesus as ἠγανάκτησεν ("indignant" or "angry"), ἰδὼν δὲ ὁ Ἰησοῦς ἠγανάκτησεν καὶ εἶπεν αὐτοῖς.[478] The Lukan narrator omits Jesus' "anger" or "indignation" by simply stating, ὁ δὲ Ἰησοῦς προσεκαλέσατο αὐτὰ λέγων (18:16).[479]

Many scholars who have recognized the Lukan redaction (of Jesus' indignation) have argued that the omission universalizes or generalizes the passage.[480] Marshall, seemingly following Jeremias, notes that in stressing that the children were infants (βρέφη instead of Mark's παιδία), along with the omissions of Jesus' annoyance at the

---

[478] ἀγανακτέω was a common verb in antiquity, "to be indignant" or "to be angry," BADG, 4. The same verbal description (ἀγανακτῶν) is used by Luke (special L material) to describe the ruler of the synagogue (ὁ ἀρχισυνάγωγος) in response to Jesus healing the crippled woman on the Sabbath in Luke 13:14.

[479] Bovon states that Luke "évite de dessiner un maître qui ne domine pas ses passions" in *Saint Luc 15,1-19,27*, 196.

[480] Other commentators recognize the Lukan omission of indignation, though they provide no further comment: Johnson, *Gospel of Luke*, 275-76; Fitzmyer does not elaborate on his general comments above in *Luke X-XXIV*, 1191-92; Schweizer, *Good News according to Luke*, 285; Craig A. Evans, *Luke*, 272.

disciples and his embracing of the children, Luke ―generalizes the story, and stresses its significance for the character of adults."[481] C. F. Evans likewise remarks the purely ―stylistic alterations" to the Markan source in arguing that Luke takes a ―more universal form."[482] Nolland also contends that it is quite natural for Luke to develop and apply Mark's version more thoroughly to adults. Nolland argues that the Lukan προσεκαλέσατο αὐτά, which displaces Jesus' anger in Mark, signifies a more

welcoming attitude, especially toward the parents and adults.[483] Though I contend the primary reason for the Lukan omission of Jesus' indignation is the suppression of Jesus' emotions, the redactions in general do serve to shift the focus towards parents and adults.

Other scholars have postulated a Lukan pattern of preserving the dignity or honor of the disciples. Frederick W. Danker contends that Luke's removal of ―Jesus' displeasure over the disciples" is in harmony with ―Luke's rather consistent removal of features that are unnecessarily embarrassing to the *apostles*" [emphasis added].[484] Goulder similarly states that Luke ―cuts out Jesus' indignation with the disciples, in order to preserve the reputations of the latter, as often."[485] While this is true on occasion, it is far from being ―rather consistent" or ―as often." On many occasions, Luke's portrayal of the apostles could be considered more embarrassing than Mark. Even if one tenuously

---

[481] Marshall, *Gospel of Luke*, 681. Joachim Jeremias also stressed Luke's adult parental focus of the passage in *Die Kindertaufe in den ersten vier Jahrhunderten* (Göttingen: Vandenhoeck und Ruprecht, 1958), 53-56.

[482] C.F. Evans, *Saint Luke*, 646.

[483] Nolland, *Luke 9:21-18:34*, 881-82.

[484] Frederick W. Danker, *Jesus and the New Age* (Philadelphia: Fortress, 1988), 298.

[485] Goulder, *Luke: A New Paradigm II*, 667.

accepts the general scholarly consensus that the disciples gradually become more aware of who Jesus is and gain greater understanding as Luke's narrative progresses,[486] the disciples' portrayal in Luke is mixed.[487] Contrarily, Joel B. Green (pace Danker and Goulder) argues that the removal of Jesus' anger at the disciples is indicative of the opposite principle; Luke actually indicts the disciples and their lack of understanding even more than Mark.[488]

Similar to the first passage (Mark 3:5//Luke 6:10), the Lukan version of the passage is much closer to Mark linguistically than Matthew is to Luke, though Matthew does follow Luke in removing Jesus' indignation (Mt 19:14). Luke reproduces the Markan wording quite closely, and has been labeled ―pure Markan material.‖[489] Though less clear-cut than the pericope concerning the man with the withered hand, it seems that Matthew also removes Jesus' indignation for the same reason as Luke – the suppression of emotion.

273. The Cleansing of the Temple

Mark 11:15-17	Luke 19:45-46

---

[486] Fitzmyer sees in the question in 8:25 ―the beginning of a sense of awareness‖ in the disciples in *Luke I-IX*, 730. Pace Fitzmyer, Arthur A. Just Jr. argues that ―Luke shows a gradual movement toward total misunderstanding and silence. By the end of the gospel, Luke has demonstrated that the disciples are completely confused concerning the purpose of Jesus' Messiahship‖ in *Luke 1:1-9:50* (St. Louis: Concordia, 1996), 393.

[487] As late as the transfiguration (9:32-33), they are not fully aware and respond inappropriately; see further Tannehill, ―Jesus and the Disciples‖ in *Narrative Unity Vol.1*, 203-274, esp. 225-228. See also the transference of Jesus' distress in Mark to the disciples in Luke in the Garden narrative (Mark 14:37//Luke 22:45); see further chapter five.

[488] Joel B. Green, *The Gospel of Luke* (Grand Rapids, Mich.: Eerdmans, 1997), 650-52.

[489] Tim Schramm states that the pericope ―ist wahrscheinlich als reiner Mark-Stoff zu beurteilen‖ in *Der Markus-Stoff bei Luka*, 141.

Καὶ ἔρχονται εἰς Ἱεροσόλυμα. Καὶ εἰσελθὼν εἰς τὸ ἱερὸν ἤρξατο ἐκβάλλειν τοὺς πωλοῦντας <u>καὶ τοὺς ἀγοράζοντας ἐν τῷ ἱερῷ,</u> <u>καὶ τὰς τραπέζας τῶν κολλυβιστῶν</u> <u>καὶ τὰς καθέδρας τῶν πωλούντων</u> <u>τὰς περιστερὰς κατέστρεψεν,</u> <u>καὶ οὐκ ἤφιεν ἵνα τις διενέγκῃ</u> <u>σκεῦος διὰ τοῦ ἱεροῦ</u> καὶ ἐδίδασκεν καὶ ἔλεγεν αὐτοῖς οὐ γέγραπται ὅτι ὁ οἶκός μου οἶκός προσευχῆς κληθήσεται πᾶσιν τοῖς ἔθνεσιν; ὑμεῖς δὲ πεποιήκατε αὐτὸν σπήλαιον λῃστῶν.	Καὶ εἰσελθὼν εἰς τὸ ἱερὸν ἤρξατο ἐκβάλλειν τοὺς πωλοῦντας λέγων αὐτοῖς γέγραπται καὶ ἔσται ὁ οἶκός μου οἶκός προσευχῆς ὑμεῖς δὲ αὐτὸν πεποιήκατε σπήλαιον λῃστῶν.

The most famous and striking example of Luke's redactional tendency toward removing violent and angry actions is the scene in which Jesus ―cleanses" the temple (Mark 11:15-17//Luke 19:45-46). By the omission of Jesus' preliminary inspection (Mark 11:11), and of the enigmatic cursing of the fig tree (Mark 11:12-14), Luke presents us with a much abbreviated version of the so-called cleansing of the temple.[490] In the Markan source, Jesus' anger is not shown primarily through the narrator's comments, but

---

[490] The temple mount or courts are cleansed by Jesus so that he may take them over for his own purposes of *teaching* at the center of Judaism; see further below and C.F. Evans, *Saint Luke*, 686-688. The actions of Jesus are so sanitized in the Lukan version, that some commentators have labeled the pericope in figurative terms; Nolland terms it ―Symbolic Protest in the Temple" in *Luke 18:35-24:53*, 933; see also Lieu, *Gospel of Luke*, 156-57. Other commentators have correctly shown that even the symbolism in Luke is exscinded and have avoided ―cleansing" or ―protest" terminology altogether, thus Green's label ―Preparation of the Temple for Teaching" in *Gospel of Luke*, 691. See analysis of the cursing of the fig tree below.

through Jesus' actions.[491] Both accounts begin with the exact same language, but the Markan account includes Jesus overturning the money-changers' tables and the pigeon-sellers' seats, καὶ τὰς τραπέζας τῶν κολλυβιστῶν καὶ τὰς καθέδρας τῶν πωλούντων τὰς περιστερὰς κατέστρεψεν (Mark 11:15b).[492] Mark's narrative also includes, καὶ οὐκ ἤφιεν ἵνα τις διενέγκῃ σκεῦος διὰ τοῦ ἱεροῦ (v.16), implying violent intervention and resistance to other Temple activities. In his abbreviated version of the cleansing narrative, Luke omits these violent details (Mark 11:15b-16),[493] in order to portray Jesus as honorable, self-controlled and not prone to violence. Since Luke basically removes any deeper meaning (i.e., eschatological, see below) to the temple event, I. Howard Marshall similarly concludes that Luke ―may well have played down the details of the action in order to avoid any suspicion that Jesus was man of violence."[494]

Comparison with Mark's version of the cleansing reveals a number of important Lukan motifs and emphases, many of which are directly related to my primary task of

---

[491] Tannehill correctly points out, ―the short Lukan version removes all violent details from the scene," and further argues that Matthew's ―somewhat longer" version is a type of middle ground in *Luke*, 286. Matthew's Jesus overturns the money-changers' tables and the pigeon-sellers' seats (Mt 21:12), but stops short of physically keeping those carrying anything through the temple.

[492] Like most of the analyzed texts in this chapter, what remains, after the redactions, of the account follows the Markan text closely. See further Culpepper, *Gospel of Luke*, 373-74.

[493] The Lukan text is expanded in many manuscripts to include those buying as well as selling (ἐν αὐτῷ καὶ ἀγοράζοντας). An even longer addition is found in D *pc* it (ἐν αὐτῷ καὶ ἀγοράζοντας καὶ τὰς τραπέζας τῶν κολλυβιστῶν ἐξέχεεν καὶ τὰς καθέδρας τῶν πωλούντων τὰς περιστερὰς). The variants seem to be later editorial attempts at harmony. For example, ἐξέχεεν is probably taken from the Johanine version of the temple cleansing.

[494] Marshall, *Gospel of Luke*, 721.

revealing the Lukan pattern of removing strong emotion. Mark makes specific reference to Jesus' violent stopping of the very routine of worship (Mark 11:15-16). This has led many scholars to conclude that the temple cult per se is under attack in Mark's gospel.[495] In Luke, Jesus condemns the *abuse* of the temple by those described as "robbers" (λῃστῶν, v.46), not legitimate worship. J. Bradley Chance summarizes, "In short, while Mark portrays Jesus' encounter with the temple virtually as a *cursing*, Luke views it more as an actual *cleansing*" [emphasis his].[496] Though commenting on the *theological* significance of the Lukan redactions, Hans Conzelmann likewise asserts, "Bei Lukas handelt es sich nicht um das eschatologische Ende des Tempels, sondern um seine Reinigung; d. h. Jesus bereitet ihn für sich selbst als Aufenthalt zu und hält sich von nun an in diesem seinem Eigentum auf."[497]

While an in-depth analysis of Luke's complex political apologetical stance is certainly beyond the scope of this redactional analysis, Luke's version of the temple cleansing is characteristic of his apologetic agenda in that it serves a dual apologetic purpose. I have argued briefly in the introduction that Luke's primary apology is to Rome (based in part upon Luke's emotional redactions), though Luke minimizes any sense in which Jesus might be seen as critical of the Jerusalem temple[498] and consistently

---

[495] See especially F.D. Weinert, "The Meaning of the Temple in the Gospel of Luke" (Ph.D. diss. Fordham University, 1979), 23-41.

[496] J. Bradley Chance, *Jerusalem, the Temple, and the New Age in Luke*-Acts (Macon, Ga.: Mercer University Press, 1988), 57.

[497] Hans Conzelmann, *Die Mitte der Zeit: Studien zur Theologie des Lukas* (Tübingen: J.C.B. Mohr (Paul Siebeck), 1977), 71. Along with the absence of the fig tree cursing, the reference to the "cleansing" as an eschatological sign is also missing in Luke.

[498] See Nolland, *Luke 18:35-24:53*, 937.

stresses observance of the Mosaic Law.[499] My view (in the broad tradition of Conzelmann[500]) is perhaps closest to Charles H. Talbert.[501] Talbert argues (pace Cassidy,[502] Yoder,[503] and others) that although the Lukan Jesus shows no deference toward *political rulers* (e.g. Luke 13:31-33), he is not involved in a Gandhi-style nonviolent (or even against all textual evidence, violent,[504] as some have argued) resistance against them either.[505] While stressing his observance of Judaism, Luke's Jesus is involved in a type of *nonviolent* resistance against the *Jewish* authorities.[506]

---

[499] See the Lukan additions to the burial narrative concerning Mosaic law, especially the concluding proclamation, καὶ τὸ μὲν σάββατον ἡσύχασαν κατὰ τὴν ἐντολήν (23:56); Cf. Luke 2:21-24.

[500] While Conzelmann's theses regarding Luke's periodization of redemptive history and the delay of the parousia have been widely discussed, his corollary thesis that Luke presents a deep political apologetic received almost no attention until the late 1970's, *Die Mitte der Zeit*, 128-135. See further Willard M. Swartley, ―Politics of Peace (Eirēnē) in Luke's Gospel" in *Political Issues in Luke-Acts* (ed. Richard J. Cassidy and Philip J. Scharper; Maryknoll, N.Y.: Orbis Books, 1983), 18-37.

[501] See especially his formulation in ―Martyrdom and the Lukan Social Ethic" in *Political Issues in Luke-Acts* (ed. Richard J. Cassidy and Philip J. Scharper; Maryknoll, N.Y.: Orbis Books, 1983), 99-110.

[502] See the influential work of Richard J. Cassidy, *Jesus, Politics, and Society: A Study of Luke's Gospel* (Maryknoll, N.Y.: Orbis Books, 1978).

[503] John Howard Yoder, *The Politics of Jesus: vicit Agnus noster* (Grand Rapids, Mich.: Eerdmans, 1972), esp. chs. 2-3.

[504] Robert F. O'Toole, after a redactional analysis of Luke showing the softening of violent Markan passages including the temple cleansing, states amazingly, ―The cleansing of the temple was an act of civil disobedience *and violence*" [emphasis added] in ―Luke's Position on Politics and Society" in *Political Issues in Luke-Acts* (ed. Richard J. Cassidy and Philip J. Scharper; Maryknoll, N.Y.: Orbis Books, 1983), 14. Likewise Sharon Ringe, after stating ―Luke does not describe Jesus' actions" and ―there is no mention of the destruction of property described in the other Gospels," argues for Jesus' impassioned protest in *Luke*, 241-42.

[505] Talbert, *Reading Luke*, 193.

[506] Luke also has a type of apologetic towards the people, especially in the latter part of his gospel. Luke Timothy Johnson correctly points out, ―With only the smallest possible exception (23:13), throughout this Jerusalem account Luke will portray the populace as a whole as positive toward Jesus, and place responsibility for his death squarely and exclusively on the leadership (see esp. 24:30)" in *Gospel of Luke*, 302. In 23:13, the people, though present, do not actually play a role until 23:18-23, where they are counted with the elders, the chief priests, and the scribes (whom Luke assigns the term ―assembly," πλῆθος, in 23:1), and designated as the whole multitude shouting together (ἀνέκραγον δὲ παμπληθεί). Further, Luke painstakingly distinguishes between the people and its officials (20:1, 9, 19; 21:38; 22:2).

Though confrontation is frequent in Luke's gospel (e.g., 5:12-6:11; 11:37-54; 13:10-17; 14:1-24; 16:14-15; 19:47-20:47), only at the cleansing of the temple (Luke 19:45) is there any hint of possible violence, and Luke has so shaped the cleansing story, that it becomes merely Jesus' entry into the site of his subsequent teaching (19:47-21:38).[507] Talbert summarizes:

> Nonviolent confrontation aimed at dialogue and hoping for a change of behavior seems the best description of the Lukan Jesus' stance toward the Jewish structures. This was doubtless due to the fact that Jesus and the Jews shared common assumptions about God and values.[508]

The removal of Jesus' angry and violent actions in cleansing the Temple (along with the cursing of the fig tree) radically alters the portrait of Jesus. While other Lukan pericopae have omitted Jesus' anger when describing Jesus' actions,[509] Luke's version of the temple cleansing most clearly shows his aversion to anger in that he removes the actual actions associated with Jesus' anger in Mark.

Even though, as previously stated, the crucifixion is demanded by all (23:18-23), Luke distinguishes the populace (23:4, 13) from the leaders (23:2, 5). See further Schweizer, *The Good News according to Luke*, 302. In my view, this increased favorable portrayal towards the people, stresses the Lukan theme of Jesus' innocence both by the Roman authorities and the general population.

[507] Moreover, Luke 22:49-51 has Jesus explicitly reject violence against Jewish authority. The Lukan version keeps the Markan violence by Jesus' followers in cutting off the ear of the high priest's slave, but (contrary to both Mark and Matthew) has Jesus actually heal his ear as well as exclaim –ἐᾶτε ἕως τούτου" (v.51). In keeping with my general redactional principles, the violence (and potential violence) *toward* Jesus is greatly reduced, even though the violence by one of Jesus' followers is kept, pace Fitzmyer's claim that *anything* associated with violence or strong emotion is redacted. Luke omits the crowd with swords and clubs (Mark 14:43// Mt 26:47), the potential seizing (κρατήσατε αὐτὸν καὶ ἀπάγετε ἀσφαλῶς, Mark 14:44 // κρατήσατε αὐτόν, Mt 26:48), and the actual seizing and laying on of hands (Mark 14:46// Mt 26:50). Matthew keeps all of these elements and even increases the violence (and potential violence) with the addition of 26:52-54.

[508] Talbert, –Lukan Social Ethic," 108.

[509] For example, Jesus still heals on the Sabbath (Mark 3:5//Luke 6:10), though does so without anger.

42. The Cleansing of the Leper

Mark 1:43-4a	Luke 5:14a
καὶ ἐμβριμησάμενος αὐτῷ **εὐθὺς ἐξέβαλεν αὐτόν,** καὶ λέγει αὐτῷ,	καὶ αὐτὸς παρήγγειλεν αὐτῷ
ὅρα μηδενὶ μηδὲν εἴπῃς	μηδενὶ εἰπεῖν

Jesus' anger is also expressed in Mark through the use of stern speech, which is consistently eliminated (or at least significantly softened) by the Lukan redactor. Most commentators cast aside these redactions as merely stylistic changes by Luke, [510] but a consistent pattern emerges in the linguistic depiction of a less emotional Jesus. In the scene where Jesus heals a leper (Mark 1:40-45//Luke 5:12-16), the Markan Jesus sternly warns[511] the healed leper and then sends him away at once (καὶ ἐμβριμησάμενος αὐτῷ

---

[510] Though Cadbury does not include many of the proposed emotional speech redactions (see above list), he argues convincingly for a subtle Lukan *stylistic* pattern (in addition to the analyzed pericopae) that attributes to the overall depiction of Jesus as an authoritative, yet calm and self-controlled leader. Luke frequently makes less abrupt and peremptory the commands and requests found in his sources by avoiding such words as ὕπαγε, δεῦτε, ἴδε, and by the subtle use of vocatives. These changes "quite accord with motives of style, lending grace and smoothness to the dialogue . . . but *they also affect the impression* we get of the speakers, both Jesus himself and those who address him" [emphasis added] (91). He includes the following in accordance with his proposed pattern: Mark 11:3, εἴπατε // Luke 19:31, οὕτως ἐρεῖτε; Mark 14:14, εἴπατε // Luke 22:11, ἐρεῖτε; Mark 14:36, παρένεγκε τὸ ποτήριον τοῦτο // Luke 22:42, εἰ βούλει παρενέγκαι τοῦτο τὸ ποτήριον; Mark 12:15, τί με πειράζετε // Luke 20:24 omits; Mark 13:9, βλέπετε δὲ ὑμεῖς ἑαυτούς // Luke 21:12 omits.

[511] The exact translation of ἐμβριμάομαι is the source of debate among scholars, especially the *tone* of the verb. BADG (254) cites Lucian's *Necyomant.* 20 and Pseudo-Libanius' *Declam.* 40 as examples of a general expression of anger and displeasure, thus provides the translation "warn sternly" for Mark 1:43. Henry Barclay Swete has classically argued that ἐμβριμάομαι connotes speaking or acting sternly, but *without* the idea of anger being inherent in the term in *The Gospel according to St. Mark: The Greek Text with Introduction, Notes, and Indices* (London: Macmillan, 1909), 112. Carl W. Conrad has suggested since the active root-element is BPI with a fundamental sense of "weight," the import of ἐμβριμάομαι is

εὐθὺς ἐξέβαλεν αὐτόν, 1:43-44a), while the narrator of Luke states generically that

Jesus forbids the leper to tell anyone (καὶ αὐτὸς παρήγγειλεν αὐτῷ μηδενὶ εἰπεῖν).[512]

The Markan choice carries with it a much stronger emotional connotation.[513] Further, the

Markan account uses direct discourse with Jesus charging, ―ὅρα μηδενὶ μηδὲν εἴπῃς‖

(1:44a), giving the charge more literary force, compared with Luke generically having the

narrator comment, ―And he charged him to tell no one‖ (5:14a).[514] Luke significantly

softens the tone of Jesus' speech in Mark in order to emphasize calmness and emotional

composure even when making an authoritative charge.[515]

Though not as consistent as Luke nor to the same degree, Matthew makes many

---

―to act with intensity.‖ He further takes a middle position, ―This would not necessarily imply anger, but it could‖ in *Biblical Greek Digest* V1 #945 (10 Nov 1995); Online: cwconrad@artsci.wustl.edu. My translation, pace Swete and his great influence, is in line with BADG as a general expression of anger. On the harshness of the expression, see Matthew Black, *An Aramaic Approach to the Gospels and Acts* (Oxford: Clarendon, 1967), 240-243. C.S. Mann suggests ―stern warning‖ due to his understanding of ἐμβριμάομαι as a ―strong word, for which there is no satisfactory English equivalent‖ in *Mark*, 219.

[512] Luke also omits another emotional participle, σπλαγχνισθείς (Mark 1:41), from the Markan text, which is discussed in detail below concerning the characterization of Jesus and the positive emotions.

[513] παραγγέλλω with μή and an infinitive implies a general forbidding to do something. It does not carry the emotional weight of the Markan ἐμβριμάομαι, see BADG, 613. Ulrich Busse comments that παραγγέλλω with an infinitive (with and without μή) is a common Lukan vocabulary selection used to emphasize the command of a person who possesses authority in *Die Wunder des Propheten Jesus: Die Rezeption, Komposition, und Interpretation der Wundertradition im Evangelium des Lukas* (FB 24; Stuttgart: Katholisches Bibelwerk, 1979), 106-7. In commenting on the Lukan changes, Nolland observes that ―Luke omits Mark's rather *violent-sounding* dismissal of the man‖ [emphasis added] in *Luke 1-9:20*, 227. Goulder further argues that Luke suppresses Mark 1:43 because it might appear ―excessively fierce‖ in *Luke: A New Paradigm I*, 329.

[514] I.H. Marshall contrarily contends that the Lukan switch to indirect discourse is purely stylistic, though fails to explain the immediate use of direct discourse in the same verse (5:14) in *Gospel of Luke*, 209.

[515] In François Bovon's abstruse view, Luke softens (by vocabulary choice and the movement to indirect speech) the emotional command in Mark because Luke did not understand its significance in Mark though provides no further explanation in *Saint Luc 1-9*, 176.

of the Lukan redactional changes concerning emotional speech (probably for similar reasons). Like some of the preceding pericopae, though the Lukan version of the passage is much closer to Mark linguistically than Matthew is to Mark, Matthew does follow Luke in removing the references to compassion and stern speech (Matt 8:3-4). Matthew even omits the Lukan παρήγγειλεν, preferring the simple Markan λέγει (without καὶ ἐμβριμησάμενος αὐτῷ εὐθὺς ἐξέβαλεν αὐτόν, 4a), though he does retain a concise version of the Markan direct command, ὅρα μηδενὶ εἴπῃς, 4a).[516]

113. Jesus Heals Multitudes by the Sea

Mark 3:12	Luke 6:19?
Καὶ πολλὰ ἐπετίμα αὐτοῖς **ἵνα μή αὐτὸν φανερὸν ποιήσωσιν**	Luke omits

Mark 3:11b-12	Luke 4:41b?
προσέπιπτον αὐτῷ	
καὶ ἔκραζον λέγοντα	Κραυγάζοντα καὶ λέγοντα
ὅτι σὺ εἶ ὁ υἱὸς τοῦ θεοῦ	ὅτι σὺ εἶ ὁ υἱὸς τοῦ θεοῦ
καὶ **πολλὰ** ἐπετίμα αὐτοῖς	καὶ ἐπιτιμῶν οὐκ εἴα αὐτὰ λαλεῖν,
ἵνα μή αὐτὸν φανερὸν ποιήσωσιν	ὅτι ᾔδεισαν τὸν χριστὸν αὐτὸν εἶναι

On the occasion before the ―Sermon on the Plain" in Luke, Jesus healed many

---

[516] See further Goulder, *A New Paradigm I*, 328-30.

who were troubled with unclean spirits (6:17-19). In a possible parallel account[517] in

Mark (3:7-12, which is placed before Jesus' appointing of the twelve disciples), Jesus

again exhorts those healed (or possibly the spirits themselves) with stern speech, Καὶ

πολλὰ ἐπετίμα αὐτοῖς ἵνα μή αὐτὸν φανερὸν ποιήσωσιν (3:12), even using πολλά as

an intensifying adverb (absent from the similar exhortation in Mark 1:44). This entire

statement is omitted from the Lukan version.

Though most scholars recognize the dependence of Luke on the Markan source

(3:7-12), this passage is missing from many redactional analyses primarily due to setting

of the healing before the _Sermon on the Plain' in public in front of a great crowd of

disciples and a great multitude of people from all Judea, Jerusalem, and the coast of Tyre

and Sidon (v.17). Further, there is no messianic proclamation, no occasion for rebuke,

and therefore the command of silence is unnecessary, either directed towards those

healed or the spirits themselves or both.[518] The emphasis is on the crowd in Luke, the

people who came to hear Jesus, an element not found in the Markan parallel.[519] Luke has

so thoroughly recast this passage that it basically functions as little more than an

introduction to Jesus' teaching (20-49).[520]

In light of the above discussion, my view is that this pericope does not provide

---

[517] One possibility for the Mark 3:11-12 parallel is Luke 6:19ff. It is listed as parallel 113 in *Synopsis Quattuor Evangeliorum*, 159. The ‑parallel" text in Mathew bears little resemblance.

[518] Mark 3:11-12, the remainder of the Markan summary statement, has already been used in Luke 4:41. See Goulder, *A New Paradigm I*, 345; also Culpepper, *Gospel of Luke*, 142

[519] See further Craig A. Evans, *Luke*, 107.

[520] See for example, Johnson, *Gospel of Luke*, 110; Marshall, *Gospel of Luke*, 241-42; Green, *Gospel of Luke*, 260-63; Nolland, *Luke 1-9:20*, 274-77; C.F. Evans, *Saint Luke*, 320-22. Bovon, *Saint Luc 1-9*, 212-14.

primary evidence of Luke's pattern of emotional speech redaction, however there is another parallel possibility.[521] An attentive redactional analysis by Michael Goulder provides fodder for consideration. He emphasizes, ―It is to be noted how carefully Luke has included all of Mark 3.7-12: vv.7-8, 10-11a are here; v.9 is at Luke 5.1f.; *vv. 11b-12 at Luke 4.41*" [emphasis added].[522] If we tentatively accept the notion that the Mark 3:12 parallel is located at Luke 4:41, we can analyze the Lukan redactions according to the proposed redactional principles concerning emotional speech. Luke preserves the Markan verb ἐπιτιμάω in stating καὶ ἐπετιμῶν οὐκ εἴα αὐτὰ λαλεῖν (41b).[523] But, in keeping with his redactional tendency of softening Jesus' speech, Luke omits the intensifying adverb πολλά.

137. The Gerasene Demoniac

Mark 5:18b-5:19a	Luke 8:38-39a
παρεκάλει αὐτὸν ὁ δαιμονισθείς	ἐδεῖτο δὲ αὐτοῦ ὁ ἀνὴρ ἀφ' οὗ ἐξεληλύει τὰ δαιμόνια

---

[521] Besides being listed as parallel 113, it is also listed as parallel 48, *Synopsis Quattuor Evangeliorum*, 69.

[522] Goulder, *A New Paradigm I*, 345. Culpepper makes a similar contention, ―the remainder of the Markan summary [3:11-12] has already been used in Luke 4:41" in *Gospel of Luke*, 142.

[523] ἐπιτιμάω generically connotes ―rebuke" or ―reprove," and specifically when followed by ἵνα or ἵνα μή connotes a censure or warning, often relating to demons; BADG, 302; LSJ, 305. It is a common Lukan (and Markan and to a lesser extent Matthean) verb (Luke 4:35, 39, 41//Mark 1:28, 31, 3:12; Luke 8:24//Mark 4:39; Luke 9:21//Mark 8:30, 32, 33; Luke 9:42//Mark 9:35; Luke 9:55; Luke 17:3//Matt 18:15; Luke 18:15//Matt 10:13; Luke 18:39//Matt 10:48; Luke 19:39; Luke 23:40) and usually means ―rebuke," but Luke also uses ἐπιτιμάω as ―to charge, speak seriously" (e.g. 9:21).

ἵνα μετ' αὐτοῦ ᾖ καὶ οὐκ *ἀφῆκεν* αὐτόν, ἀλλὰ λέγει αὐτῷ *ὕπαγε* εἰς τὸν οἶκόν σου πρὸς τοὺς σούς	εἶναι σὺν αὐτῷ *ἀπέλυσεν* δὲ αὐτὸν λέγων *ὑπόστρεφε* εἰς τὸν οἶκόν σου

Similar to the passage where Jesus heals a leper (Mark 1:40-45//Luke 5:12-16), Luke softens the Markan emotional language in the pericope concerning the Gerasene Demoniac (Mark 5:1-20//Luke 8:26-39). The Lukan narrator omits Jesus' strong refusal in Mark (καὶ οὐκ ἀφῆκεν αὐτόν, 5:19), choosing instead a general dismissal (ἀπέλυσεν δὲ αὐτόν, 8:38b), which significantly lessens the stringent tone of Mark in the ensuing dialogue.[524] Luke also chooses a different imperative for Jesus' direct command to the formerly demon-possessed Gerasene, though the senses of the verbs are similar.[525]

138. Jairus' Daughter and the Woman with a Hemorrhage

Mark 5:40, 43	Luke 8:53, 56

---

[524] ἀπολύω is a general term meaning simply to send away. It is often used in antiquity in dismissing an assembly. In certain contexts, it can even connote ―pardon," ―set free," or ―release," BADG, 96. ἀφίημι is similar in meaning, but slightly stronger in tone. It was used more frequently in antiquity, sometimes in a legal sense to ―cancel" or ―remit," or ―to leave" or ―to abandon," BADG, 125-26. Nolland likewise contends a softened tone adding that the ―man is not turned down, but redirected" in *Luke 1-9:20*, 413. Similarly see further Marshall, *Gospel of Luke*, 341; and C.F. Evans, *Saint Luke*, 387.

[525] One could possibly construe the Lukan ὑποστρέφω (to return) as more polite than the Markan ὑπάγω (to go), but my view is that it is a simple stylistic change. Bovon contends Luke chose ὑποστρέφω to achieve a dramatic literary effect to parallel Jesus' return in 8:37 in *Saint Luc 1-9*, 378-79. See further Goulder, *Luke: A New Paradigm I*, 423. Matthew's shortened version ends with the crowd begging Jesus to leave and omits the last few verses of the Markan account.

[40] καὶ κατεγέλων αὐτοῦ. **αὐτὸς δὲ ἐκβαλὼν πάντας παραλαμβάνει τὸν πατέρα τοῦ παιδίου καὶ τὴν μητέρα καὶ τοὺς μετ' αὐτοῦ,** **καὶ εἰσπορεύεται ὅπου ἦν τὸ παιδίον.** [43] *καὶ διεστείλατο αὐτοῖς πολλὰ* ἵνα μηδεὶς γνοῖ τοῦτο, καὶ εἶπεν δοθῆναι αὐτῇ φαγεῖν.	[53] καὶ κατεγέλων αὐτοῦ, εἰδότες ὅτι ἀπέθανεν [56] καὶ ἐξέστησαν οἱ γονεῖς αὐτῆς· *ὁ δὲ παρήγγειλεν αὐτοῖς* μηδενὶ εἰπεῖν τὸ γεγονός.

In the charge to tell no one, concerning Jesus' healing of Jairus' daughter (Mark 5:21-43//Luke 8:40-56), Luke significantly softens the tone of Jesus' speech. Mark reads, καὶ διεστείλατο αὐτοῖς πολλὰ ἵνα μηδεὶς γνοῖ τοῦτο (5:43), while Luke reads, ὁ δὲ παρήγγειλεν αὐτοῖς μηδενὶ εἰπεῖν τὸ γεγονός (8:56). Luke not only changes the verb from διαστέλλω[526] to παραγγέλλω,[527] but also omits the intensifying πολλά.[528]

---

[526] διαστέλλω is a particularly harsh term for giving a command. The intensity of the command is missing from many English translations; see BADG, 188. Hence, I prefer "strictly ordered" or "strictly commanded." However, διαστέλλω does not quite have the emotional intensity of ἐμβριμάομαι (Mark 1:43), which Luke also redacts (see above).

[527] παραγγέλλω with μή and an infinitive implies a general forbidding to do something. See above analysis on the scene where Jesus heals a leper (Mark 1:40-45//Luke 5:12-16), where Luke changes the Markan ἐμβριμάομαι to παραγγέλλω.

[528] In commenting on the Lukan changes, Nolland observes that "Luke reproduces the command to silence in a softened form" in *Luke 1-9:20*, 422. The Matthean version of the pericope is so abbreviated and so different in general, Matthew's changes are irrelevant except perhaps that the Markan secrecy motif, retained in a softened form by Luke, is completely absent. At the end of the radically abbreviated account,

Luke further omits the complete Markan description of Jesus ejecting the mourners from the house.[529]

142. Commissioning the Twelve

Mark 6:7-9	Luke 9:1-3
Καὶ προσκαλεῖται τοὺς δώδεκα,	Συγκαλεσάμενος δὲ τοὺς δώδεκα
καὶ ἤρξατο αὐτοὺς	
ἀποστέλλειν δύο δύο,	
καὶ ἐδίδου αὐτοῖς ἐξουσίαν	ἔδωκεν αὐτοῖς δύναμιν καὶ ἐξουσίαν
τῶν πνευμάτων τῶν ἀκαθάρτων,	ἐπὶ πάντα τὰ δαιμόνια
	καὶ νόσους θεραπεύειν
	καὶ ἀπέστειλεν αὐτοὺς κηρύσσειν
	τὴν βασιλείαν τοῦ θεοῦ καὶ ἰᾶσθαι
καὶ *παρήγγειλεν* αὐτοῖς	καὶ *εἶπεν* πρὸς αὐτούς
ἵνα μηδὲν αἴρωσιν εἰς ὁδὸν	μηδὲν αἴρετε εἰς τὴν ὁδόν,
εἰ μὴ ῥάδον μόνον,	μήτε ῥάβδον μήτε πήραν
μὴ ἄρτον, μὴ πήραν,	μήτε ἄρτον μήτε ἀργύριον
μὴ εἰς τὴν ζώνην χαλκόν,	
ἀλλὰ ὑποδεδεμένους σανδάλια,	
καὶ μὴ ἐνδύσησθε δύο χιτῶνας	μήτε ἀνὰ δύο χιτῶνας ἔχειν

Another subtle instance of Luke changing the speech of the Markan source and a possible example of Luke softening the emotional language of his source occurs in the

---

Matthew states, καὶ ἐξῆλθεν ἡ φήμη αὕτη εἰς ὅλην τὴν γῆν ἐκείνην (9:26). See Goulder, *Luke: A New Paradigm I*, 427.

[529] The strong verb used for this ejection, ἐκβάλλω, is also often employed for the exorcism of demons; see analysis above and further Joel Markus, *Mark 1-8* (AB 27A; New York: Doubleday, 2000), 372.

scene where Jesus commissions the twelve (Mark 6:6b-13//Luke 9:1-6). The Lukan

account reads generically, καὶ εἶπεν πρὸς αὐτούς (9:3), while Mark reads, καὶ

παρήγγειλεν αὐτοῖς (6:8). Luke has altered Mark's general verb of command

(παραγγέλλω) with an indirect command (a simple λέγω) followed by direct

imperatives.[530] John Nolland contends, ―Luke softens Mark's ‗commanded' to ‗said' and

moves the account into direct speech."[531] While I agree with Marshall and Nolland that

Luke has slightly ―softened" the Markan language, which is perfectly in line with my

main thesis concerning the emotional redactions by Luke, the Lukan ―softening" is a

rather odd linguistic choice.[532] Two of my previous examples of the Lukan principle of

omitting or softening Jesus' stern speech (Mark 1:43//Luke 5:14; Mark 5:43//Luke 8:56)

showed Luke changing the Markan ἐμβριμάομαι //διαστέλλω to παραγγέλλω. I

further argued (along with Busse) that παραγγέλλω is a common Lukan vocabulary

selection (especially with an infinitive) used to emphasize the command of a person who

possesses authority. Here, Luke removes παραγγέλλω in order to ―soften" even further

---

530 I. Howard Marshall argues that the change to softer language may be due to Luke possibly following Q rather than deliberately altering Mark in *Gospel of Luke*, 352-53. See also Heinz Schürmann, *Das Lukasevangelium* (HTKNT; Freiburg: Herder, 1969), 501.

531 Nolland, *Luke 1-9:20*, 426. Nolland, like Marshall and others, sees Luke influenced by Q in this narrative.

532 A discussion of the linguistic change is understandably missing from many commentators, given the subtlety of the change and the complexity of the pericope's provenance and themes, though Tannehill does similarly describe the Lukan wording as ―strange" in *Luke*, 152.

the language describing Jesus' commands.[533] Thus, although the Lukan changes to Jesus'

speech do fit with my thesis, I view the change primarily as stylistic preference, and I do

not count this pericope as primary evidence of the proposed pattern.

161. The Transfiguration

Mark 9:8-10a	Luke 9:36
καὶ ἐξάπινα περιβλεψάμενοι οὐκέτι οὐδένα εἶδον εἰ μὴ τὸν Ἰησοῦν μόνον μεθ᾽ ἑαυτῶν Καὶ καταβαινόντων αὐτῶν ἐκ τοῦ ὄρους **διεστείλατο αὐτοῖς** **ἵνα μηδενὶ ἃ εἶδον διηγήσωνται** εἰ μὴ ὅταν ὁ υἱὸς τοῦ ἀνθρώπου ἐκ νεκρῶν ἀναστῇ καὶ τὸν λόγον ἐκράτησαν πρὸς ἑαυτούς	καὶ ἐν τῷ γενέσθαι τὴν φωνὴν εὑρέθη Ἰησοῦς μόνος καὶ αὐτοὶ ἐσίγησαν καὶ οὐδενὶ ἀπήγγειλαν ἐν ἐκείναις ταῖς ἡμέραις οὐδὲν ὧν ἑώρακαν

In the transfiguration pericope (Mark 9:2-10//Luke 9:28-36), Luke significantly

alters the Markan source concerning the narrative description of Jesus' speech.[534]

---

[533] Matthew omits any narrator description of Jesus ‑charging" or even ‑saying" due to the addition of a series of imperatives not found in Mark or Luke. Before Jesus' charge, Μὴ κτήσησθε χρυσὸν μηδὲ ἄργυρον μηδὲ χαλκὸν εἰς τὰς ζώνας ὑμῶν (v.9), Jesus' commands include κηρύσσετε (v.7); θεραπεύετε, καθαρίζετε, ἐγείρετε, ἐκβάλλετε, δότε (v.8). In my opinion, all three versions seem to be different due to stylistic preferences.

[534] For a complete analysis of all the Lukan redactions concerning the transfiguration, see Barbara Reid, *The Transfiguration: A Source and Redaction-Critical Study of Luke 9:28-36* (Paris: Gabalda, 1993).

Though the result of both passages is that Peter, James, and John do not tell anyone what they have seen, the emotion portrayal of Jesus and his words is radically different. Luke removes Mark's harsh language, διεστείλατο αὐτοῖς ἵνα μηδενὶ ἃ εἶδον διηγήσωνται (Mark 9:9).[535] The Lukan text generically states, καὶ αὐτοὶ ἐσίγησαν καὶ οὐδενὶ ἀπήγγειλαν ἐν ἐκείναις ταῖς ἡμέραις οὐδὲν ὧν ἑώρακαν (9:36), *without* Jesus charging them to tell no one.[536]

Many scholars recognize Luke's redactional change, but provide little actual commentary.[537] John Nolland, among others, has argued that Luke does not reproduce from Mark Jesus' call to silence because Luke ―is consistently less interested in the messianic secret."[538] Space does not permit a full discussion on the theme in general, but I can say that Nolland's statement (at least in the broadest understanding) is not true for

---

[535] For the emotional intensity of διαστέλλω, see previous analysis of the pericope concerning Jairus' daughter (Mark 5:40, 43//Luke 8:53, 56), where Luke likewise omits διαστέλλω.

[536] Importantly, Matthew, pace Luke, keeps Mark's actual charge of silence, Καὶ καταβαινόντων αὐτῶν ἐκ τοῦ ὄρους ἐνετείλατο αὐτοῖς ὁ Ἰησοῦς λέγων, Μηδενὶ εἴπητε τὸ ὅραμα (17:9). Matthew's linguistic choice – the aorist indicative form of ἐντέλλω with λέγω along with Jesus' direct discourse – is at least as emotionally trenchant (along the lines of ―command emphatically") as the Markan version, which itself carries significant emotional weight; see BADG, 268; LSJ, 266.

[537] Schweizer states plainly ―Luke omits Jesus' demand for silence; the disciples are silent of their own accord" in *Good News according to Luke*, 161. Even Bovon states that this verse (Luke 9:36) shows Luke's ―redactional peculiarities" concerning the silence of the disciples, though doesn't actually state what these are in *Saint Luc 1-9*, 477. Contra Ringe (in *Luke*, 142; see also Morris, *Luke*, 189), who states that all questions within the narrative have been resolved, hence no words are necessary. Nolland rightly asserts the experience of the disciples in Luke is more puzzling than illuminating, and interprets the silence more along the lines of bewilderment. Commentators that recognize the Lukan redaction though provide little analysis include: C.F. Evans, *Saint Luke*, 421; Culpepper, *Gospel of Luke*, 207; Green, *Gospel of Luke*, 384-85; Radl, *Das Evangelium nach Lukas: 1,1-9,50*, 635-36.

[538] Nolland, *Luke 9:21-18:34*, 502.

this passage.[539] While Luke omits Jesus' *command* of silence, thus linguistically softening the tone of Jesus' emotional portrayal, he deliberately maintains the *actual* silence of Peter John, and James.[540] In fact, the theme of silence is one of the few Markan themes in this passage that Luke *does not* suppress.[541]

Luke Timothy Johnson contends the silence of the disciples in Luke 9:36 is in obedience to Jesus command in Luke 9:21.[542] Jesus' command of silence in Luke 9:21 is interpreted by many commentators as evidence contrary to my proposed thesis of Luke softening Jesus' speech in Mark, but the following lexical analysis reveals the opposite.

158. Peter's Confession

Mark 8:27b-30	Luke 9:18b-21
τίνα με λέγουσιν οἱ ἄνθρωποι εἶναι	τίνα με οἱ ὄχλοι λέγουσιν εἶναι
οἱ δὲ εἶπαν αὐτῷ λέγοντες ὅτι	οἱ δὲ ἀποκριθέντες εἶπαν
Ἰωάννην τὸν βαπτιστήν,	Ἰωάννην τὸν βαπτιστήν,
καὶ ἄλλοι Ἡλίαν,	ἄλλοι δὲ Ἡλίαν,
ἄλλοι δὲ ὅτι εἷς τῶν προφητῶν.	ἄλλοι δὲ ὅτι προφήτης
	τις τῶν ἀρχαίων ἀνέστη.
καὶ αὐτὸς ἐπηρώτα αὐτούς	εἶπεν δὲ αὐτοῖς
ὑμεῖς δὲ τίνα με λέγετε εἶναι;	ὑμεῖς δὲ τίνα με λέγετε εἶναι;
ἀποκριθεὶς ὁ Πέτρος λέγει αυτῷ	Πέτρος δὲ ἀποκριθεὶς εἶπεν
σὺ εἶ ὁ χριστός.	τὸν χριστὸν τοῦ θεοῦ

---

[539] Craig A. Evans explicitly states when commenting on this verse that Luke borrows the messianic secrecy motif from Mark, not only in this passage, but in general, though Luke does redirect it for his purpose in *Luke*, 154.

[540] For an in-depth discussion of how Luke has deliberately kept the silence and re-interpreted the theme according to his intentions, see Marshall, *Gospel of Luke*, 388-89.

[541] Michael Goulder contends it is the only theme Luke does not suppress from Mark 9:9-13 except for the initial themes of descent from the mountain in *Luke: A New Paradigm I*, 445.

[542] Johnson makes his intriguing assertion in light of the entire literary unit, which he terms ‑recognizing Jesus" (Luke 9:18-36) in *Gospel of Luke*, 150-156.

καὶ *ἐπετίμησεν αὐτοῖς*	ὁ δὲ *ἐπιτιμήσας αὐτοῖς παρήγγειλεν*
ἵνα μηδενὶ λέγωσιν περὶ αὐτοῦ	μηδενὶ λέγειν τοῦτο

At the end of the passage usually labeled Peter's confession (Mark 8:27-30//Luke 9:18-21) and before Jesus' prediction of his passion (Mark 8:31-33//Luke 9:22), Jesus charges the disciples to remain silent. Mark states καὶ ἐπετίμησεν αὐτοῖς ἵνα μηδενὶ λέγωσιν περὶ αὐτοῦ (8:30), which Luke redacts to ὁ δὲ ἐπιτιμήσας αὐτοῖς παρήγγειλεν μηδενὶ λέγειν τοῦτο (9:21).[543] Most English translations correctly render Mark's aorist indicative ἐπετίμησεν αὐτοῖς, "he sternly ordered them," or "charged them" or "warned them."[544] These same translations basically ignore the Lukan participial construction ὁ δὲ ἐπιτιμήσας αὐτοῖς παρήγγειλεν in translating "he sternly ordered *and* commanded them," or "he charged them *and* commanded them" (emphases

---

[543] Importantly, Matthew increases the intensity of Jesus' charge. Matthew's Jesus states, τότε διεστείλατο τοῖς μαθηταῖς ἵνα μηδενὶ εἴπωσιν (16:20), using the emotional and typically Markan διαστέλλω. For the emotional intensity of διαστέλλω, see previous analysis of the pericopae concerning Jairus' daughter (Mark 5:40, 43//Luke 8:53, 56) and the transfiguration (Mark 9:2-10//Luke 9:28-36), where Luke removes the Markan uses of διαστέλλω. The Markan narrator uses διαστέλλω in 7:36, which has no parallel in Luke and a tenuous parallel in Matthew (in which four full verses are omitted). Mark further uses διαστέλλω in describing Jesus speech (8:15) in the narrative concerning the leaven of the Pharisees (Matt 16:5-12//Mark 8:14-21//Luke 12:1), which both Matthew (in a close textual parallel) and Mark (in a tenuous parallel) remove.

[544] See discussion of ἐπιτιμάω above in the analysis on Mark 3:7-12//Luke 6:17-19 or 4:41.

added), implying a harsher tone to Jesus' command.[545] A simple literal rendition is along the lines of, "having warned him, he charged them," which seems to be tonally similar to the Markan version, and more representative of the Greek text.[546] If Luke's command still seems more intense than the pattern I have shown in other Lukan passages, as an exception to the proposed rule, it must be seen in the context of the following passage – Peter's rebuke of Jesus and Jesus' subsequent satanic rebuke of Peter and its complete omission by Luke.

159. Jesus Foretells His Passion

Mark 8:31-33	Luke 9:22
Καὶ ἤρξατο διδάσκειν αυτούς	εἰπὼν
ὅτι δεῖ τὸν υἱὸν τοῦ ἀνθρώπου	ὅτι δεῖ τὸν υἱὸν τοῦ ἀνθρώπου
πολλὰ παθεῖν καὶ ἀποδοκιμασθῆναι	πολλὰ παθεῖν καὶ ἀποδοκιμασθῆναι
ὑπὸ τῶν πρεσβυτέρων καὶ	ἀπο τῶν πρεσβυτέρων καὶ
τῶν ἀρχιερέων καὶ τῶν γραμματέων	ἀρχιερέων καὶ γραμματέων
καὶ ἀποκτανθῆναι	καὶ ἀποκτνθῆναι
καὶ μετὰ τρεῖς ἡμέρας ἀναστῆναι	καὶ τῇ τρίτῃ ἡμέρᾳ ἐγερθῆναι

---

[545] See, for example, Arthur A. Just Jr., who in comparing the Lukan text with the Markan source, argues that Luke "heightens the messianic secret ... by adding 'commanded' to 'rebuking'," in *Luke 1:1-9:50*, 393; see also Culpepper, *Gospel of Luke*, 200.

[546] See especially John Nolland who makes a similar argument in *Luke 9:21-18:34*, 464. Because this linguistic change is not usual of Lukan style, Nolland contends Luke uses the participle form to subordinate the Markan idea of rebuke (according to the same redactional principle, Peter's rebuke of Jesus and vice versa in Mark 8:32-33 is also eliminated in Luke, see below), where the principal verb is ἐπιτιμᾶν. Thus, the command to silence comes to the fore using the common Lukan παραγγέλειν (see for example, analysis of Luke 5:14 above). I. Howard Marshall argues that the linguistic choices by Luke (participle over indicative) softens the command language to the point that the command of silence loses all importance in *Gospel of Luke*, 367.

καὶ παρρησίᾳ τὸν λόγον ἐλάλει __καὶ προσλαβόμενος ὁ Πέτρος αὐτὸν__ __ἤρξατο ἐπιτιμᾶν αὐτῷ ὁ δὲ ἐπιστραφεὶς__ __καὶ ἰδὼν τοὺς μαθητὰς αὐτοῦ__ __ἐπετίμησεν Πέτρῳ καὶ λέγει, ὕπαγε__ __ὀπίσω μου, σατανᾶ, ὅτι οὐ φρονεῖς τὰ__ __τοῦ θεοῦ ἀλλὰ τὰ τῶν ἀνθρώπων__	

The proposed Lukan principle of omitting (or at least softening) Jesus' stern and sometimes angry speech found in Mark is seen most clearly in the omission of the contentious altercation between Jesus and Peter culminating in the famous rebuke, "Get behind me Satan!" (Mark 8:33). In foretelling his impending death using self-referential "Son of Man" terminology (Mark 8:31-33//Luke 9:22), the Markan narrator states that Jesus had spoken "openly" (παρρησίᾳ) with the disciples. Jesus' predictive comments on his coming suffering provoke Peter's private rebuke of Jesus: καὶ προσλαβόμενος ὁ Πέτρος αὐτὸν ἤρξατο ἐπιτιμᾶν αὐτῷ (8:32b). Peter's private reprimand of Jesus in turn provokes Jesus' public rebuke of Peter: ὁ δὲ ἐπιστραφεὶς καὶ ἰδὼν τοὺς μαθητὰς αὐτοῦ ἐπετίμησεν Πέτρῳ (8:33a).[547] After describing the action through his narrator, Mark uses direct discourse to emphasize Jesus' already puissant admonition: ὕπαγε

---

[547] It seems Luke is making an explicit point in that Jesus turns and looks at the disciples before rebuking Peter in order to contrast Peter taking Jesus aside to rebuke him privately. Jesus' rebuke is public in the sense that it is in front of the disciples. The crowd is called immediately after Jesus' harsh rebuke of Peter.

ὀπίσω μου, σατανᾶ, ὅτι οὐ φρονεῖς τὰ τοῦ θεοῦ ἀλλὰ τὰ τῶν ἀνθρώπων (8:33b).

This entire exchange between Peter and Jesus is eliminated in Luke.[548]

Most commentators assume the reason Luke omits this passage is to enhance the portrayal of Peter.[549] Luke Timothy Johnson states, ―Luke skips the objection by Peter to Jesus‗ suffering, and Jesus‗ counter-rebuke of Peter. The portrait of Peter is thus enhanced."[550] Michael D. Goulder similarly declares, ―The omission of Peter‗s rebuke to Jesus, and its response, saves the apostle‗s blushes as usual."[551] By omitting a heated exchange with Jesus, Peter‗s portrait is perhaps slightly enhanced in this specific instance, but Peter‗s portrait is certainly not Luke‗s primary concern.[552] Luke, in

---

[548] It is important to observe that Matthew does not omit this pericope. Matthew changes certain aspects of the narrative, but if anything, Jesus‗ words are harsher in Matthew. Matthew keeps Peter‗s rebuke using similar language (16:22). Matthew removes the narration describing Jesus‗ rebuke (ἐπετίμησεν, Mark 8:33); Matthew instead reads generically, ὁ δὲ στραφεὶς εἶπεν τῷ Πέτρῳ (Matt 16:23b). However, Jesus‗ direct discourse is an even stronger rebuke in Matthew, calling Peter an ―offense" or a ―hindrance." Matthew‗s text is a close linguistic parallel to Mark, but includes the harsh words: σκάνδαλον εἶ ἐμοῦ (26:23c).

[549] Like my previous narrative analyses, even an omission as important as this one fails to elicit comment from many otherwise fine commentaries. C.F. Evans asserts that Luke ―boldly suppresses the hostile reaction of Peter to the announcement and his consequent rebuke as Satanic," but does not say why in *Saint Luke*, 407. Other important commentators that recognize the Lukan omission of Mark 8:32-33, though deny, ignore, or understate their importance: Danker, *Jesus and the New Age*, 193-194; Culpepper, *Gospel of Luke*, 200; Radl, *Das Evangelium nach Lukas*, 615.

[550] Johnson, *Gospel of Luke*, 151. I. Howard Marshall also contends, ―Peter no longer appears in a bad light" in *Gospel of Luke*, 367. Schweizer adds, ―The harsh attack on Peter found in Mark 8:32-33 he [Luke] is happy to omit in any case, so as not to speak ill of Peter in *The Good News according to Luke*, 157.

[551] Goulder, *Luke: A New Paradigm I*, 438.

[552] Peter‗s overall depiction in Luke, like the other disciples, is still mixed. See above discussion on the Lukan portrayal of the disciples in light of the Kingdom of God and children narrative (Mark 10:13-16//Luke 18:15-17). Why would Luke keep Peter‗s denial (22:54ff), along with other passages where Peter still does not understand Jesus and his message (i.e. 22:54), if his main concern were Peter? Further, the *occasion* of the pericope is Peter‗s apparent misunderstanding (or at least not full understanding) and Jesus‗ mistrust of Peter and the disciples to disseminate the message (9:18-21). The reason for the command of silence (9:21, analyzed above) in Luke seems to be the near certainty of misunderstanding if it were spread

omitting this passage, and in his omissions overall, is most concerned with *Jesus* and his characterization.[553] In light of his Markan source, it is the behavior of Jesus that Luke feels obliged to save.[554]

272. The Cursing of the Fig Tree

Mark 11:12-14	Luke 13:6-9
Καὶ τῇ ἐπαύριον	Ἔλεγεν δὲ ταύτην τὴν παραβολήν.
ἐξελθόντων αὐτῶν ἀπὸ βηθανίας	συκῆν εἶχέν τις πεφυτευμένην
ἐπείνασεν	ἐν τῷ ἀμπελῶνι αὐτοῦ,
καὶ ἰδὼν συκῆν ἀπὸ μακρόθεν	καὶ ἦλθεν ζητῶν καρπὸν ἐν αὐτῇ,
ἔχουσαν φύλλα	καὶ οὐχ εὗρεν.
ἦλθεν εἰ ἄρα τι εὑρήσει ἐν αὐτῇ,	εἶπεν δὲ πρὸς τὸν ἀμπελουργόν
	ἰδοὺ τρία ἔτη
	ἀφ' οὗ ἔρχομαι ζητῶν

abroad. See further Morris, *Luke*, 185. See also analysis of the emotional characterization of the disciples in chapter five.

[553] In fact, Luke's removal of Peter's rebuke is probably due to the third corollary (to the proposed Lukan redactional principle of subjugating Jesus' emotion) presented above in analyzing the scene at the synagogue (Mark 3:1-6//Luke 6:6-11). There is a general Lukan principle of omitting or lessening the violence (or the threat of violence) and strong emotion *to* Jesus as discussed above. Again, Luke is primarily concerned with the portrait of Jesus, Jesus' actions and the actions done to him.

[554] As previously stated, pericopae often have multiple functions. For example, I accept Schweizer's contention that the episode points forward to Luke 9:51 and thus to Jesus' journey to his cross and resurrection in *The Good News according to Luke*, 159-160. Judith Lieu sees the passage as having a two-fold purpose, ―Luke omits this [Peter's protest and Jesus' rebuke], perhaps out of kindness to the disciples but more because it enables him immediately to follow Jesus' words with the demand of discipleship" in *Gospel of Luke*, 73. I accept her latter contention, and reject the former. Similarly, I agree with Craig A. Evans when he states, ―Peter's rejection of this idea and his rebuke in turn by Jesus (Mark 8:32-33) are omitted by Luke so that the evangelist may provide a closer link between Jesus' passion pronouncement in vv.21-22 and his teaching in vv.23-26 on the suffering involved in being his follower." I disagree with him when he appends, ―It is also omitted because Luke wishes to present Peter and the other apostles in the best light possible" in *Luke*, 149.

καὶ ἐλθὼν ἐπ’ αὐτὴν οὐδὲν εὗρεν εἰ μὴ φύλλα ὁ γὰρ καιρὸς οὐκ ἦν σύκων. καὶ ἀποκριθεὶς εἶπεν αὐτῇ μηκέτι εἰς τὸν αἰῶνα ἐκ σοῦ μηδεὶς καρπὸν φάγοι. καὶ ἤκουον οἱ μαθηταὶ αὐτοῦ.	καρπὸν ἐν τῇ συκῇ ταύτῃ καὶ οὐχ εὑρίσκω ἔκκοψον αὐτήν ἱνατί καὶ τὴν γῆν καταργεῖ; ὁ δὲ ἀποκριθεὶς λέγει αὐτῷ κύριε, ἄφες αὐτὴν καὶ τοῦτο τὸ ἔτος, ἕως ὅτο σκάψω περὶ αὐτὴν καὶ βάλω κόπρια, κἂν μὲν ποιήσῃ καρπὸν εἰς τὸ μέλλον εἰ δὲ ἥ γε, ἐκκόψεις αὐτήν.

Despite the listing in *Synopsis Quattuor Evangeliorum*, the Lukan version (13:6-9) is so different from Mark‘s (11:12-14) that most scholars do not recognize the Lukan episode as a true parallel.[555] Outside of generally concerning a fig tree‘s unproductiveness, there is almost no linguistic similarity,[556] though for the purpose of this

---

[555] Aland lists the Lukan pericope in a different font size beside the Mark-Matthew parallel in ―272, Verfluchung des Feigenbaums" in *Synopsis,* 371. Luke removes the Markan narrative of the fig tree, both the cursing (11:12-14) and the lesson of the withered fig tree (11:20-25). Matthew keeps a version of both halves of the story, but removes Mark‘s intertwining of the temple cleansing; instead, Matthew puts both halves after the temple cleansing. C. Clifton Black states, ―The cursing of the fig tree (vv.12-15, 20-25) and the cleansing of the temple are interwoven, each interpreting the other" in ―Mark: Introduction," *The HarperCollins Study Bible* (New York: HarperCollins, 1993), 1940. Such narrative intertwinings are characteristic of Mark; see 2:1-12; 3:1-6; 3:19-35; 5:21-43; 6:7-30; 14:1-11; 14:53-72; 15:6-32. See further Eduard Schweizer, *The Good News according to Mark* (tran. Donald H. Madvig; Atlanta: John Knox, 1970), 230.

[556] While commenting on the Matthean parallel (21:18-19), C.S. Mann rules out the interrelation of Mark‘s cursing pericope (11:12-14) with Luke‘s parable (13:6-9): ―While there is the common feature of the unproductiveness, the language of this pericope would appear to rule out the connection. . . . There is a vividness about the narrative which is lacking in the Lucan parable" in *Mark: A New Translation with Introduction and Commentary* (AB 27; Garden City, N.Y.: Doubleday, 1986), 439-440. See also Sharon H. Ringe, *Luke* (Louisville: Westminster John Knox, 1995), 183-85. While the parallel relationship between Mark and Luke is tenuous, most scholars see the Matthew version dependent on Mark; see Albright and Mann, *Matthew,* 260-61. At the very least, the actual curse is linguistically similar in Matthew, καὶ λέγει αὐτῇ, Μηκέτι ἐκ σοῦ καρπὸς γένηται εἰς τὸν αἰῶνα (21:19b). Of special consequence is the comparison of last sentences in Matthew and Mark. While Mark states that the disciples heard the curse (11:14), Matthew states, καὶ ἐξηράνθη παραχρῆμα ἡ συκῆ (21:19c). Jesus‘

dissertation it doesn't really matter, as each interpretation yields the same result. If Luke omitted the cursing episode (the most probable explanation), he did so due to the troubling emotional depiction of Jesus irrationally cursing a tree for not having fruit during the off-season.[557] If Luke drastically redacted the Markan pericope of an irrational and emotional Jesus into a parable about a man not harming a fig tree, then he did so for the same reason.[558]

The history of interpretation of the Markan passage yields an important hermeneutical nugget which is relevant to the emotional depiction of Jesus in Mark and the need to omit the passage (or drastically alter it) in Luke. C.S. Mann notes that this pericope has been embarrassing for many commentators, both ancient and modern.[559] Some feel it necessary to explain the cantankerousness of Jesus when unreasonable demands are not met. For many commentators the whole account is a misunderstood parable, while for others there may be a desire to acquit Jesus of anything approaching a misapprehension or mistake.[560] Analogous to my proposal that we see Luke as one of many portraitists, in a certain sense, Luke was one of the first commentators on Mark's

---

curse is so mordacious in Matthew, he not only curses the tree to quit bearing fruit, he actually causes the tree to immediately wither. It is most likely ξηραίνω implies that Jesus actually killed the tree, but could also mean that the tree just immediately stopped producing fruit; see BADG, 548. The most important facet for my purposes is that the tone of Jesus' speech/curse is stronger in Matthew than Mark.

[557] Cadbury suggests this interpretation: ―Luke's omission of the cursing of the fig tree (Mark 11, 12-14, 20-25) may be due to the same motive [the omission of human emotions and expressions]" in *Style and Literary Method*, 91.

[558] Luke Timothy Johnson states that Luke's parable may derive from the same tradition, but turns it in quite a different way in *Gospel of Luke*, 211. Goulder sees the parallel passages based on thematic similarity, arguing that Luke makes the same point more gently (challenging Israel to repent) by turning a scandalous miracle in Mark into a Lukan parable in *Luke: A New Paradigm II*, 562-63.

[559] Mann, *Mark*, 439.

[560] See the somewhat dated but excellent review of scholarship, J. Duncan M. Derrett, ―Figtrees in the New Testament," *Heythrop Journal* 14:3 (1973), 249-278.

text. Like the commentators that followed him, Luke found Mark's version

embarrassing, and therefore chose to omit it (or radically alter it).

Grief / Neediness

46. Plucking Grain of the Sabbath

Mark 2:25	Luke 6:3
Καὶ λέγει αὐτοῖς, οὐδέποτε ἀνέγνωτε τί ἐποίησεν Δαυίδ, ὅτε **χρείαν ἔσχεν** καὶ ἐπείνασεν αὐτὸς καὶ οἱ μετ᾽ αὐτοῦ	καὶ ἀποκριθεὶς πρὸς αὐτοὺς εἶπεν ὁ Ἰησοῦς, οὐδὲ τοῦτο ἀνέγνωτε ὃ ἐποίησεν Δαυίδ, ὁπότε ἐπείνασεν αὐτὸς καὶ οἱ μετ᾽ αὐτοῦ ὄντες

In the first of two Sabbath controversy scenes, Jesus compares his actions to those

of David in picking grain on the Sabbath (Mark 2:23-28//Luke 6:1-5). The Markan

account reads, Καὶ λέγει αὐτοῖς, οὐδέποτε ἀνέγνωτε τί ἐποίησεν Δαυίδ, ὅτε χρείαν

ἔσχεν καὶ ἐπείνασεν αὐτὸς καὶ οἱ μετ᾽ αὐτοῦ (2:26), and the Lukan version similarly

construes, καὶ ἀποκριθεὶς πρὸς αὐτοὺς εἶπεν ὁ Ἰησοῦς, οὐδὲ τοῦτο ἀνέγνωτε ὃ

ἐποίησεν Δαυίδ, ὁπότε ἐπείνασεν αὐτὸς καὶ οἱ μετ᾽ αὐτοῦ ὄντες (6:3). The Lukan

redactor maintains the physical aspect of Jesus' hunger (ἐπείνασεν), but omits the emotional language of neediness in Mark (χρείαν ἔσχεν).[561]

There is much debate as to the exact meaning of Mark's language of neediness

(χρεία), specifically in regard to the emotional aspect and reason for Luke's omission.[562]

While most commentators either ignore the omission or arrogate it to mere stylistic

preference by Luke,[563] there is an emotional component to Luke's omission of Jesus'

description of David (χρείαν ἔσχεν).[564] Jesus' description of David is self-descriptive

and comparative. Obviously, Luke (along with the other evangelists) relies upon Davidic

language to describe Jesus and his message. Perhaps further, Luke has omitted Jesus'

description of David (as being ―needy") in order to avoid the association of Jesus with

such an emotional state.[565]

χρεία is a common Lukan word, and Luke's use of χρεία is complicated and

---

[561] BADG generically defines χρεία as ―to be in need," listing Mark 2:25 as an example, 885. See also A.J. Hultgren, ―The Function of the Sabbath Pericope in Mark 2:23-28," *JBL* 91 (1972): 38-43.

[562] There is also an obvious stylistic concern with repetition if χρεία is perceived as simply a physical need, repeating the notion of πεινάω. See classically John C. Hawkins, *Horae Synopticae: Contributions to the Study of the Synoptic Problem* (Oxford: Clarendon Press, 1899), 100-110.

[563] See Nolland, *Luke 1-9:20,* 256, who maintains χρεία is a repetitive general term. Marshall terms the Lukan redactions ―stylistic changes" in *Gospel of Luke,* 228. Goulder calls the Lukan change ―superfluous" in *Luke: A New Paradigm I,* 337, following C.M. Tuckett, *The Revival of the Griesbach Hypothesis: An Analysis and Appraisal* (SNTS 44; Cambridge: Cambridge University Press, 1983), 20, 194.

[564] Contrarily, for example, Luke clearly omits the name of the priest in Mark 2:26, Abiathar, because it is incorrect (1 Sam 21:1 reads Ahimelech). The reason for the χρεία omission is more complicated and nuanced.

[565] In his discussion of Luke's omissions, Cadbury was one of the first to argue for an impoverished emotional neediness beyond a mere physical condition in *Style and Literary Method,* 90-97; see also Radl, *Das Evangelium nach Lukas: 1,1-9,50,* 341-43.

nuanced. Sometimes it obviously implies only a general or physical need, as in the need

for a witness (22:71), or Jesus' need for a colt (19:31, 34). Sometimes the context

provides for the possibility of either a physical or an emotional/spiritual need (or even

both), as in those in need of a physician (5:31) or healing (9:11). Other times χρεία

clearly connotes both a physical and an emotional need, as it is used to describe eating,

drinking, as well as anxiety (12:30). Just as often, χρεία applies solely to a spiritual

and/or an emotional condition, as in Martha's anxiety and many troubles (10:41-42),

general friendship needs (12:30), and the need for repentence and joy (15:7). Further, as

seen by these examples, χρεία has both positive and negative connotations. Basic

physical needs and certain spiritual needs are seen as both necessary and good (e.g. food,

drink, friendship, repentence, etc.), while Martha's situation, for instance, has a more

pejorative tone. While certainly χρεία can imply a general need (either physical,

emotional, or both) without negative implications, there is evidence in antiquity of a

negative connotation with χρεία. In the previously mentioned *Progymnasmata*,

Aphthonius has an essay on *Chreia (Progymnasmata 4: Maxim)* which he concludes, ―So

we must admire Euripides, who said that it is an evil thing to be in want (χρείαν)."

While the omission of χρεία cannot serve as primary evidence that Luke has removed

emotion from the character of Jesus, it may be the case that Luke has removed χρεία

from Jesus' depiction in order to avoid associating the character of Jesus with even the perception of strong emotion.[566]

47. The Man with the Withered Hand

Mark 3:5a	Luke 6:10a
καὶ περιβλεψάμενος αὐτοὺς <u>μετ᾽ ὀργῆς</u>, **συλλυπούμενος ἐπὶ τῇ πωρώσει τῆς καρδίας αὐτῶν**, λέγει τῷ ἀνθρώπῳ ἔκτεινον τὴν χεῖρα.	καὶ περιβλεψάμενος πάντας αὐτοὺς εἶπεν αὐτῷ ἔκτεινον τὴν χεῖρα σου.

In the previously mentioned pericope concerning healing on the Sabbath (Mark 3:1-6//Luke 6:6-11), the author of Luke redacts not only the anger of Jesus (by transferring it to the scribes and Pharisees), but the classic Stoic emotion of grief (λύπη) is removed in his portrayal of Jesus. The entire Markan phrase, συλλυπούμενος ἐπὶ τῇ πωρώσει τῆς καρδίας αὐτῶν, is omitted from the Lukan narration.[567] The simple verbal form (λυπέω) of λύπη, especially in the present passive form, merely indicates ―to be grieved" or ―to be distressed."[568] With the preposition, συλλυπέω strengthens the

---

[566] Matthew also makes the same redaction, removing the Markan phrase, χρείαν ἔσχεν (12:3).

[567] Matthew's version is so different in general, it is difficult to compare emotional characterizations. Matthew omits the second half of Mark 3:4 and all of verse 5, whereas Luke removes only the specific emotional Markan phrase, συλλυπούμενος ἐπὶ τῇ πωρώσει τῆς καρδίας αὐτῶν (3:4a). Contra Luke, Matthew does retain the violence of the Pharisees at the end of the passage (12:14).

[568] LSJ, ―λυπέω," 480.

simple verb, and connotes a togetherness, ‑grieve at the same time" or ‑sympathy with," thus some translations prefer ‑sympathy" or ‑compassion."[569]

Despite the previously mentioned assertion by I. Howard Marshall that the ‑alterations made by Luke to his source are insignificant,"[570] many scholars recognize the importance of Luke's removal of Jesus' anger.[571] Some of these commentators, while noting the significance of Luke removing Jesus' anger,[572] miss the importance of Luke also removing a traditional emotion from his characterization of Jesus.[573] Almost all the commentators correctly recognize the importance of this passage in showing the authority of Jesus, culminating with the self-referential proclamation, ‑The Son of Man is lord of the Sabbath" (Mark 2:28//Luke 6:5), though they miss the fact that the removal of emotion is directly related to the authority of Jesus. Robert Tannehill, for example, who identifies the Lukan redactions, errs in this important regard, ‑*Although* Luke omits Mark's references to Jesus' anger and grief, Jesus' question is *still* challenging and his behavior provocative" [emphasis added].[574] Jesus is a challenging and provocative public

---

[569] BADG contends, ‑in συλλυπούμενος ἐπὶ τῇ πωρώσει τῆς καρδίας αὐτῶν Mark 3:5 the prep. surely has no other force than to strengthen the simple verb *deeply grieved at the hardening of their heart*," 777.

[570] Marshall, *Gospel of Luke*, 233.

[571] Even François Bovon admits that Luke tones down both of Jesus' emotions (Mark 3:5: μετ' ὀργῆς, συλλυπούμενος; ‑with anger, he was grieved," despite contending earlier that the claim of Luke suppressing emotions is mistaken. See Bovon, *Saint Luc 1-9*, 266, 23.

[572] This is partly due to the sheer number of instances of Luke removing or softening Jesus' anger. Metzger, commenting solely on the textual critical traditions, exclaims that Luke could not admit that Jesus showed anger in *A Textual Commentary on the Greek New Testament*, 140.

[573] Scholars who note the redaction of Jesus' anger but not his grief include C.F. Evans, *Saint Luke*, 316-17; Green, *Gospel of Luke*, 251-257; Ringe, *Luke*, 86-88; Culpepper, *Gospel of Luke*, 135.

[574] Tannehill, *Luke*, 111.

figure *because* he embodies the unemotional ideal.

154. The Pharisees Seek a Sign

Mark 8:12a	Luke 12:54?
καὶ ἀναστενάξας τῷ πνεύματι αὐτοῦ λέγει	omits

As stated in the introduction to the Lukan redactions, I do not include the pericope of the Pharisees seeking a sign (Mark 8:11-13//Luke ?) as primary evidence for the proposed pattern. Along with most scholars, I do not view it as a true parallel,[575] as it is part of the block of texts termed "the great omission" or "big omission." At the very least, however, it does demonstrate Mark's Jesus as showing strong emotion. When the Pharisees come to Jesus seeking a sign from heaven in the Markan narrative (8:11-13), the narrator tells the reader (8:12) that Jesus καὶ ἀναστενάξας τῷ πνεύματι," "sighed deeply in his spirit" or "let out a deep groan from his spirit" connoting an emotional disturbance, a mix of sadness and slight anger, conceivably even frustration.[576]

---

[575] It is listed in *Synopsis Quattuor Evangeliorum* as no. 154, pp. 225-26. The Lukan column consists of three separate blocks of text: 11:16; 12:54-56; 11:29.

[576] See "ἀναστενάζω," BAGD, 61. See also Mark 7:34, "Then looking up to heaven, he sighed (ἐστέναξεν) and said to him" (7:34a). See further Cadbury, *Style and Literary Method*, 96. Matthew's version(s) are also tenous parallels, but in both cases, there is no mention of Jesus' sighing deeply in spirit (16:2, 12:39).

212

"Positive" Emotions

42. The Cleansing of the Leper

Mark 1:41	Luke 5:13a
καὶ **σπλαγχνισθεὶς**	καὶ
ἐκτείνας τὴν χεῖρα αὐτοῦ ἥψατο	ἐκτείνας τὴν χεῖρα ἥψατο αὐτοῦ
καὶ λέγει αὐτῷ θέλω, καθαρίσθητι	λέγων θέλω, καθαρίσθητι

Not only has the Markan source been redacted to eliminate the so-called
"negative" emotions from Jesus in Luke's account, but Jesus' feelings of compassion,
mercy, and love, as well as Jesus showing general affection, have also been removed
from the Lukan narrative.[577] In the aforementioned scene where Jesus cleanses a leper
(Mark 1:40-45//Luke 5:12-16), not only is the tone of Jesus' speech significantly softened
(Mark 1:43-44//Luke 5:14), but Jesus' pity/tenderness/compassion is removed.[578] Jesus
is "moved with compassion" in the Markan account (1:41), but σπλαγχνισθεὶς is
omitted from the Lukan text (5:13), which is otherwise almost identical to Mark's

---

[577] For a helpful discussion of the "positive" and "negative" emotions from a literary perspective, see
Powell, *What Are They Saying about Luke*, 19-20.

[578] My analysis is complicated by text critical concerns in Mark 1:41. The term σπλαγχνισθεὶς,
which is removed by Luke (and Matthew), has been altered to ὀργισθεὶς in various manuscripts, or vice
versa. Some textual traditions (D a ff² r¹), especially the western, read ὀργισθεὶς instead of
σπλαγχνισθεὶς, perhaps to remove the perceived conflict with Jesus' stern order (ἐμβριμησάμενος) in v.
43; see C.F. Evans, *Saint Luke*, 294. See further Metzger, who (pace Evans and Markus) prefers
σπλαγχνισθεὶς, but recognizes the possibility of ὀργισθεὶς in *A Textual Commentary on the Greek New
Testament*, 76-77. See discussion in Radl, *Das Evangelium nach Lukas: 1,1-9,50*, 308 n.155. In fact,
Markus argues for ὀργισθεὶς, in part, because he argues that Matthew and Luke would have included
σπλαγχνισθεὶς in their parallels, since they use the term elsewhere of Jesus (Matt 9:36; Luke 7:13). See
my comments below on the special Lukan material and Matthew's further use of σπλαγχνίζομαι.

version.[579] The root verb σπλαγχνίζομαι is related to the noun σπλάγχνον, which

generically is a term for inner parts or entrails, but was a technical philosophical term for

the ―seat of the emotions" in some traditions.[580]

Similar to the healing on the Sabbath incident (Mark 3:1-6//Luke 6:6-11), many

commentators correctly recognize the Lukan emphasis on Jesus' power and authority in

this cleansing pericope (Mark 1:40-45//Luke 5:12-16), but fail to show how the Lukan

emotional redactions contribute to this emphasis.[581] Indicative of this tendency, I.

Howard Marshall discusses both the Lukan readactional changes and the authority of

Jesus. Marshall rightly points out that Luke omits ―Mark.'s σπλαγχνισθείς (v.l.

ὀργισθείς)" along with the ―difficult use of ἐμβριμησάμενος" because Luke ―avoids

expressions of Jesus' emotions," and the fact that the passage shows Jesus ―breaking

down barriers" and is representative of his increased reputation and ―becomes a

---

[579] Matthew makes the same omission of Jesus' emotion as Luke. Bovon applies the same reason for this omission to both Matthew and Luke – either a lack of understanding or an intolerance towards Jesus' wrath in *Saint Luc 1-9*, 233.

[580] BADG, ―σπλάγχνον," 763; it can also connote general love and affection; see Josephus, *Ant.* 15.359.

[581] C.F. Evans states the passage presents the ―single theme of Jesus wielding power and authority," though he describes the redactions as ―accidental" in *Saint Luke*, 293-94. Similarly, Luke Timothy Johnson notes the significance of the Lukan Jesus' *exousia* (power), explicitedly stated in 5:24, but contends ―Luke's alterations of his source are minimal, consisting mainly of clarifications" in *Gospel of Luke*, 94-95. Léopold Sabourin also emphasizes Jesus' authority without recognizing the significance of the Lukan redactions in *L'Évangile de Luc: Introduction et commentaire* (Roma: Editrice Pontificia Università Gregoriana, 1985), 145-47. See also Lieu, *Gospel of Luke*, 39-40, who states the main theme is ―Jesus' authority," and rightly identifies that ―Luke does not speak of Jesus' compassion," but does not associate the two. Craig A. Evans sees the main Lukan theme is a question of true authority in *Luke*, 87-93. He also discusses this theme in relation to the ―private" Jesus and the ―public" Jesus. Puzzlingly, Craig A. Evans, *Luke*, fails to note the redactional changes concerning emotion in an otherwise close textual analysis with respect to a Greco-Roman audience and milieu. Evans descants (91) on Luke's redactional change of a tiled roof (5:19) from Mark's digging through the roof (2:4), ―Luke puts it this way probably for the sake of his Greco-Roman readers who would have been more familiar with tile roofs."

214

testimony to the fulfillment of the promise of the messianic age,"[582] but does not link the *apatheia* of Jesus with this described authority. Robert C. Tannehill does not *directly* link Jesus' *apatheia* with his authority as a public leader, but does discuss the ―two expressions of strong emotion by Jesus" dropped by Luke in the general context of Jesus' courage.[583] In analyzing Luke 5:13, Walter Radl first comments on Jesus acting without hesitation and with authority, and immediately notes Luke's Jesus as being without emotion, then discusses the contrasting setting elements of publicness and isolation, though he never directly links these concepts.[584] Eduard Schweizer lists ―no reference to Jesus' emotions (Mark 1:41, 43)," along with Jesus' praying and the removal of the disobedience of the healed leper in his contention: ―perhaps in order to emphasize his intimate relationship with God at the very beginning of the conflict that follows" which he ultimately concludes points to Jesus' ―authority (5:17, 24)."[585] In light of this pericope where Jesus cleanses a leper (Mark 1:40-45//Luke 5:12-16) and the previous healing on the Sabbath incident (Mark 3:1-6//Luke 6:6-11), Luke's portrayal of an unemotional Jesus is intricately linked to his portrayal of Jesus as the ultimate authority figure.

---

[582] Marshall, *Gospel of Luke*, 209; 210; 206-7. Bovon (again, despite his initial contention that Luke has not quelled Jesus' emotions) similarly discusses ―le courage et la souveraineté de Jésus" immediately after his statements: ―Le lépreux fait appel à cette volonté active, non à de bons sentiments. Quant à l'irritation de Jésus telle qu'elle apparaît chez Marc (Mc 1,41), Luc ne la comprend pas ou ne la supporte pas," though Bovon does not connect Jesus' emotionlessness with Jesus' courage in *Saint Luc 1-9*, 175.

[583] Tannehill, *Luke*, 102-3.

[584] Radl states of Luke's redactional agenda, ―Lukas erwähnt auch keinerlei Gemütsbewegung bei ihm (diff Mark 1,41)" in *Das Evangelium nach Lukas: 1,1-9,50*, 308.

[585] Schweizer, *The Good News according to Luke*, 110. Joseph Fitzmyer connects the ―omission of Jesus' human emotions" with the ―developing christological awareness in the early community, by the time Luke writes" which emphasizes ―Jesus' power and will, not his emotions" in *Luke I-IX*, 572-574. While Christology is certainly related to authority and power, I argued above against a simplistic human/divine distinction as related to the emotions in the pericope concerning the legality of healing on the Sabbath (Mark 3:1-6//Luke 6:6-11).

146. Five Thousand are Fed

Mark 6:34	Luke 9:11a
Καὶ ἐξελθὼν εἶδεν πολὺν ὄχλον, καὶ *ἐσπλαγχνίσθη* ἐπ᾽ αὐτοὺς ὅτι **ἦσαν ὡς πρόβατα μὴ ἔχοντα ποιμένα** καὶ ἤρξατο διδάσκειν αὐτοὺς πολλά	οἱ δὲ ὄχλοι γνόντες ἠκολούθησαν αὐτῷ καὶ *ἀποδεξάμενος* αὐτοὺς ἐλάλει αὐτοῖς περὶ τῆς βασιλείας τοῦ θεοῦ

As in the preceding pericope where Jesus heals a leper (Mark 1:40-45//Luke 5:12-16), Jesus' compassion is also redacted in Jesus' feeding of the multitudes (Mark 6:32-44//Luke 9:10b-17).[586] Whereas Mark's version states καὶ ἐσπλαγχνίσθη ἐπ᾽ αὐτοὺς (6:34), the Lukan account reads καὶ ἀποδεξάμενος αὐτοὺς (9:11).[587] Luke replaces the more emotional verb, σπλαγχνίζομαι (he had compassion or sympathy) with the more neutral ἀποδέχομαι (he welcomed).[588] Luke further removes the powerful emotional

---

[586] The root verb σπλαγχνίζομαι is removed from Mark 1:41(aorist participle σπλαγχνισθείς) in Luke 5:13 and from Mark 6:34 (aorist indicative ἐσπλαγχνίσθη) in Luke 9:11. See above for etymological analysis.

[587] Probably to reciprocate the crowd welcoming Jesus in 8:40 (ἀπεδέξατο αὐτὸν ὁ ὄχλος). See Sabourin, *L'Évangile de Luc*, 199.

[588] ἀποδέχομαι has a positive connotation (to ―receive favorably,‖ usually by a person of higher rank) without the emotional baggage of σπλαγχνίζομαι. See BADG, ―ἀποδέχομαι,‖ 90; also Bovon, *Saint Luc 1-9*, 356.

language of sheep (πρόβατα) needing a shepherd (ποιμένα).[589] Matthew does not

follow Luke in removing the Markan Jesus' compassion, but in line with Luke, he does

remove all reference to sheep needing a shepherd.[590]

Consistent with his redactional tendencies, Luke omits any hint of compassion or

pity or sentimentality in his depiction of Jesus, yet maintains his authority as a public

figure. Without endeavoring to be redundant, many commentators, as in the leper

cleansing (Mark 1:40-45//Luke 5:12-16), rightly acknowledge the Lukan emphasis on

Jesus' power and authority and the portrayal of a considerably less emotional Jesus, but

do not manifest how the Lukan emotional redactions augment this accentuation.[591] In a

primarily theological analysis, R. Alan Culpepper examines Luke's omission of ―Jesus'

compassion and the allusion to the people being like sheep without a shepherd in Mark

6:34" within the context of how the feeding pericope as a whole shows the ―full

revelatory power" of Jesus, but doesn't directly link these concepts.[592] I. Howard

Marshall asserts, ―Luke's narrative is closely dependent upon that of Mark. …. The main

---

[589] This is significant as a sheep without a shepherd is a common metaphor and Hebrew Bible phrase for the Israel/Yahweh relationship. See Num 27:15-17; 1 Kgs 22:17; 2 Chr 18:16; Ezek 34:1-31; Jdt 11:19. In fact, the Markan version of the story (along with his version of the four thousand) is deeply colored by Hebrew Bible stories of the feeding of Israel by Yahweh. See C.F. Evans literary analysis with OT parallels in *Saint Luke*, 400. While again refusing to fully acknowledge the emotion redactions, Bovon does state, ―Luc remplace … le style biblique par une expression grecque de l'hospitalité" in *Saint Luc 1-9*, 456.

[590] The first half of Matthew 14:14 is identical to the first half of Mark 6:34, Καὶ ἐξελθὼν εἶδεν πολὺν ὄχλον, καὶ ἐσπλαγχνίσθη ἐπ᾽ αὐτούς. See further Goulder, *Luke: A New Paradigm I*, 434.

[591] Of course, there are a plethora of commentaries that examine the authority of Jesus but surprisingly fail to avow the Lukan redactions concerning Jesus' emotion. See Schweizer, *The Good News according to Luke*, 154-55. Green, *Gospel of Luke*, 362-63. Tannehill, *Luke*, 154-57.

[592] Culpepper, *Gospel of Luke*, 195-96. Sabourin argues the passage increases the messianic character of Jesus, but this is not linked to his contention that Jesus is without compassion in *L'Évangile de Luc*, 199. See also Lieu, *Gospel of Luke*, 70-72. Craig A. Evans assays the ―power of Jesus" in referencing the distinctions with Mark 6:34, but doesn't directly associate them in *Luke*, 143-45.

difference lies in the enhanced christological stress." He later recognizes, ―Luke omits

mention of Jesus' sympathy for the crowds, and also the detail that he saw them as sheep

without a shepherd,"[593] though does not link these two Lukan themes. A paragraph

before his discussion of Jesus' power (*Macht*), Radl notes, ―Er nimmt sie freundlich auf.

Nach Mark 6,34 hat er Mitleid mit ihnen, weil sie wie Schafe ohne Hirte sind."[594] Joseph

Fitzmyer contends the Lukan version has a greater emphasis on the ―power of Jesus,"

though does not speculate why Luke removed Jesus' emotion, ―For some reason Luke

omits mention of the compassion of Jesus (cf. Mark 6:34)."[595] Luke removes Jesus'

emotion *in order* to accentuate Jesus' power.

Further evidence of the difference between Matthew and Luke is their use of

σπλαγχνίζομαι. While Matthew does follow Luke in removing Jesus' compassion in the

scene where Jesus cleanses a leper (Matt 8:1-4//Mark 1:40-45//Luke 5:12-16), Matthew

does not follow Luke's consistent redactional program in other pericopae. In the feeding

passages, Matthew retains the Markan usage of σπλαγχνίζομαι. Not only has Matthew

retained Jesus' compassion in Jesus' feeding of the five thousand (Matt 14:13-21// Mark

6:32-44//Luke 9:10b-17), but he has also retained Jesus' compassion in the great

omission text of Jesus feeding the four thousand (Matt 15:32-39//Mark 8:1-10). Both

---

[593] Marshall, *Gospel of Luke*, 359-360. Similarly John Nolland notes, ―Luke makes no use of Mark's statement of Jesus' compassion nor of the linked likening of the crowd to sheep without a shepherd (6:34)," then immediately analyzes how Luke ―concentrates on the Christological focus of the pericope," but doesn't state if and/or how Jesus' lack of compassion relates to his increased Christological authority in *Luke 1-9:20*, 440-41.

[594] Radl, *Das Evangelium nach Lukas: 1,1-9,50*, 598-99.

[595] Fitzmyer, *Luke I-IX*, 764, 766.

Matthew and Mark have the identical description of Jesus' emotion, σπλαγχνίζομαι ἐπὶ

τὸν ὄχλον ὅτι ἤδη ἡμέραι τρεῖς προσμένουσίν μοι καὶ οὐκ ἔχουσιν τί φάγωσιν

(Matt 15:32b//Mark 8:2).

137. The Gerasene Demoniac

Mark 5:19b-20	Luke 8:39
ὕπαγε εἰς τὸν οἶκόν σου πρὸς τοὺς σούς,	ὑπόστρεφε εἰς τὸν οἶκόν σου,
καὶ ἀπάγγειλον αὐτοῖς	καὶ διηγοῦ
ὅσα *ὁ κύριός* σοι πεποίηκεν	ὅσα σοι ἐποίησεν *ὁ θεός.*
καὶ ἠλέησέν σε	
καὶ ἀπῆλθεν	καὶ ἀπῆλθεν
καὶ ἤρξατο κηρύσσειν ἐν τῇ Δεκαπόλει	καθ' ὅλην τν πόλιν κηρύσσων
ὅσα ἐποίησεν αὐτῷ ὁ Ἰησοῦς,	ὅσα ἐποίησεν αὐτῷ ὁ Ἰησοῦς.
καὶ πάντες ἐθαύμαζον	

In the previously mentioned pericope concerning the Gerasene Demoniac (Mark

5:1-20//Luke 8:26-39), not only does Luke soften the tone of the Markan narrators'

portrayal of Jesus' speech and actions, he also removes Jesus' self-described

mercy/compassion. My interpretation is complicated by the exact referent of ὁ κύριός in

Mark 5:19.[596] Jesus tells the man to return home and announce what ―the Lord" has just

---

[596] The simplest and most accepted interpretation is that Jesus is speaking in the third person, and therefore it is *Jesus'* emotion of mercy that is described by Mark. See below. The Markan narrator states in the next verse (5:20) that the man responded to Jesus' command to tell how much the Lord has done for you (in 5:19), by telling how much *Jesus* had done for him (ὅσα ἐποίησεν αὐτῷ ὁ Ἰησοῦς), using ὁ κύριός in 5:19 synonymously with ὁ Ἰησοῦς in 5:20; see Schweizer, *The Good News according to Mark,*

done (i.e. an exorcism) *and* of the compassion "the Lord" had on him (καὶ ἀπάγγειλον

αὐτοῖς ὅσα ὁ κύριός σοι πεποίηκεν καὶ ἠλέησέν σε, 5:19b). In Luke, Jesus tells the

man to return home, but only says generically to tell what "God" has done for you (καὶ

διηγοῦ ὅσα σοι ἐποίησεν ὁ θεός, 8:39). Luke redacts Mark's ὁ κύριός to ὁ θεός,

while removing Jesus'/God's mercy.[597] Mark seems to employ ὁ κύριός and ὁ Ἰησοῦς

synonymously (with Jesus speaking in the third person in 5:19, see note above), while

Luke (despite also using ὁ Ἰησοῦς to describe the man's response in 8:39b) does not use

ὁ θεός and ὁ Ἰησοῦς equivalently. Though Luke's particular christological position is

beyond our scope, the question relevant to my redactional analysis of the emotions is the

determination of whose ἔλεος has been omitted.

Recognition of Luke's removal of Jesus' mercy from the Markan source is

missing from almost all of the secondary literature, including the heavily relied-upon

monographs and commentaries of Henry Cadbury, Joseph Fitzmyer, Walter Radl, and

---

114-15. Contrarily, C.S. Mann contends ὁ κύριός refers to God only, who is the one who had mercy and is the source of the miracle, but does not explain Mark's seemingly interchangeable use of ὁ Ἰησοῦς in Mark 5:20, *Mark*, 280-81. I prefer the straight-forward interpretation of Schweizer based on the synonymous use of ὁ κύριός and ὁ Ἰησοῦς by the narrator in Mark 5:20. Of course, the Luke narrator also uses in ὁ Ἰησοῦς in 8:39b, yet no one would argue Luke is using ὁ Ἰησοῦς synonymously with ὁ θεός in v.39a.

[597] ἐλεέω was a common verb (ἔλεος, "mercy/compassion/pity" was a common noun) in antiquity with a straight-forward definition, "have mercy or pity," BADG, 249; LSJ, 249. See above quotation of Epictetus' advocacy of removing mercy (ἔλεος) absolutely in "On the Cynic" (*Diatr.* 3.22.13).

Michael Goulder, perhaps due to the hermeneutical question put forward.[598] The few scholars who recognize the Lukan redactions usually attribute them to Lukan stylistic conventions or fail to ascribe any meaning at all. John Nolland asserts, "Luke speaks simply of what 'God did', whereas Mark has 'the Lord has done and has had mercy on you',"[599] without further comment either on the ὁ κύριός / ὁ θεός switch or the removal of mercy. I. Howard Marshall speaks tersely of Luke's emotional redaction: "…. and he omits Mark's awkward καὶ ἠλέησέν σε."[600] François Bovon notes the redactions, but dismisses them as mere linguistic preference, "Il renonce à la miséricorde de Dieu (καὶ ἠλέησέν σε, Mc 5,19) pour une raison grammatical, parce que ἐλεέω ne peut pas avoir ὅσα (<<tout ce que …>>) comme complément d'objet direct."[601] While Bovon is

---

[598] The scholarly lack of acknowledgment being due to Luke's complication in preferring ὁ θεός over Mark's ὁ κύριός is pure speculation. See Cadbury, *Style and Literary Method*, 91, who lists other passages where Jesus' pity is omitted; also Fitzmyer, *Luke I-IX*, 733-740; Radl, *Das Evangelium nach Lukas: 1,1-9,50*, 560-62; Goulder, *Luke: A New Paradigm I*, 423. Other commentators who fail to acknowledge Luke's removal of Jesus' mercy: Green, *Gospel of Luke*, 341-42; C.F. Evans, *Saint Luke*, 387; Culpepper, *Gospel of Luke*, 187-88; Sabourin, *L'Évangile de Luc*, 191-92; Danker, *Jesus and the New Age*, 184-85; Ringe, *Luke*, 121; Tannehill, *Luke*, 147-48; Craig A. Evans, *Luke*, 138; Morris, *Luke*, 172-73; Lieu, *Gospel of Luke*, 64-66.

[599] Nolland , *Luke 1-9:20*, 413.

[600] Marshall, *Gospel of Luke*, 341. Somehow he also contends that these three passages (calming the storm, 8:22-25; Gerasene Demoniac, 8:26-39; Jairus' daughter and woman with hemorrhage, 8:40-56) reveal Jesus' authority and compassion. I have argued throughout how Luke's unemotional Jesus adds to his authority, but question how these texts reveal his compassion, especially when Luke specifically removes his mercy in this text. The revealing aspect of the texts is how Jesus physically saves, heals, exorcizes without showing mercy or compassion.

[601] Bovon, *Saint Luc 1-9*, 325; He later contends that the healed man correctly interprets the act of God (39a) Christologically (39b). This seems to be the best interpretation of Luke's Christological view, as David Tiede similarly declares, "The former demoniac declares what *God* has done in terms of what *Jesus* has done" [emphasis his] in "The Gospel according to Luke," *HarperCollins Study Bible* (New York: HarperCollins, 1993), 1974.

correct concerning ἐλεέω and ὅσα (and in further stating the accusative following ἐλεέω indicates the person receiving mercy), Luke hypothetically keeping a version of ἐλεέω (or even ἔλεος) and rewording the text to make it grammatically correct would constitute a linguistic stylistic change. Luke choosing to omit Jesus' and/or God's mercy is an important thematic redaction.

As to whose mercy is actually being removed, for the broad purpose of showing Luke's removal of Mark's emotion concerning the character of Jesus, it doesn't really matter, as each interpretation yields a similar result (comparable to the contention put forward in my analysis of the cursing of the fig tree, Mark 11:12-14//Luke 13:6-9).[602] In Mark, the most straightforward reading of the text is that Jesus' speaks in the third person and is the one who shows mercy, and this is troubling for Luke. If Luke alters ὁ κύριός to ὁ θεός purely as a stylistic change, and thus equates ὁ Ἰησοῦς with ὁ θεός (as Mark equates ὁ Ἰησοῦς with ὁ κύριός), it is clearly Jesus' mercy that Luke removes. Since Luke regularly uses ὁ κύριός to refer to Jesus, my preferred interpretation (following Bovon and Tiede above) is that Luke modifies the Markan ὁ κύριός in order to clarify his christological convictions, that ὁ Ἰησοῦς is not equivalent to ὁ θεός (God performs

---

[602] It is also an *argumentum ex silentio*, because the mercy (no matter whose it is) doesn't exist in Luke, thus the inclusion of the passage in my analysis.

222

the exorcism through Jesus or Jesus' works reveal the power of God, etc.).[603] This interpretation of Luke's christology yields a similar view of Jesus'/God's compassion. It is God's mercy as revealed by Jesus or Jesus' compassion reveals divine mercy, etc. Or to be more precise in terms of Luke's christology with respect to his redactions concerning Jesus' emotions, Jesus' *apatheia* demonstrates self-control and rationality and is evidence of his merit as a public authoritative representative of God who endows Jesus with the power to perform exorcisms, miracles, etc.

254. The Rich Young Man

Mark 10:20-22	Luke 18:21-23
ὁ δὲ ἔφη αὐτῷ διδάσκαλε,	ὁ δὲ εἶπεν
ταῦτα πάντα ἐφυλαξάμην	ταῦτα πάντα ἐφύλαξα
ἐκ νεότητός μου.	ἐκ νεότητός.
ὁ δὲ Ἰησοῦς ἐμβλέψας αὐτῷ	ἀκούσας δὲ ὁ Ἰησοῦς
ἠγάπησεν αὐτὸν	
καὶ εἶπεν αὐτῷ,	εἶπεν αὐτῷ
ἕν σε ὑστερεῖ	ἔτι ἕν σοι λείπει
ὕπαε, ὅσα ἔχεις πώλησον	πάντα ὅσα ἔχεις πώλησον
καὶ δὸς τοῖς πτχοῖς,	καὶ διάδος πτωχοῖς,
καὶ ἔξεις θησαυρὸν ἐν οὐρανῷ,	καὶ ἔξεις θησαυρὸν ἐν τοῖς οὐρανοῖς,
καὶ δεῦρο ἀκολούθει μοι.	καὶ δεῦρο ἀκολούθει μοι.
ὁ δὲ στυγνάσας ἐπὶ τῷ λόγῳ	ὁ δὲ ἀκούσας ταῦτα
ἀπῆλθεν λυπούμενος,	περίλυπος ἐγενήθη,
ἦν γὰρ ἔχων κτήματα πολλά	ἦν γὰρ πλούσιος σφόδρα

In the encounter of the rich man with Jesus (Mark 10:17-22//Luke 18:18-23),

---

[603] In this view Luke separates Jesus from the Markan emotion in two ways – in his understanding that κύριός equals θεός in Mark, and through the actual removal of the emotional phrase, καὶ ἠλέησέν σε.

before Jesus tells him the one thing he lacks, the Markan narrator tells us that after

looking upon him, Jesus —loved" him. Luke omits Mark's ἠγάπησεν αὐτόν.[604] The

Markan text has been redacted from ὁ δὲ Ἰησοῦς ἐμβλέψας αὐτῷ ἠγάπησεν αὐτὸν

καὶ εἶπεν αὐτῷ (10:21a) to the more generic, ἀκούσας δὲ ὁ Ἰησοῦς εἶπεν αὐτῷ (Luke

18:22a). As in the previous passage concerning the Gerasene Demoniac (Mark 5:1-

20//Luke 8:26-39) and the removal of Jesus' mercy, Luke makes the important omission

of Jesus' love.[605]

Linguistically, Luke follows the Markan text closely, save for —small touches"

---

[604] ἀγάπη / ἀγαπάω were common terms, especially used by early Christians, but also in antiquity in general, which connoted just about every type of love (brotherly, between humans/deities, among deities, etc.), but was usually not associated with erotic love; BADG, 4-6. Luke and Mark use ἀγάπη often, but not to describe Jesus' emotion. ἀγάπη is used in God's direct description of Jesus at the Baptism of Jesus (Mark 1:11//Luke 3:22) and the Transfiguration (Mark 9:7//Luke 9:35, some manuscripts read ἐκλελεγμένος instead of ἀγαπητός; see Metzger, *A Textual Commentary on the Greek New Testament*, 148). The vineyard owner's son is termed —beloved" (Mark 12:6//Luke 20:13). In the passage dealing with Jesus and the questions concerning the commandments, ἀγάπη is used four times (Mark 12:30//Luke 10:27; Mark 12:31, 33). In Luke's sermon on the plain, Jesus teaches on ἀγάπη four times (6:27, 32, twice in 35). Jesus heals a centurion's servant; the centurian —loves" the Jewish people (7:5). In teaching on forgiving a sinful woman, Jesus uses ἀγάπη two times (7:42, 47). Jesus describes the love of God is his denouncement of the Pharisees (11:42), and he states that the Pharisees love to have the seat of honor (11:43). In his teaching on serving two masters, Jesus uses ἀγάπη once (16:13).

[605] Joseph Fitzmyer states that Luke —eliminates the mention of Jesus' emotional reaction (see Mark 10:21, as he often does elsewhere," though does not elaborate how this would add to Jesus' —nobility" or —christological awareness" or even —power," terms he uses elsewhere in commenting on other redactions concerning the emotions in *Luke X-XXIV*, 1196. C.F. Evans argues that the Lukan redactions are meant to cast the rich *ruler* in a less favorable light, but does not mention how they affect the character of *Jesus* in *Saint Luke*, 649. Marshall states that Luke —omits mention that Jesus looked at the man and loved him, then contends, —The emotion shown by Jesus is ignored and in this way the story is generalized," though no further explanation is given in *Gospel of Luke*, 685. Matthew's version also removes Jesus' love, though he significantly redacts larger portions of surrounding text. Interestingly, Matthew is the only one to add the phrase, καί, ἀγαπήσεις τὸν πλησίον σου ὡς σεαυτόν, after his list of commandments to the rich man (19:19b).

(including the removal of Jesus' ἀγάπη), though these scintillae drastically alter the tone

and indeed the entire explication of the passage. Luke Timothy Johnson notes:

> Luke deliberately accentuates the contrast [between the rich man and children], by making the rich man a ‗ruler' (*archōn*). This small touch changes the character of the story … Rather than a sincere request to learn about discipleship – to which Jesus responds with ‗love' as in Mark – we recognize the sort of testing question posed by the lawyer in 10:25.[606]

By making Mark's ―man" a ―ruler," Luke emphasizes the larger civic responsibilities of

which the ruler is capable as a person of wealth, thus the ―testing" runs both ways.

Before Jesus puts the ruler to the test with the ultimate request (v.22), the ruler states he

has observed the commandments ―from his youth." This serves to show the ruler's

exceptional merit, as men of remarkable distinction in antiquity would on occasion be

praised for manifestion of virtue ―from their youth."[607] Only another person of the

highest distinction could make such a claim on the wealthy ruler.

 Not only does the rejection of Jesus' request by the rich ruler show the superiority

(in virtue, benefaction, etc.) of one public authority figure (Jesus) over another (the ruler),

the emotional portrayal of the two civic characters in Luke highlights this distinction. As

analyzed above, due to the removal of the Markan narrator's description of Jesus'

response to the rich man's self-description of prodigious virtue (ἐμβλέψας αὐτῷ

ἠγάπησεν αὐτόν), the Lukan Jesus shows no emotion. This is contrasted to the strong

---

[606] Johnson, *Gospel of Luke*, 280. I would add a more explicit mention of the contrast in emotions shown by the public authority figure of Jesus (no love) and the public rich ruling authority figure (deep sorrow, 18:23). Luke retains the rich ruler's περίλυπος (the only time Luke uses *perilypos*), see chapter five.

[607] See Danker, *Jesus and the New Age*, 299-300. See, for example, the pericope of the boy Jesus in the Temple (2:41-52), a story unique to Luke.

emotion shown by the rich ruler in Luke after Jesus' ultimate request; Luke (περίλυπος

ἐγενήθη, 18:23) retains Mark's description (ἀπῆλθεν λυπούμενος, 10:22) of the ruler's

reaction.[608] Due to his two small redactional ―touches" (of man to ruler and the omission

of Jesus' love), Luke provides the reader with an unemotional public leader, who is

rational and self-controlled, in direct contrast to the rich public ruler.

166. True Greatness

Mark 9:36-37	Luke 9:47b-48a
καὶ λαβὼν παιδίον	ἐπιλαβόμενος παιδίον
ἔστησεν αὐτὸ ἐν μέσῳ αὐτῶν	*ἔστησεν αὐτὸ παρ' ἑαυτῷ,*
καὶ ἐναγκαλισάμενος αὐτὸ	
εἶπεν αὐτοῖς	καὶ εἶπεν αὐτοῖς
ὃς ἂν ἓν τῶν τοιούτων παιδίων	ὃς ἐὰν δέξηται τοῦτο τὸ παιδίον
δέξηται ἐπὶ τῷ ὀνόματί μου,	ἐπὶ τῷ ὀνόματί μου,
ἐμὲ δέχεται	ἐμὲ δέχεται
καὶ ὃς ἂν ἐμὲ δέχηται,	καὶ ὃς ἂν ἐμὲ δέξηται,
ουκ ἐμὲ δέχεται	δέχεται
ἀλλὰ τὸν ἀποστείλαντά με	τὸν ἀποστείλαντά με

Just as Jesus' anger is communicated to the Markan reader through his actions

---

[608] As analyzed above, λύπη (grief, distress, pain) was one of the four main categories of emotion in Stoicism (appetite or desire, ἐπιθυμία; fear, φόβος; and pleasure, ἡδονή being the other three). See especially Epictetus, for whom overcoming grief was a sign of self-control and autonomy in *Diatr.* 4.6.16.

(such as in the important pericope of the temple cleansing), Jesus' love and affection are likewise communicated through his actions. In keeping with the redactional pattern of removing Jesus' emotion (both the traditionally negative as well as the positive), these behavioral signs of Jesus' love and affection are extirpated from the Lukan account. In the infamous dialogue among the disciples concerning who is the greatest (Mark 9:33-37//Luke 9:46-48), Jesus responds to them by telling them that they should receive children in his name (Mark 9:37//Luke 9:48). Before this direct speech to the disciples, he takes a child as a type of visual aid (Mark 9:36//Luke 9:47). In the Markan text, Jesus grasps the child, puts him in the middle of the group, and then dramatically takes the child in his arms, καὶ λαβὼν παιδίον ἔστησεν αὐτὸ ἐν μέσῳ αὐτῶν καὶ

ἐναγκαλισάμενος αὐτὸ (9:36), but in the Lukan version, Jesus, less literarily striking, less emotionally, only puts the child by his side (ἐπιλαβόμενος παιδίον ἔστησεν αὐτὸ

παρ᾽ ἑαυτῷ, 9:47).[609] Matthew's account (18:1-5) is a type of middle ground. Pace Luke, he retains the Markan placement of the child in the middle of the group, but in line with Luke, he removes reference of Jesus taking the child in his arms.

Many scholars identify the Lukan changes to the Markan text, but fail to recognize fully their significance in portraying an unemotional Jesus and how this

---

[609] Luke Timothy Johnson concludes that "there is nothing sentimental therefore in Jesus' saying about the child received in his name." He further argues (pace Craig A. Evans, who contends that Luke redeems Mark's negative portrayal of the disciples in this passage in *Luke*, 157-59) that the Lukan omissions result in Luke being "more directly derogatory of the disciples' pretensions," which evidences my previous contention that the disciples depiction in Luke is mixed. In *Gospel of Luke*, 160.

portrayal contributes to Luke's understanding of the person of Jesus.[610] Joseph Fitzmyer, without remarking further, simply states, ―As usual, he [Luke] omits the emotional, the embrace of the child by Jesus (see Mark 9:36ff).[611] John Nolland affirms:

> The significant changes are that the child is now placed beside himself, and not in the midst of the disciples, and that the Markan embrace of the child disappears (… as it does also in [the parallel to] Mark 10:16). … In Luke's account we cannot yet know what Jesus is seeking to achieve with this action.[612]

Though I have argued against his ultimate conclusion on numerous occasions above, I. Howard Marshall accurately recognizes that Luke is concerned not only with Jesus' *message* concerning status and benefaction, but also with how Jesus is *perceived* by his Greco-Roman auditors.[613] Compatible with his view towards many of the Lukan redactions concerning Jesus' emotion, Marshall analyzes them in terms of humanity/divinity. He argues that ―the action [of Jesus' putting the child by his side which he suggests is a place of honor for the child] replaces the description of Jesus' embracing the child which is found in Mark, a rather human trait which Luke omits (and

---

[610] Scholars who recognize the redactions: C.F. Evans mentions the redactional changes, but gives no weight to them in *Saint Luke*, 428; Radl points out Jesus' different use of children in Luke, without additional comment in *Das Evangelium nach Lukas: 1,1-9,50*, 651-52; Jacob Kremer notes the redactions, but doesn't assign any significance to them in *Lukasevangelium* (Würzburg: Echter Verlag, 2000), 111-12. Goulder, who has identified the Lukan redactions in almost all of the pericopae examined, unfathomably states (in his close textual reading of this passage, in which he actually points out the Lukan changes on emotion above, addressing the Lukan emotional redactions as a whole), ―there is little justification for thinking that Luke suppresses signals of emotion in Jesus," in *Luke: A New Paradigm*, 451.

[611] Fitzmyer, *Luke I-IX*, 816.

[612] Nolland, *Luke 9:21-18:34*, 519. He later interprets Jesus' actions in terms of honoring and respecting a humble child in a way that would honor and respect Jesus himself. Nolland construes the Lukan message, ―The pericope sets out to show that receiving and honoring the lowly does not mark one as inferior, but rather exalts one, because in doing so one receives Jesus" (519-520).

[613] Marshall (pace Morris, *Saint Luke*, 66 et al.) consistently argues that Luke removes Jesus' emotion in order to make him more divine in *Gospel of Luke*, 396. I have argued against this view on numerous occasions above, see analysis of the scene at the synagogue (Mark 3:1-6//Luke 6:6-11) in particular.

Luke's general avoidance of attributing human emotions to Jesus)."[614] Though

commentators correctly acknowledge the Lukan theme of Jesus challenging existing

notions of status (evidenced by his use of children as representations of the lowly),[615]

they fail to recognize how a significantly less emotional Jesus underscores his status as a

rational and self-controlled public authority figure.

253. Jesus Blesses the Children

Mark 10:15-16	Luke 18:17
ἀμὴν λέγω ὑμῖν ὃς ἂν μὴ δέξηται τὴν βασιλείαν τοῦ θεοῦ ὡς παιδίον, οὐ μὴ εἰσέλθῃ εἰς αὐτήν. **καὶ ἐναγκαλισάμενος αὐτὰ κατευλόγει τιθεὶς τὰς χεῖρας ἐπ᾽ αὐτά**	ἀμὴν λέγω ὑμῖν ὃς ἂν μὴ δέξηται τὴν βασιλείαν τοῦ θεοῦ ὡς παιδίον, οὐ μὴ εἰσέλθῃ εἰς αὐτήν.

In a passage similar to the previous episode (of Jesus' response to the disciples

arguing who is the greatest involving a child as a visual teaching device, Mark 9:33-

37//Luke 9:46-48), Jesus again uses a child as a pedagogical tool (Mark 10:13-16//Luke

18:15-17). In an exact linguistic parallel, Jesus states that one must receive the kingdom

of God like a child, ἀμὴν λέγω ὑμῖν ὃς ἂν μὴ δέξηται τὴν βασιλείαν τοῦ θεοῦ ὡς

παιδίον, οὐ μὴ εἰσέλθῃ εἰς αὐτήν (Mark 10:15//Luke 18:17). In the Markan source,

---

[614] Marshall, *Gospel of Luke*, 396.

[615] For the low status of children in antiquity see Carolyn Osiek and David L. Balch, *Families in the New Testament World: Households and House Churches* (Louisville: Westminster John Knox Press, 1997), 68-74, 136-140. See also Beryl Rawson, ed., *The Family in Ancient Rome: New Perspectives* (Ithaca, N.Y.: Cornell University Press, 1986); and Beryl Rawson, ed. *Marriage, Divorce, and Children in Ancient Rome* (New York: Oxford University Press, 1991).

Jesus takes the children into his arms and blesses them. The passage ends with Mark emphasizing Jesus physically laying his hands upon the children. In accordance with the common Lukan redactional scheme of removing strong emotion from Jesus (emotions with both positive and negative connotations), Luke not only removes Jesus' anger (Mark 10:14//Luke 18:16, see above), but also removes Jesus' affective actions. Luke omits the entire Markan verse, καὶ ἐναγκαλισάμενος αὐτὰ κατευλόγει τιθεὶς τὰς χεῖρας ἐπ᾽ αὐτά (10:16).[616] As in the previous pericope, Matthew's emotional portrayal of Jesus is intermediary between Mark's and Luke's (19:13-15). Matthew's account ends with Jesus' laying hands on the children but without blessing them, καὶ ἐπιθεὶς τὰς χεῖρας αὐτοῖς ἐπορεύθη ἐκεῖθεν (v.15).

Consistent with his redactional tendencies of disassociating Jesus with strong emotion, Luke omits any hint of affection (as he also does in the disciples' discussion of who is the greatest, Mark 9:33-37//Luke 9:46-48) or sentimentality (as in Jesus' feeding of the multitudes, Mark 6:32-44//Luke 9:10b-17). Comparable to their commentary on the preceding passage concerning the use of a child as an aid in Jesus' teaching, many scholars recognize the Lukan redactions along with such themes of status, benefaction, the kingdom of God, and Jesus' authority, but fail to correlate them.[617] Joel B. Green

---

[616] Nolland states, "The wording here is identical to Mark 10:15, but Luke drops the Markan completion of the episode in 10:16," but doesn't comment on how either Lukan omission (anger or affection) contributes hermeneutically in *Luke 9:21-18:34*, 881-82.

[617] Charles Talbert comes close in that he loosely associates these in his discussion of the Lukan version of the pericope in light of the general theme of status reversal and the kingdom of God in *Reading Luke*, 170-71. As with most of the so-called positive emotional redactions, Joseph Fitzmyer does not elaborate how they contribute to various Lukan themes, "Luke follows the Marcan account of Jesus' blessing of the little children fairly closely. ... However, Luke eliminates the details of Jesus' anger and

touches upon all these themes, but does not link these with Luke's omission of Mark's final verse. In his introduction to this pericope, he states, "Polarity regarding status honor has just occupied Jesus, and he closes his parabolic teaching with a reaffirmation of value-transposition effective through his ministry (18:9-14; cf. 1:46-55; 14:11)."[618] He then discusses the important role of "hospitality" in the Lukan narrative, Jesus' teaching on the "kingdom," how its leaders ought to function, and the "agency" of Jesus, though does not link nay of these to the Lukan emphasis on a less emotional Jesus through his redaction of Jesus' affective actions.[619] Robert C. Tannehill recognizes the "close parallel to Mark 10:13-16," with certain Lukan specifications, and examines the passage with regard to the status of children in antiquity and in relation to the status and power of the kingdom of God, but does not connect them. Jesus' status as a public figure with the authority to challenge the current system of status and power is dependent on his characterization as a rational and self-controlled leader without emotion.

Jesus' Emotions in the Special Lukan Material

Scriba mansuetudinis Christi – Dante Alighieri, *De monarchia* 1.18

The emphasis of this examination has been on Luke's use of the Markan source, and though a full analysis of Luke is perhaps slightly beyond the scope, it is necessary to

---

affection." In *Luke X-XXIV*, 1191. Lieu recognizes the lessening of Jesus' signs of affection and emphasis on the "status of Jesus," but does not link them in *Gospel of Luke*, 141-43. Goulder seemingly contends Luke redacted Mark due to concerns for emphasis and brevity, "Because he is not interested in the story of the children for itself, but only for the moral of humility, he leaves out Mark's final verse, and taking them in his arms, laid his hands on them, and blessed them'," in *Luke: A New Paradigm II*, 667; Schweizer states, "The idyllic picture of Jesus, the friend of children, laying his hands on them in blessing (Mark 10:16), is absent in Luke," though does not provide a compelling explanation in *Good News according to Luke*, 285. Marshall suggests by omitting Jesus' embracing of the children, Luke somehow "generalises the story" in *Gospel of Luke*, 681.

[618] Green, *Gospel of Luke*, 650.

[619] Ibid., 651-652.

consider briefly the presentation of Jesus' emotions in Luke's special material.[620] This is especially important in passages which might portray an emotional Jesus and would seemingly provide counter-evidence to the proposed pattern. Simply, why would Luke consistently and methodically remove emotion from the Markan Jesus, only to have another source characterize an emotional Jesus and not make the same redactional changes? Or why would Luke present his audience with an unemotional Jesus through major exclusions, minor omissions, and subtle changes to the Markan text, only to create with his own hand a Jesus opposite of his painstakingly redacted characterization?

This possible counter evidence in the special Lukan material primarily concerns the so-called ‑positive" emotions of mercy and compassion. The redactions concerning the removal of Jesus' positive emotions are particularly important for locating Luke's themes, auditors, and the traditions on which Luke relies in constructing his gospel. In my analysis of the emotional portrait of Jesus, I noted two occasions on which Luke removed variations of σπλαγχνίζομαι from the Markan text.[621] Seemingly

contradictory, Luke uses versions of σπλαγχνίζομαι / σπλάγχνον four times in his special material to describe God's/Jesus' mercy/compassion. Similarly, Luke omitted Jesus' self-described ἔλεος in the passage concerning the Gerasene Demoniac (Mark 5:1-

---

[620] Without getting bogged down with the technical details concerning the complex composition of Luke's gospel, I use ‑L" to connote the third main source (in the broadest sense) for his gospel material. For the purpose of my dissertation, this is simply the material not from Mark or ‑Q." ‑L" could have been written or oral or even the free composition of Luke or some combination of these. See Fitzmyer, *Luke 1-IX*, 63-133, esp. 82-85.

[621] Luke removes σπλαγχνισθείς (Mark 1:41//Luke 5:13) from the passage where Jesus cleanses a leper (Mark 1:40-45//Luke 5:12-16); and ἐσπλαγχνίσθη (Mark 6:34//Luke 9:11) from Jesus' feeding of the multitudes (Mark 6:32-44//Luke 9:10b-17).

20//Luke 8:26-39), by omitting the Markan phrase "καὶ ἠλέησέν σε" (Mark 5:19//Luke 8:39), while in the special "L" material, Luke uses a variation of ἔλεος six times to describe Jesus'/God's mercy.[622]

The special "L" passages in particular have been influential in leading many scholars to follow Dante's general analysis of Luke as "the scribe of the gentleness of Christ." In the history of Lukan scholarship, influential commentators from Ernest Renan to D.A. Hays to C.K. Barrett have accepted this broad designation.[623] Even Fitzmyer, who acknowledges the consistent removal of Jesus' emotion,[624] somewhat puzzlingly claims, "The qualities of mercy, love, charm, joy, and delicacy are part of the Lucan portrait of Jesus in the Third Gospel."[625] While recognizing the importance and granting the essence of their scholarly contributions in general, I will argue against these claims concerning the *character* of Jesus.

Luke's Infancy Narratives

In the first chapter of his gospel, Luke describes the mercy and compassion of God numerous times through poetry and general narrator comments. In Mary's Magnificat, Mary poetically describes God's mercy: τὸ ἔλεος αὐτοῦ (v.50); μνησθῆναι

---

[622] This doesn't include the description of Father Abraham's mercy in Luke 16:24; see below. Additionally, in a passage sometimes used to show the strong emotional presentation of a distraught Jesus, Luke describes Jesus weeping over the city of Jerasulem (19:41-44).

[623] Renan writes of the Lukan gospel, "C'est le plus beau livre qu'il y ait," *Les Evangiles et la seconde génération chrétienne* (3rd ed.; Paris: Calmann Lévy, 1877), 283; Hayes, *The Most Beautiful Book Ever Written: The Gospel According to Luke.* New York: Eaton & Mains, 1913). C. K. Barrett, *Luke the Historian in Recent Study* (Philadelphia, Fortress Press, 1970).

[624] As previously mentioned, Fitzmyer importantly notes the removal of Jesus' emotions, "even if they are expressions of love, compassion, or tenderness [emphasis added]" in *Luke I-IX*, 95.

[625] Ibid., 258.

ἐλέους (v.54). The Lukan narrator states that Elizabeth conceived and bore John the

Baptist due to the Lord's great mercy, ἐμεγάλυνεν κύριος τὸ ἔλεος αὐτοῦ μετ' αὐτῆς

(v.57). In Zechariah's Benedictus (Luke 1:67-79), Luke describes the compassion/mercy

of God, using two words he has consistently removed from his Markan source –

σπλάγχνον and ἔλεος. Luke states, ποιῆσαι ἔλεος μετὰ τῶν πατέρων ἡμῶν καὶ

μνησθῆναι διαθήκης ἁγίας αὐτοῦ (v.72) and, διὰ σπλάγχνα ἐλέους θεοῦ ἡμῶν

(v.78). Though Luke uses ἔλεος and σπλάγχνον numerous times to describe mercy and

compassion, ἔλεος and σπλάγχνον are used only of God, a fact which will become

increasingly important as I examine Jesus' emotional characterization in further special

–Ł" passages.

Positive Emotions in Special "L" Parables

The special Lukan parables are often used as evidence of a compassionate,

merciful, and loving Jesus in Luke's gospel.[626] In the parable of the two debtors, an –Ł"

passage interpolated into the passage concerning the woman with the ointment (7:36-50),

Jesus teaches on forgiveness and love, using the analogy of creditor/debtor. Luke

associates the forgiveness of debts with the forgiveness of sins and this forgiveness with

---

[626] Fitzmyer (*Luke I-IX*, 258) even has a *termina technique* for these parables – –Lucan parables of mercy," which for him includes the two debtors (7:41-43), the good Samaritan (10:29-37), the barren fig tree (13:6-9), the lost sheep (15:3-7), the lost silver coin (15:8-10), the prodigal son (15:11-32), and the Pharisee and the Toll-Collector (18:9-14), which are all analyzed below.

—love" (ἀγάπη), μὴ ἐχόντων αὐτῶν ἀποδοῦναι ἀμφοτέροις ἐχαρίσατο, τίς οὖν

αὐτῶν πλεῖον ἀγαπήσει αὐτόν (v.42).[627] Later in the narrative, Jesus states, οὗ χάριν

λέγω σοι, ἀφέωνται αἱ ἁμαρτίαι αὐτῆς αἱ πολλαί, ὅτι ἠγάπησεν πολύ: ᾧ δὲ ὀλίγον

ἀφίεται, ὀλίγον ἀγαπᾷ (v.47). Despite the interpretation by the Pharisees in the

pericope that it is Jesus who has forgiven her sins (v.49), most commentators[628] have

correctly noted the careful linguistic choices (i.e. the theological passive) by Luke to

convey to the reader that is it God, and not Jesus who has forgiven her sins.[629] Though

ἀγάπη certainly is an important theme is this pericope, the parable is not self-referential.

Jesus is not using the parable of the debtors and the passage as a whole to convey his

powers of forgiveness and most important for my analysis – his love. As in the use of

---

[627] Luke's use of ἀγάπη in this case can connote —thankfulness" instead of, or at least in addition to, —love." See Marshall, *Gospel of Luke*, 311.

[628] See, for example, Culpepper, *Gospel of Luke*, 172; C.F. Evans, *Saint Luke*, 301, 364; Marshall, *Gospel of Luke*, 313; Green, *Gospel of Luke*, 313-14; Just, *Luke 1-9:50*, 324-25; Fitzmyer, *Luke I-IX*, 583, 692-93; Johnson, *Gospel of Luke*, 127-28. Bovon, somewhat contrarily, argues that the passage reveals the Christological roots for the forgiveness of sins in *Saint Luc 1-9*, 379-80. Nolland argues a type of —both and" position. He contends that forgiveness certainly comes from God as communicated through the theological passive, but eschatologically realized in Jesus in *Luke 1-9:20*, 357-58.

[629] The theological passive is a typical Lukan construction connoting divine action, which is clearly seen, for example, in his redaction of the healing of the paralytic (Matt 9:1-8//Mark 2:1-12//Luke 5:17-26), especially in light of Matthew's version. In the Markan account, Jesus' sees the faith of those bringing the paralytic man, then he states, Τέκνον, ἀφίενταί σου αἱ ἁμαρτίαι (2:5). Luke changes the Markan form ἀφίενταί to the Doric-Ionic dialectical form of the perfect passive ἀφέωνταί as the Lukan Jesus says, Ἄνθρωπε, ἀφέωνταί σοι αἱ ἁμαρτίαι σου (5:20); see further technical analysis in BDF 97.3, 340.

Matthew retains the Markan verbal form, Θάρσει, τέκνον: ἀφίενταί σου αἱ ἁμαρτίαι (9:2). In Luke 7:47 therefore, the perfect tense expresses the state of her forgiveness, which Jesus declares, and the passive alludes to the divine agency, hence a literal translation, —Her many sins have been forgiven by God." See further Max Zerwick and Joseph Smith, *Biblical Greek* (Rome: Biblical Institue, 1963), 236.

ἔλεος and σπλάγχνον in the infancy narratives, Luke uses ἀγάπη solely to describe

God, carefully avoiding this emotionally charged designation for the character of Jesus.

In the parable of the Good Samaritan, Jesus describes the Good Samaritan as

ἐσπλαγχνίσθη (10:33), and concludes by asking, Ὁ ποιήσας τὸ ἔλεος μετ' αὐτοῦ

(v.37). While the hermeneutical examination of the compassion of the Samaritan (10:30-

35) is often interpreted as a self-contained and isolated pericope, the passage is intimately

connected with the preceding one by the introductory question by the lawyer to Jesus, καὶ

τίς ἐστίν μου πλησίον (v.29).[630] Thus the story is basically a controversy narrative, with

the lawyer challenging Jesus (v.25).[631] Jesus' response to the lawyer after the initial

challenge is to contrast the lack of compassion shown by two members of the Jewish

priesthood with that of a Samaritan. Another main tenet of the passage is that the

Samaritan is presented as an example to be followed, hence Jesus' concluding

exhortation to the lawyer, πορεύου καὶ σὺ ποίει ὁμοίως (v.37).[632] With respect to the

long and varied history of allegorically identifying the Samaritan with Jesus, especially in

[630] Numerous scholars have shown the parallel structure of Luke10:25-28 with 29-37; see Green, *Gospel of Luke*, 426-27.

[631] Like the previous passage concerning the woman with the ointment (7:36-50), Luke has used special ⌐L" material, the parable proper, to expound upon Markan material (12:28-34). See Marshall, *Gospel of Luke*, 440-50.

[632] It is specifically an *exemplum*, providing a practical model for conduct with often radical demands and the approval/rejection of certain modes of action. The point of the story is not conveyed by some analogy to a spiritual truth, but by the narrative thrust of the ―example" itself; see Fitzmyer, *Luke X-XXIV*, 883. Pace John Dominic Crossan, who argues that the parable, taken on its own, is not primarily an example to follow but a means of showing that the coming of the kingdom of God demands the complete upturning of conventional opinions, such as the impossibility of a Jew bringing himself to talk of a *good* Samaritan in ―Parable and Example in the Teaching of Jesus," *NTS* 18 (1971-72): 285-307.

the Church Fathers, as Luke presents the parable, it is not self-referential.[633] Jesus is not

speaking of himself as compassionate or merciful, but imploring others to ―do‖ mercy.[634]

Similar to his description of the Good Samaritan, Jesus describes the father in the

parable of the prodigal son (Luke 15:11-32) as ἐσπλαγχνίσθη (v.20). There is general

agreement in scholarship that the parable presents the father in the parable as a symbol of

God.[635] As we have seen within the larger Lukan narrative, in text after text, God (often

as ―father‖)[636] has consistently been correlated with mercy and compassion,[637] while

Jesus, again, is not associated with these emotions. Just as the parable of the Good

---

[633] See Christopher Wordsworth, *The New Testament of our Lord and Saviour Jesus Christ: in the original Greek* (often reprinted; orig. London: Rivingtons, 1859), ad loc; see also Karl Barth, Geoffrey William Bromiley, and Thomas F. Torrance, *Church Dogmatics. Vol. 1, Part 2 The Doctrine of the Word of God* (Edinburgh: Clark, 1956), 429; and John Duncan Martin Derrett, *Law in the New Testament* (London: Darton, Longman & Todd, 1970), 208ff.

[634] In response to Jesus‗ question of which of the three had become a neighbor to the one having fallen among the robbers, the lawyer states, Ὁ ποιήσας τὸ ἔλεος μετ' αὐτοῦ (v.37a). By using the parable as an *exemplum*, Luke‗s primary purpose is not to illuminate the compassion of God either, as seems to be the case in the parable of the prodigal son.

[635] Fitzmyer further states, ―His [the father in the parable] ready, unconditioned, and unstinted love and mercy are manifested not only towards the repentant sinner (the younger son) but toward the uncomprehending critic of such a human being‖ in Luke X-*XXIV*, 1085. Marshall profoundly states, ―Of all the parables this one is perhaps the easiest to interpret in broad outline and yet the most open to a variety of interpretation…In its present context it is meant to illustrate the pardoning love of God that cares for the outcasts‖ in *Gospel of Luke*, 604. See also Joachim Jeremias, *The Parables of Jesus* (2nd ed.; New York: Scribner, 1966), 128-31. Other scholars, who might question this interpretive supposition, do not associate Jesus with the father, which is ultimately the point of my analysis; see C.F. Evans, *Saint Luke*, 588-94.

[636] A primary image of God in the Lukan travel narrative (9:51-18:14) has been God the Father (e.g. 11:1-13; 12:22-34); see Green, *Gospel of Luke*, 579. In the finale pericope to the travel narrative, the parable of the Pharisee and the Toll-Collector (18:9-14), a toll-collector asks God for mercy, Ὁ θεός, ἱλάσθητί μοι τῷ ἁμαρτωλῷ (v.14). This is the only Lukan usage of ἱλάσκομαι, to be ―propitious‖ or ―merciful‖ BADG, 375. Earlier in the Lukan text, in the passage where Jesus cleanses ten lepers (17:11-19), the lepers call out to Jesus, ἐπιστάτα, ἐλέησον ἡμᾶς (v.13). Though the lepers plead for mercy, Luke does not describe Jesus as acting out of mercy or compassion, as he does in Luke 7:13 below. In the parable of the rich man and Lazarus (16:19-31), the rich man dies and goes to Hades where he pleads with Father Abraham, ἐλέησόν με (v.24a).

[637] See ch.1; 6:36; 8:51; 11:2, 11, 13; 12:30, 32.

Samaritan proper (10:29-37) is linked by Luke to the lawyer's questioning of Jesus (25-28), Luke intricately links the parable of the prodigal son with the two parables preceding it – the parable of the lost sheep (15:3-7) and the parable of the lost coin (8-10). The three contribute to the Lukan themes of God's mercy/compassion and joy over finding that which was lost, and provide further evidence that while Jesus teaches on mercy and compassion (especially God's), he does not show mercy or compassion himself. In fact, the ―joy" associated with this finding of lost items in the first two parables, is explicitly applied to God in the concluding verse of each (vv.7, 10).[638] Further, John Nolland synthesizes these concepts when he contends, ―The ‗joy in heaven' in vv 7, 10 orients the reader to link the father's experience in the present parable [of the Good Samaritan] with that divine joy."[639] In short, the two antecedent parables anticipate the parable of the prodigal son, in theme, as well as in association of the parables' compassion with God.

Jesus Weeps

After Jesus' triumphal entry into Jerusalem and immediately before the temple cleansing, the Lukan narrator states, Καὶ ὡς ἤγγισεν, ἰδὼν τὴν πόλιν ἔκλαυσεν ἐπ' αὐτήν (19:41). Many commentators correctly stress the prophetic and judgment themes of this passage. Luke Timothy Johnson views the weeping over the city purely as a

---

[638] See Fitzmyer, *Luke X-XXIV*, 1071-72;

[639] Nolland, *Luke 9:21-18:34*, 780.

238

prophetic gesture, with strong allusions to the LXX.[640] Likewise, Joseph Fitzmyer

contends that Jesus' weeping is to be seen as a prophetic sign.[641] Jack T. Sanders even

claims that since the function of the passage is prophetic, "there is present no element of

sadness."[642]

While Jesus' weeping is clearly symbolic and prophetic and perhaps even

eschatological, there does seem to be genuine sorrow in the character of Jesus over the

impending fate of Jerusalem.[643] My position is similar to that of Robert Tannehill, who

states, "In spite of the general Lukan tendency to remove Jesus' expressions of emotion

in Mark (cf. Fitzmyer 1981, 95), Jesus is depicted as weeping over Jerusalem."[644] In

terms of my analysis concerning Jesus' emotion, it is significant that Jesus' emotion here

occurs directly before his rather unemotional "cleansing" of the temple, and his general

lack of emotion going forward. It is further important that Jesus' sorrow mirrors the

intense mourning of his interlocutors in Luke 23:27-31.[645]

Similar to his reason for having Jesus show emotion in the following analyzed

pericope (compassion for the woman at Nain in Luke 7:11-17), Luke has Jesus show

---

[640] Jesus' weeping is followed by three verses of various allusions to oracles of destruction, possibly including 2 Kings 8:11-12; Neh 1:4; Ps 136:1, 137:9; Isa 29:3-10, 48:18; Jer 6:6-20, 8:18-21, 9:1, 15:5, 23:38-40; 13:17; Lam 1:1, 16; see Johnson, *Gospel of Luke*, 298.

[641] Fitzmyer, *Luke X-XXIV*, 1256. Joel Green terms it a "prophetic threat oracle" in *Gospel of Luke*, 689. L.T. Johnson calls Jesus' weeping a "prophetic gesture" in *Gospel of Luke*, 298. See also David L. Tiede, *Prophecy and History in Luke-Acts* (Philadelphia: Fortress Press, 1980), 82.

[642] J.T. Sanders, *The Jews in Luke-Acts* (Philadelphia: Fortress, 1987), 210.

[643] See Marshall, *Gospel of Luke*, 717-18.

[644] Tannehill, *Luke*, 284.

[645] For the connection of Jesus' weeping in Luke 19:41-44 with the women wailing in Luke 23:27-31, see especially Culpepper, *Gospel of Luke*, 371-75 and 450-53; and Schweizer, *Good News according to Luke*, 357.

emotion to emphasize the importance and significance of the passage. In one of the very few depictions of Jesus expressing emotion, Luke reveals to his audience how important the destruction of Jerusalem is to his view of history, eschatology, and christology. On his walk toward crucifixion (23:26-33), Luke's Jesus explicitly refocuses the women's wailing from him onto themselves (v.28) As Tannehill contends, "The Lukan audience is being asked to show compassion and sympathy for the Jewish women and children who died in Jerusalem."[646] This same principle is at work in Jesus' weeping in Luke 19:41-44. Sharon Ringe states, "Jesus' lament over the city (19:42-44) is Luke's lament as he looks back through the intervening years of war and destruction, especially during the Jewish-Roman War (66-70 C.E.)."[647] While Jesus' sorrow (shown through his weeping) is certainly contrary to my proposed pattern of Jesus as an *exemplum* of *apatheia* in Luke, Luke "saves" Jesus' emotion in order to emphasize certain facets of his message, including the importance of women in his gospel, and the significance of the destruction of the Temple.

The Widow's Son at Nain

Most of the previously analyzed "L" passages concerning emotion have straight-forward explanations (i.e. it is God's compassion) and clearly do not contradict the

---

[646] Tannehill, *Luke*, 339. In doing so, he also singles out the women. As in the woman at Nain passage, Jesus' emotion is importantly saved for women and children. See Morris, *Luke*, 355. Pace Nolland, who contends that the women are merely part of the larger crowd of people, that "we should not mark any clear separation between the People and the women in *Luke 23:26-32*, 1136. See further Jerome H. Neyrey, "Jesus' Address to the Women of Jerusalem (Lk. 23.27-31): A Prophetic Judgment Oracle." *NTS* 29 (1983), 75-76.

[647] Ringe, *Luke*, 241. Tannehill similarly concludes, "In this way the narrator suggests to the Lukan audience the attitude that should take toward the destruction of Jerusalem by the Romans in AD 70" in *Luke*, 284.

proposed pattern of Luke portraying Jesus as unemotional, the epitome of *apatheia*. The pericope of Jesus raising the son of a widow from the dead (7:11-17), however, does provide an example that contradicts my proposed pattern.[648] Using the same verb he used to describe the compassion of the Good Samaritan and the father of the prodigal son, Luke reads, καὶ ἰδὼν αὐτὴν ὁ κύριος ἐσπλαγχνίσθη ἐπ' αὐτῇ καὶ εἶπεν αὐτῇ, μὴ κλαῖε (v.13). Not only does the Lukan narrator describe Jesus' emotional state as one of compassion, but the emotion is the actual impetus for the healing.[649]

There has been no acceptable scholarly explanation for this odd case, even from the few commentators who similarly acknowledge the Lukan principle of removing emotion from Jesus. Fitzmyer simply states, "Thus the motive of the miracle is presented. It proceeds from Jesus' spontaneous compassion for the woman."[650] Not only is the compassion of Jesus the motive for the miracle, the miracle is the first occasion on which Luke, as narrator, calls Jesus Lord.[651] Thus the authority of Jesus is linked to his compassion is this episode, which is also contrary to my proposal that the authority of

---

[648] Along with the previously discussed passage concerning Jesus' weeping, Luke seems to be using the very few instances of Jesus expressing emotion for important emphasis.

[649] The most obvious "source" for this special Lukan miracle was the raising of the widow of Sarepta's son from the dead by the prophet Elijah (1 Kings 17:20-24). There is both a structural similarity, and a number of deliberate echoes (7:12, 15), but importantly there is no mention of compassion or any emotion on the part of Elijah. If this story was the primary source for the story, Luke has actually added an emotion, one not present in the source text, and on he has extirpated from his Markan source on numerous occasions.

[650] Does this imply spontaneity somehow is the reason for this non-redaction? Further, Fitzmyer argues against Martin Dibelius, who sought to ascribe v.13 to Luke, by indicating that Luke often omits the emotions of Jesus that are in his sources as well as the fact that the Lukan occurrences of the verb σπλαγχνίζομαι are all found in "L" passages, but tellingly, Fitzmyer doesn't actually provide explanation for the occurrence of compassion in the character of Jesus. See Martin Dibelius, *From Tradition to Gospel* (New York: Scribner, 1965), 75; Fitzmyer, *Luke I-IX*, 656-59.

[651] Just, *Luke 1:1-9:50*, 308.

241

Jesus is usually directly allied to his lack of emotion in Luke. Along with the previously

discussed passage concerning Jesus' weeping, Luke seems to be using the very few

instances of Jesus expressing emotion for important emphasis.

The "L" Evidence

With the whole of the evidence of the special Lukan material concerning Jesus'

emotion laid out, the obvious observation is that most of the passages *do not* concern

Jesus at all.[652] The infancy narratives are undoubtably a reference to the character of

God; many of the parables reference God, not Jesus. With respect to commentators and

theologians throughout history who have linked Jesus with the Good Samaritan, the

parable is clearly meant as an *exemplum* by Luke. Jesus' weeping is a symbolic and

prophetic oracle of judgment, but also an important counter-example of emotion used for

emphasis by Luke in communicating to his auditors how utterly devastating was the

destruction of Jerusalem. It is just as clear that the compassion shown by Jesus as the

impetus for the raising of the widow's son is certainly contrary to the proposed pattern,

and also seems to be used for emphasis.

The Preponderance of the Evidence: Luke's Redactional Pattern Emerges

In the introduction, I quoted Donald Capps, who stated, ―A portraitist's decision

whether or not to incorporate a given image is an important statement about who the

---

[652] A distinction must be made between the emotional portrayal of God and Jesus, as well as a distinction between the depiction of Jesus as a character in Luke's composition and the emotional and practical expectations of his followers as found especially in his teachings.

portraitist understands Jesus to have been."[653] I further proposed that we see Luke as one

such portraitist, in whose decisions of what to incorporate and what to remove from his

Markan source, in whose redactions concerning the emotional depiction of Jesus, we see

an important statement of who Luke understands Jesus to have been. Though the Lukan

redactions are sometimes subtle, the pericopae put forward as evidence often have

multiple interpretations, and the form of these Lukan redactions varies greatly,[654] a clear

pattern emerges. Through a close textual comparison of the Lukan and Markan texts, I

have shown that Luke consistently redacts Mark in his portrait of a Jesus that shows little

or no emotion, a portrait of Jesus in line with the philosophical concept of *apatheia*.

Anger

Luke consistently removes emotions that I have termed traditionally "negative,"

for lack of a better term, including the philosophically important emotions of anger,

strong speech, and grief. In a scene at the synagogue (Mark 3:1-6//Luke 6:6-11), Luke

omits the Markan narrator's "with anger" (μετ᾽ ὀργῆς) as well as Jesus' grief ("grieved

at their hardness of heart," συλλυπούμενος ἐπὶ τῇ πωρώσει τῆς καρδίας αὐτῶν) in

---

[653] Capps, *Jesus*, 7.

[654] The *forms* of the texts that Luke redacts include narrative descriptions of Jesus' emotional state (anger and grief, Mark 3:5//Luke 6:10; anger/indignation: Mark10:14//Luke 18:16; compassion: Mark 1:41//Luke 5:13, 6:34//Luke 9:11; love: Mark 10:21//Luke 18:22), narrative descriptions of Jesus' actions (anger/violence: Mark 11:15-16//Luke 19:45; affection: Mark 9:39//Luke 9:47-48, Mark 10:15-16//Luke 18:17), narrative descriptions of Jesus' speech (Mark 3:12//Luke 6:19/4:41, Mark 5:19//Luke 8:38, Mark 6:8//Luke 9:3, Mark 9:9//Luke 9:36, Mark 8:30//Luke 9:21), direct discourse (stern rebuke: Mark 11:14//Luke 13:6-9), narrative description *and* direct discourse (sternness: Mark 1:43-44//Luke 5:14; mutual rebuke: Mark 8:32-33//Luke 9:22), and self-descriptive speech (neediness: Mark 2:25//Luke 6:3; mercy: Mark 5:19-20//Luke 8:39).

referring to how Jesus looked at the Pharisees (Mark 3:5//Luke 6:10). Similarly, the

Lukan narrator omits Jesus' ―anger/indignation" (ἠγανάκτησεν) from his Markan source

(Mark 10:14//Luke 18:16) concerning Jesus' teaching on the kingdom of God and

children (Mark 10:13-16//Luke 18:15-17).

While these Lukan pericopae have omitted Jesus' anger as a narrator description,

Luke's version of the temple ―cleansing" most clearly shows his aversion to anger in that

he removes the actual actions associated with Jesus' anger in Mark (Mark 11:15-17//Luke

19:45-46). The Markan account includes Jesus angrily overturning the money-changers'

tables and the pigeon-sellers' seats (Mark 11:15b), as well as ―καὶ οὐκ ἤφιεν ἵνα τις

διενέγκη σκεῦος διὰ τοῦ ἱεροῦ" (v.16), implying violent intervention and resistance to

other Temple activities. In his abbreviated version of the cleansing narrative, Luke omits

these emotional details (Mark 11:15b-16), in order to portray Jesus as self-controlled and

not prone to violence.

Stern Speech

Jesus' anger is also shown in Mark through the use of stern speech, which is

consistently eliminated (or at least significantly softened) by Luke. Although it was

noted that most commentators discard these often subtle redactions as merely stylistic

changes by Luke, a consistent pattern emerges of a less emotional Jesus with regard to his

speech. In the scene where Jesus heals a leper (Mark 1:40-45//Luke 5:12-16), the

Markan Jesus, using direct discourse, ―sternly warns" (ἐμβριμησάμενος) the healed

244

leper and then sends him away at once (1:43-44a), while the narrator of Luke states generically that Jesus —forbids" (παρήγγειλεν) the leper to tell anyone. The Lukan narrator similarly softens Jesus' strong refusal in Mark (καὶ οὐκ ἀφῆκεν αὐτὸν, 5:19), choosing instead a general dismissal (ἀπέλυσεν δὲ αὐτὸν, 8:38b) in the passage concerning the Gerasene Demoniac (Mark 5:1-20//Luke 8:26-39). In the charge to tell no one in the passage concerning Jesus' healing of Jairus' daughter (Mark 5:21-43//Luke 8:40-56), Luke significantly softens the tone of Jesus' speech, changing the Markan, καὶ διεστείλατο αὐτοῖς πολλὰ ἵνα μηδεὶς γνοῖ τοῦτο (5:43), to ὁ δὲ παρήγγειλεν αὐτοῖς μηδενὶ εἰπεῖν τὸ γεγονός (8:56). Luke changes the verb from διαστέλλω to παραγγέλλω, and also omits the intensifying πολλὰ. Another case providing evidence of Luke's subtle softening of Jesus' speech occurs in the scene where Jesus commissions the twelve (Mark 6:6b-13//Luke 9:1-6).

In the transfiguration pericope (Mark 9:2-10//Luke 9:28-36), Luke (9:36) removes Mark's harsh command language, διεστείλατο αὐτοῖς ἵνα μηδενὶ ἃ εἶδον διηγήσωνται (Mark 9:9). With a modification in verbal construction, Luke provides a tonally softer charge (καὶ ἐπετίμησεν αὐτοῖς ἵνα μηδενὶ λέγωσιν περὶ αὐτοῦ, Mark 8:30 // ὁ δὲ ἐπιτιμήσας αὐτοῖς παρήγγειλεν μηδενὶ λέγειν τοῦτο, Luke 9:21) by Jesus to the disciples at the end of the narrative usually labeled Peter's confession (Mark 8:27-

30//Luke 9:18-21). In a tenuous parallel (Mark 11:12-14//Luke 13:6-9), Luke either

radically changes the pericope of an irrational and emotional Jesus cursing a fig tree into

a parable about a man not harming a fig tree, or most probably simply omits the episode

altogether. Luke has consistently softened the tone of Jesus' speech in Mark in order to

emphasize calmness and emotional self-control even when making an authoritative

charge.

It is important to point out that many of the stern speech redactions include

Markan texts usually labeled under the category of "messianic secret." Thus, many

commentators explain these Lukan redactions as Luke's unconcern with this Markan

theme. Obviously, Luke has reapportioned these texts for his particular purpose(s), but it

is of vital import to note that of the *five* Markan texts dealing with secrecy of some sort

that Luke has redacted, Luke has *retained* the secrecy element at least *four* times. In fact,

the only instance of Luke completely removing a Markan messianic secrecy text is a

tenuous one. If the Lukan parallel to Jesus' healings by the sea (Mark 3:7-12) is 6:17-19,

then Luke has removed the secrecy motif. But if the Lukan parallel is 4:41, which seems

more likely, then Luke has retained the motif, and thus Luke has retained every

occurrence. At the very least Luke retains Mark's secrecy theme in the leper healing

(Mark 1:40-45//Luke 5:12-16), the healing of the ruler's daughter (Mark 5:43//Luke

8:56), the transfiguration (Mark 9:9//Luke 9:36), and Peter's confession (Mark

8:30//Luke 9:21). Therefore, the reason for the Lukan redactions in these texts is

definitively not the lessening of Mark's messianic secret. What Luke does change,

importantly, is the *emotional tone* of the secrecy commands; it is softened in every single

case.

The Lukan principle of omitting (or at least softening) Jesus' stern and sometimes angry speech in Mark is seen most clearly in the *total omission* of the mutual rebukes between Jesus and Peter in the pericope concerning Jesus' prediction of his passion (Mark 8:31-33//Luke 9:22). Jesus' predictive comments on his coming suffering provoke Peter's private rebuke of Jesus: καὶ προσλαβόμενος ὁ Πέτρος αὐτὸν ἤρξατο ἐπιτιμᾶν αὐτῷ (8:32b). Peter's private reprimand of Jesus in turn provokes Jesus' public rebuke of Peter: ὁ δὲ ἐπιστραφεὶς καὶ ἰδὼν τοὺς μαθητὰς αὐτοῦ ἐπετίμησεν Πέτρῳ (8:33a). Then Jesus directly admonishes Peter by declaring, ὕπαγε ὀπίσω μου, σατανᾶ, ὅτι οὐ φρονεῖς τὰ τοῦ θεοῦ ἀλλὰ τὰ τῶν ἀνθρώπων (8:33b).

Grief

Not only is Luke's portrait of Jesus drastically different than Mark's anent Jesus' anger, Luke also completely alters the emotional characterization of Jesus regarding neediness and the important philosophical emotion of grief or distress (λύπη). In the controversy scene of Jesus comparing his actions to those of David in picking grain on the Sabbath (Mark 2:23-28//Luke 6:1-5), Luke maintains the physical aspect of Jesus' hunger (ἐπείνασεν, 6:3), but omits the emotional language of neediness in Mark (χρείαν ἔσχεν, 2:26). In another Sabbath controversy scene (Mark 3:1-6//Luke 6:6-11), Luke removes –συλλυπούμενος" (Mark 3:5//Luke 6:10).

In summary concerning λύπη, Luke never uses any form of λύπη for the

character of Jesus. Luke removes every Markan form of λύπη for the *character of*

Jesus. It is also important, as will be shown in greater detail in chapter five concerning

the emotions and characters other than Jesus, that Luke redacts Mark (and avoids in the

special Lukan material) concerning grief in the *character of Jesus only*.[655] For Luke does

use λύπη for other characters and retains every Markan usage of λύπη concerning other

characters (see analysis above of the rich man and Jesus, Mark 10:17-22//Luke 18:18-23,

and further chapter five) save for one.[656]

Positive Emotions

---

[655] There is an important text critical note, and possible exception to my proposed redactional rule, in Luke 18:24. Some manuscripts add περίλυπον γενόμενον to the beginning of v.24, so that it reads —When Jesus saw that he was filled with grief, he said…" Though it does not concern Jesus, it does speak to Luke's overall redactional agenda, and is directly relevant to my contention that the Lukan redactional program concerning the emotions primarily concerns the character of Jesus. The best manuscript evidence favors the shorter text (B L fl 1241 *al*) and the variety of positions of περίλυπον γενόμενον suggest that the words περίλυπον γενόμενον were introduced by copyists, probably from v.23 (περίλυπος ἐγενήθη). However, given Cadbury's observation that Luke often repeats a word or phrase in adjacent passages, in English translations, the phrase περίλυπον γενόμενον is often not omitted entirely, but enclosed in brackets. See Metzger, *A Textual Commentary on the Greek New Testament*, 168-69.

[656] The one mention of the other characters and λύπη removed by Luke concerns the narrative of Jesus foretelling his betrayal (Mark 14:18-21//Luke 22:21-23). Two explanations are the most probable. Mark could have removed the disciples grief (λυπεῖσθαι, v.19), along with vv. 18-19 entirely, to emphasize a divine determinism which is much more forceful in the Lukan version; see Nolland, *Luke 18:35-24:53*, 1058-1060. The two texts are so different linguistically, many scholars have argued that Luke was not literarily dependent on Mark, but relied on other traditions; see Friedrich Rehkopf, *Die Lukanische Sonderquelle: Ihr Umfang und Sprachgebrauch* (WUNT 5; Tübingen: J.C.B. Mohr, 1959), 7-30; and Vincent Taylor, *The Passion Narrative of St. Luke: A Critical and Historical Investigation* (NTS 19; Cambridge: Cambridge University Press, 1971), 59-61. For the pericopae that do fit the proposed pattern, see the passage on the rich young man (Mark 10:17-22//Luke 18:18-23), where Luke removes the Markan description of Jesus' love (v.21, see below), but retains the Markan description of the rich man's grief (λυπούμενος, Mark 10:22) in 18:23 (περίλυπος). See also the Gethsemane narrative (Mark 14:32-42//Luke 22:39-46) discussion in chapter one, where Luke actually transfers Jesus' grief in Mark 14:34 (περίλυπος) to the disciples in Luke 22:45 (λύπη).

In my analysis of Luke as a portraitist, special attention was given to his redactions concerning the ‑positive" emotions of the Markan Jesus, including compassion, mercy, and affection.[657] In the pericope where Jesus cleanses a leper (Mark 1:40-45//Luke 5:12-16), Luke removes Jesus' ‑compassion" (σπλαγχνισθείς) as found in Mark 1:41 (c.f. Luke 5:13). Jesus' compassion is also redacted in Jesus' feeding of the multitudes (Mark 6:32-44//Luke 9:10b-17). Luke replaces the more emotional σπλαγχνίζομαι with the more neutral ἀποδέχομαι (‑to welcome," Mark 6:34//Luke 9:11), and also removes the sentimental language of sheep (πρόβατα) needing a shepherd (ποιμένα). In the passage concerning the Gerasene Demoniac (Mark 5:1-20//Luke 8:26-39), Luke removes Jesus' self-described mercy (ἔλεος), by omitting the Markan phrase ‑καὶ ἠλέησέν σε" (Mark 5:19//Luke 8:39). Luke omits the Markan description of Jesus' love (αὐτῷ ἠγάπησεν, Mark 10:21//Luke 18:22) in the encounter of the rich man with Jesus (Mark 10:17-22//Luke 18:18-23). In the last two pericopae examined, Luke removes Jesus' actions of affection toward children. When the disciples argue over greatness (Mark 9:33-37//Luke 9:46-48), the Markan Jesus grasps the child, puts him in the middle of the group, and then dramatically takes the child in his arms (9:36), and similarly, in teaching on the Kingdom of God (Mark 10:13-16//Luke 18:15-17), the Markan Jesus takes the children into his arms, blesses them, and then lays his

---

[657] These redactions concerning the removal of Jesus' positive emotions will be particularly important in chapter six in the attempt to specifically locate the audience and the philosophical tradition(s) on which Luke relies in constructing his gospel.

hands upon the children (10:15-16); the Lukan Jesus does not.

While some scholars, even when providing evidence to the contrary, have stubbornly failed to acknowledge the broad Lukan redactional *program* of removing emotion from the character of Jesus (e.g. Bovon, Goulder), many scholars have identified at least some of these *Tendenzen*. Though commentators may recognize the Lukan changes regarding emotion, they fail to understand fully their significance in portraying a phlegmatic Jesus and how this portrait contributes to who Luke and his audience understood Jesus to have been. Some scholars even identified these redactions in pericopae designed to show the authority of Jesus,[658] but do not demonstrate how the Lukan emotional redactions contribute to this emphasis. A key aspect to the Lukan emotional redactions is that Jesus is seen as publically authoritative *because* of his lack of emotion, not in spite of it.[659] Jesus is able to break down barriers and challenge contemporary notions of status, precisely because he is portrayed as a public leader full of rationality and self-control, evident in his depiction as a man of *apatheia*.

---

[658] The pericopae where the Lukan redactions serve to increase the authority of Jesus (e.g. removing Jesus' anger depicts a calmer authority figure with greater self-control) could include all the pericope assayed, in one way or another, but this is especially true in confrontational narratives with other authorities (6:1-5, 6-11; 19:45-46), public healing/miracle/exorcism episodes (5:12-16; 6:17-19; 8:26-39; 9:10b-17), and public teaching passages (9: 46-48; 18:15-17, 18-23;). Pericopae are listed according to Lukan purposes, as Markan intentions are often reassigned.

[659] For example, in his commentary of the passage concerning the cleansing of the leper (Mark 1:4-45//Luke 5:12-16), John Nolland does connect Jesus' authority to his lack of emotion, albeit in a manner exactly the opposite of my proposed relationship. Luke -omits here from the Markan account the words that express Jesus' inner feelings" which Nolland *contrasts* with Luke's -public claims" of Jesus in the -public realm" as signs of -public authentication" in *Luke 1-9:20*, 227-28. He seems to be relying on Pesch for the Lukan redactions concerning emotion; see Rudolf Pesch, *Jesu ureigene Taten? Ein Beitrag zur Wunderfrage* (Freiburg: Herder, 1970), 103; see further chapter six.

CHAPTER 5
LUKE'S REDACTIONS OF MARK:
THE SUPPORTING CHARACTERS

Introduction

[C]ertain redactional modifications of the Marcan source material can be seen to stem from a delicate sensitivity which tends to make Luke eliminate anything that smacks of the violent, the passionate, or the emotional."[660]

---

[660] Joseph Fitzmyer, *Luke I-IX*, 94.

We have seen that almost without exception Luke has removed the emotion from the Markan Jesus. Text by text, I have presented evidence that Luke has consistently omitted (or at least drastically softened) Jesus' anger, grief, and stern speech, and the actions which result from these. Further I have presented evidence that Luke has systematically taken away Jesus' compassion, love, and affection. Though most biblical scholars have failed to acknowledge Luke's redactional program, Henry Cadbury, and Joseph Fitzmyer in particular, have correctly recognized many of these redactions. In the attempt to account for this redactional program, Fitzmyer has stated that Luke eliminates *anything* that smacks of the violent, the passionate, or the emotional. This chapter will argue that this is simply not true, it is only true for the character of Jesus.

As discussed in chapter four, Fitzmyer, following Cadbury, notes many (but not all) of the proposed Lukan redactions concerning the emotions of Jesus.[661] However, Fitzmyer, pace Cadbury, in keeping with his contention that Luke has eliminated anything associated with passion, further declares, ―A similar restraint [Luke's elimination of Jesus' emotion in Mark] is manifested at times toward the disciples of Jesus."[662] As evidence he offers the Lukan omission (18:31) of the disciples' wonder and fear (ἐφοβοῦντο) at Jesus' traveling to Jerusalem in Mark (10:32b) and also, ―the

---

[661] Fitzmyer states, ―Similarly, the description of Jesus moved by human emotions in the Marcan Gospel is normally eliminated in the Lucan story, even if they are expressions of love, compassion, or tenderness," in *Luke I-IX*, 95. Cadbury writes, ―Human emotions and expressions of feeling on Christ's part are omitted by Luke, even when they are love and pity," in *Style and Literary Method*, 91.

[662] Fitzmyer, *Luke I-IX*, 95. He tempers his assertion with ―at times," with which I would basically agree, however, from context it is clear that by ―at times" he means most of the time, or even all the time, just not as many occurrences as Jesus. At the very least, it happens enough for him to declare it a consistent pattern. Contrarily, I contend there is not a pattern, as more often, Luke retains or even intensifies their emotions. Further, as I argued briefly in chapter four, there is not an agenda in Luke to preserve the character or honor of the apostles; see further below.

embarrassed silence of the disciples (Mark 9:34) is passed over by Luke (9:47)."[663] While the omission of the disciples' fear and amazement is a possible emotional redaction,[664] the reference to the disciples' silence has nothing to do with their emotions, but with their overall presentation as a favorable or unfavorable character, or more precisely the level of their understanding, which I have consistently argued is mixed.[665]

Fitzmyer further tenders the Lukan omission of the rebuke of Simon Peter (Mark 8:33//Luke 9:22) and the disciples' accusation of Jesus' lack of concern about them (Mark 4:38//Luke 8:24) as evidence for his proposed theorem. As analyzed previously, the omission of Jesus'/Peter's mutual rebuke is primarily due to Luke's concern with the portrayal of Jesus and has little if anything to do with the characterization of Peter.[666]

---

[663] Ibid.

[664] Luke has obviously removed the disciples' fear and amazement, though the reason is simple geography. Luke doesn't retain a similar version of the verse without the emotion, he removes the entire verse (Mark 10:32) for geographic reasons. It could also be to highlight the theme of the *failure* of the disciples to appreciate what was going to happen in Jerusalem (Luke 19:11); see Marshall, *Gospel of Luke*, 689. At the very least it doesn't seem to in any way contribute to a more positive or more honorable portrait as Fitzmyer implies, which is what the Jesus redactions consistently do.

[665] The depiction is so mixed, commentators have opined completely opposite positions. Fitzmyer argues for a gradual increase in apostolic awareness with Luke 8:25 as "the beginning of a sense of awareness" in *Luke I-IX*, 730. Arthur A. Just Jr. argues that "Luke shows a gradual movement toward total misunderstanding and silence. By the end of the gospel, Luke has demonstrated that the disciples are completely confused concerning the purpose of Jesus' Messiahship" in *Luke 1:1-9:50*, 393. In the analysis of Jesus' teaching on the kingdom of God and children (Mark 10:13-16//Luke 18:15-17), Frederick W. Danker and Michael D. Goulder argue that the passage portrays the apostles in a less embarrassing light, while Joel B. Green argues Luke's account is a further indictment on the disciples. See Green, *Gospel of Luke*, 650-52; Danker, *Jesus and the New Age*, 298; Goulder, *Luke: A New Paradigm II*, 667.

[666] See detailed analysis in chapter four. Peter's overall depiction in Luke, like the disciples as a general group, is mixed. Why would Luke keep Peter's denial (22:54ff), along with other passages where Peter still does not understand Jesus and his message (e.g. 22:54), if his main concern were Peter? Further, the *occasion* of the pericope is Peter's apparent misunderstanding (or at least not full understanding) and Jesus' mistrust of Peter and the disciples to disseminate the message (9:18-21). In fact, Luke's removal of Peter's rebuke is probably due (at least in part) to the third corollary (to the proposed Lukan redactional principle of subjugating Jesus' emotion) as presented in chapter four. Luke oftens omits or lessens the violence (or the threat of violence) and strong emotion *to* Jesus. Again, pace Fitzmyer, Luke is primarily concerned with the portrait of Jesus, Jesus' actions, and the actions done to him. Fitzmyer contends, "Luke has further omitted Peter's protest ... because he undoubtedly considered the rebuke unflattering to Peter;

Likewise, Luke's removal of the disciple's accusation has more to do with Jesus' appearing not to care and Jesus, as a person of authority, being spoken to in that manner than concern over the disciples' whining.[667] Further, though different language is used, the disciples' actual emotion in the pericope (Mark 4:35-41//Luke 8:22-25) is retained:

136. Stilling the Storm[668]

Mark 4:40-41	Luke 8:25
καὶ εἶπεν αὐτοῖς	εἶπεν δὲ αὐτοῖς
τί *δειλοί* ἐστε οὕτως	
πῶς οὐκ ἔχετε πίστιν	ποῦ ἡ πίστις ὑμῶν
καὶ *ἐφοβήθησαν φόβον* μέγαν	*φοβηθέντες δὲ ἐθαύμασαν*
καὶ ἔλεγον πρὸς ἀλλήλους	λέγοντες πρὸς ἀλλήλους
τίς ἄρα οὗτός ἐστιν	τίς ἄρα οὗτός ἐστιν
ὅτι καὶ ὁ ἄνεμος ἡ θάλασσα	ὅτι καὶ τοῖς ἀνέμοις καὶ τῷ ὕδατι
ὑπακούει αὐτῷ	καὶ ὑπακούουσιν αὐτῷ

In Mark, Jesus asks them why they are afraid (δειλοί) and then they are described

as being afraid (ἐφοβήθησαν φόβον, 40-41). Luke describes their reaction as fear and

---

he deliberately omits as much as he can in his Gospel that may sound blameworthy in Peter's conduct (and often of the apostles as well)" in *Luke I-IX*, 777. This is simply not true.

[667] Fitzmyer even acknowledges "the Lucan form of Jesus' words to the disciples takes some of the edge off his reply; the sternness of his answer in Mark 4:40 corresponds to the disciples' query in v.38c whether he cared about them or not" in *Luke I-IX*, 728.

[668] All Greek texts and parallel numbers/titles are taken from Kurt Aland, *Synopsis Quattuor Evangeliorum* (13th revidierte Auflage; Stuttgart: Deutsche Bibelgesellschaft, 1985), based on the Greek text of Nestle-Aland 26th edition. All English translations are mine (based on the NRSV), unless otherwise noted. The word(s) underlined in red indicate material omitted in Luke's version; dashed underlined in blue indicates emotion transferred from Jesus to another person or group; double-underlined in green indicates the omission or lessening of violence or emotion *to* Jesus; *italicized in orange* indicates a different word choice; waved underline in purple indicates emotional special "L" material.

marvel (φοβηθέντες δὲ ἐθαύμασαν, v.25). Fitzmyer contends that ―the disciples'

cowardice and great fear" is one of the Markan elements Luke omits which ―are not

essential to the story."[669] How essential Luke's emotional portrayal is to the pericope is

perhaps up for debate, but Luke has not removed the disciples' fear, he has repositioned it

for his purpose. Luke's mention of their fear is certainly reduced, as Mark includes their

fear in Jesus' direct question and uses both a verbal and an accusative form (with μέγαν)

for further emphasis.[670] But Luke adds ἐθαύμασαν – the only place where Luke

combines ―awe" and ―fear" – not to increase (or even out) the emotional portrayal of the

disciples, but to clarify the depiction of Jesus, whose work inspires wonder as well as

fear. My contention, bluntly, is that Luke is just not concerned with portraying the

disciples without emotion, or even in depicting them as more favorable than Mark, or

even favorable in general. The only thing consistent about the disciples' portrait is that,

from beginning to the end, their characterization is consistently sundry.

In further support for his contention that Luke has eliminated the disciples'

emotion along with Jesus', Fitzmyer states, ―Luke not only omits the request of the sons

of Zebedee (Mark 10:35-40), but also – what is extraordinary – all reference to the

apostles' deserting of Jesus and their flight (Mark 14:49)."[671] This omission certainly

---

[669] Fitzmyer, *Luke I-IX*, 727.

[670] This is a common Septuagintism, which Luke, though he redacts this instance, does use once – to describe the shepherds' response to the angel of the Lord (2:9). Luke shifts an indicative to a participle followed by an indicative, which is perhaps merely a stylistic change, but also serves to clarify their reaction to Jesus question. At the end of Peter's confession (Mark 8:27//Luke 9:21), Luke uses a similar construction to clarify Jesus' charge to the disciples; see chapter four.

[671] Fitzmyer, *Luke I-IX*, 95.

speaks directly to the character of the disciples and Jesus, and perhaps indirectly to their emotions (fear? grief?), though the Lukan changes to the pericope immediately prior to the disicples' fleeing would seem to negate the necessity of them taking flight.[672] He also offers as proof of his proposed principle the omission by Luke of the story of the youth who ran off naked, which he terms "a Marcan detail symbolizing the utter dereliction of Jesus (14:51-52)."[673] Even if we accept his tenuous interpretation, this would speak to Luke's agenda concerning Jesus, not the disciples. In brief, most of Fitzmyer's evidence has nothing to do with the emotions of the disciples, and the few instances that do concern the disciples and the emotions have straight-forward explanations that do not speak to the manifestation of a general principle.

More important than refuting Fitzmyer's evidence, I will present two strands of evidence in order to show that there is not an over-riding Lukan program of eliminating emotion in general and neither is there a specific program of eliminating the disciples' emotion. (1) Luke, on occasion, employs a technique where he eliminates the emotion from Jesus and then transfers the same emotion to another person or group in the same pericope.[674] There is not a net *elimination* of emotion. It is either a zero sum transfer or

---

[672] In accordance with the previously mentioned corollary to the proposed redactional principle that Luke has consistently removed strong emotion from the character of Jesus, Luke keeps the Markan violence by Jesus' *followers* in cutting off the ear of the high priest's slave, but (contrary to both Mark and Matthew) has Jesus actually heal his ear as well as exclaim ἐᾶτε ἕως τούτου (v.51). The violence (and potential violence) *toward* Jesus is greatly reduced, even though the violence by one of Jesus' followers is kept. Since Jesus healed the slave's ear and put an end to the violence, there is really no reason for the disciples to be fearful and flee.

[673] Ibid.

[674] The transferred emotion is taken from Jesus and either given to the disciples (in the garden, Mark 14:43-52//Luke 22:47-53), the people who speak well of him (in the synagogue, Mark 6:1-6//Luke 4:16-30), or to the scribes and Pharisees (in the synagogue, Mark 3:1-6//Luke 6:6-11). Thus, there doesn't seem to be an agenda as to who receives the emotion (i.e. Jesus' enemies or friends). Overall, Luke is

occasionally Luke even intensifies the transfer so that there is a net *gain* of emotion. Besides presenting evidence from Luke's ―transference technique," (2) I will also show that Luke often merely maintains characters' emotion. Whether the characters are essentially deemed positive, negative, or neutral/mixed by Luke, he is frankly just not that concerned with their emotional portrait. Conversely, Luke is extremely interested in the manner in which he portrays Jesus. Luke is concerned with presenting an unemotional Jesus to demonstrate Jesus' self-control, to manifest his rationality, and ultimately to reveal and proclaim the virtuous authority of Jesus.

Luke's Transference Technique[675]

330. Gethsemane

Mark 14:33-34, 37	Luke 22:45
καὶ παραλαμβάνει τὸν Πέτρον καὶ τὸν Ἰάκωβον καὶ τὸν Ἰωάννην μετ' αὐτοῦ, καὶ ἤρξατο **ἐκθαμβεῖσθαι** καὶ **ἀδημονεῖν**, καὶ λέγει αὐτοῖς περίλυπός ἐστιν ἡ ψυχή μου ἕως θανάτου	Luke omits

---

unconcerned who shows emotion, as long as it is not Jesus, as favorable characters, unfavorable characters, and those with neutral or mixed characterizations all show emotion.

[675] The transference technique put forward seems to be an amalgamation of two broader Lukan principles. Obviously, based on the survey of the Lukan emotional redactions in chapter four, Luke wants to present the reader with a Jesus without emotion. Luke also transfers phrases in Mark to different locations in his version as a general principle. See Johannes Henricus Scholten. *Das Paulinische Evangelium: kritische Untersuchung des Evangeliums nach Lucas und seines Verhältnisses zu Marcus, Matthäus und der Apostelgeschichte* (Elberfeld: R.L. Friderichs, 1881), 26-41, 143ff. Cadbury further contends, ―In the following cases, Luke seems to have transferred a phrase in such a manner as to alter the meaning" in *Style and Literary Method*, 97. Though he does not list our four passages (Luke also transfers the amazement of the women at the tomb in Mark to the disciples in his account; see analysis below) concerning emotion, such a transfer is not without precedence.

καὶ ἔρχεται	ἐλθὼν πρὸς τοὺς μαθητὰς
καὶ εὑρίσκει αὐτοὺς καθεύδοντας,	εὗρεν κοιμωμένους αὐτοὺς
	ἀπὸ τῆς λύπης
καὶ λέγει τῷ Πέτρῳ	καὶ εἶπεν αὐτοῖς
Σίμων, καθεύδεις;	τί καθεύδετε;

In the pericope that began our analysis of the Lukan redactions concerning Jesus'

emotion, Jesus in the garden (Mark 14:32-42//Luke 22:39-46), Luke transfers Jesus' grief

from Jesus (Mark 14:33-34) to the disciples (Luke 22:45).[676] After he took Peter, James,

and John with him, the Markan narrator describes Jesus as greatly distressed and troubled

(ἐκθαμβεῖσθαι καὶ ἀδημονεῖν, v.33). The Markan Jesus then says to them, ―My soul is

very sorrowful, even to death (περίλυπός ἐστιν ἡ ψυχή μου ἕως θανάτου, v.34).

These two verses are removed by Luke.[677] Later in the pericope, Jesus finds them (Peter,

James, and John in Mark//all the disciples in Luke) sleeping and asks them why they

were asleep (Mark 14:37//Luke 22:45-46). The Lukan version is a close textual parallel,

---

[676]See further Sterling, ―Mors philosophi," 393.

[677] Many commentators maintain that, since the details of Luke's version are so different than the Markan account, it derived from an independent account. So Adolf Schlatter, *Das Evangelium des Lukas aus s. Quellen erkl* (Stuttgart: Calwer Vereinsbuchh, 1931), 432-33; Alfred Loisy, *L'Évangile selon Luc* (8th ed.; Frankfurt: Minerva, 1971), 525; Walter Grundmann, *Das Evangelium nach Lukas* (THKNT 3; Berlin: Evangelische Verlagsanstalt, 1981), 411; Vincent Taylor and Owen E. Evans, *The Passion Narrative of St Luke: A Critical and Historical Investigation* (London: Cambridge University Press, 1972), 69-72. I (following Linnemann et al) contend that, especially if one prescinds from the text-critical problem of vv.43-44, the rest of the Lukan verses can be easily explained through Lukan redactions/omissions of Mark and special composition. See especially Eta Linnemann, *Studien zur Passionsgeschichte* (FRLANT 102; Göttingen: Vandenhoeck u. Ruprecht, 1970), 34-40; also Erich Klostermann, *Das Lukasevangelium* (HNT 5; Tübingen: J.C.B. Mohr (Paul Siebeck), 1929), 215; Gerhard Schneider, *Das Evangelium nach Lukas* (3 vols.; Gütersloh: Gütersloher Verlagshaus Mohn, 1977-1992), 457.

only he provides an important emotional reason for their sleeping – grief (ἀπὸ τῆς

λύπης, v.45).

It is of vital import that Luke gives no explanation why the disciples should be

grieving, nor why Jesus withdrew to pray, whereas in the Markan version Jesus reveals to

Peter, James, and John that he withdraws because his soul is περίλυπός ἐστιν ἡ ψυχή

μου ἕως θανάτου (Mark 14:34). As he is in general, Luke here is primarily concerned

with the emotional portrait of Jesus. Thus he transfers Jesus' emotion to the disciples.

This transference leaves the text slightly awkward, as now there is no reason for Jesus'

withdrawal and no reason for the disciples to be grieved.[678] It is simply the result of the

Lukan redactional agenda concerning Jesus' emotions.

47. The Man with the Withered Hand

Mark 3:4-5	Luke 6:9-10
καὶ λέγει αὐτοῖς ἔξεστιν τοῖς σάββασιν ἀγαθὸν ποιῆσαι ἢ κακοποιῆσαι, ψυχὴν σῶσαι ἢ ἀποκτεῖναι; οἱ δὲ ἐσιώπων. καὶ περιβλεψάμενος αὐτοὺς <u>μετʼ ὀργῆς,</u> **<u>συλλυπούμενος ἐπὶ τῇ πωρώσει</u>** **<u>τῆς καρδίας αὐτῶν,</u>** λέγει τῷ ἀνθρώπῳ	εἶπεν δὲ ὁ Ἰησοῦς πρὸς αὐτούς ἐπερωτῶ ὑμᾶς εἰ ἔξεστιν τῷ σαββάτῳ ἀγαθοποιῆσαι ἢ κακοποιῆσαι, ψυχὴν σῶσαι ἢ ἀπολέσαι; καὶ περιβλεψάμενος πάντας αὐτοὺς εἶπεν αὐτῷ

---

[678] See further Fitzmyer, *Luke X-XXIV*, 1442.

ἔκτεινον τὴν χεῖρα.	ἔκτεινον τὴν χεῖρα σου.
καὶ ἐξέτεινεν,	ὁ δὲ ἐποίησεν,
καὶ ἀπεκατεστάθη ἡ χεὶρ αὐτοῦ.	καὶ ἀπεκατεστάθη ἡ χεὶρ αὐτοῦ.
καὶ ἐξελθόντες οἱ φαρισαῖοι	αὐτοὶ δὲ
εὐθὺς μετὰ τῶν Ἡρῳδιανῶν	ἐπλήσθησαν ἀνοίας,
συμβούλιον ἐδίδουν κατ' αὐτοῦ,	καὶ διελάλουν πρὸς ἀλλήλους
ὅπως αὐτὸν ἀπολέσωσιν.	τί ἂν ποιήσαιεν τῷ Ἰησοῦ.

Another example of Luke's ―transference technique" occurs in the previously mentioned scene between the Pharisees (and scribes in Luke) and Jesus (Mark 3:1-6//Luke 6:6-11). Luke has not just removed Jesus anger, but taken away this anger and given it to Jesus' enemies (v.11).[679] In the last verse of the Markan pericope, the Pharisees went out, and held counsel with the Herodians on how to destroy Jesus (v.6). Luke's gospel is comparable with the scribes and Pharisees discussing what they might do to Jesus, though significantly, the Lukan narrator adds the phrase ―they were filled with rage" (αὐτοὶ δὲ ἐπλήσθησαν ἀνοίας, v.11). Mark's account reads, καὶ

ἐξελθόντες οἱ φαρισαῖοι εὐθὺς μετὰ τῶν Ἡρῳδιανῶν συμβούλιον ἐδίδουν κατ'

αὐτοῦ, ὅπως αὐτὸν ἀπολέσωσιν (3:6), while the Lukan version states, αὐτοὶ δὲ

ἐπλήσθησαν ἀνοίας, καὶ διελάλουν πρὸς ἀλλήλους τί ἂν ποιήσαιεν τῷ Ἰησοῦ

---

[679] Luke never uses ὀργή/ ὀργίζεσθαι of Jesus. Luke further removes the one Markan reference to Jesus' ὀργή (3:5). Luke actually uses ὀργή more than Mark. See John the Baptizer's proclamation to the crowd about the wrath to come (Luke 3:7); the owner of the house who throws the great dinner is described as angry when his invitations are refused in Jesus' parable (Luke 14:21); Jesus' foretelling of Jerusalem's destruction and its wrath against the people (21:23).

(6:11).

The lack of recognition of Luke's transference technique by the scholarly

community in this passage is probably due to the linguistic choice by Luke concerning

the description of the Pharisees' and scribes' anger.[680] Luke uses ἐπλήσθησαν ἀνοίας

to characterize their emotional state – a term Luke only uses here, and in antiquity,

usually connoted a mix of anger and ignorance.[681] Though at first glance it may seem

odd, Luke's choice fits the context of the narrative as they clearly don't fully

understand.[682] Further, Luke lessens the threat of violence to Jesus as the scribes and

Pharisees only discuss what they might do (τί ἂν ποιήσαιεν) to Jesus (6:11), whereas

Mark states they counseled with the Herodians how they might destroy (ἀπολέσωσιν)

Jesus (3:6).[683] Thus Luke must depict Jesus' enemies with a type of anger that reveals

their character,[684] or more importantly reveals Jesus' character, as the Lukan Jesus'

---

[680] Commentators discuss the ἄνοια of the scribes and Pharisees, but not in comparison to the Markan Jesus' ὀργή. See Bovon, *Saint Luc 1-9*, 204-5, C.F. Evans, *Saint Luke*, 316-7; Culpepper, *Gospel of Luke*, 135; Just, *Luke 1:1-9:50*, 253; Lieu, *Gospel of Luke*, 48; Marshall, *Gospel of Luke*, 236;. L.T. Johnson, *Gospel of Luke*, 104; Green, *Gospel of Luke*, 262; , Goulder, *Luke: A New Paradigm I*, 339-40; Morris, *Luke*, 136-7; Craig A. Evans, *Luke*, 138; 102, Radl, *Das Evangelium nach Lukas: 1,1-9,50*, 348-351; Schweizer, *The Good News according to Luke*, 113.

[681] BADG, ἄνοια, 70. Plato (*Tim.* 86B) distinguishes two forms: μανία (fury, madness) and ἀμᾱθία (ignorance, folly). Due to the context, I, following Fitzmyer et al, prefer the former.

[682] Frederick W. Danker sees the word choice (ἄνοια) as a play on the word for –good will" (ἔννοια) in *Jesus and the New Age*, 134; as a further contrast, ἔννοια also connotes knowledge and insight, BADG, 267.

[683] See further chapter four for discussion of this corollary principle where Luke omits or lessens the violence (or the threat of violence) to Jesus as mentioned above.

[684] Sharon H. Ringe comes close to recognizing that Luke omits Jesus' emotion and violence *done to* Jesus, but not *everything or anything* associated with emotion or violence, with her contention: –The rage

261

calmness (a Jesus without anger or grief) is the antithesis of the scribe's and Pharisees' angry ignorance.[685]

139. Jesus is Rejected at Nazareth

Mark 6:2,6	Luke 4:22
² καὶ γενομένου σαββάτου ἤρξατο διδάσκειν ἐν τῇ συναγωγῇ καὶ πολλοὶ ἀκούοντες **ἐξεπλήσσοντο** λέγοντες, πόθεν τούτῳ ταῦτα ⁶ καὶ ἐθαύμασεν διὰ τὴν ἀπιστίαν αὐτῶν	 καὶ πάντες ἐμαρτύρουν αὐτῷ καὶ ἐθαύμαζον ἐπὶ τοῖς λόγοις τῆς χάριτος τοῖς ἐκπορευομένοις ἐκ τοῦ στόματος αὐτοῦ

A close textual analysis reveals a subtle, but important, example of Luke's transference technique. Luke has removed the amazement (ἐξεπλήσσοντο, 6:2) of the people who hear him in Mark and replaced it with the astonishment of the Markan Jesus (ἐθαύμασεν in Mark 6:6 is transferred to ἐθαύμαζον in Luke 4:22).[686] The net effect is

---

of the opponents is clear in Luke's concluding comment (6:11), but he has tempered Mark's outright statement that they conspired to destroy Jesus (Mark 3:6)" in *Luke*, 88.

[685] See Tannehill, *Narrative Unity I*, 176: ―The choice of the word ἄνοια [not in the parallel passages in Matthew and Mark], which can refer to foolishness and a general lack of comprehension as well as madness, may prepare readers for a later manifestation of a fateful ignorance (ἄγνοια) which will lead to Jesus' death."

[686] There is also a form of this technique present in the post-Easter narratives concerning ―amazement" and the women at the tomb and the response of Peter and two of the disciples (Mark 16:1-8//Luke 24:1-35). The passage is not included as primary evidence for Luke's transference technique because it does not specifically concern the character of Jesus, though an analysis is included below as this pericope is also illustrative of Luke's redactions concerning fear.

that Jesus' astonishment is removed from Luke's depiction, and the amazement of those

listening to Jesus is retained, albeit with slightly different language.[687] Jesus was teaching

in the synagogue on the Sabbath and the response of those who heard him was

ἐξεπλήσσοντο (Mark 6:2) and ἐθαύμαζον (Luke 4:22). After his self-referential speech

anent a prophet being rejected in his own country, the Markan Jesus ―was amazed

(ἐθαύμασεν) at their unbelief" (v.6).

Though the simple recognition of Luke's transference technique in portraying a

less emotional Jesus is our primary concern, the transference of Jesus' θαῦμα sheds light

on a number of Lukan redactional themes. The transference of Jesus' amazement

complicates an already hermeneutically complex text, which has led to a variety of

interpretations of Luke 4:22 in particular. As stated above, θαυμάζω and ἐκπλήσσω

depend greatly on context for exact meaning. The Markan usage of both terms is

generally interpreted negatively as a straight-forward reading of the passage reveals a

number of ways in which Mark reveals the rejection of Jesus.[688] Luke softens many of

the Markan characteristics which has led to the multifarious expositions.[689] Luke greatly

reduces the number of questions asked by the people (Mark 6:2-3//Luke 4:22) and omits

---

[687] θαυμάζω and ἐκπλήσσω are common to and seem to be used synonymously by both Mark and
Luke, as both can be taken positively or more negatively based on context. Their emotional connotations
are also based on context, as both can include an element of fear or panic. See BADG, 244, 353; LSJ, 243,
359.

[688] See Schweizer, *Good News according to Mark*, 122-25.

[689] About the only thing commentators do agree on concerning this passage is that Luke ―has exercised
considerable editorial and compositional control in adapting a conflict story." In L.T. Johnson, *Gospel of
Luke*, 80-81.

the blunt assertion of the Markan narrator, καὶ ἐσκανδαλίζοντο ἐν αὐτῷ (v.3). Luke

also shortens Jesus' speech, removing the reference to Jesus being without honor

(ἄτιμος), and omits verses 5-6. Further, Jesus elicits an emotional response (v.28) only

later in the narrative after he implicitly passes judgment on them (25-27).

The exact meaning of καὶ ἐθαύμαζον is even further obfuscated by the awkward

transition within the verse itself from ―high approval to some sort of disapproval."[690] At

the beginning of the verse, the approval is total as πάντες ἐμαρτύρουν αὐτῷ.[691]

Though Joel B. Green criticizes those who read the negativity of the Markan source

material into their Lukan commentary, most scholars do exactly that concerning the

people's question: ―Is this not Joseph's son" (v.22c). Joseph Fitzmyer is representative in

that he recognizes the possibility of a positive rendering (―pleasant surprise or

admiration"), but ultimately refuses on source-critical grounds.[692] With respect to the

plethora of issues involved and to the complexity of these hermeneutical issues, I read the

initial response as positive (pace Jeremias and Marshall),[693] the use of ἐθαύμαζον as

---

[690] C.F. Evans, *Saint Luke*, 272-73. Contra Evans, see Green, *Gospel of Luke*, 214-15, who argues that their question, ―Is this not Joseph's son," should be interpreted positively as a source of communal pride.

[691] There is disagreement whether the αὐτῷ in the phrase ἐμαρτύρουν αὐτῷ is a dative of advantage (―they attested to him") or a dative of disadvantage (―they testified against him"). See discussion in Just, *Luke 1:1-9:50*, 195.

[692] Fitzmyer, *Luke I-IX*, 535.

[693] Joachim Jeremias, *Jesus' Promise to the Nations* (SBT 24; London: SCM Press, 1958), 44-46; Marshall, *Gospel of Luke*, 185-86. My view is based on my linguistic reading of αὐτῷ as a dative of advantage, interpreting the phrase ἐμαρτύρουν αὐτῷ as ―they attested to him," as opposed to ―they testified against him" (a dative of disadvantage).

neutral,[694] and the question as the beginning of the increasingly negative reaction that follows.[695]

Luke's Supporting Cast

A similar restraint [Luke's elimination of Jesus' emotion in Mark] is manifested at times toward the disciples of Jesus."[696]

In the effort to show that there is *not* an over-riding Lukan pattern of eliminating *anything* emotional, I will offer as evidence the Lukan emotional redactions (or more often, the lack there of) concerning the portrayals of the minor characters in Luke, which essentially includes everyone, save for Jesus. As the following list attests, the most frequent editorial action on the part of Luke is inaction. Most of the time, Luke simply chooses to retain the existing Markan emotion of the supporting cast. In fact, about as often as he *removes* emotion from the supporting players, he *adds* emotion to their characterization. The most important facet of our research is the Lukan emotional portrait of Jesus, especially in comparison to his Markan source. Therefore, the evidence

---

[694] This is a more positive rendering than the Markan narrator's description of Jesus' response, which I read more pejoratively. This is an example of Luke recasting a transferred phrase for his purpose, as noted below.

[695] Following Fitzmyer and to the chagrin of Green, I do rely partially on Luke's source material for the negative reading. I also rely on a literary reading that must account for the ultimate θυμός of the people later in the pericope (v.28), and on Malina and Neyrey's interpretation of the people's response as hostile within a matrix of challenge-reposte in ―Honor and Shame,‖ 53-54.

[696] Fitzmyer, *Luke I-IX*, 95; see analysis of quote above.

concerning the other characters is not meant to be exhaustive, but simply to provide further evidence that there is not a general principle in Luke of removing the emotions. Luke is only concerned with the emotional portrayal of Jesus as a model of self-control and rationality, an exemplar of *apatheia*.

"Supporting" Characters' Emotions

Mark 4:40-1	Luke 8:25	Luke retains the disciples' fear
Mark 5:15	Luke 8:35	Luke retains the people's fear
Mark 5:17	Luke 8:37	Luke adds the people's fear
Mark 5:33	Luke 8:47	Luke removes the woman's fear, retains her trembling
Mark 5:36	Luke 8:50	Luke retains the man's fear
Mark 5:38-9	Luke 8:52	Luke retains the people's weeping and wailing
Mark 5:42	Luke 8:56	Luke retains the parents' amazement
Mark 9:6-7	Luke 9:34-5	Luke retains the fear of the disciples
Mark 9:32	Luke 9:45	Luke retains the fear of the disciples
Mark 9:27-30	Luke 9:43	Luke adds astonishment / marvel of the people
Mark 10:22	Luke 18:23	Luke removes the general sadness and increases the grief of the rich man
Mark 11:18	Luke 19:47-8	Luke removes fear of chief priests and scribes
Mark 12:12	Luke 20:19	Luke retains fear of the chief priests and scribes
Mark 14:72	Luke 22:62	Luke increases intensity of Peter's weeping[697]

---

[697] There is scholarly debate whether or not the Lukan account of Peter's denial portrays a more emotional Peter and whether Luke portrays him more or less favorable; see Fitzmyer, *Luke X-XXIV*, 1465. My view is that the two versions of this pericope are a microcosm of the two gospels in general. Luke

Mark 16:5-8   Luke 24:5-9   Luke retains the fear of the women at the tomb

137. Gerasene Demoniac

Mark 5:15b-17	Luke 8:35b-37b
καὶ ἐφοβήθησαν.	*καὶ ἐφοβήθησαν.*
καὶ διηγήσαντο αὐτοῖς οἱ ἰδόντες	ἀπήγγειλαν δὲ αὐτοῖς οἱ ἰδόντες
πῶς ἐγένετο τῷ δαιμονιζομένῳ	πῶς ἐσώθη ὁ δαιμονισθείς.
καὶ περὶ τῶν χοίρων.	
καὶ ἤρξαντο παρακαλεῖν αὐτὸν	καὶ ἠρώτησεν αὐτὸν ἅπαν τὸ πλῆθος
	τῆς περιχώρου τῶν Γερασηνῶν
ἀπελθεῖν ἀπὸ τῶν ὁρίων αὐτῶν.	ἀπελθεῖν ἀπ' αὐτῶν,
	ὅτι φόβῳ μεγάλῳ συνείχοντο

In a passage previously analyzed to show the removal of Jesus' emotion, Luke actually *increases* the fear of the people who came to see Jesus after the exorcism of the Gerasene Demoniac (Mark 5:1-20//Luke 8:26-39). Luke significantly lessens the stringent tone of Mark concerning Jesus' refusal (Mark 5:19a//Luke 8:38b) and more importantly, he also removes Jesus' self-described mercy/compassion (ἔλεος, Mark 5:19//Luke 8:39). Though Luke softens Jesus' speech and removes his emotion, he not only includes the Markan description of the people's fear, but adds a further expression

---

sometimes portrays the disciples as more honorable than Mark, other times he does not. The evidence in this passage is mixed, as Luke removes Peter's self-imposed curse (Mark 14:71//Luke 22:60), but increases the intensity of his weeping (Mark 14:72//Luke 22:62). Further, it underscores how various commentators have come to completely opposite conclusions when it concerns the disciples even within the same passage. Fitzmyer interprets Peter's "going out" (ἐξελθὼν ἔξω) as Peter abandoning Jesus. Green sees a certain redemption in the Lukan version as Luke emphasizes divine agency in Peter's actions, making him less culpaple in *Gospel of Luke*, 788-89. L.T. Johnson sees the Lukan account as both a harsher verdict on Peter and the beginning of his redemption in *Gospel of Luke*, 358-62. There are also textual and redactional concerns that have ultimately led to the exclusion of this pericope from my analysis; see Marshall, *Gospel of Luke*, 844-45.

of their fear.[698] The Markan narrator describes the people's reaction to Jesus' exorcism as καὶ ἐφοβήθησαν (5:15b); the Lukan narrator identically as καὶ ἐφοβήθησαν (8:35b).

The people then ask Jesus to depart from them in both versions, with Luke adding an expression of their strong emotion when doing so: ὅτι φόβῳ μεγάλῳ συνείχοντο (v.37b).[699]

138. Jairus' Daughter and the Woman with a Hemorrhage

Mark 5:33, 36, 38b-39, 42b	Luke 8:47, 50, 52, 56
[33] ἡ δὲ γυνὴ **φοβηθεῖσα** καὶ *τρέμουσα*, εἰδυῖα ὃ γέγονεν αὐτῇ, ἦλθεν καὶ *προσέπεσεν αὐτῷ*	[47] *τρέμουσα* ἦλθεν καὶ *προσπεσοῦσα αὐτῷ*
[36] ὁ δὲ Ἰησοῦς παρακούσας τὸν λόγον λαλούμενον λέγει τῷ ἀρχισυναγώγῳ, *μὴ φοβοῦ*, μόνον πίστευε.	[50] ὁ δὲ Ἰησοῦς ἀκούσας ἀπεκρίθη αὐτῷ, *μὴ φοβοῦ*, μόνον πίστευσον
[38] καὶ θεωρεῖ *θόρυβον* καὶ *κλαίοντας καὶ ἀλαλάζοντας* πολλά, [39] καὶ εἰσελθὼν λέγει αὐτοῖς, τί *θορυβεῖσθε καὶ κλαίετε*;	[52] *ἔκλαιον δὲ πάντες καὶ ἐκόπτοντο* αὐτήν ὁ δὲ εἶπεν, *μὴ κλαίετε*,

---

[698] Fitzmyer notes this addition but tellingly doesn't comment on it, *Luke I-IX*, 740.

[699] Luke often uses φόβος to express the reaction of bystanders to a manifestation of God's or Jesus' power; see 1:65; 5:26; 7:16; 8:25; also Acts 2:43; 5:5, 11; 19:17. See Marshall, *Gospel of Luke*, 335. ὅτι φόβῳ μεγάλῳ συνείχοντο is a particular Lukan phrase; ―great fear" is also found in Luke 2:9 and Acts 5:5. See also Bovon, *Saint Luc 1-9*, 324; C.F. Evans, *Saint Luke*, 387. For the responses to healing episodes in particular, see Kindalee Pfremmer De Long, ―Surprised by God: Praise Responses in the Narrative of Luke-Acts (Ph.D. diss., The University of Notre Dame, 2007), esp.254-277.

⁴² καὶ *ἐξέστησαν* εὐθὺς *ἐκστάσει* μεγάλῃ.	⁵⁶ καὶ *ἐξέστησαν* οἱ γονεῖς αὐτῆς

In the passage following the Gerasene Demoniac (Mark 5:1-20//Luke 8:26-39) – concerning Jairus' daughter and the woman with a hemorrhage (Mark 5:21-43//Luke 8:40-56) – Jesus' emotional depiction is slightly altered,[700] but importantly, Luke keeps most of the emotion of the woman with a hemorrhage, all of the fear of the ruler of the synagogue, all the wailing and weeping of the people, and all of the amazement of the girl's parents found in the Markan account. After the woman's hemorrhage is healed, she came in ~~fe~~ar and trembling (φοβηθεῖσα καὶ τρέμουσα) and fell down before him" (Mark 5:33). After removing her fear,[701] Luke similarly states, ~~s~~he came trembling (τρέμουσα), and falling down before him" (Luke 8:47).[702] Later in the passage Jesus'

---

[700] The emotion of Jesus' speech is slightly different, though the redactions appear to be stylistic changes, and not significant enough for inclusion as primary evidence for the proposed pattern. Jesus' response to the people's weeping and wailing is abbreviated in Luke (Mark 5:39//Luke 8:52b), and the Markan narrator's description of Jesus putting the people outside before Jesus ~~heals~~" the girl is omitted by Luke (Mark 5:40//Luke 8:54); for Jesus' charge at the end of the pericope, see chapter four.

[701] This is one of the few instances that Luke removes emotion from someone other than Jesus. The most obvious explanation is literary, for Luke has transposed the order of Jesus' realization that someone had touched him and his question of who that was. In Mark, the narrator states that Jesus felt the touch (thus the other characters do not know this), and then his direct question (along with looking around) is perceived as more of an accusation; ergo, the woman is described as fearful. Adversely, the Lukan Jesus first asks the question then *directly* states why he asks the question – his perception of the healing; the result is a less apprehensive tone negating the need for the woman to fear. A slightly different literary interpretation is provided by Marshall who argues that the Lukan woman shows no fear because she knows who Jesus is in *Gospel of Luke*, 346. Surprisingly, Fitzmyer does not comment or even acknowledge this redaction, even though it is one of the few instances that support his overall contention in *Luke I-IX*, 746-47.

[702] Fear and trembling was a common expression in antiquity and in the biblical texts (esp. LXX, φόβος or φοβέω with τρόμος or τρέμω). The full expression is not used in Luke; this is the only time τρέμω is used. This is the only time Mark uses the full expression; he uses τρόμος in 16:8. BADG, 827, 864-65.

269

command to the man (from the ruler's house in Luke, the actual ruler of the synagogue in Mark), ―Do not fear" (Mark 5:36//Luke 8:50), is kept by Luke. Then in response to Jesus coming out of the man's house, Mark describes the ―commotion (θόρυβον), people weeping (κλαίοντας) and wailing loudly (ἀλαλάζοντας πολλά)" (v.38) and then Jesus' direct command, ―Why do you make a commotion (θορυβεῖσθε) and weep (κλαίετε)" (v.39). The Lukan narrator recounts their reaction, ―They were all weeping (ἔκλαιον) and wailing (ἐκόπτοντο) for her" (v.52a), and Jesus' command, ―Do not weep (κλαίετε)" (52b).[703] The parents' concluding amazement (ἐξέστησαν) in Mark 5:42 is retained by Luke (ἐξέστησαν, 8:56).[704]

161. The Transfiguration

Mark 9:6-7a	Luke 9:34-35
οὐ γὰρ ᾔδει τί ἀποκριθῇ,	ταῦτα δὲ αὐτοῦ λέγοντος
ἔκφοβοι γὰρ ἐγένοντο, καὶ	
ἐγένετο νεφέλη ἐπισκιάζουσα αὐτοῖς,	ἐγένετο νεφέλη καὶ ἐπεσκίαζεν αὐτούς,
	ἐφοβήθησαν δὲ
	ἐν τῷ εἰσελθεῖν αὐτοὺς εἰς τὴν νεφέλην
καὶ ἐγένετο φωνὴ ἐκ τῆς νεφέλης,	καὶ φωνὴ ἐγένετο ἐκ τῆς νεφέλης
	λέγουσα,

---

[703] Marshall argues that the Lukan account expresses a more intense description of Jewish mourning in *Gospel of Luke*, 347.

[704] See further Schürmann, *Das Lukasevangelium*, 495-98.

Οὗτός ἐστιν ὁ υἱός μου ὁ ἀγαπητός, ἀκούετε αὐτοῦ.	Οὗτός ἐστιν ὁ υἱός μου ὁ ἐκλελεγμένος, αὐτοῦ ἀκούετε.

In the Transfiguration scene (Mark 9:2-10//Luke 9:28-36), Luke removes Mark's harsh language concerning Jesus' speech, but the fear of Peter, James, and John is retained. In Mark the narrator describes their fear as ἔκφοβοι γὰρ ἐγένοντο (v.6); in Luke it is termed ἐφοβήθησαν (v.34). While many commentators have emphasized the basic theophanic element to the disciples' fear in both versions,[705] other scholars have seen unique Lukan elements. Fitzmyer uses this retention of their fear as an example of Luke retaining a Markan element and repositioning it for his own purpose. The fear in Mark is associated with lack of understanding, while in Luke it is created by the cloud's presence, and perhaps has an apocalyptic element to it.[706] Likewise, Bovon concludes, "Luc n'a fait que déplacer et render explicite le motif de Mc 9, 6-8."[707] The important hermeneutical aspect of those (including me) who see a Lukan appropriation of the Markan source is that, despite this re-interpretation, Luke has retained the emotional

---

[705] While scholarship is split concerning who actually enters the cloud, most interpret the fear as a standard response to a theophany. See Green, *Gospel of Luke*, 384, 71-72; Just, *Luke 1:1-9:50*, 401; Ringe, *Luke*, 141-42; L.T. Johnson, *Luke*, 153; Schweizer, *The Good News according to Luke*, 161; Danker, *Jesus and the New Age*, 200-1; See further Horst Balz and Günther Wanke, "φοβέω κτλ," *TDNT* 9:189-219.

[706] Fitzmyer, *Luke I-IX*, 802. See also Schürmann, *Das Lukasevangelium*, 561. Nolland states, "Luke introduces here the fear motif and links it to the experience of being enveloped by the cloud, which becomes much more prominent in Luke's telling" in *Luke 9:21-18:34*, 501. Though C.F. Evans argues against an apocalyptic interpretation, he emphasizes the uniqueness of Luke's account, which speaks to the significance of Luke's retention of the fear, despite all of the other changes he has made in *Saint Luke*, 419-20.

[707] Bovon, *Saint Luc 1-9*, 487.

element of the pericope.

164. Jesus Foretells His Passion again

Mark 9:31-32	Luke 9:43-45
	ἐξεπλήσσοντο δὲ πάντες
	ἐπὶ τῇ μεγαλειότητι τοῦ θεοῦ.
	πάντων δὲ *θαυμαζόντων*
ἐδίδασκεν γὰρ τοὺς μαθητὰς αὐτοῦ	ἐπὶ πᾶσιν οἷς ἐποίει
καὶ ἔλεγεν αὐτοῖς	εἶπεν πρὸς τοὺς μαθητὰς αὐτοῦ
	θέσθε ὑμεῖς εἰς τὰ ὦτα ὑμῶν
	τοὺς λόγους τούτους,
ὅτι ὁ υἱὸς τοῦ ἀνθρώπου	ὁ γὰρ υἱὸς τοῦ ἀνθρώπου μέλλει
παραδίδοται εἰς χεῖρας ἀνθρώπων,	παραδίδοσθαι εἰς χεῖρας ἀνθρώπων.
<u>καὶ ἀποκτενοῦσιν αὐτόν,</u>	
<u>καὶ ἀποκτανθεὶς μετὰ τρεῖς</u>	
ἡμέρας ἀναστήσεται.	
οἱ δὲ ἠγνόουν τὸ ῥῆμα	οἱ δὲ ἠγνόουν τὸ ῥῆμα τοῦτο,
	καὶ ἦν παρακεκαλυμμένον
	ἀπ' αὐτῶν ἵνα μὴ αἴσθωνται αὐτό,
καὶ *ἐφοβοῦντο* αὐτὸν ἐπερωτῆσαι	καὶ *ἐφοβοῦντο* ἐρωτῆσαι αὐτὸν
	περὶ τοῦ ῥήματος τούτου

In the pericope where Jesus' foretells his ―passion"[708] (Mark 9:30-32//Luke 9:43b-45), Luke retains the disciples' fear (Mark 9:32//Luke 9:45), and even adds the astonishment and marvel of the people (Luke 9:43). At the end of the previous passage

---

[708] This passage also evidences the Lukan principle of lessening the violence (or threat of violence) done *to* Jesus, as Luke removes the Markan prediction that Jesus will be killed. The passive constructions by Luke (9:44, 45) further speak to the Lukan theme of the passion being part of a divine plan, stressing the innocence of Jesus, and removing the blame from the Roman authorities in particular; see Zerwick and Smith, *Biblical Greek*, 236.

(Luke 9:37-43a), the Lukan narrator states, ἐξεπλήσσοντο δὲ πάντες ἐπὶ τῇ μεγαλειότητι τοῦ θεοῦ (43a). At the beginning of the following narrative (Luke 9:43b-45), the narrator similarly states, πάντων δὲ θαυμαζόντων ἐπὶ πᾶσιν οἷς ἐποίει εἶπεν πρὸς τοὺς μαθητὰς αὐτοῦ (43b).[709] Neither description is in the Markan texts. Later in the passage, after the disciples are described as not understanding (Mark 9:32a//Luke 9:45a), Mark declares, καὶ ἐφοβοῦντο αὐτὸν ἐπερωτῆσαι (32b), while Luke likewise alleges, καὶ ἐφοβοῦντο ἐρωτῆσαι αὐτὸν περὶ τοῦ ῥήματος τούτου (45c).[710]

254. The Rich Young Man

Mark 10:21-22	Luke 18:22-23
ὁ δὲ Ἰησοῦς ἐμβλέψας αὐτῷ	ἀκούσας δὲ ὁ Ἰησοῦς εἶπεν αὐτῷ,

---

[709] The most straight-forward reading of the text is that the first half of the verse references amazement of God and the second Jesus, though the most important aspect for our purposes concerns the simple fact the people's amazement is present in Luke and not Mark. See Marshall, *Gospel of Luke*, 392-93.

[710] The actual reason for their fear is a matter of scholarly debate. See Schürmann, *Das Lukasevangelium*, 573. John Nolland argues that Luke actually re-situates the disciples' fear as a sign of at least partial understanding, ―whatever it is that Jesus is saying, it disturbs acutely their sense of how things should be‖ in *Luke 9:21-18:34*, 514. Similarly Fitzmyer asks, ―Is the fear retained by Luke because he wants to hint that the disciples are beginning to realize that the destiny facing Jesus may have implications for them too?‖ in *Luke I-IX*, 814. Tannehill contrarily argues that due to the Lukan redactions, the disciples' utter failure to understand is now the main emphasis in *Narrative Unity I*, 226; see also Green, *Gospel of Luke*, 390-91. L.T. Johnson importantly notes that in Mark they are afraid of Jesus himself and in Luke only of Jesus' words. He further argues, ―As a result [of the Lukan redactions], the reader focuses completely on the incapacity of the disciples‖ in *Gospel of Luke*, 158-59. C.F. Evans finds it odd that Luke retains the fear since Luke seems to imply that fear is the ―cause of the intellectual incomprehension,‖ even though the Lukan narrator states matter-of-factly that understanding was (divinely) concealed from them in *Saint Luke*, 426.

ἠγάπησεν αὐτὸν	
καὶ εἶπεν αὐτῷ,	
Ἕν σε ὑστερεῖ· ὕπαγε ὅσα	Ἔτι ἕν σοι λείπει· πάντα ὅσα
ἔχεις πώλησον	ἔχεις πώλησον
καὶ δὸς τοῖς πτωχοῖς,	καὶ διάδος πτωχοῖς,
καὶ ἕξεις θησαυρὸν ἐν οὐρανῷ,	καὶ ἕξεις θησαυρὸν ἐν [τοῖς] οὐρανοῖς,
καὶ δεῦρο ἀκολούθει μοι.	καὶ δεῦρο ἀκολούθει μοι.
ὁ δὲ **στυγνάσας** ἐπὶ τῷ λόγῳ	ὁ δὲ ἀκούσας ταῦτα
ἀπῆλθεν *λυπούμενος*,	*περίλυπος* ἐγενήθη,
ἦν γὰρ ἔχων κτήματα πολλά.	ἦν γὰρ πλούσιος σφόδρα.

In the encounter of the rich man with Jesus (Mark 10:17-22//Luke 18:18-23), Luke omits Jesus' emotion and retains the rich man's. Luke removes Jesus ―love," but not the rich man's sorrow. Luke somewhat abbreviates, and almost totally rewords, his Markan source.[711] He removes the introductory participle στυγνάσας describing the rich man's general sadness (στυγνάσας), though significantly, retains his sadness/grief – the important philosphical λύπη. Mark reads, ὁ δὲ στυγνάσας ἐπὶ τῷ λόγῳ ἀπῆλθεν λυπούμενος (v.22), while Luke reads tersely, περίλυπος ἐγενήθη (v.23).

While Mark uses two words to emphasize the rich man's sadness, Luke uses just one, but the variation on the classic emotion he uses – περίλυπος – connotes, ―a deep level of distress."[712] In fact, this is the only time Luke uses the compound verb, probably

---

[711] See Nolland, *Luke 9:21-18:34*, 887.

[712] L.T. Johnson, *Gospel of Luke*, 277.

to parallel the intensifier he uses to describe the rich ruler's wealth – σφόδρα. By

describing the man as a ruler (as opposed to just a man in Mark),[713] by stressing his

extreme wealth and extreme grief,[714] and even by not having the rich ruler "go away,"[715]

Luke provides his auditors with a public ruling figure with whom to compare Jesus.

274. The Chief Priests and Scribes Conspire against Jesus

Mark 11:18	Luke 19:47-48
	Καὶ ἦν διδάσκων τὸ καθ' ἡμέραν ἐν τῷ ἱερῷ.
καὶ ἤκουσαν οἱ ἀρχιερεῖς καὶ οἱ γραμματεῖς,	οἱ δὲ ἀρχιερεῖς καὶ οἱ γραμματεῖς
καὶ ἐζήτουν πῶς αὐτὸν ἀπολέσωσιν	ἐζήτουν αὐτὸν ἀπολέσαι καὶ οἱ πρῶτοι τοῦ λαοῦ καὶ οὐχ εὕρισκον τὸ τί ποιήσωσιν,
ἐφοβοῦντο γὰρ αὐτόν, πᾶς γὰρ ὁ ὄχλος **ἐξεπλήσσετο** ἐπὶ τῇ διδαχῇ αὐτοῦ.	ὁ λαὸς γὰρ ἅπας ἐξεκρέματο αὐτοῦ ἀκούων.

In a subtle but telling move, after the temple "cleansing" and in response to Jesus'

---

[713] See chapter four.

[714] In contrast, Jesus' love is removed in this passage, and Jesus' anger is omitted in the previous passage (Mark 10:13-16//Luke 18:15-17).

[715] Pace I. Howard Marshall (*Gospel of Luke*, 683) and George Bradford Caird (*The Gospel of St. Luke* (PNTC A490; Baltimore: Penguin Books, 1963-65), 205), the magistrate is not said to have gone off, as in Mark 10:22 and Matthew 19:22. The result is that Jesus' subsequent pronouncement is not only an occasion for providing instruction to the disciples but a direct rebuke against the ruler; see further M.J. Lagrange, *Évangile selon Saint Luc* (Paris: Études bibliques, 1927), 479. See ἀπέρχομαι, LSJ, 92.

teaching, Luke omits the fear (ἐφοβοῦντο) of the chief priests and scribes,[716] as well as the emotional astonishment (ἐξεπλήσσετο) of the crowd. After the leaders sought to destroy him, Mark states, ἐφοβοῦντο γὰρ αὐτόν, πᾶς γὰρ ὁ ὄχλος ἐξεπλήσσετο ἐπὶ τῇ διδαχῇ αὐτοῦ (11:18), while Luke writes only that they could not do anything because the people hung upon his words (ὁ λαὸς γὰρ ἅπας ἐξεκρέματο αὐτοῦ ἀκούων, 19:48).

Fitzmyer uses this passage to support his overall claim that Luke removes anything emotional. He thus provides no reason for this Lukan redaction besides this supposed overarching agenda.[717] The real reason for the Lukan redactional changes is the Lukan principle of omitting or lessening the violence (or the threat of violence) and strong emotion *to* Jesus as previously discussed.[718] The role of the crowd's emotional response to the teaching of Jesus in Mark is to *provoke the leaders* to fear him and therefore seek to destroy him. Thus it also represents at least a partial explanation of the leadership's response to the temple incident.[719] In Luke, the role of the response is to

---

[716] Luke adds ‑the leaders of the people" (οἱ πρῶτοι τοῦ λαοῦ), presumably the lay elders of the people, the third group in the Sanhedrin. See Marshall, *Gospel of Luke*, 722.

[717] Fitzmyer, *Luke X-XXIV*, 1269-70.

[718] This passage also evinces another general principle that Jesus' harsh *teaching* in Mark is mitigated by Luke, and exacerbated in Matthew. Jesus' teaching causes astonishment in Mark, while in Luke it captivates his audience. See further chapter four.

[719] Nolland, *Luke 18:35-24:53*, 940.

stand in the way, at least temporarily, of the leaders' plan to destroy Jesus.[720]

278. The Parable of the Wicked Husbandmen

Mark 12:12	Luke 20:19
Καὶ ἐζήτουν αὐτὸν κρατῆσαι,	Καὶ ἐζήτησαν οἱ γραμματεῖς
	καὶ οἱ ἀρχιερεῖς ἐπιβαλεῖν
	ἐπ' αὐτὸν τὰς χεῖρας ἐν αὐτῇ τῇ ὥρᾳ,
καὶ *ἐφοβήθησαν* τὸν ὄχλον	καὶ *ἐφοβήθησαν* τὸν λαόν
ἔγνωσαν γὰρ ὅτι πρὸς αὐτοὺς	ἔγνωσαν γὰρ ὅτι πρὸς αὐτοὺς
τὴν παραβολὴν εἶπεν.	εἶπεν τὴν παραβολὴν ταύτην.
καὶ ἀφέντες αὐτὸν ἀπῆλθον.	

In the parable of the tenants (Mark 12:1-12//Luke 20:9-19), the emotional reaction of the authorities is identically described as fear (ἐφοβήθησαν, Mark 12:12//Luke20:19) by both Mark and Luke. After the parable proper, the authorities (chief priests, scribes, and elders in Mark; scribes and chief priests in Luke) perceive the parable has been told against them, and therefore want to arrest him, but do not, for they fear the crowd/people. The form (parable and response in both), content (textually similar), and function (Luke has not repositioned it as he has many of the passages under examination) of the Lukan and Markan pericopae are basically the same. It is precisely the sameness of the two narratives that is important for our purposes as Luke *has not removed* anything that

---

[720] Further, the fear of the chief priests and the scribes (and the lay elders) could imply that the plot and ultimate destruction of Jesus was justified, whereas Luke stresses the utter innocence of Jesus as part of a divine plan.

smacks of the emotional, just the emotion concerning the character of Jesus.[721]

352. The Women at the Tomb

Mark 16:5-6a, 8	Luke 24:4-5, 12, 22
⁵ καὶ εἰσελθοῦσαι εἰς τὸ μνημεῖον	⁴ καὶ ἐγένετο ἐν τῷ ἀπορεῖσθαι αὐτὰς περὶ τούτου καὶ ἰδοὺ
εἶδον νεανίσκον καθήμενον ἐν τοῖς δεξιοῖς	ἄνδρες δύο ἐπέστησαν αὐταῖς
περιβεβλημένον στολὴν λευκήν, καὶ *ἐξεθαμβήθησαν*.	ἐν ἐσθῆτι ἀστραπτούσῃ. ⁵ *ἐμφόβων* δὲ γενομένων αὐτῶν καὶ κλινουσῶν τὰ πρόσωπα εἰς τὴν γῆν
⁶ ὁ δὲ λέγει αὐταῖς, Μὴ *ἐκθαμβεῖσθε*· Ἰησοῦν ζητεῖτε τὸν Ναζαρηνὸν τὸν ἐσταυρωμένον	εἶπαν πρὸς αὐτάς, Τί ζητεῖτε τὸν ζῶντα μετὰ τῶν νεκρῶν
⁸ καὶ ἐξελθοῦσαι ἔφυγον ἀπὸ τοῦ μνημείου, εἶχεν γὰρ αὐτὰς *τρόμος* καὶ *ἔκστασις* καὶ οὐδενὶ οὐδὲν εἶπαν, *ἐφοβοῦντο* γάρ.	
	¹²Ὁ δὲ Πέτρος ἀναστὰς ἔδραμεν ἐπὶ τὸ μνημεῖον, καὶ παρακύψας βλέπει τὰ ὀθόνια μόνα; καὶ ἀπῆλθεν πρὸς ἑαυτὸν *θαυμάζων* τὸ γεγονός.
	²² ἀλλὰ καὶ γυναῖκές τινες ἐξ ἡμῶν

[721] Frankly, I do not understand Fitzmyer's comment: "Though Luke has reworded the conclusion and *eliminated the mention of their fear*, he retains in his own way the pointed reference to the leaders found in Mark'," [emphasis added] in *Luke X-XXIV*, 1282. He later says [1286], "Luke now introduces the note of fear which he eliminated in v.32. I assume he speaks of the narrator's description of the authorities in Mark 11:32 as being afraid of the people. Although Luke does omit the actual phrase, ἐφοβοῦντο τὸν ὄχλον (Mark 11:32), he replaces it with an arguably stronger phrase, ὁ λαὸς ἅπας καταλιθάσει ἡμᾶς (Luke 20:6). Instead of general fear, the authorities are fearful of death.

	ἐξέστησαν ἡμᾶς

In the last pericope of the shortened version of Mark, Mary Magdalene, Mary the mother of James, and Salome, enter the empty tomb and are described as ―alarmed‖ (ἐξεθαμβήθησαν, 16:5). The angel (νεανίσκον) further states, μὴ ἐκθαμβεῖσθε (v.6). Then when the women flee the tomb, Mark narrates, εἶχεν γὰρ αὐτὰς τρόμος καὶ ἔκστασις καὶ οὐδενὶ οὐδὲν εἶπαν, ἐφοβοῦντο γάρ (v.8). Importantly, Luke retains the fear (ἐμφόβων, 24:5) of the women (Mary Magdalene, Joanna, Mary the mother of James, and the ―other women,‖ 24:10).[722]

Similar to how Luke has, on occasion, transferred the emotion of Jesus to other persons or groups, the amazement of the women (ἐκθαμβέω, 16:5; ἔκστασις, 16:8) in Mark has been transferred to the disciples in Luke.[723] After the women tell Peter what

---

[722] I. Howard Marshall calls the Lukan choice ―a fuller description of the fear felt by the women‖ for reasons of emphasis in *Gospel of Luke*, 885. See also Richard J. Dillon, *From Eye-Witnesses to Ministers of the Word: Tradition and Composition in Luke 24* (AnBib 82; Rome: Biblical Institute Press, 1978), 224-28.

[723] Two explanations, which are not mutually exclusive, make the most sense. Because Luke has more story with which to work, he simply delays the astonishment as a literary device, perhaps to emphasize the divine providence aspect to his narrative; he often describes their lack of belief or misunderstanding as divinely sanctioned (esp. 24:26, 31-32, 45). By transferring the amazement (θαυμάζω, a typically Lukan word: 1:21, 63; 2:18, 33; 4:22; 7:9; 8:25; 11:4, 38; 20:26; Acts 2:7; 4:13) to the disciples, he emphasizes their unbelief (24:11, 25, 38, 41), further evidence that even a few verses from the end of Luke, the disciples still don‘t understand. Though not using the term transference, Frans Neirynck, in putting forth his case for the Johannine (20:3-10) dependence on Luke (24:12), makes a similar argument to the one proposed, as he sees a ―parallel‖ between the experience of the women in Mark and Peter in Luke; see ―Marc 16, 1-8: Tradition et Rédaction,‖ *ETL* 56 (1980): 56-88; and ―John and the Synoptics: The Empty Tomb Stories,‖ *NTS* 30 (1984): 161-87.

they have seen, he runs to the tomb and the Lukan narrator says he was amazed (θαυμάζων) at what had happened.[724] In Luke 24:22, the women's amazement has been transferred both redactionally and literarily as Cleopas states, "Moreover, some women in our group astounded (ἐξέστησαν) us."[725]

Fitzmyer's Thesis Revisited

The purpose of this chapter is to clarify further Luke's redactional program concerning the emotions. I methodically and systematically presented evidence in chapter four showing that Luke has consistently removed emotion from his Markan source in his characterization of Jesus. But this pattern is only true for Jesus; it is not representative of a broader principle of eliminating *anything* associated with the passionate or emotional. As evidence for this proposition, I have supplied evidence of Luke removing emotion from Jesus and giving it to another character or group, which I have termed Luke's "transference technique." I have also showed that Luke's primary *modus operandi* is simply to retain the Markan characters' emotion; there are even instances of Luke increasing the emotional portrayal of characters in Mark, such as the

---

[724] This verse is missing from many ancient texts. Westcott and Hort called it a "Western non-interpolation" and their weighty opinion held sway (it is still missing from the 27th edition of the Novum Testamentum Graece) until the discovery of P75, and is now viewed as genuine by the majority of scholarship including Aland and Metzger. See Klyne Snodgrass, "Western Non-Interpolations," *JBL* 91 (1972): 369-79. See discussion in Morris, *Luke*, 366-67.

[725] The verb ἐξίστημι is a strong one implying both surprise and confusion; see L.T. Johnson, *Gospel of Luke*, 395. Though not specific redactions or transferences, the disciples are often characterized as showing strong emotion in Luke's post-Easter narratives. In Luke 24:17, two of them (not part of the eleven apostles) are described as sad (σκυθρωποί). The eleven are designated πτοηθέντες and ἔμφοβοι when Jesus appears to them, and Jesus responds by asking, τί τεταραγμένοι ἐστέ (24:37-38).

addition of the people's fear (Mark 5:17//Luke 8:37). There are also a few examples of Luke removing the emotion from characters other than Jesus, including the fear of the hemorrhaging woman (Mark 5:33//Luke 8:47). Some of these omissions have simple straight-forward explanations and some of them perhaps are exceptions that prove the Lukan rule, or are just evidence that Luke is unconcerned with the supporting characters' emotion – most of the time it is retained, sometimes increased, sometimes omitted.

Along with the important acknowledgment of Luke's ―transference technique" and the recognition of Luke's normal procedure of merely maintaining the status quo, of simply retaining the emotion of the supporting characters, it is important to point out, with regard to the few times that he does omit/increase the Markan emotion, that there is no pattern or overarching agenda. Favorably portrayed characters sometimes show strong emotion; unfavorable characters sometimes show little emotion. As a concluding evidentiary example, I offer the women at the tomb in Luke. Luke Timothy Johnson says of the women, ―Luke eliminates completely any negative nuance concerning the women he might have found in Mark. They are not commanded to tell anyone, yet they report everything they have experienced. The problem of disbelief is not that of the women but of the men."[726] Whether we can accept the totality of his statement (the question in 24:5 is one of rebuke),[727] I can agree that overall the portrayal of the women is positive, and further, through the above mentioned redactional changes, it is certainly more positive than Mark's depiction. And yet, after all the redactional changes, Luke tellingly retains the fear of the women.[728]

---

[726] L.T. Johnson, *Gospel of Luke*, 391.

[727] See Danker, *Jesus and the New Age*, 388; Goulder, *Luke: A New Paradigm II*, 778.

[728] The opposite is also true, as Luke has on occasion actually removed the emotion of his chief enemies in Luke – the chief priests and scribes (i.e. Mark 12:12//Luke 20:19).

CHAPTER 6

LUKE'S REDACTIONS OF MARK

IN LIGHT OF HELLENISTIC PHILOSOPHY

Conclusions: The Lukan Redactions in Light of Roman Stoicism

The real voyage of discovery consists not in seeking new landscapes, but in having new eyes.[729]

---

[729] Often seen translated in the above shortened form, the extended quote is, ―The only true voyage of discovery… would be not to visit new landscapes, but to possess other eyes, to see the universe through the eyes of another, of a hundred others, to see the hundred universes that each of them sees." In Marcel Proust, *The Captive* (vol. 5 of *In Search of Lost Time*; trans. C.K. Scott Moncrieff & Terence Kilmartin; rev. D.J. Enright; London: Vintage, 1996), 291. Based on ―Le seul véritable voyage … ce ne serait pas d'aller vers de nouveaux paysages, mais d'avoir d'autres yeux, de voir l'univers avec les yeux d'un autre, de cent autres, de voir les cent univers que chacun d'eux voit," in ―La Prisonnière" in *À la recherche du temps perdu* (1913-27). In Roger Shattuck, *Marcel Proust* (New York: Viking Press, 1974), 131. See also Inge Crosman Wimmers, *Proust and Emotion: The Importance of Affect in A La Recherche Du Temps Perdu* (University of Toronto Romance Series; Toronto: University of Toronto Press, 2003).

My main contention is that Luke has redacted Mark in terms of the emotional characterization of Jesus. Luke has consistently removed strong emotion from the character of Jesus (and only Jesus), including both the traditionally-viewed negative emotions such as anger and grief, and the more positively viewed emotions including compassion and love. In the humble attempt to answer the important scholarly question of *why* Luke has presented his Greco-Roman auditors with an unemotional Jesus, I offered evidence from the Hellenistic, Jewish, and Roman philosophical traditions on the subject of emotions (in chapters two and three). In light of the philosophical evidence, I argue that it is primarily the Stoic traditions on which the author of Luke relies, and in particular the popular rendering of these in the Roman imperial authors and rhetoricians. It is my contention that Luke, knowledgeable in common literary and rhetorical conventions, drew upon these philosophical traditions in order to present his audience (which at the very least was able to respond appropriately) with a drastically less emotional Jesus (which is seen in comparison to his Markan source) perfectly in line with prevailing notions of honor and virtue according to Roman Stoicism.

I locate the Lukan redactions within the Roman Stoic tradition for a number of reasons. Importantly, especially for our purposes, the Stoics emphasized the cognitive *ability* of one to control one's emotions. This ability was emblematic of a rationality and, especially in the Stoics of the Roman period, a self-control that the best humans possessed. In the Roman authors and rhetoricians, this self-willed control was particularly necessary in public, civic, and/or political figures of authority. And perhaps most importantly, it is in the Stoics of the first century that the traditionally ‑positive"

283

emotions, including love and mercy, are most often listed alongside the negative emotions as "diseases of the soul," to be eradicated at all costs.

Anger Revisited

We have seen the importance of anger as a philosophical concept in antiquity, from Democritus to Luke's contemporary Josephus. Many emotions were viewed pejoratively in the philosophical traditions, but anger in particular. The Stoics called for the complete eradication of anger, a type of passionlessness (*apatheia*), which was the mark of the true sage. Even the moderation of emotion found in Aristotle and the Peripatetics proclaimed an exclusive hard-to-justify anger: "... but to be angry with the right person, to the right extent, at the right time, for the right moment and in the right manner is not something which anyone can do and it is not easy" (*Eth. nic.* 1109a26). Anger is pernicious in 4 Maccabees, being common to both pleasure and pain. Perhaps most indicative of the bridge between earlier Stoic philosophy and Roman imperial values, what I termed the "philosophy in the air" ethos of the first century, was Seneca's explication of anger. Seneca construed anger as:

> ... the most hideous and frenzied of all the emotions (*affectum*). For the other emotions have in them some element of peace and calm ... this one is wholly violent (*De Ira* 1.1).
> Anger is temporary madness, for it is equally devoid of self-control (*aeque enim impotens sui est*) ... closed to reason and counsel (*rationi consiliisque praeclusa*) (*De ira* 1.2).

Luke follows the overwhelming majority view in Hellenistic philosophy by looking upon anger as an irrational emotion devoid of self-control, an emotion he consistently removes from his characterization of Jesus. For example, in the pericope concerning Jesus' teaching on the kingdom of God and children (Mark 10:13-16//Luke 18:15-17), Luke simply omits Jesus' "anger/indignation" (ἠγανάκτησεν) from his Markan source. Importantly (as seen in chapter five), anger, like the other emotions, both the traditionally "positive" and "negative," is removed from the character of Jesus only. Jesus is held up as the authority figure, the civil leader who must not show emotion. Jesus' lack of emotion is closely linked with his persona as the ultimate human figure of authority.[730] A telling example of this is the scene at the synagogue (Mark 3:1-6//Luke 6:6-11), where Luke omits the Markan narrator's "with anger" (μετ' ὀργῆς) and transfers the anger to the Pharisees (a type of maddening rage, ἐπλήσθησαν ἀνοίας, Luke 6:11).

Luke depicts Jesus as the true authority figure, while the Pharisees, as revealed by their emotional anger, do not have the emotional disposition necessary for true leadership.

While Luke has omitted Jesus' anger in the *narrator's description* of Jesus' actions in the above pericopae,[731] Luke's version of the temple cleansing most clearly shows his aversion to anger in that he removes the *actual actions* associated with Jesus' anger in Mark.[732] In fact, this is a perfect test case for Aristotle's (and subsequent

---

[730] This contention, that Jesus' authority is revealed through his *apatheia*, is more clearly seen in passages discussed below.

[731] For example, Jesus still heals on the Sabbath (Mk 3:5//Lk 6:10), though does so without anger.

[732] Cadbury uses this incident to argue for a type of "both/and" in describing Luke's relationship with Rome and Judaism. The removal of Jesus' angry and violent actions in cleansing the Temple (along with the cursing of the fig tree) portrays Jesus as more honorable in the eyes and ears of his Roman audience, while the softening of Jesus' actions from cursing in Mark to a mild cleansing in Luke presents the gospel perfectly amenable with Judaism. Cadbury suggests, in the gospel, as in Acts, Luke wished to present Christianity as in no way hostile to Judaism, but even as faithful to its requirements in *Style and Literary Method*, 91. See further the classic Paul Wernle, *Die synoptische Frage* (Freiburg: J.C.B. Mohr (Paul

philosophic formulations of) justifiable anger, for the Lukan criticism against the sellers is quite severe. Luke draws upon the prophetic tradition (esp. Isa 56:7) and borrows a phrase from Jeremiah 7:11 in charging them with turning the temple into a σπήλαιον ληστῶν (19:46). Oppressing the downtrodden (7:6), stealing, murder, adultery and idolatry (7:8-9) are among those iniquitous practices which Jeremiah condemns in describing his ―den of robbers."

For Jeremiah, as well as for Luke's first-century readers, a ―den of robbers" recalls the caves to which people of violence retreat in order to escape justice.[733] While omitting much of the violent action, the Lukan narrator simply describes Jesus' action, ἤρξατο ἐκβάλλειν τοὺς πωλοῦντας, in the same way that he ―drove out" demons as though the sellers were similarly oppressive and profane.[734] Thus, the charge against those doing business in the temple is scathing, and a strong argument could be made that considering the charge, Jesus' violent actions in Mark and Matthew would be justified according to Aristotle. In effect, not to be angry (as Jesus is portrayed in Luke) under

---

Siebeck), 1899), 105. There are also scholars who argue that Luke is defending Rome to the Christians, see for example Paul W. Walaskay, ―And so We Came to Rome": The Political Perspective of St. Luke (SNTSMS 49; Cambridge: Cambridge University Press, 1983), and B.J. Hubbard, ―Luke, Josephus and Rome: A Comparative Approach to the Lukan Sitz im Leben," *SBL Seminar Papers, 1979* (2 vols.; SBLSP 16; Chico, Calif.: Scholars Press, 1979), 1:59-68. Jacob Jervell argues that Luke wished to defend Christianity as *religio licita*, that Luke sought for Christianity to become a privileged religion in the Roman Empire in the same manner as Judaism in ―Retrospect and Prospect in Luke-Acts Interpretation" *SBL Seminar Papers, 1991* (SBLSP 30; Atlanta: Scholars Press, 1991), 383-404. Philip Francis Esler has convincingly argued against both notions in *Community and Gospel in Luke-Acts: The Social and Political Motivations of Lucan Theology* (SNTS 57; Cambridge: Cambridge University Press, 1987), 208-14. See also Robert L. Maddox, *The Purpose of Luke-Acts* (Göttingen: Vandenhoeck & Ruprecht, 1982), 91-93.

[733] Josephus recounts Herod's battles with Antigonus, and ensuing pursuit of the robbers who dwelt in caves, *A.J.* 14.415, 421.

[734] For ἐκβάλλω, see Lk 9:40, 49; 11:14-20; 13:32; See also Green, *Gospel of Luke*, 692-94.

such circumstances, would have been an unethical act according to the Peripatetic tradition. With regard to the portrayal of Jesus and anger, the ―most hideous and frenzied of all the emotions," Luke consciously and consistently depicts an unemotional Jesus over and against his Markan source. At this point, we cannot say with certainty that Jesus' characterization most fully aligns with the Stoic tradition, as anger was problematic to a broad range of philosophical traditions, though we can say without hesitation that Luke's representation of Jesus is not compatible with Aristotelian moral philosophy.

Though perhaps most resonant with the Roman Stoic presentation, the Lukan redactions concerning anger could fit many philosophical traditions (including the complex presentation of Plato and maybe even the nuanced position of Philodemus), with the notable exception of Aristotle and the Peripatetic tradition. The consistent removal of anger by Luke in the character of Jesus[735] (in a variety of ways) is incompatible (even as it pertains to justifiable anger) with the moderation of the Aristotelian mean. Anger is omitted or drastically softened through explicit comment by the Lukan narrator, by Jesus' actions or lack thereof, as well as with the following direct speech omissions.

Stern Speech Revisited

Jesus' anger is also depicted in Mark through the use of stern speech, which is consistently eliminated (or at least significantly softened) by the Lukan redactor. While

---

[735] François Bovon states, ―Luc n'admettrait guère une colère de Jésus" in *L'Évangile selon Saint Luc 1-9* (Commentaire du Nouveau Testament 3a; Genève: Labor et Fides, 1991), 202 n.12.

some of these redactions are related to stylistic changes by Luke,[736] a consistent pattern emerges in the linguistic depiction of a less emotional Jesus, which again is used by Luke to bolster Jesus' persona as a public figure of great authority. In the scene where Jesus heals a leper (Mark 1:40-45//Luke 5:12-16), Luke significantly softens the tone of Jesus' speech in Mark in order to emphasize calmness and emotional composure even when making an authoritative charge.[737] In line with this contention, C.F. Evans cites this passage as evidence for the Lukan depiction of a less emotional and violent Jesus in the introduction to his commentary, "If Luke avoids associating Jesus with violent emotions (cf. 5:12-16 with Mark 1:40-45), that may reflect the Greek ideal of equanimity in great men."[738]

In the pericope concerning Jesus' prediction of his passion (Mark 8:31-33//Luke 9:22), the Lukan principle of omitting (or at least softening) Jesus' stern and sometimes angry speech in Mark is seen most clearly in the *total omission* of the mutual rebukes between Jesus and Peter. In chapter three, we analyzed Josephus as a parallel contemporary to show that Luke is not alone in his general enterprise of rewriting his religious tradition to make it more acquiescent to a Roman milieu. We demonstrated that

---

[736] See detailed analysis in chapter four. While some of the proposed redactions may be due primarily to stylistic concerns, most deal directly with the emotional characterization.

[737] In François Bovon's abstruse view, Luke softens (by vocabulary choice and the movement to indirect speech) the emotional command in Mark because Luke did not understand its significance in Mark, though he provides no further explanation in *Saint Luc 1-9*, 176.

[738] C.F. Evans, *Saint Luke*, 66. Though C.F. Evans doesn't recognize the scope of the Lukan redactions and ultimately argues that the less emotional characterization of Jesus by Luke shows the Lukan emphasis on the "humanity" of Jesus, he does associate the concept of public authority in antiquity with *apatheia* or lack of emotion (though doesn't use the term). Evans discusses the concept of "Man" at length, arguing that Luke places great prominence upon Jesus humanity (pace Schweizer, Fitzmyer, Morris, et al). In excursus D above, I argued against the emotions being used as evidence for either a more human or divine figure. I.H. Marshall similarly suggests Luke omits Mark's σπλαγχνισθείς (1:41) and ἐμβριμησάμενος (1:43), "possibly to avoid describing the emotions of Jesus" in *Gospel of Luke*, 209, but does not associate this avoidance to Jesus' authority.

Josephus, along with recasting certain biblical stories according to his purposes, also omitted numerous biblical stories, especially those potentially seen to be disconcerting for his Greco-Roman audience and/or embarrassing to the Jewish people. The Lukan omission of the verbal confrontation between Jesus and Peter (Mark 8:32-33) is reminiscent of Josephus' omission of the golden calf incident (Exod 32). Yahweh's consuming hot burning wrath (ויתר - אפי בהם) and Moses' hot burning anger (ויחר אף משה) were not directed at each other, as were Jesus' and Peter's, but at the Israelites, which culminates in the greatest national hero (according to Josephus) commanding and watching as the clan of Levi killed three thousand people (vv.27-28). The anger and violence (both from Moses the national hero and Yahweh the universal God) would have been embarrassing to the Jewish people and troubling to the Romans, so instead of radically rewriting the incident, Josephus omits the narrative altogether. Luke redacts many troubling aspects of the Markan narrative, but Peter's and especially Jesus' anger depicted through their mutual rebukes and harsh language is so troubling that Luke simply chose to omit the problematic emotional episode altogether.

Grief / Neediness Revisited

Perhaps not as universally condemned as anger, grief was the subject of many philosophical discussions of the emotions and ethics in antiquity. In general, grief, sadness, pain, and emotional neediness, were looked upon pejoratively in ancient contexts. Specifically to philosophy and especially to the Stoics, λύπη (grief, distress, pain) was one of the four main categories of emotion in Stoicism (appetite or desire, ἐπιθυμία; fear, φόβος; and pleasure, ἡδονή being the other three), and of course was to

be eradicated by all means necessary.[739] In the Roman period, Arius Didymus lists the

four types of πάθη, ―First in genus are these four: appetite [ἐπιθυμία], fear [φόβος],

pain [λύπη], and pleasure [ἡδονή]."[740] In his *Diatribai* (*Dissertationes*), Epictetus, like

Arius Didymus and traditional Stoicism, the emotions from which one is to be freed

include: fear [φόβος], desire [ἐπιθυμία], grief [λύπη], and pleasure [ἡδονή] (1.4).

Further, overcoming grief was a sign of self-control and autonomy for Epictetus,

―However, the necessary principles, those which enable a man, if he sets forth from them,

to get rid of grief, fear, passion, hindrance, and become free…" (4.6.16).

Before revisiting specific passages in light of Roman Stoic values, a recapitulation

of Luke's redactional pattern concerning λύπη will provide valuable insight into Luke's

redactional program and further locate his redactional agenda within the Stoic tradition.

Luke does not use λύπη (in any form) for the *character of Jesus*. Luke removes every

Markan usage of λύπη for the *character of Jesus* (i.e. Mark 3:1-6//Luke 6:6-11). As was

the case with his use of anger, Luke redacts Mark (and avoids in the special Lukan

material) concerning grief in the *character of Jesus only*. Luke does use λύπη for other

---

[739] See Ioannes von Arnim, *Stoicorum veterum fragmenta* (4 vols.; Leipzig: B.G.Teubner, 1905-1924), 3.377-420; for similar lists, see Stobaeus 2.57.13-116.18; and Cicero *Tusc.* 4.11-22.

[740] Arius Didymus 10 = Stobaeus, *Ecl.* 2.88; translation from Pomeroy, *Arius Didymus*, 57. See Krentz, ―Πάθη and ἀπάθεια in Early Roman Empire Stoics," 125.

characters and retains every Markan usage of λύπη concerning the other characters

except for the one previously mentioned scene (Jesus foretelling his betrayal, Mark

14:18-21//Luke 22:21-23).

In the controversy scene concerning Jesus picking grain on the Sabbath (Mark

2:23-28//Luke 6:1-5), the Lukan redactor maintains the physical aspect of Jesus' hunger

(ἐπείνασεν), but omits the emotional language of neediness in Mark (χρείαν ἔσχεν).

While recognizing that χρεία can certainly imply a general need (either physical,

emotional, or both) without negative implications, there is evidence in antiquity of a

negative connotation with χρεία. In the previously mentioned *Progymnasmata*,

Aphthonius has an essay on *Chreia (Progymnasmata 4: Maxim)* which he concludes, ―So

we must admire Euripides, who said that it is an evil thing to be in want (χρείαν)."

In the previously mentioned pericope concerning healing on the Sabbath (Mark

3:1-6//Luke 6:6-11), the author of Luke redacts not only the anger of Jesus (by

transferring it to the scribes and Pharisees), but the classic Stoic emotion of grief (λύπη)

is removed in his portrayal of Jesus. Despite the assertion by I. Howard Marshall that the

―alterations made by Luke to his source are insignificant,"[741] many scholars recognize the

importance of Luke's removal of Jesus' anger.[742] Some of these commentators, while

---

[741] Marshall, *Gospel of Luke*, 233.

[742] Even François Bovon admits that Luke tones down both of Jesus' emotions (Mark 3:5: μετ' ὀργῆς, συλλυπούμενος; ―with anger, he was grieved," despite contending earlier that the claim of Luke suppressing emotions is mistaken. See Bovon, *Saint Luc 1-9*, 266, 23.

noting the significance of Luke removing Jesus' anger,[743] miss the importance of Luke also removing a traditional emotion from his characterization of Jesus.[744] Almost all the commentators correctly recognize the importance of this passage in showing the authority of Jesus, culminating with the self-referential proclamation, —The Son of Man is lord of the Sabbath" (Mark 2:28//Luke 6:5), though they miss the fact that the removal of emotion is directly related to the authority of Jesus. Robert Tannehill, for example, who identifies the Lukan redactions, errs in this important regard, —*Although* Luke omits Mark's references to Jesus' anger and grief, Jesus' question is *still* challenging and his behavior provocative" [emphasis added].[745] Jesus is a challenging and provocative public figure *because* he embodies the unemotional ideal.

While recognizing the text critical debate of Luke 22:43-44, the pericope of Jesus praying at Gethsemane is still of vital import no matter the ultimate text critical decision. In the Lukan text, no explanation is given why the disciples should be grieving, nor why Jesus withdrew to pray, whereas in the Markan version Jesus reveals to Peter, James, and John that he withdraws because his soul is περίλυπός ἐστιν ἡ ψυχή μου ἕως θανάτου (Mark 14:34). As he is in general, Luke here is primarily concerned with the emotional portrait of Jesus. Thus he transfers Jesus' emotion to the disciples. This transference leaves the text slightly awkward, as now there is no reason for Jesus' withdrawal and no

---

[743] This is partly due to the sheer number of instances of Luke removing or softening Jesus' anger. Metzger, commenting solely on the textual critical traditions, exclaims that Luke could not admit that Jesus showed anger in *A Textual Commentary on the Greek New Testament*, 140.

[744] Scholars who note the redaction of Jesus' anger but not his grief include C.F. Evans, *Saint Luke*, 316-17; Green, *Gospel of Luke*, 251-257; Ringe, *Luke*, 86-88; Culpepper, *Gospel of Luke*, 135.

[745] Tannehill, *Luke*, 111.

reason for the disciples to be grieved.[746] It is simply the result of the Lukan redactional

agenda concerning Jesus' emotions. This further example of Luke transferring emotion

to other characters is reminiscent of Philo's two-stage ethical program or Galen's view

that not everyone can achieve *apatheia*, only the best of humanity.[747]

"Positive" Emotions Revisited

In short, say no to all emotions, positive or negative, in all areas of life.
(Epictetus, *Diatr.* 3.22.13)

Not only has the Markan source been redacted to eliminate the so-called

‑negative" emotions from Jesus in Luke's account, but Jesus' feelings of compassion,

mercy, and love, as well as Jesus showing general affection, have also been removed

from the Lukan narrative.[748] We have seen how the Lukan redactions analyzed thus far

perhaps *most fully* align with the Stoics, but those concerning anger, indignation, and

grief, could fit a variety of philosophical traditions. This is particularly true of the

idealistic representations of the schools, for an ideal philosopher or sage or statesmen in

Epicureanism, Cynicism, Platonism, or Stoicism, or an ideal national hero like Moses to

Philo and Josephus, could look very similar with regard to the ideal state of

imperturbability (*apatheia*).[749] The Lukan redactions that are most representative and

---

[746] See further Fitzmyer, *Luke X-XXIV*, 1442.

[747] Loveday Alexander states, ‑It is important for Galen that not everyone can escape or be ‑cured" from these morbid conditions, but only the _best or wisest'. (Passions 1.3)" in ‑The Passions in Galen," 176-78; see also Bobzien, *Determinism and Freedom*, 359.

[748] For a helpful discussion of the ‑positive" and ‑negative" emotions from a literary perspective, see Powell, *What Are They Saying about Luke*, 19-20.

distinctive of a popular Roman Stoicism are those concerning the "positive" emotions of compassion, mercy, love and affection.

The Roman Stoics in particular emphasized the *ability* of one to control one's emotions.[750] This emotional aptitude was representative of a rationality and self-control that the best of humanity possessed, the best philosophers, the best political leaders, the best citizens. [751] This self-willed control was necessary, especially in political leaders,[752] with regard to the traditionally negative ones, such as anger or grief or fear, as well as the traditionally positive emotions. Epictetus listed positive emotions, including love and mercy, with those emotions to be avoided or eradicated. Associating *apatheia* with public citizenship and leadership in "On the Cynic," he stated:

> It is necessary for you to remove desire absolutely, to turn your avoidance to the things that within the province of your choice (ὄρεξιν ἆραί σε δεῖ παντελῶς, ἔκκλισιν ἐπὶ μόνα μεταθεῖναι τὰ προαιρετικά); you should have no anger, no wrath, no envy, no mercy (σοὶ ὀργὴν μὴ εἶναι, μὴ μῆνιν, μὴ Φθόνον, μὴ ἔλεον); no little girl should appear fair to you, no little public reputation, no young boy, no little darling [μὴ κοράσιόν σοι φαίνεσθαι καλόν, μὴ δοξάριον, μὴ παιδάριον, μὴ πλακουντάριον]. (*Diatr.* 3.22.13)

---

[749] Sharper distinctions among the philosophical schools were certainly easier when dealing with the general populace or whether *apatheia* was possible in reality, but Luke certainly holds Jesus in high regard and comparisons with other heroes (Zeno or Socrates or Moses) whether political, philosophical, or national, seems apropos.

[750] We see this especially in the Stoic contention of the necessity of assent or judgment (what Nussbaums labels the "cognitive" aspect of Stoicism) to emotion.

[751] Pfitzner called the struggle of self-control with regard to the emotions the struggle of life itself: "The true Agon of the sage is one of the most frequently recurring pictures in the moral discourses of Epictetus, Seneca, Marcus Aurelius, and Plutarch. The contest into which a man struggles against the desires and passions, and the whims of fortune which threaten to disrupt his peace of mind, is the Olympic contest of life itself." In *Paul and the Agon Motif*, 29.

[752] See the criticism of Caligula and his lack of self-control (especially regarding his anger) in Seneca, *On the Firmness of the Wise Person* XVII-XVIII.

Galen, the second-century philosophically minded doctor, working from a

Platonic psychology and a (—mostly Stoic") ethical framework[753] somewhat similar to

Philo's,[754] calls the traditional Stoic emotions of —anger and wrath [θυμός and ὀργή] and

fear and grief and envy and excessive desire" nothing less than —diseases of the soul"

(*Passions* 1.3). It is important for Galen that not everyone can escape or be —cured" from

these morbid conditions, but only the —best or wisest," through a system of —training"

(ἄσκησις), with an emphasis on both rationality and self-control, comparable to a

—prolonged course of training in rhetoric or medicine" (*Passions* 1.4).[755] He describes

this training in rational self-control:

> If you do this, some day you will be able to tame and calm that power of passion
> within you which is as irrational as some wild beast.... Can you not take and tame
> this thing which is not some beast from outside yourself but an irrational power
> within your soul, a dwelling it shares at every moment with your power of
> reason? It would be a terrible thing if you could not. (*Passions* 1.5)

Galen further articulates the important concept of condemnation of positive

emotions along with the traditionally negative ones, a notion emblematic of popular

Stoicism of the first and second centuries CE. Galen argues that —loving or hating

anything too much" should also be regarded as a *pathos*, a disease of the soul (*Passions*

1.3). In his commentary on Epictetus' use of ἀταραξία and ἀπάθεια as representative of

---

[753] See Alexander, —The Passions in Galen," 175; and Brennan, —Stoic Epistemology," 115-120.

[754] See Hankinson, —Affection, Emotion, and Moral Self-management in Galen's Philosophical Psychology," 160-63; and Tieleman, *Galen and Chrysippus on the Soul*, 119-124.

[755] Alexander (177) states this *askēsis* in self-control —ultimately will enable the addressee to live a life in which the passions are firmly under the control of the rational mind" in —The Passions in Galen," 176-78; see also Bobzien, *Determinism and Freedom*, 359.

Stoicism during the Roman period,[756] Edgar Krentz contends:

> By these, however, he [Epictetus] does not mean noninvolvement or disinterestedness; rather they describe imperturbability, *the triumph of mind over disturbance arising from without*, the mastery of circumstances, against which anger, fear, *love*, hatred, despair, *friendship*, desire, and the like work. One should not be apathetic like a statue; no one must keep the natural and acquired states, *as a pious person*, a son, a brother, a father, *a citizen*. [emphasis added][757]

Krentz includes three areas representative of Roman Stoicism in the late first/early second century C.E.: (1) an emphasis on the cognitive quality of emotion, (2) the inclusion of positive emotions in the understanding of *apatheia*, and (3) the vinculum of *apatheia* with piety and citizenship.[758] A revisitation of the Lukan redactional program concerning the ―positive" emotions in light of these three tenets will locate the redactions within Roman Stoicism.

In the pericope where Jesus cleanses a leper (Mark 1:40-45//Luke 5:12-16), Luke removes Jesus' ―compassion" (σπλαγχνισθείς). Similar to the healing on the Sabbath incident (Mark 3:1-6//Luke 6:6-11), many commentators correctly recognize the Lukan emphasis on Jesus' power and authority, but fail to show how the Lukan emotional redactions contribute to this emphasis.[759] Indicative of this tendency, I. Howard Marshall

---

[756] This representation of Roman Stoicism in the late first/early second century C.E. included an emphasis on the cognitivity of emotion, the inclusion of positive emotions in the understanding of *apatheia*, and the vinculum of *apatheia* to piety and citizenship in Krentz, ―Πάθη and ἀπάθεια in Early Roman Empire Stoics," 128-131.

[757] *Diatr.* 3.2.4, in Krentz, ―Πάθη and ἀπάθεια in Early Roman Empire Stoics," 130.

[758] See discussion in ibid., 128-131.

[759] C.F. Evans states the passage presents the ―single theme of Jesus wielding power and authority," though he describes the redactions as ―accidental" in *Saint Luke*, 293-94. Similarly, Luke Timothy Johnson notes the significance of the Lukan Jesus' *exousia* (power), explicitedly stated in 5:24, but contends ―Luke's alterations of his source are minimal, consisting mainly of clarifications" in *Gospel of Luke*, 94-95. Léopold Sabourin also emphasizes Jesus' authority without recognizing the significance of the Lukan

discusses both the Lukan readactional changes and the authority of Jesus. Marshall

rightly points out that Luke omits ―Mark's σπλαγχνισθείς (v.l. ὀργισθείς)" along with

the ―difficult use of ἐμβριμησάμενος" because Luke ―avoids expressions of Jesus'

emotions," and the fact that the passage shows Jesus ―breaking down barriers" and is

representative of his increased reputation and ―becomes a testimony to the fulfillment of

the promise of the messianic age,"[760] but does not link the *apatheia* of Jesus with this

described authority. Robert C. Tannehill does not *directly* link Jesus' *apatheia* with his

authority as a public leader, but does discuss the ―two expressions of strong emotion by

Jesus" dropped by Luke in the general context of Jesus' courage.[761] In analyzing Luke

5:13, Walter Radl first comments on Jesus acting without hesitation and with authority,

and immediately notes Luke's Jesus as being without emotion, then discusses the

contrasting setting elements of publicness and isolation, though he never directly links

these concepts.[762] Eduard Schweizer lists ―no reference to Jesus' emotions (Mark 1:41,

---

redactions in *L'Évangile de Luc*, 145-47. See also Lieu, *Gospel of Luke*, 39-40, who states the main theme is ―Jesus' authority," and acknowledges that ―Luke does not speak of Jesus' compassion," but does not associate the two. Craig A. Evans sees the main Lukan theme is a question of true authority in *Luke*, 87-93. He also discusses this theme in relation to the ―private" Jesus and the ―public" Jesus. Puzzlingly, Craig A. Evans, *Luke*, fails to note the redactional changes concerning emotion in an otherwise close textual analysis with respect to a Greco-Roman audience and milieu. Evans descants (91) on Luke's redactional change of a tiled roof (5:19) from Mark's digging through the roof (2:4), ―Luke puts it this way probably for the sake of his Greco-Roman readers who would have been more familiar with tile roofs."

[760] Marshall, *Gospel of Luke*, 209; 210; 206-7. Bovon (again, despite his initial contention that Luke has not quelled Jesus' emotions) similarly discusses ―le courage et la souveraineté de Jésus" immediately after his statements: ―Le lépreux fait appel à cette volonté active, non à de bons sentiments. Quant à l'irritation de Jésus telle qu'elle apparaît chez Marc (Mc 1,41), Luc ne la comprend pas ou ne la supporte pas," though Bovon does not connect Jesus' emotionlessness with Jesus' courage in *Saint Luc 1-9*, 175.

[761] Tannehill, *Luke*, 102-3.

[762] Radl states of Luke's redactional agenda, ―Lukas erwähnt auch keinerlei Gemütsbewegung bei ihm (diff Mark 1,41)" in *Das Evangelium nach Lukas: 1,1-9,50*, 308.

43)," along with Jesus' praying and the removal of the disobedience of the healed leper in his contention: ‒perhaps in order to emphasize his intimate relationship with God at the very beginning of the conflict that follows" which he ultimately concludes points to Jesus' ‒authority (5:17, 24)."[763] In light of this pericope where Jesus cleanses a leper (Mark 1:40-45//Luke 5:12-16) and the previous healing on the Sabbath incident (Mark 3:1-6//Luke 6:6-11), Luke's portrayal of an unemotional Jesus is intricately linked to his portrayal of Jesus as the ultimate authority figure.[764]

Jesus' compassion is also redacted in Jesus' feeding of the multitudes (Mark 6:32-44//Luke 9:10b-17). Consistent with his redactional tendencies, Luke omits any hint of compassion or pity or sentimentality in his depiction of Jesus, yet maintains his authority as a public figure. Many commentators, as in the leper cleansing (Mark 1:40-45//Luke 5:12-16), rightly acknowledge the Lukan emphasis on Jesus' power and authority and the portrayal of a considerably less emotional Jesus, but do not manifest how the Lukan emotional redactions augment this accentuation.[765] In a primarily theological analysis, R. Alan Culpepper examines Luke's omission of ‒Jesus' compassion and the allusion to the people being like sheep without a shepherd in Mark 6:34" within the context of how the

---

[763] Schweizer, *The Good News according to Luke*, 110. Joseph Fitzmyer connects the ‒omission of Jesus' human emotions" with the ‒developing christological awareness in the early community, by the time Luke writes" which emphasizes ‒Jesus' power and will, not his emotions" in *Luke I-IX*, 572-574. While christology is certainly related to authority and power, I argued above against a simplistic human/divine distinction as related to the emotions in the pericope concerning the legality of healing on the Sabbath (Mark 3:1-6//Luke 6:6-11).

[764] John Nolland does connect Jesus' authority to his lack of emotion, albeit in a manner exactly the opposite of the proposed relationship. Luke ‒omits here from the Markan account the words that express Jesus' inner feelings" which Nolland contrasts with Luke's ‒public claims" of Jesus in the ‒public realm" as signs of ‒public authentication." In *Luke 1-9:20*, 413. In light of Roman Stoic values (especially those preferred in civic leaders), Jesus is seen as publicly authoritative because of his lack of emotion.

[765] Of course, there are a plethora of commentaries that examine the authority of Jesus but surprisingly fail to explain the Lukan redactions concerning Jesus' emotion. See Schweizer, *The Good News according to Luke*, 154-55. Green, *Gospel of Luke*, 362-63. Tannehill, *Luke*, 154-57.

feeding pericope as a whole shows the "full revelatory power" of Jesus, but doesn't directly link these concepts.[766] I. Howard Marshall asserts, "Luke's narrative is closely dependent upon that of Mark. …. The main difference lies in the enhanced Christological stress." He later recognizes, "Luke omits mention of Jesus' sympathy for the crowds, and also the detail that he saw them as sheep without a shepherd,"[767] though does not link these two Lukan themes. A paragraph before his discussion of Jesus' power (*Macht*), Radl notes, "Er nimmt sie freundlich auf. Nach Mark 6,34 hat er Mitleid mit ihnen, weil sie wie Schafe ohne Hirte sind."[768] Joseph Fitzmyer contends the Lukan version has a greater emphasis on the "power of Jesus," though he does not speculate why Luke removed Jesus' emotion, "For some reason Luke omits mention of the compassion of Jesus (cf. Mark 6:34)."[769] Luke removes Jesus' emotion *in order* to accentuate Jesus' power.

In the encounter of the rich man with Jesus (Mark 10:17-22//Luke 18:18-23), Luke omits the Markan description of Jesus' love. In commenting on this passage, Luke Timothy Johnson notes:

> Luke deliberately accentuates the contrast [between the rich man and children], by making the rich man a _ruler' (*archōn*). This small touch changes the character of

---

[766] Culpepper, *Gospel of Luke*, 195-96. Sabourin argues the passage increases the messianic character of Jesus, but this is not linked to his contention that Jesus is without compassion in *L'Évangile de Luc*, 199. See also Lieu, *Gospel of Luke*, 70-72. Craig A. Evans assays the "power of Jesus" in referencing the distinctions with Mark 6:34, but doesn't directly associate them in *Luke*, 143-45.

[767] Marshall, *Gospel of Luke*, 359-360. Similarly John Nolland notes, "Luke makes no use of Mark's statement of Jesus' compassion nor of the linked likening of the crowd to sheep without a shepherd (6:34)," then immediately analyzes how Luke "concentrates on the Christological focus of the pericope," but doesn't state if and/or how Jesus' lack of compassion relates to his increased christological authority in *Luke 1-9:20*, 440-41.

[768] Radl, *Das Evangelium nach Lukas: 1,1-9,50*, 598-99.

[769] Fitzmyer, *Luke I-IX*, 764, 766.

the story ... Rather than a sincere request to learn about discipleship – to which Jesus responds with ‗bve‘ as in Mark – we recognize the sort of testing question posed by the lawyer in 10:25.[770]

Not only does the rejection of Jesus‘ request by the rich ruler show the superiority (in virtue, benefaction, etc.) of one public authority figure (Jesus) over another (the ruler), the emotional portrayal of the two civic characters in Luke highlights this distinction. The unemotional Lukan Jesus is contrasted to the strong emotion shown by the rich ruler in Luke after Jesus‘ ultimate request; Luke (περίλυπος ἐγενήθη, 18:23) retains Mark‘s description (ἀπῆλθεν λυπούμενος, 10:22) of the ruler‘s reaction.[771] Luke provides the reader with an unemotional public leader, who is rational and self-controlled, in direct contrast to the rich public ruler.

In the last two pericopae examined, Luke removes Jesus‘ actions of affection toward children. When the disciples argue over greatness (Mark 9:33-37//Luke 9:46-48), the Markan Jesus grasps the child, puts him in the middle of the group, and then dramatically takes the child in his arms (9:36), and similarly, in teaching on the Kingdom of God (Mark 10:13-16//Luke 18:15-17), the Markan Jesus takes the children into his arms, blesses them, and then lays his hands upon the children (10:15-16); the Lukan Jesus does not. In Mark 9:36, many scholars identify the Lukan changes to the Markan text, but fail to recognize fully their significance in portraying an unemotional Jesus and how this

---

[770] Johnson, *Gospel of Luke*, 280.

[771] As analyzed above, λύπη (grief, distress, pain) was one of the four main categories of emotion in Stoicism (appetite or desire, ἐπιθυμία; fear, φόβος; and pleasure, ἡδονή being the other three). See especially Epictetus, for whom overcoming grief was a sign of self-control and autonomy in *Diatr.* 4.6.16.

portrayal contributes to a first-century understanding of Jesus in light of Roman Stoic values.[772] Though commentators correctly acknowledge the Lukan theme of Jesus challenging existing notions of status (evidenced by his use of children as representations of the lowly),[773] they fail to recognize how a significantly less emotional Jesus underscores his status (especially along Stoic lines) as a rational and self-controlled public authority figure. In Mark 10:15-6, Jesus' status as a public figure with the authority to challenge the current system of status and power is dependent on his characterization as a rational and self-controlled leader without emotion. Jesus' depiction is in line with the current (first-century Roman Stoic) status system that values an *apatheia* which evidences a certain rationality and just as importantly, the virtue of self-control.[774]

Provisional Judgments and Topics for Further Inquiry

Luke's Authorial Audience Revisited

Luke's authorial audience, while probably unable themselves to reproduce these rhetorical devices in composition, were nevertheless able to respond to their

---

[772] Scholars who recognize the redactions: C.F. Evans mentions the redactional changes, but gives no weight to them in *Saint Luke*, 428; Radl points out Jesus' different use of children in Luke, without additional comment in *Das Evangelium nach Lukas: 1,1-9,50*, 651-52; Jacob Kremer notes the redactions, but doesn't assign any significance to them in *Lukasevangelium*, 111-12. Goulder, who has identified the Lukan redactions in almost all of the pericopae examined, unfathomably states (in his close textual reading of this passage, in which he actually points out the Lukan changes on emotion above, addressing the Lukan emotional redactions as a whole), ―there is little justification for thinking that Luke suppresses signals of emotion in Jesus,‖ in *Luke: A New Paradigm*, 451.

[773] For the low status of children in antiquity see Osiek and Balch, *Families in the New Testament World*, 68-74, 136-140. See also Beryl Rawson, ed., *The Family in Ancient Rome: New Perspectives* (Ithaca, N.Y.: Cornell University Press, 1986); and Beryl Rawson, ed. *Marriage, Divorce, and Children in Ancient Rome* (New York: Oxford University Press, 1991).

[774] See further Tannehill, *Luke*, 267-69.

efforts. Since Luke's authorial audience presumably knew how to respond appropriately (if unconsciously) to persuasive rhetoric, we should determine then how that same authorial audience would have understood his rhetorical strategies and literary conventions.[775]

Of course I am not the first scholar to suggest that Luke was aware of and influenced by the philosophical and rhetorical traditions in composing Luke-Acts. This is especially true for scholarship on Acts, particularly concerning the speeches in Acts. Starting with George Kennedy's brief chapter on the speeches in Acts in his *New Testament Interpretation through Rhetorical Criticism*,[776] scholars have shown convincingly that the author of Acts was familiar with the devices and strategies of ancient rhetoric as practiced during the Hellenistic period.[777] If we can assume according to scholarly consensus that Luke was more than competent in his rhetorical composition in the speeches in Acts, I maintain it would be fair to conclude, at the very least, that Luke was knowledgeable in the general *progymnasmata* tradition.[778]

The *progymnasmata* were ―handbooks that outlined ‗preliminary exercises' designed to introduce students who had completed basic grammar and literary studies to

---

[775] Mikeal Parsons, *Luke: Storyteller, Interpreter, Evangelist* (Peabody, Mass.: Hendrickson, 2007), 19.

[776] George Kennedy, *New Testament Interpretation through Rhetorical Criticism* (Chapel Hill: University of North Carolina Press, 1984), 114-40.

[777] See for example Jerome H. Neyrey, ―The Forensic Defense Speech and Paul's Trial Speeches in Acts 22-26: Form and Function," in *Luke-Acts: New Perspectives from the Society of Biblical Literature Seminar* (ed. Charles H. Talbert; New York: Crossroad, 1984), 210-24; Marion L. Soards, *The Speeches in Acts: Their Content, Context, and Concerns* (Louisville: Westminster John Knox, 1994). Philip E. Satterthwaite concludes (378): ―At point after point Acts can be shown to operate according to conventions similar to those outlined in classical rhetorical treatises" in ―Acts against the Background of Classical Rhetoric," in *The Book of Acts in its Ancient Literary Setting* (eds. Bruce W. Winter and Andrew D. Clarke; vol. 1 of *The Book of Acts in its First Century Setting*, ed. Bruce W. Winter; Grand Rapids, Mich.: Eerdmans, 1993), 337-79.

[778] See Parsons, *Luke: Storyteller*, 15-39. R.O.P. Taylor argued that as a Hellenic citizen, the ―Christian was bound to pursue the art of pleading, both in his own defense and in the work of persuading others. … It was only natural that he should use the methods in vogue. And in the work of the Rhetores, we have an exposition of their methods." In *Groundwork for the Gospels* (Oxford: Blackwell, 1946), 75.

the fundamentals of rhetoric that they would then put to use in composing speeches and prose."[779] These exercises were probably intended to facilitate the transition from grammar school to the more advanced study of rhetoric.[780] It is important for our purposes to stress that some of the exercises in the *progymnasmata* are clearly intended for both oral *and* written forms of communication. For example, Aelius Theon comments:

> So then, I have presented these things, not thinking that they are all suitable for all beginners, but in order that we might know that training in the exercises is absolutely necessary, not only for those who are going to be orators, but also if anyone wishes to practice the art of poets or prose-writers (λογοποιῶν), or any other writers. These things are, in effect, the foundation of every form of discourse.[781]

Further, George Kennedy has remarked that the curriculum described in the *progymnasmata* and other philosophical works was the source of facility and training in written and oral expression for many persons in public and private life. Kennedy adds:

> Not only the secular literature of the Greeks and Romans, but the writings of early Christians beginning with the gospels and continuing through the patristic age, and of some Jewish writers as well, were molded by the habits of thinking and writing learned in schools.[782]

---

[779] Willi Braun, *Feasting and Social Rhetoric in Luke 14* (SNTSNS 85; Cambridge: Cambridge University Press, 1995), 146. Surviving *progymnasmata* include those by Aelius Theon (1st c.), Hermogenes of Tarsus (2nd c.), Aphthonius of Antioch (4th c.), and Nicholaus of Myra (5th c.), along with a fifth document, a commentary on Apthonius' *Progymnasmata* attributed to John of Sardis. English translations are from George Kennedy, *Progymnasmata: Greek Textbooks of Prose Composition Introductory to the Study of Rhetoric* (Fort Collins, Colo.: Chez l'auteur, 1999).

[780] Quintilian refers to the preliminary exercises as part of the educational curriculum of young boys (*Inst.* 1.9). On rhetoric and philosophy in the educational curricula of antiquity, see S.F. Bonner, *Education in Ancient Rome* (Berkeley: University of California Press, 1977).

[781] "On the Education of Young Students," 70.24-30; James R. Butts correctly observes: "This statement is clear evidence that Theon understood the *progymnasmata* as providing instruction for literary activity ranging far beyond the technical parameters of rhetoric" in *The Progymnasmata of Theon: A New Text with Translation and Commentary* (Ph.D. diss., The Claremont Graduate School, 1986), 181 n.36.

[782] Kennedy, *Progymnasmata*, v.

It is reasonable to assert that if Kennedy's statements are at least partially true and Luke

(at the very least, among the gospel writers) was familiar with the philosophical and

rhetorical exercises of the time, then an investigation into the rhetorical and philosophical

conventions in Luke's gospel (not only his sequel) is both legitimate and fruitful,

especially when we have available Luke's major source in which to compare.[783]

Conversely, a number of scholars have provided strong warning against this type

of scholarly enterprise. F. Scott Spencer cautions:

> ... it is possible for modern scholars to become in effect too competent or literate.
> Redaction critics, for example, presuppose a professional scholar-reader like
> themselves poring over every detail of the Lukan narrative surrounded by Gospel
> parallel texts, concordances and other lexical aids – a scenario scarcely
> conceivable to Luke's original audience.[784]

Heeding Spencer's warning against redactional critical analyses, I have analyzed Luke in

light of Philo, Josephus, and 4 Maccabees, along with the larger philosophical corpus in

order to prevent the imposing of modern precepts on the ancient text. Importantly, we do

have Luke's major source which he has recast for his purpose.[785] I have followed the

---

[783] For example, on the speeches in the gospel of Luke, see the recent extensive and well-researched Patrick E. Spencer, *Rhetorical Texture and Narrative Trajectories of the Lukan Galilean Ministry Speeches* (LNTS; New York: T&T Clark, 2007).

[784] Spencer, ―Acts and Modern Literary Approaches,‖ in *The Book of Acts in its Ancient Literary Setting* (eds. Bruce W. Winter and Andrew D. Clarke; vol. 1 of *The Book of Acts in its First Century Setting*, ed. Bruce W. Winter; Grand Rapids, Mich.: Eerdmans, 1993), 413.

[785] I am not (nor is any scholar in which I am aware) suggesting any literary dependence between Luke and Aelius Theon of Alexandria (ca. 50-100 C.E., roughly contemporary to Luke), only that he was generally aware of the rhetorical and philosophical traditions. I see the same relationship between Luke and Theon as I do between Luke and the Roman Stoics. Theon's text represents the kind of rhetorical exercises practiced in the first century, many of which had been practiced earlier, thus, some (if not most) of what Theon states about these rhetorical exercises was not unique to Theon. Theon acknowledges that others had written on the subject of preliminary exercises (1.15-16) and even refers to traditional exercises (1.18).

general methodology proposed by Craig A. Evans and James Sanders in their combined investigation of Luke's methods of construction in light of Jewish traditions. Denouncing clear-cut categories of comparison of the Gospels to *targumin* or *midrashim*, for example, they prefer to recognize that Luke's process contains elements that are ―targumic" and ―midrashic."[786] I am not claiming that Luke was a professional philosopher or rhetorician, only that he knew enough philosophy to employ certain patterns, allusions, and typologies, familiar to semi-educated people (see discussion of audience below), in order to rewrite Mark's Jesus more in line with a Stoic sage, or more specifically for his audience, a Stoic Roman statesman.

Spencer's warning also concerns Luke's perceived audience and the degree of their philosophical sophistication. Luke's audience has always been a matter of great contention within scholarship. My contention is that Luke has redacted and constructed his Jesus by having drawn upon a general Stoic philosophical ethos which permeated the first century of the Common Era.[787] The closest scholarly discussion of ―authorial audience"[788] and Luke's use of philosophical techniques to my thesis is Mikeal Parsons' description of Luke and the ―rhetoric in the air" that permeated antiquity.[789] Similar to my contention that Luke drew upon common philosophical themes and topics, Parsons

---

[786] Craig A. Evans and James Sanders, *Luke and Scripture: The Function of Sacred Tradition in Luke-Acts* (Minneapolis: Fortress, 1993), 1-13.

[787] See further Sedley, ―The School, from Zeno to Arius Didymus," 30-36.

[788] For methodological concerns on the concept ―authorial audience," see Peter J. Rabinowitz, ―Truth in Fiction: A Reexamination of Audience," *Critical Inquiry* 4 (1977), 126; Mary Ann Tolbert, *Sowing the Gospel: Mark's World in Literary-Historical Perspective* (Minneapolis: Fortress, 1989), 52-55; Charles H. Talbert, ―Conversion in the Acts of the Apostles: Ancient Auditors' Perceptions," in *Literary Studies in Luke-Acts: Essays in Honor of Joseph B. Tyson* (ed. Richard P. Thompson and Thomas E. Phillips; Macon, Ga.: Mercer University Press, 1998), 141-54.

[789] Parsons, *Luke: Storyteller*, 18-20. See also further R.O.P. Taylor, *Groundwork for the Gospels*, 75.

argues that Luke drew upon common rhetorical techniques of the first century CE.

Parsons further makes the interesting postulation that the —rhetoric in the air"
quality applies to the *audience* as well as the author. Parsons defines —authorial
audience" as the audience Luke had in mind when he wrote Luke-Acts, which for him is
a general Christian audience, living in the Roman Empire near the end of the first
century.[790] While calling for a study of Luke in light of ancient conventions, Parsons,
pace Spencer, makes the previously mentioned contention that due to the pervading first-
century ethos of rhetoric, Luke's audience could understand or at the very least respond
suitably to Luke's rhetorical conventions.

Parsons argument is compelling in that it responds to the question of why Luke
would use conventions, be they rhetorical devices or philosophical strategies, his
audience would not understand at any level.[791] I contend, in short, he would not.
Likewise, I maintain Luke intentionally removes emotion from Jesus to make a character
more presentable in the eyes and ears of his audience, whether they are semi-educated (as
I previously put forward) and can fully understand the Lukan characterization techniques,
or are only able to —respond appropriately" (even if only unconsciously). In a kind of
stream-of-consciousness musing, Henry J. Cadbury makes a consonant hypothesis. In
discussing popular ancient forms in light of literary types, Cadbury remarks at the
extraordinary persistence of the *Jewish* characteristics of the Lukan text when it would
have been more natural to remove them considering the *prevalence of popular philosophy*

---

[790] Parsons, *Luke: Storyteller*, 19. See also Richard Bauckham, —For Whom Were the Gospels
Written?" in *The Gospel for All Christians: Rethinking the Gospel Audiences* (ed. Richard Bauckham;
Grand Rapids, Mich.: Eerdmans, 1998), 9-48; Luke Timothy Johnson, —On Finding the Lukan Community:
A Cautious Cautionary Essay," *SBLSP* (ed. Paul J. Achtemeier; Missoula, Mont.: Scholars Press, 1979),
87-100.

[791] Parsons, *Luke: Storyteller*, 19-20.

and readily available rhetoric in the first century. He states, ―In the simple popular philosophic speech of the Stoic and Cynic pamphlet, the Hellenistic world had at hand a style of its own, as informal as that of the Jewish scribes. . .and survives in the works of Seneca, Epictetus, and others."[792]

Luke's Christology Revisited

The omission of the mention of Jesus emotions probably results from a developing Christological awareness in the early community.[793]

Among the select few scholars who not only recognize at least some of the Lukan redactions concerning the emotional portrayal of Jesus but also offer account for their removal, most attribute them to a line of argument concerning christology, usually in terms of human/divine characteristics. This rationale probably began with Henry Cadbury's brief introduction to his list of Luke's redactions as discussed in detail in my discussion of the Lukan redactional program in chapter four. In a sub-section entitled ―Changes Perhaps Attributable to Religious Motives," his one-sentence introduction reads, ―Human emotions and expressions of feeling on Christ's part are omitted by Luke, even when they are love and pity."[794] Even without further comment, his direct reference to ―human" emotions, his use of ―Christ" instead of Jesus (which Cadbury most often uses), and the title of the sub-section, have led most scholars to interpret Cadbury's

---

[792] Cadbury, *Making of Luke-Acts* (London: SPCK, 1961), 152.

[793] Fitzmyer, in response to Luke removing Jesus' emotions in the cleansing of the leper pericope (Mk 1:40-45//Lk 5:12-16), *Luke I-IX*, 572.

[794] Cadbury, *Style and Literary Method*, 90-91.

limited analysis as I have suggested – christologically. More specifically, this christological frame is basically interpreted in the simplistic sense that the expression of emotion is associated with humanity and phlegmaticness with divinity.

Fitzmyer, who admittedly follows Cadbury closely in his redactional examination concerning Jesus' emotion, states in the proem to his redactional list:

> Similarly, the description of Jesus moved by *human* emotions in the Marcan Gospel is normally eliminated in the Lucan story, even if they are expressions of love, compassion, or tenderness. The Marcan episodes depict Jesus in a more *human* way, perhaps too *human* for the nobility of character that Luke sought to depict. [emphasis added][795]

I argued above that the use of ―nobility" in describing the Lukan agenda concerning the persona of Jesus and emotion is useful and applicable, and certainly related to (if not synonymous with) my preferred term ―honor." In contrast, the analysis of the Lukan redactions concerning Jesus' emotional characterization using the oversimplified humanity/divinity frame is not that useful and, in light of my exploration of the special ―L" material in particular, sometimes not even applicable.[796]

While Cadbury, Fitzmyer, and Powell, have argued, as a general principle, that a less emotional Jesus is a more divine Jesus, some important commentators have followed this line of argumentation in specific scenes. As previously mentioned, in his analysis of

---

[795] Fitzmyer, *Luke I-IX*, 95. He also states (96), ―For further details in this sort of study of Luke's use of his sources, see H. J. Cadbury, *Style and Literary Method*, 73-205."

[796] In his analysis of Fitzmyer, Mark Allan Powell agrees not only with Fitzmyer's redational list but also with his explanation. ―References to Jesus' emotions are also omitted. Mark's descriptions of Jesus as stern (1:43), angry (3:5; 10:14), distressed (14:33-34) and sad (3:5) seem inappropriate to Luke, but not just because they are ―negative" emotions. Luke also omits references to Jesus feeling compassion (Mk 1:41) and love (Mk 10:21). Fitzmyer suggests that, for this evangelist, the attribution of any *human* emotion to Jesus detracted *in some way* from his nobility. [emphasis added]" In *What Are They Saying about Luke*, 19-20. As with Fitzmyer, Powell does not discuss nor explain the association of emotion with humanity and the lack of emotion with divinity.

308

the scene at the synagogue (Mark 3:1-6//Luke 6:6-11), Leon Morris uses the omission of

Jesus' anger and grief in Luke to claim, ―Mark is franker in depicting Jesus' humanity,"

though no further analysis or citation is provided to show how a definition of

humanity/divinity applies to emotion.[797] In his interpretation of the dialogue among the

disciples concerning who is the greatest (Mark 9:33-37//Luke 9:46-48), I. Howard

Marshall argues that Luke's removal of the Markan description of Jesus' embrace of a

child is symbolic of ―Luke's general avoidance of attributing *human* emotions to Jesus

[emphasis added],"[798] though he doesn't elaborate on the connection between humanity

and emotion. While certainly not a complete list of scholars following the

humanity/divinity hermeneutical frame, this explanation has become a type of *de facto*

argument for those select scholars who recognize the omission of Jesus' emotions in

Luke. Thus, it is necessary to offer evidence against this popular interpretation, at least

as a be-all end-all explanation of the Lukan agenda.

In response to the Leon Morris declaration discussed in chapter four (and repeated

above) concerning the pericope at the synagogue (Mark 3:1-6//Luke 6:6-11), I briefly

provided two reasons why the emotional redactions by Luke should not be framed in

terms of humanity/divinity. (1) There is ample evidence that divine beings in antiquity

were portrayed as very emotional beings, both in Greek mythology and in the Hebrew

Bible. For example, see the extended analysis of the Josephan omissions of embarrassing

biblical narratives with regard to emotion, especially the omission of Yahweh's

emotional anger in the golden calf incident, in chapter three. In the Roman Stoics

---

[797] Morris, *Luke*, 53.

[798] Marshall, *Gospel of Luke*, 396.

309

particularly, *apatheia* was found ideally in the best of *humanity* – the best philosophers, the best citizens, and especially the best public, civic, and/or political figures of authority.[799] (2) With respect to christology in early Christian documents, especially the gospel texts, John's Jesus, for example, is characterized both as more divine and more emotional than Luke's. A closer analysis of the Lukan text, particularly the ―L‖ material, provides further elaboration of these general propositions.

In our analysis of the ―L‖ material, our primary conclusion was that the emotional language used in the infancy narratives and the parables did not concern Jesus at all, but instead was used to describe the emotions of God. A necessary distinction was made between the emotional portrayal of God and the unemotional depiction of Jesus, especially in regards to the ―positive‖ emotions of love, mercy and compassion. Luke describes the mercy and compassion of God numerous times in the first few chapters, using two words he has consistently removed from his Markan source, especially concerning Jesus' character – σπλάγχνον and ἔλεος. Even throughout his gospel, Luke

uses parables (the two debtors interpolated into the passage concerning the woman with the ointment – Luke 7:36-50; the prodigal son – Luke 15:11-32; the Good Samaritan – Luke 10:25-37) to describe the love, mercy, and compassion of God, while consistently removing Jesus' love, compassion, and affection (Mark 1:41// Luke 5:13; Mark 6:34//Luke 9:11a; Mark 5:19-20//Luke 8:39; Mark 10:21//Luke 18:22; Mark 9:36//Luke 9:47-48; Mark 10:15-16//Luke 18:17).[800]

---

[799] See detailed discussion above.

[800] As more evidence against this popular contention, ἀγάπη / ἀγαπάω were common terms, especially used by early Christians, but also in antiquity in general, which connoted just about every type of love (brotherly, between humans/deities, among deities, etc.), but was usually not associated with erotic

310

In brief, the persona of the divinity in Luke is very emotional; the character of Jesus is unemotional in Luke's gospel. How is removing the emotion from Jesus making him more divine in Luke's eyes if Luke consistently describes God using these same human emotions? Fittingly, the very emotions that locate the Lukan redactions most specifically within the Roman Stoic traditions, the so-called "positive" emotions, are the ones that show the most popular scholarly explanation of the Lukan redactions concerning the emotions of Jesus – that they were removed to make Jesus more divine and less human – is insufficient and often simply not true.

Though I argue strongly against seeing Jesus' *apatheia* solely, or even primarily, in human/divine terms, Luke's portrayal of Jesus' emotions is certainly related to his christology. Luke does make strong christological claims about Jesus, and his depiction of Jesus as *apatheia* contributes to these claims. In fact, an important corollary to Luke's removal of Jesus' emotion is that Luke removes *only* Jesus' emotion (as shown in chapter five). Jesus' persona is unique, in his emotional characterization, in his title of κύριος, in

the resurrection, and in the ascension/enthronement. My contention that Luke presents his auditors with a Jesus as an ideal representation of a Stoic statesman does not diminish our perception of Luke's christology, but contributes to our understanding of it, especially in how he chose to present his christology to his Greco-Roman audience.[801]

---

love; BADG, 4-6. Luke and Mark use ἀγάπη often, but not to describe Jesus' emotion. ἀγάπη is used in God's direct description of Jesus at the Baptism of Jesus (Mark 1:11//Luke 3:22) and the Transfiguration (Mark 9:7//Luke 9:35, some manuscripts read ἐκλελεγμένος instead of ἀγαπητός; see Metzger, *A Textual Commentary on the Greek New Testament*, 148.

[801] I suggest Luke's re-characterization of Jesus as an ideal Stoic public leader is analogous to Luke's pericope concerning Paul's reaction to the unknown altar (Acts 17:16-34). Luke communicates his theological/christological views in terms (more) recognizable and acceptable to Greeks and Romans. Luke's god is a god Greeks have already known, to a certain degree. Luke, through Paul, professes this knowledge manifest (Acts 17:22-31). Luke's Jesus is the manifestation of an ideal they have already

Conclusions: The Import of the Lukan Redactions

In the *status quaestionis* in the general introduction, I noted the promising —historical psychological" approach of Klaus Berger in *Identity and Experience in the New Testament* (originally *Historische Psychologie des Neuen Testaments*). Berger's analysis is representative of the majority of previous scholarship on the emotions concerning Jesus, for despite the —new" approach, Berger basically provides a general overview of the emotions in the NT (and by NT, he means primarily Paul, but really everything *except* the gospels).[802] His brief remarks concerning Jesus and the emotions are so typical, so informative, and so important to our concluding remarks, I quote them in full:

> Next to Mark 14:34, Mark 3:5 is the most explicit statement about emotions on the part of Jesus (—He looked around at them with anger; he was grieved at their hardness of heart…"). Here Mark alerts his readers to an important conflict, indeed a turning point. (The parallel passages in Matthew and Luke do not offer – or have left out – any such reference to the emotions of Jesus). The emphasis in Mark arises from the combining of sorrow with anger, a juxtaposition that would have been unsuitable for a sage in antiquity. Ephesians 4:31 speaks in the same vein.[803]

---

known in a sense. Jesus is the embodiment of the ideal philosopher, the ideal sage, the ideal statesman. In my opinion, Luke is not making claims beyond his Judaism, he is presenting these notions as consonant with prevailing perceptions of virtue and honor. See E.P. Sanders, *Judaism: Practice and Belief, 63 BCE-66 CE* (London: SCM Press, 1992), 45-314, esp. 45-47; Martin Dibelius and K. C. Hanson, —Paul on the Areopagus," in *The Book of Acts: Form, Style, and Theology* (Fortress Classics in Biblical Studies; Minneapolis: Fortress Press, 2004), 95-128; Eduard Norden, *Agnostos Theos: Untersuchungen zur Formengeschichte religiöser Rede* (Leipzig [u.a.]: Teubner, 1913); Mircea Eliade and Charles J. Adams, eds., —Agnōstos Theos," in *The Encyclopedia of Religion* (New York: Macmillan, 1987), 135-137.

[802] In his 50-page chapter entitled —Emotions," he begins with —Paul on Feelings" and ultimately spends less than a page on Jesus, which is indicative of scholarship in general concerning the NT and the emotions; see chapter one.

[803] Berger, *Identity and Experience*, 175-76.

Berger is most important in what he doesn't say, what he dismisses, and the connections he doesn't make, but *prima facie*, he references the two most important texts for our redactional analysis. The pericope of Jesus' praying before his betrayal and arrest (Mark 14:32-42//Luke 22:39-46), as the first passage analyzed using redaction criticism in the general introduction, served as the model from which my proposed pattern was first extrapolated. The Markan text is significant because it portrays an emotionally distraught Jesus. I followed Sterling (pace Neyrey) in arguing that the Lukan version removes this intense emotion, which is indicative of his redactional program of consistently omitting Jesus' emotion.

Berger's next highlighted passage, the scene at the synagogue where the scribes and Pharisees were watching Jesus to see if he would heal on the Sabbath (Mark 3:1-6//Luke 6:6-11), as the first passage analyzed in our redactional analysis proper (chapter four), specifically evidences the three main Lukan redactional principles that I have offered for consideration. Most importantly, Luke eliminates Jesus' troubling emotions of anger and grief (ὀργή, λύπη; important foundational passions of the Stoic tetrachord),

as he consistently does throughout his gospel. This passage also provides evidence of two general principles I used to support my thesis that the Lukan emotional redactions concern only the character of Jesus (pace Fitzmyer). Jesus' anger in Mark 3:5 is transferred to the scribes and Pharisees in Luke 6:11, highlighting Luke's ―transference principal" (see also garden text above).[804] This text evinces the Lukan principle of

---

[804] It is an amazing case of serendipity that the two texts which Klaus Berger contends are the most explicit statements about Jesus' emotion (which they are) not only are our two highlighted texts for the above reasons, but are also the two texts on which Luke applies his transference principle. I view this as no mere coincidence as, of course, Luke would remove the emotion from Jesus in the texts that serve as the most egregious examples of Mark's emotional Jesus.

removing or lessening the violence (or the threat of violence) and strong emotion *to* Jesus. Luke does not ―eliminate *anything* that smacks of the violent, the passionate, or the emotional [emphasis added]," only that which smacks of the violent, the passionate, or the emotional concerning the character of Jesus.

As stated previously, Berger is most informative, not in his actual commentary on the Markan passage, but for what he almost dismissively says about the Lukan redactions. He references the fact that Luke has ―left out any such reference to the emotions of Jesus" and further states that said emotion ―would have been unsuitable for a sage in antiquity." Even further, he remarkably quotes Epictetus to substantiate his claim:

> Epictetus, *Discourse*, 3.13.11: The emperor can grant only external peace, but the philosopher offers another kind. The philosopher says, ―when you heed me, you people – wherever you are, or whatever you might be doing – you cease to be troubled, you are not angry, you are not constrained, you are not hindered, you live without passion and in freedom from all things." Also: ―Pay attention to yourself in everything, that you need not remain hidden when you … are beside yourself with sorrow or become furious through anger …" (*Sentences of Moschion* 1).[805]

Like many scholars and commentators, he recognizes certain Lukan changes concerning the emotional portrayal of Jesus, but just cannot put these contentions together. The emotional references were left out by Luke *precisely because* they were unsuitable for a person of Jesus' stature.

Other important scholars, even when providing evidence to the contrary, have failed to acknowledge the broad Lukan redactional *program* of removing emotion from

---

[805] Ibid., 276 n.80.

the character of Jesus (e.g. Bovon, Goulder), many scholars have identified at least some

of these *Tendenzen*. Though commentators may recognize the Lukan changes regarding

emotion, they fail to understand fully their significance in portraying an unemotional

Jesus and how this portrait contributes to who Luke and his audience understood Jesus to

have been in light of first-century Roman Stoic values. Some scholars even identified

these redactions in pericopae designed to show the authority of Jesus,[806] but do not

demonstrate how the Lukan emotional redactions contribute to this emphasis.[807] In

keeping with Roman Stoic values (especially those preferred in civic leaders), Jesus is

seen as publically authoritative *because* he is able, through his self-control and

rationality, to be an exemplar of *apatheia* (which is further indicative of his "honorable"

character). Further, Jesus' imperturbability is seen through the important redactions

concerning the "positive" emotions, which become a major area of emphasis in Roman

Stoicism of the late first/early second century C.E. Somewhat ironically, Jesus is able to

break down barriers and challenge contemporary notions of status, precisely because he

himself is portrayed as an idealized Roman of merit, a public leader full of rationality and

---

[806] The pericopae where the Lukan redactions serve to increase the authority of Jesus (e.g. removing Jesus' anger depicts a calmer authority figure with greater self-control) could include all the pericope assayed, in one way or another, but this is especially true in confrontational narratives with other authorities (6:1-5, 6-11; 19:45-46), public healing/miracle/exorcism episodes (5:12-16; 6:17-19; 8:26-39; 9:10b-17), and public teaching passages (9: 46-48; 18:15-17, 18-23;). Pericopae are listed according to Lukan purposes, as Markan intentions are often reassigned.

[807] The scholars who come the closest to my thesis that the Lukan redactions portray Jesus as more "honorable" and authoritative within a Roman Stoic framework, are those that recognize (at least some of) the redactions and *attempt* to comment on how they contribute to Luke's characterization of Jesus. Of course my thesis is based on Sterling, Neyrey, and Kloppenborg, who argue the emotional redactions in specific Lukan scenes contribute to some aspect of Jesus' increased honor or nobility. Though I ultimately disagreed with their human/divine distinction concerning the emotions (granted that this interpretation is certainly along the lines of honor and authority), scholars including Marshall, Nolland, Morris, and C.F. Evans, sometimes argued the removal of emotion by Luke contributed to Jesus' portrayal as more divine (or more human in Evans' view). Nearly equivalent to my main contention are Cadbury, who contends they increase the "reverence" of Jesus and Fitzmyer (and Powell), who assert(s) that the attribution of emotion detracted from Jesus' nobility; however, their interpretations argued for a Lukan redactional program of a much smaller scale.

self-control, evident in his depiction as a man of *apatheia*.

BIBLIOGRAPHY

Aland, Kurt. *Synopsis Quattuor Evangeliorum.* 13th revidierte Auflage. Stuttgart: Deutsche Bibelgesellschaft, 1985.

Albright, W. F., and C.S. Mann. *Matthew: Introduction, Translation, and Notes.* Anchor Bible 26. Garden City, N.Y.: Doubleday, 1971.

Alexander, Loveday. ―In Journeying Often': Voyaging in Acts of the Apostles and in Greek Romance." Pages 17-49 in *Luke's Literary Achievement.* Edited by C.M. Tuckett. Journal for the Study of the New Testament: Supplement Series 116. Sheffield: Sheffield Academic Press, 1995.

Alexander, Loveday. ―The Passions in Galen and the Novels of Chariton and Xenophon." Pages 251-88 in *Passions and Moral Progress in Greco-Roman Thought.* Edited by John T. Fitzgerald. New York: Routledge, 2008.

Allen, Willoughby Charles. *A Critical and Exegetical Commentary on the Gospel according to St. Matthew.* Edinburgh: T & T Clark, 1912.

Anderson, H. ―4 Maccabees: A New Translation and Introduction." Pages 531-64 in *The Old Testament Pseudepigrapha, Vol.2.* Edited by James H. Charlesworth. 2 vols. Garden City, N.Y.: Doubleday, 1983.

Anderson, William. *Anger in Juvenal and Seneca.* Berkeley: University of California Press, 1964.

André, J.M. ―Les écoles philosophiques aux deux premiers siècles de l'Empire." *ANRW* 36.1: 53. Part 2, *Principat*, 36.1. Edited by H. Temporini and W. Haase. New York: de Gruyter, 1990.

Annas, Julia. *Hellenistic Philosophy of the Mind.* Berkeley: University of California Press, 1992.

Annas, Julia. ―Epicurean Emotions." *Greek, Roman, and Byzantine Studies* 30 (1989): 145-64.

Annas, Julia. *The Morality of Happiness.* New York: Oxford University Press, 1993.

Armstrong, David. ―Be Angry and Sin Not: Philodemus Versus the Stoics on Natural Bites and Natural Emotions.‖ Pages 79-121 in *Passions and Moral Progress in Greco-Roman Thought*. Edited by John T. Fitzgerald. New York: Routledge, 2008.

Arnold, Edward. *Roman Stoicism: Being Lectures on the History of the Stoic Philosophy* Cambridge: Cambridge University Press, 1911.

Attridge, Harold W. *The Interpretation of Biblical History in the Antiquities Judaicae of Flavius Josephus*. Missoula: Scholars Press, 1976.

Aune, David C. ―Mastery of the Passions: Philo, 4 Maccabees and Earliest Christianity.‖ Pages 125-158 in *Hellenization Revisited: Shaping a Christian Response within the Greco-Roman World*. Edited by Wendy Helleman. Lanham, Md.: University Press of America, 1994.

Aune, David E. *The New Testament in its Literary Environment*. Philadephia: Westminster, 1987.

Aune, David E. ―The Problem of the Passions in Cynicism.‖ Pages 48-66 in *Passions and Moral Progress in Greco-Roman Thought*. Edited by John T. Fitzgerald. New York: Routledge, 2008.

Aune, David E., ed. *The Westminster Dictionary of New Testament and Early Christian Literature and Rhetoric*. Louisville: Westminster John Knox Press, 2003.

Babut, Daniel. *Plutarch: De la vertu éthique*. Paris: Les Belles Lettres, 1969.

Babut, Daniel. ―Xénophane critique des poètes.‖ *L'Antiquité Classique* 43 (1974): 83-117.

Babut, Daniel. *Plutarque et le Stoicisme*. Paris: Presses Universitaires de France, 1979.

Baily, D.R. Shackleton, ed. and trans. *Cicero: Letters to Quintus and Brutus, Letter Fragments, Letter to Octavian, Invectives, Handbook of Electioneering*. Cambridge: Harvard University Press, 2002.

Barrett, C. K. *Luke the Historian in Recent Study*. Philadelphia, Fortress Press, 1970.

Barth, Karl, Geoffrey William Bromiley, and Thomas F. Torrance. *Church Dogmatics: Vol. 1, Part 2: The Doctrine of the Word of God*. Edinburgh: Clark, 1956.

Barton, Carlin. *Roman Honor: The Fire in the Bones*. Berkeley: University of California Press, 2001.

Barton, Carlin. *The Sorrows of the Ancient Romans: The Gladiator and the Monster.* Princeton: Princeton University Press, 1993.

Bauckham, Richard. "For Whom Were the Gospels Written?" Pages 9-48 in *The Gospel for All Christians: Rethinking the Gospel Audiences*. Edited by Richard Bauckham. Grand Rapids, Mich.: Eerdmans, 1998.

Bauer, W., F.W. Danker, W.F. Arndt, and F.W. Gingrich. *Greek-English Lexicon of the New Testament and Other Early Christian Literature*. 3rd edition. Chicago: Chicago University Press, 1999.

Beall, Todd S. *Josephus' Description of the Essenes Illustrated by the Dead Sea Scrolls.* Cambridge: Cambridge University Press, 1988.

Becchi, F. "L'ideale della metriopatheia nei testi pseudopitagorici: A proposito di una contraddizione nella Ps.-Archita." *Prometheus* 18 (1992): 102-20.

Begg, Christopher T. *Josephus' Account of the Early Divided Monarchy (Ant. 8, 212-420): Rewriting the Bible*. Leuven: Leuven University Press, 1993.

Berger, Klaus. *Identity and Experience in the New Testament*. Minneapolis, Minn.: Fortress Press, 2003.

Berkowitz, Luci, et al. *Thesaurus Linguae Graecae: Canon of Greek Authors and Works*. New York: Oxford University Press, 1986.

Bickerman, E. "The Date of Fourth Maccabees." Pages 131-161 in *Louis Ginzberg Jubilee Volume*. Edited by S. Lieberman et al. New York: The American Academy for Jewish Research, 1945.

Bilde, Per. "Contra Apionem 1.28-56: Josephus' View of His Own Work in the Context of the Jewish Canon." Pages 94-114 in *Josephus' Contra Apoinem*. Edited by Louis H. Feldman and John R. Levison. Leiden: Brill, 1996.

Birnbaum, Ellen. *The Place of Judaism in Philo's Thought: Israel, Jews, and Proselytes*. Atlanta: Scholars Press, 1996.

Black, C. Clifton. "Mark: Introduction." Pages 1722-24. *The HarperCollins Study Bible*. Edited by Wayne A. Meeks et al. New York: HarperCollins, 1993.

Black, Matthew. *An Aramaic Approach to the Gospels and Acts*. Oxford: Clarendon, 1967.

Blowers, P.M. "Gentiles of the Soul: Maximus the Confessor on the Substructure and Transformation of the Human Passions." *Journal of Early Christian Studies* 4 (1996): 57.

Bobzien, Susanne. *Determinism and Freedom in Stoic Philosophy*. Oxford: Oxford University Press, 1998.

Bonner, S.F. *Education in Ancient Rome*. Berkeley: University of California Press, 1977.

Bons, Jeroen and R.T. Lane. ―Quintilian VI.2: On Emotion.‖ Pages 131-54 in *Quintilian and the Law: The Art of Persuasion in Law and Politics*. Edited by Olga Tellegen-Couperus. Leuven: Leuven University Press, 2003.

Booth, A. Peter. ―The Voice of the Serpent: Philo's Epicureanism.‖ Pages 159-172 in *Hellenization Revisited: Shaping a Christian Response within the Greco-Roman World*. Edited by Wendy Helleman. Lanham, Md.: University Press of America, 1994.

Borg, Marcus J. ―Portraits of Jesus.‖ Pages 18-43 in *Jesus in Contemporary Scholarship*. Valley Forge, Penn.: Trinity, 1994.

Borgman, Paul. *The Way according to Luke: Hearing the Whole Story of Luke-Acts*. Grand Rapids, Mich.: Eerdmans, 2006.

Bovon, François. *L'Évangile selon Saint Luc 1-9*. Genève: Labor et Fides, 1991.

Braun, Willi. *Feasting and Social Rhetoric in Luke 14*. Society for New Testament Studies Monograph Series 85. Cambridge: Cambridge University Press, 1995

Braund, Susanna. *Beyond Anger: A Study of Juvenal's Third Book of Satires*. Cambridge: Cambridge University Press, 1988.

Braund, Susanna, and Christopher Gill, eds. *The Passions in Roman Thought and Literature* Cambridge: Cambridge University Press, 1997.

Braund, Susanna, and Glenn Most, eds. *Ancient Anger: Perspectives from Homer to Galen*. Yale Classical Studies 32. Cambridge: Cambridge University Press, 2003.

Bréhier, Émile. *Les idées philosophiques et religieuses de Philon d'Alexandrie*. Paris: J. Vrin, 1925.

Breitenstein, Urs. *Beobachtungen zu Sprache, Stil und Gedankengut des Vierten Makkabäerbuchs*. Basel/Stuttgart: Schwabe, 1978.

Brennan, Tad. ―The Old Stoic Theory of Emotions.‖ Pages 21-70 in *The Emotions in Hellenistic Philosophy*. Edited by Juha Sihvola and Troels Engberg-Pedersen. Dordrecht: Kluwer Academic Publishers, 1998.

Brilliant, Richard. *Portraiture*. Cambridge: Harvard University Press, 1991.

Brink, C.O. —Oikeiosis and Oikeiotes: Theophrastus and Zeno on Nature and Moral Theory." *Phronesis* 1 (1955): 12-145.

Broadie, Sarah. *Ethics with Aristotle*. New York: Oxford University Press, 1991.

Brodie, Thomas L. *Luke the Literary Interpreter: Luke-Acts As a Systematic Rewriting and Updating of the Elijah-Elisha Narrative in 1 and 2 Kings*. Rome: Angelicum, 1981.

Burchard, Christoph. —Joseph and Aseneth: A New Translation and Introduction." Pages 194-95 in *The Old Testament Pseudepigrapha, Vol.2*. Edited by James H. Charlesworth. 2 vols. Garden City, N.Y.: Doubleday, 1983.

Burnet, John. *Early Greek Philosophy*. New York: Meridian Books, 1957.

Busse, Ulrich. *Die Wunder des Propheten Jesus: Die Rezeption, Komposition, und Interpretation der Wundertradition im Evangelium des Lukas*. Forschung zur Bibel 24. Stuttgart: Katholisches Bibelwerk, 1979.

Butts, James R. *The Progymnasmata of Theon: A New Text with Translation and Commentary*. Ph.D. diss., The Claremont Graduate School, 1986.

Cadbury, Henry J. —Four Features of Lucan Style." Pages 87-102 in *Studies in Luke-Acts: Essays Presented in Honor of Paul Schubert*. Edited by Leander E. Keck and J. Louis Martyn. Nashville: Abingdon Press, 1966.

Cadbury, Henry J. *Making of Luke-Acts*. London: SPCK, 1961.

Cadbury, Henry J. *The Style and Literary Method of Luke*. Cambridge: Harvard University Press, 1920.

Caird, George Bradford. *The Gospel of St. Luke*. Pelican New Testament Commentaries A490. Baltimore: Penguin Books, 1963-65.

Cairns, Douglas. *AIDŌS: The Psychology and Ethics of Honour and Shame in Ancient Greek Literature*. Oxford: Clarendon, 1993.

Caizzi, Fernanda Decleva. —Protagoras and Antiphon: Sophistic Debates on Justice." Pages 311-331 in *The Cambridge Companion to Early Greek Philosophy*. Edited by A.A. Long. Cambridge: Cambridge University Press, 1999.

Capps, Donald. *Jesus: A Psychological Biography*. St. Louis, Miss.: Chalice Press, 2000.

Cassidy, Richard J. *Jesus, Politics, and Society: A Study of Luke's Gospel*. Maryknoll, N.Y.: Orbis Books, 1978.

Centrone, Bruno. *Introduzione a i Pitagorici*. Rome: Laterza, 1996.

Chadwick, Henry. ―Philo.‖ Pages 137-57 in *The Cambridge History of Later Greek and Early Medieval Philosophy*. Edited by A.H. Armstrong. Cambridge: Cambridge University Press, 1976.

Chance, J. Bradley. *Jerusalem, the Temple, and the New Age in Luke-Acts*. Macon, Ga.: Mercer University Press, 1988.

Charlesworth, James H., ed. *The Old Testament Pseudepigrapha*. 2 vols. Garden City, N.Y.: Doubleday, 1985.

Chesnutt, Randall D. *From Death to Life: Conversion in Joseph and Aseneth*. Journal for the Study of the Pseudepigrapha: Supplement Series 16. Sheffield: Sheffield Academic Press, 1995.

Cicero on the Emotions: Tusculan Disputations 3 and 4. Translated with commentary by Margaret Graver. Chicago: University of Chicago Press, 2002.

Clay, Diskin, ―The Philosophical Inscription of Diogenes of Oenoanda: New Discoveries 1969-1983.‖ *ANRW* 36.4: 2499. Part 2, *Principat*, 36.4. Edited by H. Temporini and W. Haase. New York: de Gruyter, 1983.

Cohen, Shaye J. D. *Josephus in Galilee and Rome*. Leiden: Brill, 2002.

Cohen, Shaye J. D. ―Respect for Judaism by Gentiles according to Josephus.‖ *Harvard Theological Review* 80 (1987): 420-25.

Cohn, Leopold. Yiẕḥak Heinemann, and Maximilian Adler, eds. *Die Werke Philos von Alexandria in deutscher Übersetzung*. 6 vols. Breslau: M. & H. Marcus, 1909.

Colish, M.C. *The Stoic Tradition form Antiquity to the Early Middle Ages*. 2 vols. Leiden: Brill, 1985.

Collins, John. *Between Athens and Jerusalem*. New York: Crossroad, 1983.

Collins, John. ―Jewish Ethics in Hellenistic Dress: The Sentences of Pseudo-Phocylides.‖ Pages 158-177 in *Jewish Wisdom in the Hellenistic Age*. Louisville: Westminister John Knox, 1997.

Conrad, Carl W. *Biblical Greek Digest* V1 #945 (10 Nov 1995); Online: cwconrad@artsci.wustl.edu.

Conzelmann, Hans. *Die Mitte Der Zeit.* Tübingen: Mohr Siebeck, 1953.

Conzelmann, Hans. *The Theology of St. Luke.* London: Faber and Faber, 1960.

Cooper, J.M. ―Eudaimonism, the Appeal to Nature, and _Moral Duty' in Stoicism." Pages 261-84 in *Aristotle, Kant, and the Stoics: Rethinking Duty and Happiness.* Edited by Stephen Engstrom and Jennifer Whiting. Cambridge: Cambridge University Press, 1996.

Cooper, John M. ―Posidonius on Emotions." Pages 71-112 in *The Emotions in Hellenistic Philosophy.* Edited by Juha Sihvola and Troels Engberg-Pedersen. Dordrecht: Kluwer Academic Publishers, 1998.

Cooper, John M. *Reason and Emotion: Essays on Ancient Moral Psychology and Ethical Theory.* Princeton: Princeton University Press, 1999.

Crossan, John Dominic. *The Birth of Christianity: Discovering What Happened in the Years Immediately After the Execution of Jesus.* San Francisco: HarperSanFrancisco, 1998.

Crossan, John Dominic. ―Parable and Example in the Teaching of Jesus," *New Testament Studies* 18 (1971-72): 285-307.

Crossan, John Dominic, and Jonathan L. Reed. *In Search of Paul: How Jesus's Apostle Opposed Rome's Empire with God's Kingdom, A New Vision of Paul's Words & World.* San Francisco: HarperCollins, 2004.

Crouch, James. *The Origen and Intention of the Colossian Haustafel.* Göttingen, Vandenhoeck & Ruprecht, 1972.

Culpepper, R. Alan. *The Gospel of Luke: Introduction, Commentary, and Reflections. The New Interpreter's Bible* 9. Nashville: Abingdon Press, 1995.

D'Angelo, Mary R. ―*Eusebeia*: Roman Imperial Family Values and the Sexual Politics of 4 Maccabees and the Pastorals." *Biblical Interpretation* 11 (2003): 139.

Danker, Frederick W. *Jesus and the New Age.* Philadelphia: Fortress, 1988.

Darwin, Charles. *The Expression of the Emotions in Man and Animals.* 3rd edition with a preface by Konrad Lorenz. Chicago: University of Chicago Press, 1998.

De Long, Kindalee Pfremmer, ―Surprised by God: Praise Responses in the Narrative of Luke-Acts." Ph.D. diss., The University of Notre Dame, 2007.

Duncan, John, and Martin Derrett. ―Figtrees in the New Testament." *Heythrop Journal* 14:3 (1973): 249-278.

Duncan, John, and Martin Derrett. *Law in the New Testament.* London: Darton, Longman & Todd, 1970.

de Silva, David A. *4 Maccabees.* Sheffield: Sheffield Academic Press, 1998.

de Silva, David A. *4 Maccabees: Introduction and Commentary on the Greek Text in Codex Sinaiticus.* Boston: Brill, 2006.

de Silva, David A. ―The Noble Contest: Honor, Shame, and the Rhetorical Strategy of *4 Maccabees*," *Journal for the Study of the Pseudepigrapha* 13 (1995): 31-57.

de Silva, David A. ―The Perfection of ‗Love for Offspring': Greek Representations of Maternal Affection and the Achievement of the Heroine of 4 Maccabees." *New Testament Studies* 52 (2006): 264-67.

DeWitt, Norman Wentworth. *Epicurus and his Philosophy.* Minneapolis: University of Minneapolis Press, 1954.

Dibelius, Martin. *From Tradition to Gospel.* New York: Scribner, 1965.

Dibelius, Martin, and K. C. Hanson. *The Book of Acts: Form, Style, and Theology.* Minneapolis: Fortress Press, 2004.

Diels, Hermann. *Die Fragmente der Vorsokratiker.* 3 vols. Berlin: Weidmann, 1903.

DiCicco, Mario. *Paul's Use of Ethos, Pathos, and Logos in 2 Corinthians 10-13.* Lewiston: Mellen Biblical Press, 1995.

Dillon, John, and A. A. Long, eds. *The Question of „Eclecticism': Studies in Later Greek Philosophy.* Berkeley: University of California Press, 1988.

Dillon, John, and Abraham Terian. ―Philo and the Stoic doctrine of *Eupatheiai*." *Studia philonica* 4 (1976-77): 18-22.

Dillon, John. *The Middle Platonists: A Study of Platonism 80 B.C. to A.D. 220.* Ithaca, N.Y.: Cornell University Press, 1977 [reprint 1996].

Dillon, Richard J. *From Eye-Witnesses to Ministers of the Word: Tradition and Composition in Luke 24.* Analecta biblica 82. Rome: Biblical Institute Press, 1978.

Dillon, Richard J. ―Previewing Luke's Project from his Prologue." *Catholic Biblical Quarterly* 43 (1981): 205-208.

Dorandi, Tiziano, ―Filodemo: gil orientamenti della ricerca attuale." *ANRW* 36.4: 2349-51. Part 2, *Principat*, 36.4. Edited by H. Temporini and W. Haase. New York: de Gruyter, 1990.

Dornisch, Loretta. *A Woman Reads the Gospel of Luke.* Collegeville: The Liturgical Press, 1996).

Dreyfus, Georges. ―Is compassion an Emotion? A Cross-Cultural Exploration of Mental Typologies." Pages 31-45 in *Visions of Compassion: Western Scientists and Tibetan Buddhists Examine Human Nature.* Edited by Richard J. Davidson and Anne Harrington. Oxford: Oxford University Press, 2002.

Droge, Arthur, and James D. Tabor. *A Noble Death: Suicide and Martyrdom Among Jews and Christians in the Ancient World.* San Francisco: HarperSanFrancisco, 1991.

Dupont-Sommer, André. *Le Quatrieme Livre des Machabees.* Paris: Champion, 1939.

Edelstein, Ludwig. ―The Philosophical System of Posidonius." *American Journal of Philology* 57 (1936): 305.

Edelstein, Ludwig, and I.G. Kidd, eds. *Posidonius.* 2 vols. Cambridge: Cambridge University Press, 1988.

Egelkraut, Helmuth L. *Jesus' Mission to Jerusalem: A Redaction Critical Study of the Travel Narrative in the Gospel of Luke, Luke 9:51-19:48.* Frankfurt: Peter Lang, 1976.

Ehrman, Bart D., and Mark A. Plunkett. ―The Angel and the Agony: The Textual Problem of Luke 22:43-44." *Catholic Biblical Quarterly* 45 (1983): 401-16.

Ehrman, Bart. *The New Testament: A Historical Introduction to the Early Christian Writings.* Oxford: Oxford University Press, 2004.

Eliade, Mircea, and Charles J. Adams. *The Encyclopedia of Religion.* New York: Macmillan, 1987.

Ellis, E. Earle. *The Gospel of Luke.* New Century Bible. London: Oliphants, 1974.

Elster, Jon. *Alchemies of the Mind: Rationality and the Emotions.* Cambridge: Cambridge University Press, 1999.

Emmet, C.W. *The Fourth Book of Maccabees.* London: Society for Promoting Christian Knowledge, 1918.

Engberg-Pederson, Troels. *The Stoic Theory of Oikeiosis: Moral Development and Social Interaction in Early Stoic Philosophy*. Aarhus: Aarhus University Press, 1990.

Erskine, Andrew. "Cicero and the Expression of Grief." Pages 36-47 in *The Passions in Roman Thought and Literature*. Edited by Susanna Braund and Christopher Gill. Cambridge: Cambridge University Press, 1997.

Esler, Philip Francis. *Community and Gospel in Luke-Acts: The Social and Political Motivations of Lucan Theology*. Society for New Testament Studies Monograph Series 57. Cambridge: Cambridge University Press, 1987.

Etheridge, S.G. "Plutarch's De virtue morali: A Study in Extra-Peripatetic Aristotelianism." Ph.D. diss., Harvard University, 1961.

Evans, C.F. *Saint Luke.* Philadelphia: Trinity, 1990.

Evans, C.F. "The Central Section of St. Luke's Gospel." Pages 37-53 in *Studies in the Gospels: Essays in Memory of R.H. Lightfoot*. Edited by D.E. Nineham. Oxford: Basil Blackwell, 1955.

Evans, Craig A. *Luke.* New International Biblical Commentary on the New Testament 3. Peabody, Mass.: Hendrickson, 1990.

Evans, Craig A., and James Sanders. *Luke and Scripture: The Function of Sacred Tradition in Luke-Acts.* Minneapolis: Fortress, 1993.

Feldman, Louis H. "Abraham the Greek Philosopher in Josephus." *Transactions of the American Philological Association* 99 (1968): 146-49.

Feldman, Louis H. *Judaism and Hellenism Reconsidered.* Leiden: Brill, 2006.

Feldman, Louis H. *Philo's Portrayal of Moses in the Context of Ancient Judaism.* Notre Dame, Ind.: University of Notre Dame Press, 2007.

Feldman, Louis H. *Studies in Josephus' Rewritten Bible.* Leiden: Brill, 1998.

Feldman, Louis H. "Use, Authority, and Exegesis of Mikra in the Writings of Josephus." Pages 455-518 in *Mikra: Text, Translation, Reading, and Interpretation of the Hebrew Bible in Ancient Judaism and Early Christianity*. Edited by Jan Mulder. Philadelphia: Fortress, 1988.

Feuillet, A. "Le recit lucanien de l'agonie de Gethsemane (lc xxii. 39-46)." *New Testament Studies* 22 (1975-76): 397-417.

Fillion-Lahille, Janine. *Le De ira de Sénèque et la philosophie stoïcienne des passions*. Paris: Klincksieck, 1984.

Finley, M.I. *The Ancient Greeks: An Introduction to Their Life and Thought*. New York: Viking Press, 1969.

Fischel, Henry. *Rabbinic Literature and Graeco-roman Philosophy*. Leiden: Brill, 1973.

Fitzgerald, John T. ―The Passions and Moral Progress: An Introduction.‖ Pages 1-26 in *Passions and Moral Progress in Greco-Roman Thought*. Edited by John T. Fitzgerald. New York: Routledge, 2008.

Fitzmyer, Joseph. *The Acts of the Apostles*. Anchor Bible 31. New York: Doubleday, 1998.

Fitzmyer, Joseph. *The Gospel According to Luke: Introduction, Translation and Notes*. Anchor Bible 28-28A. 2 vols. New York: Doubleday, 1981-85.

Flintoff, Everard. ―Pyrrho and India.‖ *Phronesis* 25 (1980): 95-96.

Fortenbaugh, W.W. *Aristotle on Emotion: A Contribution to Philosophical Psychology, Rhetoric, Poetics, Politics and Ethics*. 2nd ed. London: Duckworth, 2002.

Fortenbaugh, W.W. ―Aristotle and Theophrastus on the Emotions.‖ Pages 29-47 in *Passions and Moral Progress in Greco-Roman Thought*. Edited by John T. Fitzgerald. New York: Routledge, 2008.

Fortenbaugh, W.W., P.M. Huby, R.W. Sharples, and D. Gutas, eds. *Theophrastus of Eresus: Sources for His Life, Writings, Thought, and Influence*. Leiden: Brill, 1992.

Fowler, D.P. ―Epicurean Anger.‖ Pages 16-35 in *The Passions in Roman Thought and Literature*. Edited by Susanna Braund and Christopher Gill. Cambridge: Cambridge University Press, 1997.

Franklin, Eric. ―Comparing Luke and Matthew.‖ Pages 55-77 in *Luke: Interpreter of Paul, Critic of Matthew*. Journal for the Study of the New Testament: Supplement Series 92. Sheffield: Sheffield Academic Press, 1994.

Franxman, Thomas W. *Genesis and the "Jewish Antiquities" of Flavius Josephus*. Rome: Biblical Institute Press, 1979.

Frede, Michael. ―The Stoic Doctrine of the Affections of the Soul.‖ Pages 93-110 in *The Norms of Nature: Studies in Hellenistic Ethics*. Edited by Malcolm Schofield and Gisela Striker. Cambridge: Cambridge University Press, 1986.

Galizzi, Mario. *Gesù nel Getsemani.* Zurich: Pas, 1972.

Gerson, Lloyd P. *Aristotle and Other Platonists.* Ithica, N.Y.: Cornell University Press, 2005.

Gigante, Marcello, and Dirk Obbink. *Philodemus in Italy: The Books from Herculaneum.* Ann Arbor: University of Michigan Press, 1995.

Gill, Christopher. ―Did Galen Understand Platonic and Stoic Thinking on Emotions?" Pages 113-148 in *The Emotions in Hellenistic Philosophy.* Edited by Juha Sihvola and Troels Engberg-Pedersen. Dordrecht: Kluwer Academic Publishers, 1998.

Gill, Christopher. ―Passion as Madness in Roman Poetry." Pages 213-241 in *The Passions in Roman Thought and Literature.* Edited by Susanna Braund and Christopher Gill. Cambridge: Cambridge University Press, 1997.

Gill, Christopher. ―The School in the Roman Imperial Period." Pages 33-58 in *The Cambridge Companion to the Stoics.* Edited by Brad Inwood. Cambridge: Cambridge University Press, 2003.

Gill, Christopher. *The Structured Self in Hellenistic and Roman Thought.* Oxford: Oxford University Press, 2006.

Gladman, Kimberly R., and Phillip Mitsis. *Lucretius and His Intellectual Background.* Edited by K.A. Algra, M.H. Koenen, and P.H. Schrijvers. Amsterdam: Royal Netherlands Academy of Arts and Sciences, 1997.

Ginzberg, Louis. *The Legends of the Jews.* Translated by Henrietta Szold. Philadelphia: JPS, 1952.

Gooch, Paul W. *Reflections on Jesus and Socrates: Word and Silence.* New Haven: Yale University Press, 1996.

Goodenough, Erwin R. ―Philo's Exposition of the Law and His *De Vita Mosis*." *Harvard Theological Review* 26 (1933): 109-125.

Gould, Thomas. *The Ancient Quarrel between Poetry and Philosophy.* Princeton: Princeton University Press, 1991.

Goulder, Michael. *Luke: A New Paradigm.* Journal for the Study of the New Testament: Supplement Series 20. 2 Vols. Sheffield: Sheffield Academic Press, 1989.

Green, Joel B. *The Gospel of Luke.* Grand Rapids, Mich.: Eerdmans, 1997.

Green, Joel B. "Preparation for Passover (Luke 22:7-13): A Question of Redactional Technique." Pages 154-168 in *The Composition of Luke's Gospel: Selected Studies from "Novum Testamentum."* Edited by David E. Orton. Leiden: Brill, 1999.

Greene, Stuart. "Argument as Conversation: The Role of Inquiry in Writing a Researched Argument." Pages 145-164 in *The Subject Is Research.* Edited by W. Bishop & Pavel Zemliansky. Portsmouth, N.H.: Boynton/Cook Heinemann, 2001.

Grimal, Pierre. "Seneque et le Stoicisme Romain," *ANRW* 36.3: 1962-92. Part 2, *Principat*, 36.3. Edited by H. Temporini and W. Haase. New York: de Gruyter, 1989.

Gross, D.M. *The Secret History of Emotion: From Emotion: From Aristotle's "Rhetoric" to Modern Brain Science.* Chicago: University of Chicago Press, 2006.

Grundmann, Walter. *Das Evangelium nach Lukas.* Theologischer Handkommentar zum Neuen Testament 3. Berlin: Evangelische Verlagsanstalt, 1981

Hadas, Moses. *The Third and Fourth Book of Maccabees.* New York: Harper and Bros., 1953.

Hägg, Thomas. *The Novel in Antiquity.* Berkeley: University of California Press, 1983.

Hadot, Ilsetraut. *Seneca und die griechisch-römische Tradition der Seelenleitung.* Berlin: de Gruyter, 1969.

Hadot, Pierre. *Exercices spirituels et philosophie antique.* Paris: Institut d'études augustiniennes, 1993.

Hadzsits, George Depue. *Prolegomena to a Study of the Ethical Ideal of Plutarch and of the Greeks of the First Century A.D.* Cincinnati: University of Cincinnati Press, 1906.

Haenchen, Ernst. *The Acts of the Apostles: A Commentary.* Translated by Bernard Noble and Gerald Shinn, under the supervision of Hugh Anderson. Philadelphia: Westminster Press, 1971.

Hankinson, James. "Actions and Passions: Affection, Emotion, and Moral Self-management in Galen's Philosophical Psychology." Pages 184-222 in *Passions and Perceptions.* Edited by Jacques Brunschwig and Martha Nussbaum; Cambridge: Cambridge University Press, 1993.

Harris, William. *Restraining Rage: The Ideology of Anger Control in Classical Antiquity.* Cambridge: Harvard University Press, 2001.

Hawkins, John C. *Horae Synopticae: Contributions to the Study of the Synoptic Problem.* Oxford: Clarendon Press, 1899.

Hay, David M. ―Psychology of Faith," *ANRW* 20.2: 881-925. Part 2, *Principat*, 20.2. Edited by H. Temporini and W. Haase. New York: de Gruyter, 1984.

Hayes, *The Most Beautiful Book Ever Written: The Gospel According to Luke.* New York: Eaton & Mains, 1913)

Hegel, G.W.F. *Lectures on the History of Philosophy.* Translated by E.S. Haldane. 3 vols. Lincoln: University of Nebraska, 1995.

Heinze, Max. *Die Lehre vom Logos in der griechischen Philosophie.* Oldenburg: Neudruck, 1872.

Helleman, Wendy E., ed. *Hellenization Revisited: Shaping a Christian Response within the Greco-Roman World.* Lanham, Md.: University Press of America, 1994.

Helleman ,Wendy E. ―Philo of Alexandria on Deification and Assimilation to God." *Studia philonica* 2 (1990): 51-71.

Hembold, W.C., trans. *Plutarch's Moralia.* 6 vols. London: Heinemann, 1939.

Henaut, Barry W. ―Alexandria or Athens as the Essence of Hellenization." Pages 99-106 in *Hellenization Revisited: Shaping a Christian Response within the Greco-Roman World.* Edited by Wendy E. Helleman. Lanham, Md.: University Press of America, 1994.

Hengel, Martin. *Judaism and Hellenism: Studies in their Encounter in Palestine during the Early Hellenistic Period.* Translated by John Bowden. 2 vols. London: SCM, 1974.

Henry, Denis and Elisabeth. *The Mask of Power: Seneca's Tragedies and Imperial Rome.* Warminster: Aris & Phillips, 1985.

Hershbell, Jackson P. ―De virtute morali (Moralia 440D-452D)." Pages 135-169 in *Plutarch's Ethical Writings and Early Christian Literature.* Edited by Hans Dieter Betz. Leiden: Brill, 1978.

Hornblower, Simon, and Antony Spawforth, eds. *The Oxford Classical Dictionary.* Oxford: Oxford University Press, 1996.

Hubbard, B.J. "Luke, Josephus and Rome: A Comparative Approach to the Lukan Sitz im Leben." Pages 59-68 in volume 1 of the *SBL Seminar Papers, 1979*. 2 vols. Society of Biblical Literature Seminar Papers 16. Chico, Calif.: Scholars Press, 1979.

Huck, Albert, and Heinrich Greeven. *Synopse der drei ersten Evangelien*. 13th ed. Tübingen: Mohr-Siebeck, 1981.

Hultgren, A.J. "The Function of the Sabbath Pericope in Mark 2:23-28." *Journal of Biblical Literature* 91 (1972): 38-43.

The Iliad of Homer. Translated by Richmond Lattimore. Chicago: University of Chicago Press, 1961.

Inwood, Brad. *Ethics and Human Action in Early Stoicism*. Oxford: Clarendon, 1985.

Irwin, T. H. "Stoic and Aristotelian Conceptions of Happiness." Pages 205-244 in *The Norms of Nature: Studies in Hellenistic Ethics*. Edited by Malcolm Schofield and Gisela Striker. Cambridge: Cambridge University Press, 1986.

Irwin, T.H. "Stoic Naturalism and Its Critics." Pages 345-64 in *The Cambridge Companion to the Stoics*. Edited by Brad Inwood. Cambridge: Cambridge University Press, 2003.

Irwin, T.H. "Socratic Paradox and Stoic Theory." Pages 211-232 in *Ethics: Cambridge Companions to Ancient Thought 4*. Edited by Stephen Everson. Cambridge: Cambridge University Press, 1998.

Jeremias, Joachim. *Jesus' Promise to the Nations*. Studies in Biblical Theology 24. London: SCM Press, 1958.

Jeremias, Joachim. *Die Kindertaufe in den ersten vier Jahrhunderten*. Göttingen: Vandenhoeck und Ruprecht, 1958.

Jeremias, Joachim. *The Parables of Jesus*. 2nd ed. New York: Scribner, 1966.

Jervell, Jacob. *Luke and the People of God Luke: A New Look at Luke-Acts*. Minneapolis: Augsburg, 1972.

Jervell, Jacob. "Retrospect and Prospect in Luke-Acts Interpretation." Pages 383-404 in *SBL Seminar Papers, 1991*. Society of Biblical Literature Seminar Papers 30. Edited by E.H. Lovering, Jr. Atlanta: Scholars Press, 1991.

Johnson, Luke Timothy. "On Finding the Lukan Community: A Cautious Cautionary Essay." Pages 87-100 in *SBL Seminar Papers, 1991*. Society of Biblical Literature Seminar Papers 16. Edited by Paul J. Achtemeier. Missoula, Mont.: Scholars Press, 1979.

Johnson, Luke Timothy. *Gospel of Luke.* Sacra pagina 3. Edited by Daniel J. Harrington. Collegeville, Minn.: Liturgical Press, 1991.

Johnston, David. ―The Jurists.‖ Pages 616-634 in *The Cambridge History of Greek and Roman Political Thought.* Edited by Christopher Rowe and Malcolm Schofield. Cambridge: Cambridge University Press, 2000.

Juel, Donald . *Luke-Acts: The Promise of History.* Atlanta: John Know, 1983.

Just Jr., Arthur A. *Luke 1:1-9:50.* St. Louis: Concordia, 1996.

Kahn, C.H. ―Democritus and the origins of moral psychology.‖ *American Journal of Philology 106* (1985): 1-31.

Kaster, Robert. *Emotion, Restraint, and Community in Ancient Rome.* New York: Oxford University Press, 2005.

Kee, Howard Clark. ―The Socio-Religious Setting and Aims of *Joseph and Aseneth.‖ Society of Biblical Literature Seminar Papers 10.* Edited by George MacRae. Missoula, Mont.: Scholars Press, 1976

Kennedy, George A. *Classical Rhetoric and Its Christian and Secular Tradition from Ancient to Modern Times.* Chapel Hill: University of North Carolina Press, 1980.

Kennedy, George A. *Progymnasmata: Greek Textbooks of Prose Composition Introductory to the Study of Rhetoric.* Fort Collins, Colo.: Chez l'auteur, 1999.

Kennedy, George A. *New Testament Interpretation through Rhetorical Criticism.* Chapel Hill: University of North Carolina Press, 1984.

Kenny, A.J.P. *The Aristotelian Ethics: A Study of the Relationship between the Eudemian and Nicomachean Ethics of Aristotle.* Oxford: Clarendon Press, 1978.

Kittel, Gerhard, and Gerhard Friedrich, eds. *Theological Dictionary of the New Testament.* Translated and edited by Geoffrey W. Bromiley. 10 vols. Grand Rapids, Mich: Eerdmans, 1964.

Kloppenborg, John S. ―*Exitus clari viri*: The Death of Jesus in Luke.‖ *Toronto Journal of Theology* 8 (1992): 106-20.

Klostermann, Erich. *Das Lukasevangelium.* Handbuch zum Neuen Testament 5. Tübingen: J.C.B. Mohr (Paul Siebeck), 1929.

Knight, Jonathan. *Luke's Gospel.* London and New York: Routledge, 1998.

Knuuttila, Simo. *Emotions in Ancient and Medieval Philosophy.* Oxford: Clarendon Press, 2004.

Koester, Helmut. "*Nomos Phuseōs*: The Concept of Natural Law in Greek Thought." Pages 521-41 in *Religions in Antiquity: Essays in Memory of Erwin Ramsdell Goodenough.* Edited by Jacob Neusner. Leiden: Brill, 1968.

Konstan, David. *The Emotions of the Ancient Greeks: Studies in Aristotle and Classical Literature.* Toronto: University of Toronto Press, 2006.

Konstan, David and N. Keith Rutter, eds. *Envy, Spite, and Jealousy: The Rivalrous Emotions in Ancient Greece.* Edinburgh: Edinburgh University Press, 2003.

Konstan, David. "Rhetoric and Emotion." Pages 411-25 in *A Companion to Greek Rhetoric.* Edited by Ian Worthington. Oxford: Blackwell, 2007.

Kremer, Jacob. *Lukasevangelium.* Würzburg: Echter Verlag, 2000.

Krentz, Edgar M. "Πάθη and Ἀπάθεια in Early Roman Empire Stoics." Pages 122-35 in *Passions and Moral Progress in Greco-Roman Thought.* Edited by John T. Fitzgerald. New York: Routledge, 2008.

Lada, Ismene. "Empathic Understanding: Emotion and Cognition in Classical Dramatic Audience-Response." *Proceedings of the Cambridge Philological Society* 39 (1993): 99-100.

Lagrange, M.J. *Évangile selon Saint Luc.* Paris: Études bibliques, 1927.

Lambrecht, Jan. *The Sermon on the Mount: Proclamation and Exhortation. Good News Studiesw 14.* Wilmington, Del.: Michael Glazier, 1985.

Lamour, Denis. *Flavius Josèphe.* Paris: Les Belles Lettres, 2000.

Larkin, W.J. "The Old Testament Background of Luke xxii, 43-44." *New Testament Studies* 25 (1978-79): 250-254.

Lauer, S. "*Eusebes Logismos* in 4 Maccabees." *Journal of Jewish Studies* 6 (1955): 170-71.

Lazarus, Richard. "Cognition and Motivation." *American Psychologist* 46 (1991): 353.

Leaney, Alfred Robert Clare. *A Commentary on the Gospel according to St. Luke.* London: A. & C. Black, 1958.

333

Lescow, T. ⸺Jesus im Gethsemane bei Lukas und im Hebräerbrief," *Zeitschrift für die neutestamentliche Wissenschaft und die Kunde der älteren Kirche* 58 (1967): 215-239.

Liddell, H.G., R. Scott, H.S. Jones. *A Greek-English Lexicon.* 9th ed. with revised supplement. Oxford: Oxford University Press, 1996.

Lieu, Judith. *Luke.* London: Epworth Press, 1997.

Lilla, Salvatore. ⸺Middle Platonism, Neoplatonism and Jewish-Alexandrine Philosophy in the Terminology of Clement of Alexandria's Ethics." *Archivio Italianoperia StoriaDelia Pieta* 3 (1962): 30-36.

Linnemann, Eta. *Studien zur Passionsgeschichte.* Forschungen zur Religion und Literatur des Alten und Neuen Testaments 102. Göttingen: Vandenhoeck u. Ruprecht, 1970.

Lloyd, Geoffrey Ernest Richard. *Methods and Problems in Greek Science.* Cambridge: Cambridge University Press, 1991.

Loisy, Alfred. *L'Évangile selon Luc.* 8th ed. Frankfurt: Minerva, 1971.

Long, A.A., ed. *The Cambridge Companion to Early Greek Philosophy.* Cambridge: Cambridge University Press, 1999.

Long, A.A. ⸺Carneades and the Stoic *telos.*" *Phronesis* 18 (1967): 59-90.

Long, A.A. *Epictetus: A Stoic and Socratic Guide to Life.* Oxford: Clarendon Press, 2002.

Long, A.A. *From Epicurus to Epictetus: Studies in Hellenistic and Roman Philosophy.* Oxford: Clarendon Press, 2006.

Long, A.A. and David N. Sedley. *The Hellenistic Philosophers, I-II.* Cambridge: Cambridge University Press, 1987.

Long, A.A. *Hellenistic Philosophy.* Berkeley: University of California Press, 1986.

Long, A.A. *Stoic Studies.* Cambridge: Cambridge University Press, 1996.

Lynch, J.P. *Aristotle's School: A Study of a Greek Educational Institution.* Berkeley: University of California Press, 1972.

Maddox, Robert L. *The Purpose of Luke-Acts.* Göttingen: Vandenhoeck & Ruprecht, 1982.

Maicr, Paul L. *The New Complete Works of Josephus.* Grand Rapids, Mich.: Kregel, 1999.

Malherbe, Abraham J. *The Cynic Epistles.* Society of Biblical Literature Sources for Biblical Study 12. Missoula: Scholars Press, 1977.

Malherbe, Abraham J. ―Hellenistic Moralists and the New Testament." *ANRW* 26.1:267-333. Part 2, *Principat*, 26.1. Edited by H. Temporini and W. Haase. New York: de Gruyter, 1992.

Malina, Bruce J. and Jerome H. Neyrey. ―Honor and Shame in Luke-Acts: Pivotal Values of the Mediterranean World." Pages 25-66 in *The Social World of Luke-Acts: Models for Interpretation*. Edited by Jerome H. Neyrey. Peabody, Mass.: Hendrickson, 1991.

Malina, Bruce J., and Jerome H. Neyrey. *Portraits of Paul: An Archaeology of Ancient Personality.* Louisville: Westminster John Knox Press, 1996.

Mann, C.S. *Mark: A New Translation with Introduction and Commentary.* Anchor Bible 27. Garden City, N.Y.: Doubleday, 1986.

Mansfeld, Jaap. ―Sources." Pages 9-19 in *The Cambridge History of Hellenistic Philosophy*. Edited by Keimpe Algra et al. Cambridge: Cambridge University Press, 1999.

Mansfield, Jaap. ―The Idea of the Will in Chrysippus, Posidonius, and Galen." *Boston Area Colloquium in Ancient Philosophy 7* (1991): 107-145.

Manstead, Anthony S. R., and Agneta H. Fischer. ―Social Appraisal: The Social World as Object of and Influence on Appraisal Processes." Pages 221-32 in *Appraisal Processes in Emotion: Theory, Methods, Research*. Edited by Klaus R. Scherer, Angela Schorr, and Tom Johnstone. Oxford: Oxford University Press, 2001.

Marguerat, Daniel. ―Saul's conversion (Acts 9, 22, 26) and the Multiplication of Narrative in Acts." Pages 127-55 in *Luke's Literary Achievement*. Edited by C.M. Tuckett. Journal for the Study of the New Testament: Supplement Series 116. Sheffield: Sheffield Academic Press, 1995.

Marincola, John. ―Beyond Pity and Fear: The Emotions of History." *Ancient Society* 33 (2003): 300-310.

Marshall, I. Howard. *The Gospel of Luke: A Commentary on the Greek Text.* New Internation Greek Testament Commentary 3. Grand Rapids, Mich.: Eerdmans, 1978.

Marshall, I. Howard. *Luke: Historian and Theologian.* Exeter: Paternoster Press, 1970.

Mason, Steve. *Flavius Josephus on the Pharisees: A Composition-critical Study*. Leiden: Brill, 1990.

McEvilley, Thomas. *The Shape of Ancient Thought: Comparative Studies in Greek and Indian Philosophies*. New York: Allworth Press, 2002.

Mendels, Doron. ―Hellenistic Utopia and the Essenes." *Harvard Theological Review* 72 (1979): 207-22.

Merkelbach, Reinhold. *Roman und Mysterium in der Antike*. München: Beck, 1962.

Metzger, Bruce. *A Textual Commentary on the Greek New Testament*. New York: United Bible Societies, 1975.

Milobenski, Ernst. *Der Neid in der griechischen Philosophie*. Wiesbaden: Harrassowitz, 1964.

Momigliano, Arnaldo. *The Classical Foundations of Modern Historiography*. Sather Classical Lectures 54. Berkeley: University of California Press, 1990.

Momigliano, Arnaldo. *The Development of Greek Biography*. Cambridge, Mass.: Harvard University Press, 1971.

Momigliano, Arnaldo. ―Freedom of Speech in Antiquity." Pages 252-63 in *Dictionary of the History of Ideas: Studies of Selected Pivotal Ideas, Vol.2*. Edited by Philip P. Wiener. New York: Charles Scribner's Sons, 1973.

Moore, Stephen. *Literary Criticism and the Gospels: The Theoretical Challenge*. New Haven: Yale University Press, 1989.

Moore, Stephen D., and Janice Capel Anderson. ―Taking It Like a Man: Masculinity in 4 Maccabees." *Journal of Biblical Literature* 117 (1998): 259.

Moraux, Paul. *Der Aristotelismus bei den Griechen: von Andronikos bis Alexander von Aphrodisias*. Berlin: De Gruyter, 1984.

Moraux, Paul. *Les listes anciennes des ouvrages d'Aristote*. Louvain: Éditions universitaires de Louvain, 1951.

Morgan, J.R., and R. Stoneman, eds. *Greek Fiction: The Greek Novel in Context*. London: Routledge, 1994.

Morris, Leon. *Luke: An Introduction and Commentary*. Grand Rapids, Mich.: Eerdmans, 1988.

Murray, Gilbert. *The Stoic Philosophy*. London: Watts & Co., 1915.

Navia, Luis. *Diogenes of Sinope: The Man in the Tub*. Westport, Conn.: Greenwood Press, 1989.

Neirynck, Frans. ―John and the Synoptics: The Empty Tomb Stories," *New Testament Studies* 30 (1984): 161-87.

Neirynck, Frans. ―Marc 16, 1-8: Tradition et Rédaction," *Ephemerides theologicae lovanienses* 56 (1980): 56-88.

Neyrey, Jerome H. ―The Absence of Jesus' Emotion: The Lucan Redaction of Lk. 22.39-46." *Biblica* 61 (1980): 152-71.

Neyrey, Jerome H. ―Acts, Epicureans, and Theodicy: A Study in Stereotypes." Pages 118-134 in *Greeks, Romans, and Christians*. Edited by David L. Balch, Everett Ferguson, and Wayne A. Meeks. Minneapolis: Fortress Press, 1990.

Neyrey, Jerome H. ―The Forensic Defense Speech and Paul's Trial Speeches in Acts 22-26: Form and Function." Pages 210-24 in *Luke-Acts: New Perspectives from the Society of Biblical Literature Seminar*. Edited by Charles H. Talbert. New York: Crossroad, 1984.

Neyrey, Jerome H. ―Jesus' Address to the Women of Jerusalem (Lk. 23.27-31): A Prophetic Judgment Oracle." *New Testament Studies* 29 (1983): 74-86.

Neyrey, Jerome H. *The Passion According to Luke: A Redaction Study of Luke's Soteriology*. New York: Paulist, 1985.

Neyrey, Jerome H. *The Social World of Luke-Acts: Models for Interpretation*. Peabody, Mass: Hendrickson Publishers, 1991.

Nikiprowetzky, Valentin. ―Le _De Vita Contemplativa' revisité." Pages 105-125 in *Sagesse et Religion: Colloque de Strasbourg Octobre 1976*. Edited by E. Jacob. Paris: Presses Universitaires de France, 1979.

Nolland, John. *Luke*. Word Biblical Commentary 35A-C. 3 vols. Dallas: Word, 1982-1993.

Norden, Eduard. *Agnostos Theos:Untersuchungen zur Formengeschichte religiöser Rede*. Leipzig [u.a.]: Teubner, 1913.

North, Helen. *Sophrosyne, Self-knowledge and Self-restraint in Greek Literature*. Ithaca, N.Y.: Cornell University Press, 1966.

Nussbaum, Martha. *The Therapy of Desire: Theory and Practice in Hellenistic Ethics.* Princeton: Princeton University Press, 1994.

Nussbaum, Martha. *The Fragility of Goodness: Luck and Ethics in Greek Tragedy and Philosophy.* Cambridge: Cambridge University Press, 1986.

Nussbaum, Martha. *The Poetics of Therapy: Hellenistic Ethics in its Rhetorical and Literary Context.* Edmonton: Academic, 1990.

Nussbaum, Martha, and Jacques Brunschwig, eds. *Passions and Perceptions.* Cambridge: Cambridge University Press, 1993.

Nussbaum, Martha. ―The Stoics on the Extirpation of the Passions." *Apeiron* 20 (1987): 129-77.

Nussbaum, Martha. *Upheavals of Thought: The Intelligence of Emotions.* Cambridge: Cambridge University Press, 2001.

O'Daly, Gerard, and Adolar Zumkeller, ―Affectus (*passio, pertubatio*)." Pages 166-180 in *Augustinus-Lexikon, vol.1: Aaron-Conuersio.* Edited by Cornelius Mayer. Basel: Schwabe, 1986.

O'Hagan, Andrew. ―The Martyr in the Fourth Book of Maccabees." *Studii biblici Franciscani liber annus* 24 (1974): 101.

Olbricht, Thomas and Jerry Sumney, eds. *Paul and Pathos.* Atlanta: Society of Biblical Literature, 2001.

Ortony, Andrew, Gerald Clore, and Allen Collins, eds. *The Cognitive Structure of Emotions.* Cambridge: Cambridge University Press, 1988.

Osiek, Carolyn and David L. Balch. *Families in the New Testament World: Households and House Churches.* Louisville: Westminster John Knox Press, 1997.

O'Toole, Robert F. ―Luke's Position on Politics and Society in Luke-Acts." Pages 1-17 in *Political Issues in Luke-Acts.* Edited by Richard J. Cassidy and Philip J. Scharper. Maryknoll, N.Y.: Orbis Books, 1983.

Padel, Ruth. *Whom Gods Destroy: Elements of Greek and Tragic Madness.* Princeton: Princeton University Press, 1994.

Parkinson, Brian. *Ideas and Realities of Emotion.* London: Routledge, 1995.

Parsons, Mikeal. *Luke: Storyteller, Interpreter, Evangelist.* Peabody, Mass.: Hendrickson, 2007.

Perrin, Normin, and D.C. Duling. *The New Testament: An Introduction*. New York: Harcourt Brace Jovanovich, 1982.

Pervo, Richard I. *Profit with Delight: The Literary Genre of the Acts of the Apostles.* Philadelphia: Fortress, 1987.

Pesch, Rudolf. *Jesu ureigene Taten? Ein Beitrag zur Wunderfrage*. Freiburg: Herder, 1970.

Pfitzner, Victor C. *Paul and the Agon Motif: Traditional Athletic Imagery in the Pauline Literature*. Novum Testamentum Supplements 16. Leiden: Brill, 1967.

Philo. Translated by F.H. Colson and G.H. Whitaker. 10 vols. Loeb Classical Library. 2 sup. vols. by Ralph Marcus. Harvard: Harvard University Press, 1929-1962.

Philo of Alexandria: The Contemplative Life, The Giants, and Selections. Translated by David Winston. Preface by John Dillon. New York: Paulist Press, 1981.

Philonenko, Marc. *Joseph et Aséneth: Introduction, texte critique, traduction et notes.* Leiden: Brill, 1974.

Pitt-Rivers, Julian. *The Fate of Shechem or the Politics of Sex: Essays in the Anthroplogy of the Mediterranean*. Cambridge: Cambridge University Press, 1977.

Pohlenz, Max. *Kleine Schriften.* Edited by H. Dörrie. 2 vols. Hildesheim: Olms, 1965.

Pohlenz, Max. *Die Stoa: Die Geschichte einer geistigen Bewegung*. 2 vols. Göttingen: Vandenhoeck und Ruprecht, 1948.

Pomeroy, Arthur, eds. *Arius Didymus: Epitome of Stoic Ethics*. Atlanta: Society of Biblical Literature, 1999.

Powell, Mark Allan. *Jesus as a Figure in History: How Modern Historians View the Man from Galilee*. Louisville: Westminster John Knox, 1998.

Powell, Mark Allan. *What are They Saying about Luke?* New York: Paulist Press, 1989.

Praeder, Susan M. ―Luke-Acts and the Ancient Novel.‖ *Society of Biblical Literature Seminar Papers* 20. Chico, Cal.: Scholars Press, 1981.

Procopé, John. ―Epicureans on Anger.‖ Pages 171-196 in *The Emotions in Hellenistic Philosophy*. Edited by Juha Sihvola and Troels Engberg-Pedersen. Dordrecht: Kluwer Academic Publishers, 1998.

Proust, Marcel. The Captive. Vol. 5 of *In Search of Lost Time*. Translated by C.K. Scott Moncrieff & Terence Kilmartin. Revised by D.J. Enright. London: Vintage, 1996.

Rabinowitz, Peter J. "Truth in Fiction: A Reexamination of Audience." *Critical Inquiry* 4 (1977).

Radl, Walter. *Das Evangelium nach Lukas: Kommentar, Erster Teil:1,1-9,50.* Freiburg: Herder, 2003.

Rawson, Beryl, ed. *The Family in Ancient Rome:New Perspectives.* Ithaca, N.Y.: Cornell University Press, 1986.

Rawson, Beryl, ed. *Marriage, Divorce, and Children in Ancient Rome.* New York: Oxford University Press, 1991.

Redditt, Paul L. "The Concept of *Nomos* in Fourth Maccabees." *Catholic Biblical Quarterly* 45 (1983): 249-270.

Reddy, William. *The Navigation of Feeling: A Framework for the History of the Emotions.* Cambridge: Cambridge University Press, 2001.

Reggiani, Clara Kraus. *4 Maccabei: a cura di Clara Kraus Reggiani.* Genova: Marietti, 1992.

Reggiani, Clara Kraus, and Roberto Radice. *La filosofia mosaic: La creazione del mondo secondo Mosè.* Milano: Rusconi, 1987.

Rehkopf, Friedrich. *Die Lukanische Sonderquelle: Ihr Umfang und Sprachgebrauch.* Wissenschaftliche Untersuchungen zum Neuen Testament 5. Tübingen: J.C.B. Mohr, 1959.

Reid, Barbara E. *Choosing the Better Part?* Collegeville: The Liturgical Press, 1996.

Reid, Barbara E. *The Transfiguration: A Source and Redaction-Critical Study of Luke 9:28-36.* Paris: Gabalda, 1993.

Renan, Ernest. "C'est le plus beau livre qu'il y ait." Pages 88-111 in *Les Evangiles et la seconde génération chrétienne.* 3rd ed. Paris: Calmann Lévy, 1877.

Renehan, Robert. "The Greek Philosophical Background of Fourth Maccabees." *Rheinisches Museum für Philologie* 115 (1972): 223-38.

Reydams-Schils, Gretchen. *The Roman Stoics: Self, Responsibility, and Affection.* Chicago: University of Chicago Press, 2005.

Ricken, Friedo. *Philosophie der Antike.* Stuttgart: Kohlhammer, 1988.

Riedweg, Christoph. *Pythagoras: Leben, Lehre, Nachwirkung; eine Einführung.* München: Beck, 2002.

Ringe, Sharon H. *Luke.* Louisville: Westminster John Knox, 1995.

Rist, J.M. ―Seneca and Stoic Orthodoxy," *ANRW* 36.3: 1993-2012. Part 2, *Principat*, 36.3. Edited by H. Temporini and W. Haase. New York: de Gruyter, 1992.

Rist, J.M. *Stoic Philosophy.* Cambridge: Cambridge University Press, 1969.

Rist, J.M., ed. *The Stoics.* Berkeley: University of California Press, 1978.

Rosenmeyer, Thomas G. *Seneca Drama and Stoic Cosmology.* Berkeley: University of California Press, 1989.

Runia, David T. *On the Creation of the Cosmos According to Moses.* Philo of Alexandria commentary series, vol. 1. Leiden: Brill, 2001.

Runia, David T. ―Was Philo a Middle Platonist? A Difficult Question Revisited." *Studia philonica* 5 (1993): 112 -140.

Russell, Bertrand. *A History of Western Philosophy and Its Connection with Political and Social Circumstances from the Earliest Times to the Present Day.* Great Britain: Allen & Unwin, 1961.

Rüther, Theodor. *Die sittliche Forderung der Apatheia in den beiden ersten christlichen Jahrhunderten und bei Klemens von Alexandrien.* Freiburg: Herder, 1949.

Sabourin, Léopold. *L'Évangile de Luc: Introduction et commentaire.* Roma: Editrice Pontificia Università Gregoriana, 1985.

Sach, Joe, trans. *Nichomachean Ethics.* Newbury, Mass.: Focus Pub./R. Pullins, 2002.

Sanders, Jack T. *The Jews in Luke-Acts.* Philadelphia: Fortress, 1987.

Saint Augustine: The City of God against the Pagans. Translated by David Wiesen. 3 vols. Cambridge: Harvard University Press, 1968.

Sanders, E.P. *Judaism: Practice and Belief, 63 BCE-66 CE.* London: SCM Press, 1992.

Sandmel, Samuel. *Philo of Alexandria: An Introduction.* New York: Oxford University Press, 1979.

Satterthwaite, Philip E. ―Acts against the Background of Classical Rhetoric." Pages 337-79 in *The Book of Acts in its Ancient Literary Setting.* Edited by Bruce W. Winter and Andrew D. Clarke. Vol. 1 of *The Book of Acts in its First Century Setting*. Edited by Bruce W. Winter. Grand Rapids, Mich.: Eerdmans, 1993.

Sbordone, Francesco. *Philodemi Adversus Sophistas*. Naples: Loffredo, 1947.

Schiesaro, Alessandro. ―Passion, Reason, and Knowledge in Seneca's Tragedies.‖ Pages 89-111 in *The Passions in Roman Thought and Literature*. Edited by Susanna Braund and Christopher Gill. Cambridge: Cambridge University Press, 1997.

Schneider, Gerhard. *Das Evangelium nach Lukas*. 2 vols. Würzburg: Echter-Verlag, 1984.

Schofield, Malcolm, and Gisela Striker, eds., *The Norms of Nature: Studies in Hellenistic Ethics*. Cambridge: Cambridge University Press, 1986.

Scholten, Johannes Henricus. *Das Paulinische Evangelium: kritische Untersuchung des Evangeliums nach Lucas und seines Verhältnisses zu Marcus, Matthäus und der Apostelgeschichte*. Elberfeld: R.L. Friderichs, 1881.

Schlatter, Adolf. *Das Evangelium des Lukas aus s. Quellen erkl.* Stuttgart: Calwer Vereinsbuchh, 1931.

Schneider, Gerhard. *Das Evangelium nach Lukas.* 3 vols. Gütersloh: Gütersloher Verlagshaus Mohn, 1977-1992.

Schorr, Angela. ―Appraisal: The Evolution of an Idea.‖ Pages 20-36 in *Appraisal Processes in Emotion: Theory, Methods, Research*. Edited by Klaus R. Scherer, Angela Schorr, and Tom Johnstone. Oxford: Oxford University Press, 2001.

Schramm, Tim. *Der Markus Stoff bei Lukas: Eine literarkritische und redaktionsgeschichtliche Untersuchung*. Society for New Testament Studies Monograph Series 14. Cambridge, University Press, 1971.

Schreckenberg, Heinz. *Die Flavius-Josephus-Tradition in Antike und Mittelalter*. Leiden: Brill, 1972.

Schürmann, Heinz. *Das Lukasevangelium*. Herders theologischer Kommentar zum Neuen Testament 3. Freiburg: Herder, 1969.

Schwartz, Seth. *Josephus and Judean Politics*. Leiden: Brill, 1990.

Schweizer, Eduard. ―Concerning the Speeches in Acts.‖ Pages 208-216 in *Studies in Luke-Acts*. Edited by Leander E. Keck and J. Louis Martyn. Philadelphia: Fortress, 1980.

Schweizer, Eduard. *The Good News According to Luke*. Translated by David E. Green. Atlanta: John Knox Press, 1984.

Schweizer, Eduard. *The Good News according to Mark*. Translated by Donald H. Madvig. Atlanta: John Knox, 1970.

Sedley, David N. "Metrodorus of Lampsacus," Pages 342-43 in *Encyclopedia of Classical Philosophy*. Edited by Donald J. Zeyl. Westport, Conn.: Greenwood, 1997.

Sedley, David N. "The School, from Zeno to Arius Didymus." Pages 7-32 in *The Cambridge Companion to the Stoics*. Edited by Brad Inwood. Cambridge: Cambridge University Press, 2003.

Sedley, David N. "The Stoic-Platonist Debate on *kathêkonta*." Pages 128-52 in *Topics in Stoic Philosophy*. Edited by Katerina Ierodiakonou. Oxford: Oxford University Press, 1999.

Seeley, David. *The Noble Death: Graeco-Roman Martyrology and Paul's Concept of Salvation*. Sheffield: JSOT Press, 1990.

Segal, Charles. *Language and Desire in Seneca's „Phaedra'*. Princeton: Princeton University Press, 1986.

Seim, Turid Karlsen. *The Double Message: Patterns of Gender in Luke-Acts*. Nashville: Abingdon Press, 1994.

Sherman, Nancy. "Emotional Agents." Pages 154-76 in *The Analytic Freud: Philosophy and Psychoanalysis*. Edited by Michael P. Levine. London: Routledge, 2000.

Shattuck, Roger. *Marcel Proust*. New York: Viking Press, 1974.

Siegfried, Carl Gustav Adolf. *Philo von Alexandria als Ausleger des Alten Testament: an sich selbst und nach seinem geschichtlichen Einfluss betrachtet*. Jen: Verlag von Hermann Dufft, 1875.

Sievers, Joseph. *Understanding Josephus: Seven Perspectives*. Edited by Steve Mason. Journal for the Study of the Pseudepigrapha: Supplement Series 32. Sheffield: Sheffield Academic Press, 1998.

Sihvola, Juha, and Troels Engberg-Pedersen, eds. *The Emotions in Hellenistic Philosophy*. Dordrecht: Kluwer Academic Publishers, 1998.

Snodgrass, Klyne. "Western Non-Interpolations." *Journal of Biblical Literature* 91 (1972): 369-79.

Soards, Marion L. *The Speeches in Acts: Their Content, Context, and Concerns*. Louisville: Westminster John Knox, 1994.

Solomon, Robert. *The Passions: Emotions and the Meaning of Life*. Indianapolis: Hackett, 1993.

Sorabji, Richard. *Emotion and Peace of Mind: From Stoic Agitation to Christian Temptation*. Oxford: Oxford University Press, 2000.

Spencer, Patrick E. ―Acts and Modern Literary Approaches," in *The Book of Acts in its Ancient Literary Setting*. Edited by Bruce W. Winter and Andrew D. Clarke. Vol. 1 of *The Book of Acts in its First Century Setting*. Edited by Bruce W. Winter. Grand Rapids, Mich.: Eerdmans, 1993.

Spencer, Patrick E. *Rhetorical Texture and Narrative Trajectories of the Lukan Galilean Ministry Speeches*. New York: T&T Clark, 2007.

Spilsbury, Paul. *The Image of the Jew in Flavius Josephus' Paraphrase of the Bible*. Tübingen: Mohr Siebeck, 1998.

Spivey, Robert A., D. Moody Smith, and C. Clifton Black. *Anatomy of the New Testament*. 6th ed. Upper Saddle River, N.J.: Pearson Prentice Hall, 2007.

Stanley, D.M. *Jesus in Gethsemane: The Early Church Reflects on the Suffering of Jesus*. Ramsey, N.J.: Paulist, 1980.

Stanton, Graham. *The Interpretation of Matthew*. Philadelphia: Fortress Press, 1983.

Steinmetz, Peter. ―Die Stoa in der Mitte und zweiten Hälfte des ersten Jahrhunderts vor Christus." Pages 706-16 in *Die Philosophie der Antike*. Edited by Hellmut Flashar. 4 vols. Basel: Schwabe, 1994.

Sterling, Gregory, E. *Apologetic Historiography and Self-Definition: Josephos, Luke-Acts, and Historiography*. Novum Testamentum Supplements 64. Leiden: Brill, 1992.

Sterling, Gregory, E. ―Athletes of Virtue': An Analysis of the Summaries in Acts (2:41-47; 4:32-35; 5:12-16)." *Journal of Biblical Literature* 113/4 (1994): 679-696.

Sterling, Gregory E. ―Mors philosophi: The Death of Jesus in Luke." *Harvard Theological Review* 94:4 (2001): 383-402.

Sterling, Gregory, E. ―Platonizing Moses: Philo and Middle Platonism." *Studia philonica* 5 (1993): 96-111.

Sterling, Gregory E. ―The Queen of the Virtues': Piety in Philo of Alexandria." *Studia philonica* 13 (2006): 103-23.

Sterling, Gregory, E. Review of Hans Conzelmann, *Gentiles, Jews, Christians: Polemics and Apologetics in the Greco-Roman Era.* *Studia philonica* 5 (1993): 238-242.

Stowers, Stanley K. "4 Maccabees." Pages 388-98 in *Harper's Biblical Commentary.* San Francisco: Harper and Row, 1988.

Stowers, Stanley K. "Paul and Self-Mastery." Pages 524-50 in *Paul in the Greco-Roman World: A Handbook.* Edited by J. Paul Sampley. Harrisburg, Penn.: Trinity Press International, 2003.

Striker, Gisela, ed. *Essays on Hellenistic Epistemology and Ethics.* Cambridge: Cambridge University Press, 1996.

Stuart, Duane. *Epochs of Greek and Roman Biography.* Berkeley: University of California Press, 1928.

Swartley, Willard M. "Politics of Peace (Eirēnē) in Luke's Gospel." Pages 18-37 in *Political Issues in Luke-Acts.* Edited by Richard J. Cassidy and Philip J. Scharper. Maryknoll, N.Y.: Orbis Books, 1983.

Swete, Henry Barclay. *The Gospel according to St. Mark: The Greek Text with Introduction, Notes, and Indices.* London: Macmillan, 1909.

Talbert, Charles H. "Conversion in the Acts of the Apostles: Ancient Auditors' Perceptions." Pages 141-53 in *Literary Studies in Luke-Acts: Essays in Honor of Joseph B. Tyson.* Edited by Richard P. Thompson and Thomas E. Phillips. Macon, Ga.: Mercer University Press, 1998.

Talbert, Charles H. *Literary Patterns, Theological Themes, and the Genre of Luke-Acts.* Missoula, Mont.: Scholars' Press, 1975.

Talbert, Charles H. "Martyrdom in Luke-Acts and the Lukan Social Ethic." Pages 99-110 in *Political Issues in Luke-Acts.* Edited by Richard J. Cassidy and Philip J. Scharper. Maryknoll, N.Y.: Orbis Books, 1983.

Talbert, Charles H. *Reading Luke: A Literary and Theological Commentary on the Third Gospel.* New York: Crossroad, 1982.

Tannehill, Robert C. *Luke.* Nashville: Abingdon, 1996.

Tannehill, Robert C. *The Narrative Unity of Luke-Acts.* 2 Vols. Minneapolis: Fortress Press, 1990.

Taylor, C.C.W. "The Atomists." Pages 181-204 in *The Cambridge Companion to Early Greek Philosophy.* Edited by A.A. Long. Cambridge: Cambridge University Press, 1999.

Taylor, R.O.P. *Groundwork for the Gospels*. Oxford: Blackwell, 1946.

Taylor, Vincent. *The Passion Narrative of St. Luke: A Critical and Historical Investigation. New Testament Studies*19. Cambridge: Cambridge University Press, 1971.

Tcherikover, Victor. ―Jewish Apocalyptic Literature Reconsidered." *Eos* 48 (1956): 169-93.

Thackeray, H. St. John. *Josephus: The Man and the Historian*. New York: Jewish Institute of Religion, 1929.

Thom, Johan. ―The Passions in Neopythagorean Writings." Pages 67-78 in *Passions and Moral Progress in Greco-Roman Thought*. Edited by John T. Fitzgerald. New York: Routledge, 2008.

Thomas, Johannes. *Der jüdische Phokylides: formgeschichtliche Zugänge zu Pseudo-Phokylides und Vergleich mit der neutestamentlichen Paränese*. Göttingen: Vandenhoeck & Ruprecht, 1992.

Tiede, David. ―The Gospel according to Luke." Pages 1759-61. *HarperCollins Study Bible* . Edited by Wayne A. Meeks et al. New York: HarperCollins, 1993.

Tiede, David L. *Prophecy and History in Luke-Acts*. Philadelphia: Fortress Press, 1980.

Tieleman, Teun. *Chrysippus' On Affections: Reconstructions and Interpretations*. Leiden: Brill, 2003.

Tieleman, Teun, *Galen and Chrysippus on the Soul: Argument and Refutation in the de Placitis Books II-III*. Leiden: Brill, 1996.

Theological Dictionary of the New Testament. Edited by G. Kittel and G. Friedrich. Translated by G.W. Bromiley. 10 vols. Grand Rapids, Mich.: Eerdmans, 1964-1976.

Tobin, Thomas. ―4 Maccabees." Pages 1814-15 in *The HarperCollins Study Bible*. Edited by Wayne A. Meeks et al. New York: HarperCollins, 1993.

Tolbert, Mary Ann. *Sowing the Gospel: Mark's World in Literary-Historical Perspective*. Minneapolis: Fortress, 1989.

Toohey, Peter. *Melancholy, Love, and Time: Boundaries of the Self in Ancient Literature*. Ann Arbor, Mich.: University of Michigan Press, 2004.

Townshend, R.B. ─"The Fourth Book of Maccabees." Pages 653-54 in *The Apocrypha and Pseudepigrapha of the Old Testament.* Edited by R.H. Charles. 2 vols. Oxford: Oxford University Press, 1913.

Tuckett, C.M. *The Revival of the Griesbach Hypothesis: An Analysis and Appraisal.* Society for New Testament Studies Monograph Series 44. Cambridge: Cambridge University Press, 1983.

Urmson, J.O. *The Greek Philosophical Vocabulary.* London: Duckworth, 1990.

Usener, Hermann, ed. *Epicurea.* Lipsiae: in aedibus B.G. Teubneri, 1887.

van der Horst, Pieter Willem. *Philo's Flaccus: The First Pogrom : Introduction, Translation, and Commentary.* Philo of Alexandria commentary series, vol. 2. Leiden: Brill, 2003.

van der Horst, Pieter Willem. ─"Pseudo-Phocylides: A New Translation and Introduction." Pages 565-582 in *The Old Testament Pseudepigrapha, Vol. 2.* Edited by James H. Charlesworth. 2 vols. Garden City, N.Y.: Doubleday, 1983.

van der Horst, Pieter Willem. *The Sentences of Pseudo-Phocylides.* Studia in Veteris Testamenti pseudepigrapha 4. Leiden: Brill, 1978.

van Henten, J. W., and Friedrich Avemarie, eds. *Martyrdom and Noble Death: Selected Texts from Graeco-Roman, Jewish, and Christian Antiquity.* London: Routledge, 2002.

Vermes, Geza. ─"Essenes and Therapeutae." *Revue de Qumran* 3 (1961): 495-504.

Villalba i Varneda, Pere. *The Historical Method of Flavius Josephus.* Arbeiten zur Literatur und Geschichte des hellenistischen Judentums 19. Leiden: Brill, 1986.

von Arnim, Ioannes. *Stoicorum veterum fragmenta.* 4 vols. Leipzig: B.G.Teubner, 1905-1924.

von Harnack, Adolf. *History of Dogma.* Translated by Neil Buchanan. 7 vols. Boston: Little, Brown & Co., 1896-1905.

von Harnack, Adolf. *New Testament Studies I. Luke the Physician: The Author of the Third Gospel.* Williams & Norgate; G.P. Putnam's Sons, 1907.

Wacholder, Ben Zion. ─"Josephus." Pages 383-84 in *The Oxford Companion to the Bible.* Edited by Bruce M. Metzger and Michael D. Coogan. New York: Oxford University Press, 1993.

Walaskay, Paul W. *—And so We Came to Rome": The Political Perspective of St. Luke*. Society for New Testament Studies Monograph Series 49. Cambridge: Cambridge University Press, 1983.

Walcot, Peter. *Envy and the Greeks: A Study of Human Behaviour*. Warminster: Aris & Phillips, 1978.

Wallace-Hadrill, Andrew. *Augustan Rome*. London: Bristol Classical Press, 1993.

Weinert, F.D. —The Meaning of the Temple in the Gospel of Luke. Ph.D. diss., Fordham University, 1979.

Weiss, H.F. —Pharisäismus und Hellenismus: zum Darstellung des Judentums im Geschichtswerk des jüdischen Historikers Flavius Josephus." *Orientalistische Literarzeitung* 74 (1979): 427-28.

Wendorf, Richard. *The Elements of Life: Biography and Portrait-Painting in Stuart and Georgian England*. Oxford: Clarendon, 1990.

Wernle, Paul. *Die synoptische Frage*. Freiburg: J.C.B. Mohr (Paul Siebeck), 1899.

White, Michael J. —Stoic Natural Philosophy (Physics and Cosmology)." Pages 124-52 in *The Cambridge Companion to the Stoics*. Edited by Brad Inwood. Cambridge: Cambridge University Press, 2003.

Wilken, Robert L. *Remembering the Christian Past*. Grand Rapids, Mich.: Eerdmans, 1995.

Wilson ,Walter T. *The Sentences of Pseudo-Phocylides*. New York: Walter de Gruyter, 2005.

Wimmers, Inge Crosman. *Proust and Emotion: The Importance of Affect in A La Recherche Du Temps Perdu*. University of Toronto Romance Series. Toronto: University of Toronto Press, 2003.

Winston, David. —Philo of Alexandria on the Emotions." Pages 201-20 in *Passions and Moral Progress in Greco-Roman Thought*. Edited by John T. Fitzgerald. New York: Routledge, 2008.

Winston, David. —Philo's Ethical Theory." *ANRW* 21.1:848-69. Part 2, *Principat*, 21.1. Edited by H. Temporini and W. Haase. New York: de Gruyter, 1984.

Wisse, Jakob. *Ethos and Pathos from Aristotle to Cicero*. Amsterdam: Hakkert, 1989.

Wood, H.G. ―Some Characteristics of the Synoptic Writers." Pages 134-171 in *The Parting of the Roads: Studies in the Development of Judaism and Early Christianity*. Edited by F.J. Foakes-Jackson. London: Edward Arnold, 1912.

Wordsworth, Christopher. *The New Testament of our Lord and Saviour Jesus Christ: in the original Greek*. London: Rivingtons, 1859.

The Works of Josephus. Translated by William Whiston. Peabody, Mass.: Hendrickson, 1987.

Wright, Richard A. ―Plutarch on Moral Progress." Pages 136-50 in *Passions and Moral Progress in Greco-Roman Thought*. Edited by John T. Fitzgerald. New York: Routledge, 2008.

Yoder, John Howard. *The Politics of Jesus: vicit Agnus noster*. Grand Rapids, Mich.: Eerdmans, 1972.

Young, R. D. ―The _Woman with the Soul of Abraham': Traditions about the Mother of the Maccabean Martyrs." Pages 67-81 in *Women like This: New Perspectives on Jewish Women in the Greco-Roman World*. Edited by A.J. Levine. Atlanta: Scholars Press 1991.

Xenakis, Jason. *Epictetus: Philosopher–Therapist*. The Hague: Martinus Nijhoff, 1969.

Zanker, Graham. *Modes of Viewing in Hellenistic Poetry and Art*. Madison: University of Wisconsin Press, 2004.

Zanker, Paul. *The Power of Images in the Age of Augustus*. Translated by Alan Shapiro. Ann Arbor, Mich.: University of Michigan Press, 1990.

Zerwick, Max and Joseph Smith. *Biblical Greek: Illustrated by Examples*. Rome: Biblical Institue, 1963.

CPSIA information can be obtained
at www.ICGtesting.com
Printed in the USA
LVIC010310250113
317155LV00006B

* 9 7 8 1 2 4 8 9 4 9 5 5 9 *